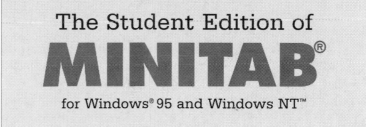

The Student Edition of

MINITAB®

for Windows® 95 and Windows NT™

John McKenzie would like to dedicate this manual to his parents, John and Elinor, and his four brothers and sisters: Bruce, Ellen, Laurie, and David.

Robert Goldman would like to dedicate this book to his wife, Maryglenn, and their daughter, Katy, with gratitude for their tolerance, support, and love.

The Student Edition of

MINITAB®

for Windows® 95 and Windows NT™

John D. McKenzie, Jr.
Babson College

Robert Goldman
Simmons College

▲ ADDISON-WESLEY

An imprint of Addison Wesley Longman, Inc.

Reading, Massachusetts • Menlo Park, California • New York • Harlow, England
Don Mills, Ontario • Sydney • Mexico City • Madrid • Amsterdam

Publishing Team
Greg Tobin, *Publisher*
Jennifer Albanese, *Sponsoring Editor*
Brenda Bravener, *Senior Marketing Manager*
Cindy Johnson, Publishing Services: *Project Manager, Developmental Editor*
Kim Ellwood, *Associate Production Supervisor*
Laura Potter, *Editorial Assistant*
Caroline Fell, *Manufacturing Coordinator*
Lisa Delgado, *Text Designer*
Barbara Atkinson, *Package Design and Illustration*
Laura Michaels, Montview Publications and Editorial Services, *Copy Editor*
Victoria Piercey, Publishing Services, *Compositor*

Minitab at Work and data set credits appear on p. I-21, which constitutes an extension of the copyright page.

Library of Congress Cataloging-in-Publication Data
McKenzie, John
The Student Edition of MINITAB for Windows User's Manual : release 12 / John D. McKenzie Jr., Robert N. Goldman.
  p.   cm.
Includes index.
ISBN 0-201-39711-0. — ISBN 0-201-39715-3 (User's Manual/Software Package)
1. Mathematical statistics—Data processing. 2. Minitab for Windows.   I. Goldman, Robert N.   II. Title.
QA276.4.M297 1998   94-8128
519.5′0285′5369—dc21   98-9915
                                  CIP

ISBN   0-201-39715-3   (User's Manual/Software Package)
          0-201-39711-0   (User's Manual)

6 7 8 9 10—CRW—0201

PREFACE

Welcome to *The Student Edition of MINITAB for Windows® 95 and Windows NT™ Release 12*.

    The Student Edition is an educational version of Minitab statistical software, Release 12. It is designed to provide students with an easy-to-learn software package to be used in describing, analyzing, and displaying the data that is so integral a part of statistical education today. It is well-suited for use in a wide variety of statistics, business, and engineering courses.

    Minitab is a powerful tool originally developed at The Pennsylvania State University as a teaching aid for introductory statistics courses. It is now one of the most widely used statistical analysis packages for college instruction, currently used at over 2,000 schools worldwide. Learning Minitab is a valuable asset for future careers. Across the globe, distinguished and successful corporations choose Minitab for quality and process improvement and for general data analysis. In fact, the majority of Fortune 500 companies rely on Minitab's award-winning software as part of their formula for success.

    The Student Edition of MINITAB for Windows® 95 and Windows NT™ Release 12 includes the following:

- Comprehensive statistical capabilities, including descriptive statistics, simulations and distributions, elementary inferential statistics, analysis of variance, regression, analysis of categorical data, nonparametric methods, control charts, and time series analysis

- A menu-driven interface providing easy access to Minitab statistical, graphical, and data management capabilities

- Data windows permitting data entry, editing, and browsing in a spreadsheet-like display

- An on-line Help facility using the Microsoft Windows Help system to provide context-specific help at the click of a mouse button

- The ability to import and export data, including data from Microsoft Excel and Microsoft Word

- Quality management tools

- Professional graphics, which enable users to produce a comprehensive array of presentation-quality graphs

Objectives

The Student Edition of MINITAB for Windows® 95 and Windows NT™ Release 12 is designed to introduce students to a powerful statistical analysis program that they can use to describe, analyze, and display data. The primary objectives of the package are as follows:

- To provide a complete educational environment for learning Minitab for Windows

- To provide students with a powerful and versatile tool that will enhance their learning experience

- To teach students the basics of Minitab in the context of case studies and *real* data drawn from business, psychology, education, engineering, health care, and the life and physical sciences

- To provide instructors with a flexible means of integrating technology into their classrooms

What's New in This Edition

The Student Edition of MINITAB for Windows® 95 and Windows NT™ Release 12 includes the standard features instructors have come to expect, but it includes more functionality than ever before, particularly those functions that would be useful in business courses. Additional capabilities for analysis include expanded basic tools such as inferences about proportions, paired t-tests, and binary logistic regression. There is also the capability to produce a wide variety of high-resolution graphs, including graphs that are built into many of the statistical procedures.

New and Revised Software Features

New! Multiple worksheets allowing up to 5,000 data points and 1,000 columns

New! The ability to both split and create subsets of worksheets

New! Projects that can store up to five data sets and unlimited graphs and plots in a single file

New! Powerful file import and export capabilities for the most common file types, including Excel and text files

New! Increased ability to handle text data

New! Sample-size and power-calculation features

New! Calculator that provides the ability to calculate mathematical equations by pointing and clicking

New! Data manipulation features that allow quick access to common operations

New! Estimations and test capabilities for paired-t and one- and two-proportion problems

New! Built-in graphs available in analysis commands

New! Graph brushing feature that allows users to see details of one or more graph points simply by highlighting them

New! On-line help that provides more "how to" information, examples, and statistical explanations for all Minitab commands

Complete Windows interface with menus, dialog boxes, and toolbars making full use of copying, cutting, and pasting text output, data, and graphs between Minitab for Windows and other applications

Data windows that allow data entry, editing, and browsing in a spreadsheet-like format

Excel compatibility

Comprehensive statistics capabilities, including inferences about proportions, power and sample size analysis, best subsets, and binary logistic regression

Professional graphics, offering a wide array of customization tools, including the *new* graph editor

Improved printing capabilities

New Features of the Student Edition Manual

- 16 hands-on, self-paced tutorials, now designed to teach students how to use greatly expanded software capabilities through a variety of approaches

- Tutorial 16 that explains the interface between the Student Edition of Minitab and other software, including Microsoft Excel and Microsoft Word

- Many new examples, case studies, Minitab at Work essays, problems, and exercises, all carefully checked for accuracy

- Over 75 real data sets chosen for their interest level as well as their applicability to the techniques under discussion

Networks

The Student Edition of MINITAB for Windows® 95 and Windows NT™ Release 12 is designed to be used by a single user on a single computer. It will not run as a shared application installed on a network server. If more than one user tries to run the Minitab software at the same time, the program will terminate.

Organization of This Manual

This manual is organized into three sections:

Part I, "Getting Started," begins with an overview in Chapter 1 of what is needed to successfully use *The Student Edition of MINITAB for Windows® 95 and Windows NT™ Release 12*. It includes a concise explanation of the conventions used throughout the manual, the system requirements needed to run the software, and information regarding technical support. It also provides complete and easy-to-use instructions for installing, starting, and exiting Minitab. Chapter 2 gives a guided tour to the program's on-line Help. Chapter 3 takes students through a sample session designed to give them an introduction to the program and the features of the manual.

Part II, "Tutorials," is the heart of the manual. It contains 16 interactive tutorials that expose students to the full power of the software through a careful, step-by-step explanation of the necessary procedures to follow. Most tutorials include case studies from business, psychology, education, engineering, health care, and/or the life and physical sciences. These case studies give students the opportunity to immediately apply their knowledge of the software within an interesting and real-life context, using real data provided for this purpose.

As students perform steps in the tutorial, screen views are shown in the manual to teach and illustrate Minitab concepts and features with as little additional outside instruction as possible. Each tutorial requires approximately 45 to 60 minutes to complete (not including end-of-chapter material). Tutorial 16 requires the use of Microsoft Word and Excel for completion. While other word processing and spreadsheet programs may be used, instructors should provide additional instructions for executing the lesson.

Each tutorial ends with a summary and review section including a Minitab command summary and a section that tests the student's mastery of material through exercises and practice problems. The exercises consist of matching and true/false questions. Data sets from the tutorial and new data sets unique to this portion of the tutorial are used in the practice problems. In selected tutorials, a Minitab at Work feature illustrates how Minitab is used in the workplace.

Students unfamiliar with Minitab should complete the sample session in "Getting Started" and the first four tutorials, dealing with data entry and manipulation and graphics, before moving on to the other tutorials. Most students will complete, in order, Tutorials 5 through 8, which cover graphics, descriptive statistics, basic probability, and elementary statistical inference. The remaining tutorials (9 through16) can be completed in any sequence. Some tutorials, however, contain case studies that are continued from earlier tutorials.

Part III, "Exploring Data," contains descriptions of all of the real data sets used in the tutorials and practice problems. It also contains descriptions of other data sets that students may want to use for additional practice.

Differences between the Student Edition and the Professional Version of Minitab for Windows

The Student Edition of MINITAB for Windows® 95 and Windows NT™ Release 12 is compatible with the Professional version, but with the following differences:

- The worksheet size is limited to 5,000 data points.

- Selected advanced commands and subcommands have not been included (see the Instructor's Manual for a complete listing).

- Matrix functions are not included.

- Minitab's macro capability (%Macros) is not included (but Exec macro capability is).

Reviewers

We would like to thank the following reviewers who assisted in the development of this publication and with prior editions:

Robert Hayden, *Plymouth State College*
Max Jerrell, *Northern Arizona University*
Milo Schield, *Augsburg College*
Lloyd Jaisingh, *Morehead State University*
Henry Reynolds, *University of Delaware*
Dan Toy, *California State University*
Calvin Williams, *Carnegie Mellon University*
Wayne Winston, *Indiana University*
Mustafa R. Yilmaz, *Northeastern University*
Jack Uurkiewicz, *Pace University*
Peter Zehna, *Naval Postgraduate School*

J. M.
R. G.

ABOUT THE AUTHORS

John McKenzie has been teaching applied statistics courses to undergraduate and MBA students at Babson College since 1978. He also provides statistical advice to the college's faculty and staff. He has used statistical software in his teaching and consulting for over 25 years, and he has been a co-editor of the Minitab User's Group Newsletter. He has also been a member of the Planning Committee of the Making Statistics More Effective in Schools of Business conferences. He has held a number of positions with the American Statistical Association, among them the representative of the Council of Chapters on its Board of Directors. In 1992, the Association presented him with a Founders Award. He has an A. B. in mathematics from Amherst College. From the University of Michigan, he has masters degrees in mathematics and statistics and a Ph.D. in statistics.

Robert Goldman has been teaching a wide variety of statistics courses at Simmons College since 1972. He is the co-author of the textbook Statistics: An Introduction and has consulted widely for a number of states and the Federal government. For the past three years, he has been the president of the Boston Chapter of the American Statistical Association. He has a B.Sc. degree in statistics from the London School of Economics and a masters degree and a Ph.D. in statistics from Harvard University.

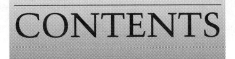

CONTENTS

PART I

GETTING STARTED

CHAPTER

Before You Begin

Checking Your Package

You can purchase *The Student Edition of Minitab® for Windows® 95/NT™* in either of two ways:

1. Without the Minitab software

   If you are planning to use a school computer with the Minitab software already loaded, you may have purchased just the manual, *The Student Edition of Minitab for Windows*. To complete the tutorials in this manual, you will also need a 3-1/2-in. high-density disk on which to store the files you create. The section entitled "Formatting Your Data Disk" in Chapter 2 of "Getting Started" provides instructions for formatting the disk.

2. With the Minitab software

   If you plan to run Minitab on your own computer, you will need to buy the entire package, which includes the Minitab software and *The Student Edition of Minitab for Windows* manual. You can save the files you create during the exercises on your personal computer's hard disk or on a separate 3-1/2-in. high-density disk.

▼ **Note** In this manual, "Minitab" refers only to the version of the software you received in *The Student Edition of Minitab for Windows* package. ▲

The package of *The Student Edition of Minitab for Windows* contains these items:

- The User's Manual (this book) called *The Student Edition of Minitab for Windows*

- A CD-ROM that contains the Minitab software and the data files you need in order to complete the tutorials in this book

- A Special Offer Upgrade Card that you return to Minitab, Inc., if you want to upgrade from the Student Edition to the Professional version (see later in this chapter for more information about the Professional version)

What's in This Book

Part I, "Getting Started," contains four chapters:

Chapter 1, "Before You Begin," familiarizes you with this manual and explains its typographical conventions.

Chapter 2, "Installing Minitab," shows you how to install the Minitab software.

Chapter 3, "Using Minitab," describes how to start and stop Minitab. It also explains how to use on-line Help to get information about the program and the statistical procedures it performs.

Chapter 4, "Sample Session," guides you through an actual Minitab session so that you can try out Minitab's capabilities before you begin the tutorials. If you have Windows experience, are familiar with on-line Help, and Minitab is already installed, you can skip directly to Chapter 4.

Part II, "Tutorials," is the heart of this book. Beginning with the simplest features of Minitab, its 16 tutorials introduce the major features of the software in a step-by-step, hands-on format. The exercises and practice problems at the end of each tutorial reinforce the concepts you've learned. Most of the tutorials and practice problems use the data sets that come with the Minitab program. You should start with Tutorials 1 through 4 to familiarize yourself with all of Minitab's basic operations, but you may then proceed from there in the order most useful to you. Some of the later tutorials continue case studies introduced in earlier ones, but you can still do most of those problems independently.

Part III, "Exploring Data," describes the data sets installed with the Minitab program. These data sets cover a variety of fields, including business, psychology, education, engineering, health care, and the life and physical sciences.

What Is the Student Edition of Minitab for Windows

The Student Edition of Minitab for Windows is an educational version of Minitab Release 12 for Windows (Professional version) that includes all but a limited number of the features and functions of the Professional version. In the Student Edition, worksheets may contain up to 5,000 cells, and up to five worksheets may be open at once. You can have up to 100 graphs open at once (if you have enough memory) and up to 1,000 columns of data in a worksheet.

A complete comparison of the features of the two versions is available in the Feature List installed with Minitab and in the Minitab folder on the Start menu.

Required Computer System

Your computer system must meet the following requirements in order to run Minitab:

- An IBM or compatible microcomputer with a 486 or higher processor

- Windows 95 or Windows NT 3.51 or 4.0

- A CD-ROM drive and one floppy disk drive

- VGA or SVGA monitor

- A mouse (required for some functions)

- A hard disk drive with at least 25MB of available space

- At least 16MB of random access memory (RAM)

- A math coprocessor (optional, but strongly recommended)

▼ **Note** The hard disk on which you install Minitab cannot be a network server, as this product does not run on a network. ▲

Typographical Conventions

Typographical conventions and symbols are used throughout this manual to make the material easier to use.

Any action that you should perform appears on a line by itself, indented, and preceded by a square bullet (■). For example:

- Type **Grades** in the "Variables" text box

- Click **Annotation**, and press Enter

Boldface type indicates letters, numbers, and/or symbols that you enter using the keyboard. Also in boldface are elements on the screen, including commands, that you are to click or select.

Quotation marks set off labels that identify text boxes in which you must enter data on the screen.

Italic type introduces a new term or concept.

"**Choose**" tells you to make a menu selection by using either the keyboard or the mouse.

"**Type**" instructs you to enter text using the keyboard. It is important to type this information *exactly* as shown, including any punctuation or spaces.

"**Press**" indicates that you should either press the specified key on the keyboard, such as Tab or Enter, or hold down the mouse button.

This book assumes you are using a mouse, although it indicates keyboard shortcuts when appropriate. (If you are unfamiliar with using a mouse or with other basic Windows operations, select Help from the Windows Start menu and choose a topic from the Contents list that appears.)

In later tutorials, as you become more familiar with Minitab, this book displays instructions in an abbreviated form using the greater than symbol (>). For example, instructions to open the Stat menu, choose Basic Statistics, and then choose Descriptive Statistics are shortened as follows:

■ Choose **Stat > Basic Statistics > Descriptive Statistics**

You can invoke commands in Minitab in a variety of ways. You should follow the tutorial instructions exactly so that you will gain experience with different ways of working with the commands. As you become familiar with them, you can then use the approach that is most comfortable for you.

Technical Support

If you encounter difficulty with installing or operating Minitab, please check the Troubleshooting section of Minitab's on-line Help (see Chapter 3 for instructions on using Help). Additional tips and technical support are available on the Minitab Web site at *www.minitab.com* and the Addison Wesley Longman Web site at *hepg.awl.com* (keyword: minitab).

Neither Addison-Wesley Publishing Company, Inc., nor Minitab, Inc., provides telephone assistance to users of Minitab. However, registered instructors who have adopted this product for their students are entitled to telephone support. You should report any problems you encounter with the Minitab software to your instructor. Be sure to note exactly what action you were performing when the problem occurred, as well as the exact error message received, if any.

If you would like to receive newsletters and product announcements from Minitab, Inc., send your name, address, and telephone number to Minitab and ask to be added to its mailing list. Mail your request to Minitab, Inc., 3081 Enterprise Drive, State College, PA 16801-3008.

CHAPTER 2

Installing Minitab

If you are using your own computer, you need to install Minitab software on your hard disk by following the instructions in the next two sections. If you are using a school computer, you can skip to the section entitled "Data Files and the Student Edition of Minitab for Windows," which presumes Minitab has already be installed. If it has not, contact your instructor or technical resource person.

▼ **Note** The hard disk on which you install Minitab cannot be on a network server, as this product does not run on a network. ▲

Before Installation

Before installing Minitab on your hard disk, you should:

- Refer to the "Checking Your Package" section in Chapter 1 for a list of the contents of your *The Student Edition of Minitab for Windows* package

- Make sure you have Windows 95 or Windows NT on your system and that your system satisfies the requirements outlined in the section "Required Computer System" in Chapter 1

▼ **Note** Because the Minitab CD-ROM contains compressed files, you must use the installation program to load the files onto your hard disk. You will not be able to use these files if you copy them directly from the CD-ROM to your hard disk. ▲

Installing Minitab

The Minitab installation program automatically installs Minitab in a directory named *Mtbwinst* on your hard disk. A *directory* is like a file folder in which you store pieces of related information. Usually when you install a program, it creates its own directory for storing its components.

To install Minitab:

- Turn on the computer, if necessary

- Be sure Windows is running but that no other applications are running

- Insert *The Student Edition of Minitab for Windows* CD-ROM in your computer's CD-ROM drive (referred to in this section as drive D; substitute the appropriate letter for your CD-ROM drive)

If your computer system is set to auto-load the CD-ROM, the Minitab Setup program may start automatically. If it does, skip the next three steps. If not, launch the Setup program:

- Click the **Start** button usually found at the bottom-left of your screen

- Choose **Run** on the Start menu that pops up

- Type **D:\SETUP** in the text box, and click **OK** (if your Minitab CD-ROM isn't in drive D, substitute the appropriate letter or use the Browse button to locate it)

The installation program loads, and the Setup program's Welcome screen appears, as shown in Figure GS-1.

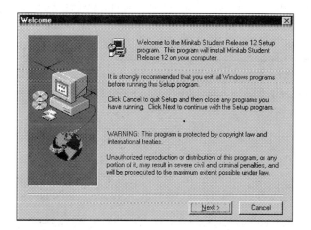

As you install Minitab, you will proceed through a series of dialog boxes that allow you to customize your installation. You can use the buttons at the bottom of each dialog box to go back to a previous step or to cancel at any time. If you did not quit any open applications before beginning, you should click the Cancel button now, quit the application(s), and then restart the installation.

The instructions that follow show you how to proceed through a normal installation.

- Click **Next** in the Welcome dialog box

Next, you are asked to select the components you wish to install in the Select Components dialog box, as shown in Figure GS-2. The default is a complete installation, which installs all five components listed in the dialog box. This will require approximately 19MB of space on your hard disk. **It is recommended that you accept the default. At a minimum, you must install the MINITAB Program Files, MINITAB Help, and the Data Set Files in order to complete the tutorials in this manual.** To deselect a component, click its check button to remove the check mark.

FIGURE GS-2

The Select Components dialog box

In the Select Components dialog box, you also specify the destination drive and directory in which Minitab will be installed. If you do not wish to accept the default location, *C:\Program Files\MTBWINST*, use the Browse button to select another drive. If you specify a new directory name, the installation program will create the directory for you.

When you are satisfied with the components and destination directory shown in the dialog box:

■ Click **Next**

The next screen asks you to select the program folder in which the Minitab Student Edition icon and menu name will be created. It is recommended that you accept the default, Minitab Student 12. To do this:

■ Click **Next**

The User Information dialog box appears.
In the User Information dialog box, personalize your Minitab installation:

■ Enter **your name** and **academic site** (school)

■ Click **Next**

The data you entered is confirmed on the next screen. If it is correct, click Yes. If not, click No and correct it in the dialog box that appears.

You have now entered the information needed to start the installation. The Start Copying Files dialog box appears to confirm the choices you have made. To change any of those choices, click the Back button until you are returned to the appropriate dialog box, where you can make the change. If all of the information is correct:

- Click **Next**

The installation program copies the files to your hard disk. This may take a minute or more, depending on your computer's speed.

- Click **OK** when you see the message "Setup is complete"

You are returned to the Windows desktop.

The Minitab Menu

If you installed Minitab to the default location, you will find a Minitab folder in the Programs folder on your Start menu. (If you did not, your folder may be located elsewhere on your Start menu.) To see the Minitab menu options:

- Click **Start**

- Click **Programs**

- Click **Minitab Student 12**

If you did a complete installation, you should see six items on the Minitab menu, as shown in Figure GS-3.

FIGURE GS-3

The Minitab menu on the Start menu

1. The "Feature List" is a comparison of the differences between *The Student Edition of Minitab for Windows* and the Professional version. In the Student Edition, worksheets may contain up to 5,000 cells, and up to five worksheets may be open at once. You can have up to 100 graphs open at once (if you have enough memory) and up to 1,000 columns of data in a worksheet.

2. "Minitab Help" is available here and also during a Minitab session from its menu bar. (You will learn more about Minitab Help in the next chapter.)

3. "Minitab Session Command Help" is available here and also during a Minitab session from its menu bar. (You will learn more about Minitab Help in the next chapter.)

4. "Minitab Student Release 12" launches your copy of Minitab.

5. The "Readme File" includes technical information that may be useful if you encounter installation difficulties.

6. "Uninstall Minitab" removes Minitab and all of its components from your hard disk.

If you performed a complete installation using the default options and do not see these items on your menu, try the installation process again.

Data Files and the Student Edition of Minitab for Windows

You will work with two different sets of files as you complete the tutorials in *The Student Edition of Minitab for Windows.*

1. The data files that were installed when you installed the Minitab software

These files do not appear on the Minitab menu but are stored in a directory called Student inside the *Mtbwinst* directory (or whatever you named your Minitab directory during installation). As you work through the tutorials, you will be asked to open files from the Student directory and work with the data they contain. If you are working on a lab computer, your instructor may have installed the data files in a different location. If so, substitute that location each time you are asked to open a file from the Student subdirectory.

2. The files that you will create as you work through the tutorials

You should save these files to a different directory than Student so that you don't accidentally overwrite a file in the Student directory that you will need later. If you are working in a school lab, you will want to save your work to a floppy disk. (You shouldn't count on saving your work on the school's computer.) If you are working on your own computer or you have an account on the school's network, create a different directory in which you will save all of your work. In the tutorials, you will be directed to save files to the location where you are saving your work — your floppy disk or the directory you create on the hard disk.

If you need help formatting a floppy disk for use with these tutorials, continue to the next section. If not, skip to the next chapter, where you will start Minitab.

Formatting Your Data Disk

You will need one 3-1/2-inch high-density formatted blank floppy disk. Most disks are already pre-formatted when you buy them (and are labeled "IBM Formatted"). If your disk is not formatted, you need to use Windows to do so. When you format a disk, you set it up so that Minitab (or any other application) can store and read information on it.

To format your disk:

- Make sure your floppy disk is not *write-protected* (the tab in the disk's corner should be closed)

- Insert your blank floppy disk into drive **A** (or other appropriate drive)

- Double-click the **My Computer** icon on the Windows desktop

- Single-click the **3 1/2 Floppy (A:)** icon (don't double-click or it will open the disk)

- Choose **File > Format** from the menu bar on the My Computer window

The Format - 3 1/2 Floppy (A:) dialog box appears, as shown in Figure GS-4, which you will use to format the disk.

- Be sure the "Capacity" box is set to **1.44 Mb**

- Click the **Full** option button

- Type a name for the disk in the "Label" text box (if desired)

- Click **Start**

FIGURE GS-4

The Format - 3 1/2 Floppy (A:) dialog box for floppy disks

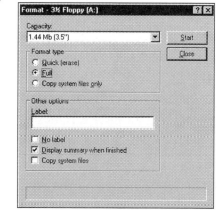

When formatting is complete, your data disk is ready to store information. The instructions in this manual assume that you will save all of the files you work with during the tutorials on this disk. If you're using your own computer, you can store your work directly on your hard drive by substituting your file's pathname for those specified in this manual.

CHAPTER 3

Using Minitab

If you have not installed Minitab on your computer's hard disk, you should do so now. Refer to Chapter 2, "Installing Minitab, in "Getting Started" for instructions on how to do so.

Starting Minitab

To start Minitab:

- Turn on your computer, if necessary

- Click **Start** to open the Start menu

- Click **Programs**, then **Minitab Student 12**, and then **Minitab Student Release 12**

▼ **Note** If you are running Minitab on a school computer, you may need to ask your instructor or technical resource person where Minitab is located on the Start menu. ▲

The Student Edition of Minitab for Windows welcome screen appears for a moment and then clears automatically. The main Minitab window opens, as shown in Figure GS-5. The Minitab *menu bar* appears near the top of the window. Each menu lists groups of related commands that you use to operate the program. Below the menu bar is the *toolbar*. The buttons on the toolbar invoke the most commonly used commands and make them available with a single click of the mouse.

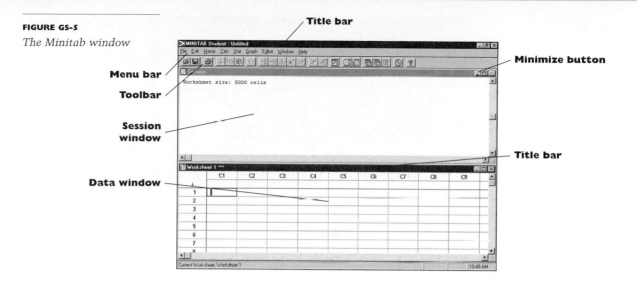

You also can see two of Minitab's open windows: the Session window and the Data window (labeled "Worksheet 1 ***"). Minitab has several kinds of windows, and any combination of them may be open at one time.

Minitab Windows

When you first start Minitab, the main Minitab window and two other windows are visible: the Session window and the Data window, as shown in Figure GS-5. Each window has its own title bar and can be moved and resized, maximized and minimized:

■ To move a window, click on its title bar and hold down the mouse button while dragging the mouse

■ To resize a window, position the mouse over the right or bottom edge until the cursor turns into a double-ended arrow, and then click and hold down the mouse button while dragging to resize the window

Two more windows, History and Info, are open but minimized. To see these windows:

■ Minimize the Session window by clicking its **minimize** button ▬

■ Minimize the Data window by clicking its **minimize** button

Your screen should look as shown in Figure GS-6, with all four windows lined up along the bottom of the screen.

Restore button

Maximize button

To return a window to its previous size, you can click on its title bar and use the menu that appears to move it, maximize it, or restore it to its previous size. You also can click its restore, maximize, or close buttons directly.

■ Click the **restore** button 🗗, shown in Figure GS-6, for the Session window

Notice that each window is identified by its name in the title bar, except the Data window. The Data window's title bar displays the name of the current data set, or *worksheet*, in this case "Worksheet 1 ***."

■ Click the Data window's **maximize** button ▢

When a window is maximized, its title is added to the Minitab window title bar. Notice that the window title is now "Minitab Student - Untitled - [Worksheet 1 ***]," as shown in Figure GS-7.

Archive cell

Status bar

When one window is maximized, its title bar is not visible, but its minimize, restore, and close buttons appear directly below those for the main Minitab window. You can use these to close or change the size of the window.

To make a different window active when one is maximized, select it by name from the Window menu on the menu bar:

■ Choose **Window > Session**

The Session window is now active and maximized, and its name appears in the Minitab title bar. To make the Data window active:

■ Choose **Window > Worksheet 1** ***

The Data window is active again.

Worksheets and the Data Window

The Data window presents a view of the data set stored in a *worksheet*. Each worksheet has its own Data window. You can have up to five worksheets — Data windows — open at once.

Like a spreadsheet, a worksheet has *columns* and *rows*. However, unlike electronic spreadsheets such as Lotus 1-2-3 and Microsoft Excel, Minitab worksheets contain only numbers and text, not formulas. Minitab worksheets can also store single-number constants, although you can't see them in the Data window.

Generally, each column lists data for one variable and each row displays a set of observations for an individual case. The worksheet has 1,000 columns and as many rows as your computer's available memory allows. However, the total number of rows times the number of columns must be less than 5,000. Columns are referred to by column numbers (C1, C2, . . . , C1000) or by names. Assigning names to the columns makes it easier to remember what they contain. (The columns in the worksheet shown in Figure GS-7 are unnamed.) Rows are referred to by number: 1, 2, and so on.

A *cell* is the intersection of a column and a row. Notice the outline around the cell in column C1 in Figure GS-7. The outline means that the cell is the *current*, or *active*, cell. You can activate any cell in the worksheet by clicking it. Minitab updates the Data window automatically whenever you make any changes to the worksheet.

Minitab commands work on the current worksheet, which is identified by the *status bar* at the bottom of the screen. Up to five worksheets and the information associated with them (in the Session, Graph, History, and Info windows) can be stored in a *project*. You will learn more about projects and how Minitab stores data as you work through Tutorials 1–4.

Entering Minitab Commands

You can enter a Minitab command by choosing it from a menu on the menu bar, clicking its toolbar button, or typing its session command in the Session window. Most menu commands open a dialog box that allows you to make further choices that relate to how the command will be carried out.

You'll learn more about the individual commands and the different ways to invoke them in the tutorials. To learn more about a particular command or to get help when you are in a dialog box, you can use Minitab's on-line Help feature.

Using Minitab Help

The Help menu, shown in Figure GS-8, offers several ways to get information about Minitab:

■ Click **Help** on the menu bar

Contents
Getting Started...
Search for Help on...
Session Command Help
How to Use Help
Minitab on the Web
About Minitab

"Contents" opens the main Minitab Help window and presents an index of topics from which to choose. All of the topic areas on the Help menu are also available from the main Help window.

"Getting Started" walks you through a typical Minitab session to get you started.

"Search for Help on" lets you select from an alphabetical index of topics or search on a particular word.

"Session Command Help" provides a list of the commands you can type in the Session window.

"How to Use Help" explains how to use the Help features.

"Minitab on the Web" opens your Web browser and, if your computer is connected to the Internet, will take you to the Minitab Web site at www.minitab.com, where additional information about Minitab can be found.

In the following sections, you will learn how to use Help to get information about commands and the data sets in the Student subdirectory.

Context-Sensitive Help

Minitab offers context-sensitive help for its commands and dialog boxes. When you press F1, the help pages for that topic appear:

- Choose **Stat** from the menu bar

- Choose **Basic Statistics**, and then choose **1-Sample Z** from the menu that appears

  The 1-Sample Z dialog box appears.
  To get help for this command:

- Press the F1 **function key** on your keyboard

Minitab Help displays the main Help window for 1-Sample Z, as shown in Figure GS-9. (Your window may be a different size when it opens. All Help windows may be moved and resized like any other window.)

FIGURE GS-9

The 1-Sample Z Help window

After a brief description of the 1-Sample Z test, each of the options in the 1-Sample Z dialog box is explained. Underlined words in the Help window are *links* to additional information. For most commands, Minitab Help offers the following links:

"overview" introduces the command and the statistical concepts related to it.

"how to" presents step-by-step instructions for using the command.

"example" shows how the steps would be carried out with a particular data set and offers help with interpreting the results.

USING MINITAB HELP GS-17

"data" describes conditions that must be met by the data set to be used with the command.

"see also" links to topics that relate to the command.

To see the step-by-step instructions for the 1-Sample Z:

- Click **how to**

The step-by-step instructions appear, as shown in Figure GS-10.

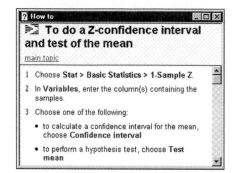

Notice at the bottom of the window the option to perform a hypothesis test. To return to the main Help window for the test:

- Click the How to window's **close button** ☒

Help Contents

You also can get help for each command on Minitab's menus by looking up that command in the list of menu commands in Help Contents. You open Help Contents by choosing it from the Help menu or, if a Help window is already open, by using the Contents button in the window.

- Click the **Contents** button in the Minitab Help window

The Contents window opens, as shown in Figure GS-11.

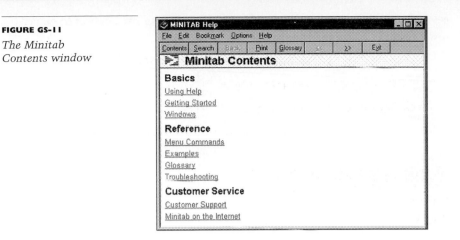

The underlined words in the Contents window *link* you to help for the basics, reference material, and customer service. You can reach all of the topics on the Help menu from the Contents window, too. To get help for a particular command, you can look it up in the Menu Commands section:

■ Choose **Menu Commands**, and then click **Stat Menu** in the window that appears

All of the commands on the Stat menu appear in order in the next window.

■ Choose **Basic Statistics**

Each item on the Basic Statistics menu is also a link.

■ Choose **1-Sample Z**

The main Help window for the test appears as you saw in the last section.

Searching for Help Topics

Another way to locate topics in Help is to search for a topic by name. You can search by choosing Search for Help On from the Help menu or by clicking the Search button in any Help window:

■ Click the **Search** button in the Minitab Help window

The Help Topics window appears with the Index tab in front. This tab allows you to choose from a list of Help topics in alphabetical order.

■ Type **menu** in the text box at the top

The list of topics changes as you type to show topics that begin with the letters you typed, as shown in Figure GS-12.

To go to a topic:

- Click **menu commands** to highlight it in the list box

- Click the **Display** button

- Click **Display** again when the list of subtopics appears

The list of menus appears as before from which you can navigate to help for a particular command.

Getting Help with Data Sets

All of the data sets you will use in this manual— and several others that are included with Minitab — are described in Minitab's Help. You can see a list of these data sets in alphabetical order by searching on the topic Sample Data Sets as you did before:

- Click **Search**

- Type **sample**

- Highlight **Sample data sets:opening**, and click **Display**

The Sample Data Sets topic appears, as shown in Figure GS-13. The alphabet buttons at the top of the window link you to a list of data sets with names that start with a given letter. (Your window may open to a different size than the window shown.)

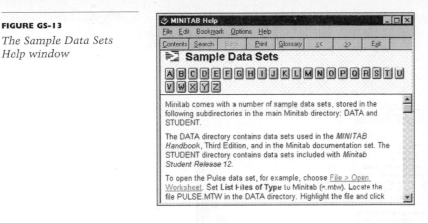

You can also type the name of the data set itself to go directly to its Help window:

- Click **Search**

- Type **music**

- Double-click ***Music.mtw*** in the list box

The description of the *Music.mtw* data set and its variables appears as shown in Figure GS-14

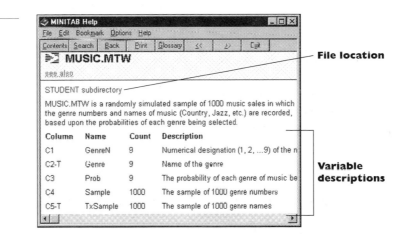

For each data set, Minitab Help tells you where the file is located; in this case, it is in the Student subdirectory. After a brief description, each variable is listed with its column name, variable name, number of different data items, and description.

When you have located a topic, you can print a copy of the information by clicking the Print button in the Help window or choosing Print from the File menu in the Help window.

If you need a definition for a term you encounter in Minitab, the Glossary button will bring up a list of terms and their definitions.

To leave Help, you can click the close button for the Help window or

- Choose **File > Exit** from the Help window menu bar

Exiting Minitab

To exit Minitab:

- Click **File** on the Minitab menu bar

- Click **Exit**

Minitab returns you to the Windows desktop.

CHAPTER
4

Sample Session

Objectives

In this sample session, you learn how to:

- open and explore an existing worksheet
- create a new variable by using basic arithmetic functions that operate on existing variables within a worksheet
- describe the characteristics of a variable by using basic statistics
- create two high-resolution graphs based on data in the worksheet
- correlate two variables in the worksheet

Getting Started

Before beginning this session, make sure that you:

- Install Minitab on your computer's hard disk (refer to Chapter 2, "Installing Minitab," for instructions)

- Format a floppy disk for storing your work (refer to "Formatting Your Data Disk" in Chapter 2 for instructions)

  To start Minitab:

- Click **Start** to open the Start menu

- Click **Programs**, then **Minitab Student 12**, and then **Minitab Student Release 12**

  The Student Edition of Minitab for Windows welcome screen appears for a moment and then clears automatically.

▼ **Note** If you are running Minitab on a school computer, you may need to ask your instructor or technical resource person where Minitab is located on the Start menu. ▲

Exploring an Existing Worksheet

In the next section you'll explore an existing worksheet named *Prof.mtw*. The tutorials in this book are based around data sets and case studies as you will see in this section.

CASE STUDY: EDUCATION—FACULTY SURVEY

As president of the student government at your school, you have just received the results of a faculty survey conducted by the student government. You want to prepare an article for the student government newsletter that describes some high points of the survey results. You decide to use Minitab to perform your preliminary analysis. (The data set used in this case study reflects the actual results of a recent survey at a U. S. university.)

  To open the file that contains the survey data:

- Click the **maximize button** in the upper-right corner of the Data window so that the Data window fills the Minitab window

- Click **File** on the Minitab menu bar

- Click **Open Worksheet**

The Open Worksheet dialog box appears.

In the "Look in" text box at the top, you should see the directory name Student. If not:

- Click the **drop-down list arrow** ▼ to the right of the "Look in" text box

- Navigate to the **Student** subdirectory where the data files for this manual are installed (you may need to ask your instructor or technical resource person where these files are located)

- Use the scroll bar at the bottom of the list box to scroll the list of filenames until you find *Prof.mtw*

- Click *Prof.mtw*

- Click **OK**

The Data window should now look as shown in Figure GS-15. Minitab displays the survey data in the Data window; the name of the current worksheet, *Prof.mtw*, is in the title bar.

FIGURE GS-15

Prof.mtw worksheet

	C1-T	C2	C3	C4	C5	C6	C7	C8	C9-T
↓	Dept	Number	Interest	Manner	Course	Instrucr	Responds	Size	Year
1	ACC	221	2.07	2.67	2.27	2.73	15	41	Soph
2	ACC	221	2.40	3.07	2.75	3.38	15	41	Soph
3	ACC	321	2.64	3.36	3.00	3.40	11	71	Junior
4	ACC	344	3.42	3.67	3.42	3.67	12	36	Junior
5	AER	101	3.25	3.50	3.13	3.13	8	52	Freshman
6	ARC	426	3.29	3.12	3.35	3.41	15	15	Senior
7	ART	111	2.47	1.73	2.33	2.00	15	22	Freshman
8	ART	111	3.00	3.42	3.08	3.17	12	21	Freshman
9	ART	211	3.17	2.00	2.67	2.33	6	15	Soph
10	ART	485	3.60	3.90	3.50	3.70	10	15	Senior
11	ATH	155	2.60	2.64	2.79	3.00	14	49	Freshman
12	ATH	212	2.92	3.09	2.83	3.17	12	46	Soph
13	CHM	111	1.44	2.78	2.00	2.78	9	68	Freshman
14	CHM	141	2.17	3.42	2.75	3.17	12	114	Freshman
15	CHM	142	1.38	0.92	1.46	1.46	13	64	Freshman
16	COM	193	3.71	3.64	3.36	3.64	14	44	Freshman
17	COM	205	3.83	3.83	3.83	3.83	6	16	Soph
18	COM	231	3.13	3.73	3.20	3.67	15	27	Soph
19	COM	359	3.30	3.00	3.00	3.20	10	29	Junior
20	COM	431	3.00	3.44	2.78	3.33	10	72	Senior

The student government randomly distributed surveys to students in 146 class sections in a variety of disciplines. The survey asked students to evaluate both the course and the instructor. Each participating section received 15 surveys. Some sections returned all 15 surveys, while others returned fewer.

The results for each section were averaged for use in this worksheet. The work-sheet consists of 9 columns and 146 rows. Each row summarizes the answers on the 1 to 15 surveys returned from a particular class. The 9 columns in the *Prof.mtw* worksheet present the information in the following table.

Number	Name	Description
C1-T	Dept	The academic department of the course to which the 15 surveys were distributed. The T following the column number C1 denotes a column that contains text (as opposed to numeric) data.
C2	Number	The course number.
C3	Interest	The section average of the surveyed students' responses to this statement: The course stimulated your interest in this area. The scale for this statement is 0 = strongly disagree, 1 = disagree, 2 = neutral, 3 = agree, and 4 = strongly agree.
C4	Manner	The section average of the surveyed students' responses to this statement: The instructor presented course material in an effective manner. The scale for this statement is 0 = strongly disagree, 1 = disagree, 2 = neutral, 3 = agree, and 4 = strongly agree.
C5	Course	The section average of the surveyed students' responses to this statement: Overall, I would rate this course as . . . . The scale for this statement is 0 = poor, 1 = below average, 2 = average, 3 = above average, and 4 = excellent.
C6	Instrucr	The section average of the surveyed students' responses to this statement: Overall, I would rate this instructor as . . . . The scale for this statement is 0 = poor, 1 = below average, 2 = average, 3 = above average, and 4 = excellent.
C7	Responds	The number of completed surveys returned out of the 15 surveys distributed to the section.
C8	Size	The number of students in the section.
C9-T	Year	The level of the course: Freshman, Soph (sophomore), Junior, or Senior.

Getting Information about a Data Set

As you work with data sets in this manual, you can read about the variables contained in them in three ways:

1. By reading about them in Part III of this manual, "Exploring Data"

2. By looking at the description in on-line Help (as you did in Chapter 3)

3. By viewing the Info window

   To display the Info window:

■ Click **Window** on the Minitab menu bar

■ Click **Info**

   The Info window, shown in Figure GS-16, is displayed in front of the Data window.

   The Info window summarizes the worksheet contents; Minitab updates it automatically as the worksheet changes. The Info window for this worksheet lists the nine variables in the worksheet, the name of each variable, the number of cells in each column (146), and the number of missing cells in each column. The number that appears in the Missing column for variable C8, for example, indicates that the size of 16 of the classes surveyed was unavailable or missing.

   To return to the Data window, use its button on the toolbar (to see the name of a button, hold your mouse over the button):

■ Click the **Current Data window** toolbar button ▦

   Minitab returns you to the Data window.

In your article, you want to report the percentage of students within a given class that completed the survey. To find this percentage, use this equation:

% of responses in the section = (number of responses in the section/ number of students in the section) * 100

The numerator in the fraction corresponds to variable C7 (Responds) in the worksheet, and the denominator corresponds to variable C8 (Size). You store the results in C10 (Percent). Using the variables in the worksheet, the equation becomes

$$C10 = (C7/C8) \times 100 \text{ (or C7/C8 * 100, in Minitab's language).}$$

To perform these calculations using the menu:

- Click **Calc** on the Minitab menu bar

- Click **Calculator**

The Calculator dialog box, shown in Figure GS-17, appears.

The blinking I-bar in the "Store result in variable" text box is the cursor. Its shape indicates that the text box is active and that you therefore can type in it.

- Type **Percent**

- Press Tab

The I-bar moves to the "Expression" text box.

- Type **C7/C8*100**

- Click **OK**

The dialog box closes, and the Data window becomes visible again, shown in Figure GS-18. The tenth column in the worksheet (you may have to scroll to see it) now shows the percentage of students in each section who completed surveys. It is properly labeled Percent.

	C4	C5	C6	C7	C8	C9-T	C10	C11	C12
→	Manner	Course	Instrucr	Responds	Size	Year	Percent		
1	2.67	2.27	2.73	15	41	Soph	36.585		
2	3.07	2.75	3.38	15	41	Soph	36.585		
3	3.36	3.00	3.45	11	31	Junior	35.484		
4	3.67	3.42	3.67	12	36	Junior	33.333		
5	3.50	3.13	3.13	8	52	Freshman	15.385		
6	3.12	3.35	3.41	16	16	Senior	100.000		
7	1.73	2.33	2.00	15	22	Freshman	68.182		
8	3.42	3.08	3.17	12	21	Freshman	57.143		
9	2.00	2.67	2.33	6	15	Soph	40.000		
10	3.90	3.60	3.70	10	15	Senior	66.667		
11	2.64	2.79	3.00	14	49	Freshman	28.571		
12	3.09	2.83	3.17	12	46	Soph	26.087		
13	7.78	2.00	2.78	9	68	Freshman	13.235		
14	3.42	2.75	3.17	12	114	Freshman	10.526		
15	0.92	1.46	1.46	13	64	Freshman	20.313		
16	3.64	3.36	3.64	14	44	Freshman	31.818		
17	3.83	3.83	3.83	6	16	Soph	37.500		
18	3.73	3.20	3.67	15	27	Soph	55.556		
19	3.00	3.00	3.20	10	29	Junior	34.483		
20	3.44	2.78	3.33	10	72	Senior	13.889		

If you scroll through the data in C10, you see that 100.00% of two classes was surveyed, but the percentage surveyed in others was as low as 6.429%. Is this the maximum and minimum? What is the average percentage surveyed? Can you summarize the results? Investigate the Percent variable further to learn more about its characteristics.

Describing a Variable By Using Basic Statistics

To find out more about the average percentage of the sections that filled out questionnaires, you decide to obtain some basic statistics for the C10 variable you just created:

- Click **Stat** on the menu bar
- Click **Basic Statistics** to display the Basic Statistics menu
- Click **Display Descriptive Statistics**

The Display Descriptive Statistics dialog box appears, as shown in Figure GS-19.

FIGURE GS-19

The Display Descriptive Statistics dialog box

Display Descriptive Statistics

C2	Number	**Variables:**
C3	Interest	
C4	Manner	
C5	Course	
C6	Instrucr	
C7	Responds	
C8	Size	
C10	Percent	

☐ **By variable:**

Select

Help   OK   Cancel   Graphs...

- Double-click **C10 Percent** in the list box on the left

  The variable name now appears in the "Variables" box on the right.

- Click **OK**

  The Session window, shown in Figure GS-20, moves to the forefront.

FIGURE GS-20

The Session window

MINITAB Student - Untitled - [Session]

File Edit Manip Calc Stat Graph Editor Window Help

```
Worksheet size: 5000 cells
Retrieving worksheet from file: C:\Program Files\MTBWinSt\Student\Prof.mtw
Worksheet was saved on Thu Jun 04 1998

Descriptive Statistics

Variable        N        N*       Mean     Median    TrMean    StDev
Percent        130       16      42.06     39.21     41.23     19.15

Variable    SE Mean   Minimum   Maximum      Q1        Q3
Percent       1.68      6.43     100.00     28.50     54.66
```

Current Worksheet: Prof.mtw   Editable   9:55 AM

The results of the Display Descriptive Statistics command appear in lower part of the session window — 11 statistics related to the C10 variable, including the mean, median, and standard deviation.

The output shown in the Session window tells you that an average of approximately 42% (Mean = 42.06) of the students were surveyed in each class. There was a fair amount of variability, as indicated by a standard deviation of 19% (StDev = 19.15). For example, in some classes, only 6% (Minimum = 6.43) of the class was surveyed — probably a large class — while in others, 100% (Maximum = 100.00) of the class was surveyed. You will learn more about these and other measures in the tutorials.

Creating Graphs

As a senior looking back over your college career, it seems like your classes this year are much more interesting than the ones you took during your first year. You wonder if this holds true for other students. To find out, you decide to see if there's any relationship between the level of a course and the students' interest in it. You create a boxplot display to examine this information:

- Choose **Graph > Boxplot**

    The Boxplot dialog box appears, as shown in Figure GS-21.

- Double-click **C3 Interest** in the list box on the left

    The variable name, Interest, appears in the Y box, and the I-bar moves to the X box.

- Double-click **C9 Year**

- Click **OK**

Minitab displays four boxplots, shown in Figure GS-22, that portray the trend in students' interest as they progressed through college.

Notice that the title bar changes to indicate the name of the Graph window that is active. All graphs are associated with a worksheet, and the name of the Graph window includes the name of the worksheet. The status bar at the bottom of the screen confirms that *Prof.mtw* is still the current worksheet.

FIGURE GS-22

Boxplots showing student interest by level of course

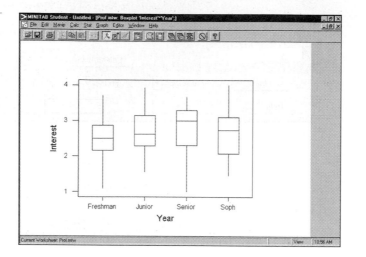

The horizontal line that divides each box in two represents the median interest level for each year. The graph indicates that senior and sophomore classes are rated as more interesting than freshman and junior classes. The ends of the "whiskers" that extend up and down from the boxes represent the largest and smallest values. Note the extensive range of interest ratings for each level. Due to the large variability in student interest, you wouldn't want to claim that seniors are more interested than first year students in their classes.

You also wonder whether students who dislike the subject matter of a course rate their instructors lower. You use a scatter plot to show the relationship between course and instructor ratings:

■ Choose **Graph > Plot**

The Plot dialog box appears as shown in Figure GS-23.

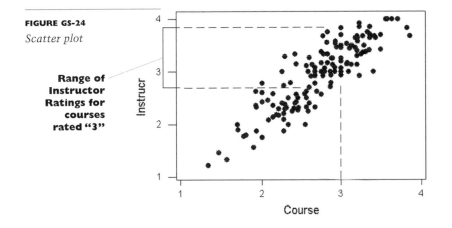

Plot

C2	Number	
C3	Interest	
C4	Manner	
C5	Course	
C6	Instrucr	
C7	Responds	
C8	Size	
C10	Percent	

Graph variables:

Graph	Y	X
1		
2		
3		

Data display:

Item	Display	For each	Group variables
1	Symbol	Graph	
2			
3			

Edit Attributes...

Select   Annotation   Frame

Help   Options...   OK   Cancel

■ Double-click **C6 Instrucr**

The variable name, Instrucr, appears in the "Y" text box.

■ Double-click **C5 Course**

That variable name appears in the "X" text box.

■ Click **OK**

Minitab displays a scatter plot, shown in Figure GS-24, that depicts the relationship between course and instructor ratings. The name in the Minitab title bar changes to reflect the new Graph window. (In this manual, graphs will be shown as they appear in Figure GS-24, without the menu and title bars, so that they are easier to see.) The boxplot you created still exists in its own window, which you can switch to by choosing its name from the Window menu.

FIGURE GS-24

Scatter plot

Range of Instructor Ratings for courses rated "3"

Your suspicions are confirmed. In general, students rate instructors relatively lower in courses they don't like than in those they do. However, regardless of course rating, there is quite a bit of variation in professor ratings. For example, students who rated the course 3.00 (a high rating) rated the instructor from approximately 2.8 to 3.8. Again, the data are highly variable.

Correlating Two Variables

To verify the apparent linear relationship between course and instructor ratings, you decide to correlate the variables you used to create the scatter plot:

■ Choose **Stat > Basic Statistics > Correlation**

The Correlation dialog box appears, as shown in Figure GS-25.

FIGURE GS-25

The Correlation dialog box

Correlation	☒

```
C2    Number        Variables:
C3    Interest      [                    ]
C4    Manner
C5    Course
C6    Instrucr
C7    Responds
C8    Size
C10   Percent


              ☑ Display p-values

     Select

   Help          OK          Cancel
```

■ Double-click **C5 Course**

■ Double-click **C6 Instrucr**

■ Click **OK**

The Session window moves to the front and displays the correlation between the Course and Instrucr variables, as shown in Figure GS-26.

```
Percent            130        16     42.06     39.21     41.23     19.15

Variable        SE Mean   Minimum   Maximum        Q1        Q3
Percent            1.68      6.43    100.00     28.50     54.66


Correlations (Pearson)


Correlation of Course and Instrucr = 0.873, P-Value = 0.000
```

The correlation value of 0.873 indicates that there is indeed a strong positive and linear relationship between course and instructor ratings.

Printing a Graph

You want to use the scatter plot in your article, so you need to print it. You can use the Window menu, which lists the names of all open windows in an application, to redisplay the scatter plot graph:

- Make sure your printer is turned on

- Choose **Window > Prof.mtw: Plot 'Instrucr'*'Course'**

    The Graph window that contains the scatter plot becomes active.

- Choose **File > Print Graph**

    Your system's Print dialog box appears.

- Click **OK** to print the plot on the printer shown at the top of the dialog box

▼ **Note** If you are using a school computer and the printer isn't directly attached to it, ask your instructor or technical resource person for the location of the printer. ▲

You now have a copy of the graph that you can include in your article to show the relationship between course and instructor ratings. You could also use Edit > Copy Graph to copy the graph to the Windows clipboard and then switch to your word processor and use Paste to insert the graph directly into your word processor.

Exiting Minitab

To exit Minitab:

- Choose **File > Exit**

   A dialog box appears, asking if you want to save the changes made to this project.

   Minitab saves individual data sets in worksheets but allows you to save up to five worksheets and all of the Graph and Session windows associated with them in a single file called a *project*. You will learn more about saving your work in the tutorials and do not need to save this session.

- Click **No**

   You have seen some of Minitab's potential. Now proceed to the tutorials, where you'll get hands-on experience using Minitab to create your own worksheets and graphs. Remember to use Minitab's on-line Help whenever you want to learn more about commands and their options.

PART II

TUTORIALS

TUTORIAL

Working with Data

This tutorial introduces the fundamentals of working with Minitab. Much of the work will be done in the Data window. You will learn how to enter data in the Data window, navigate in this window, and print data from this window.

Objectives

In this tutorial, you learn how to:

- use Minitab

- navigate the data worksheet

- enter and correct numeric and text data

- view and print data from the Data window

- save and retrieve data files

- manipulate data by using expressions

- use Minitab's Help system to find on-line information about a topic

- copy and delete columns

- insert and delete rows

- view information about a data set

▼ 1.1 Starting Minitab ▲

CASE STUDY: HEALTH MANAGEMENT — NUTRITION ANALYSIS

You have just been hired as a nutritionist for a major hospital with responsibilities for planning healthy, economical meals. The first day, your supervisor, Patricia Johnson, assigns you the task of examining some data on yogurt. The data were collected by a research company that tested 14 brands of plain yogurt. The data set consists of three variables: an overall nutritional quality rating, the cost in cents per ounce, and the number of calories per eight-ounce serving. By statistically analyzing the various brands, you hope to better understand the various yogurt products.

In this tutorial, you begin the statistical analysis by entering into Minitab the data shown in Figure 1-1. You then compute other measures using the cost and calorie variables. In a later practice problem, when you are more familiar with Minitab, you will perform more sophisticated analyses on these data.

FIGURE 1-1

Yogurt data

Row (Brand)	Nutritional Rating	Cost in Cents per Ounce	Calories per Eight-Ounce Serving
1	Excellent	11	120
2	Excellent	11	120
3	Very Good	9	100
4	Very Good	9	90
5	Poor	12	253
6	Very Good	8	250
7	Very Good	9	100
8	Excellent	7	100
9	Very Good	11	240
10	Fair	11	240
11	Fair	9	190
12	Fair	7	190
13	Poor	7	240
14	Very Good	10	160

To start Minitab:

- In Windows, click **Start** and then **Programs**

- Click **Minitab Student 12** and then **Minitab Student Release 12**

If you need help starting Minitab, refer to Getting Started, Chapter 3 of this manual.

When you start Minitab, a Session window appears in the upper half of your screen and a Data window appears in the lower half, as shown in Figure 1-2. A record of your Minitab session and much of your statistical analyses appear in the Session window. The Data window provides for easy data entry, modification, and viewing. You also will work with three other Minitab windows in these tutorials: Info, Graph, and History.

The Minitab window showing the Session and Data windows

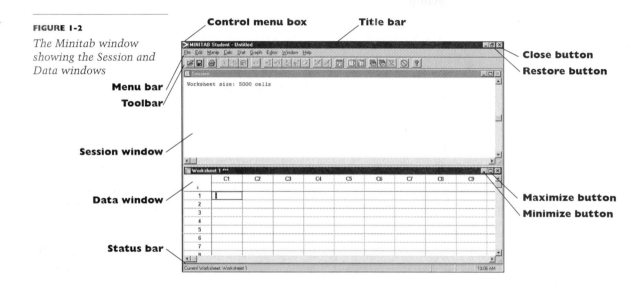

The title bar for the Minitab window reads: MINITAB Student - Untitled. The title bar for the Session window displays Session. The Data window, however, is titled Worksheet 1 *** — this is its default name. When you save your data set, the name you use replaces Worksheet 1. The three asterisks, ***, indicate that this is your active data set, that is, the one with which you are currently working. (The Student Edition of Minitab for Windows allows you to have up to five sets open at one time, but only one can be active.)

To the left of each window's title bar is its *Control menu box*. The Control menu lets you manage window size and placement. You can close a window by double-clicking its Control menu box.

To the right of each title bar are the *Minimize, Maximize,* and *Close* buttons. Clicking the Minimize button ▪ (the left-most button) reduces the window to an icon at the bottom of the Minitab window. Clicking the Maximize button ▫ (the middle button) enlarges the window to its largest size. For example, if the Minitab window does not already fill the entire screen, you can cause it to do so, or *maximize* it by clicking its maximize button.

When the Minitab window is maximized, as it is in Figure 1-2, the Maximize button becomes a Restore button ▣. You use the Restore button to return the window to its previous size.

You use the Close button ☒ only with the Data window.

Across the top of the screen and below the Minitab window title bar is a horizontal bar, the *menu bar*. The menu bar contains the names of Minitab's nine *menus*:

File

Edit

Manip

Calc

Stat

Graph

Editor

Window

Help

Each menu, when clicked, reveals a list of Minitab *commands* — the actions you perform to accomplish a task in Minitab. Minitab commands are organized by function; each menu's name reflects the type of commands it includes. The Window menu, for example, contains commands you use to manipulate and move among windows.

The row of buttons beneath the menu bar is the *toolbar*. When you click a button on the toolbar, Minitab performs the corresponding menu function. To see the function of any particular button, place your mouse pointer over the button; a *tooltip* appears, indicating the button's function. Single-clicking toolbar buttons is a fast way to select commonly used operations. Because toolbars sometimes operate slightly differently from the corresponding menus, notice how they work as you use them in these tutorials. In addition, one Minitab window may have a different toolbar from another Minitab window. The toolbar for the Data window is shown in Figure 1-3.

FIGURE 1-3

The toolbar for the Data window

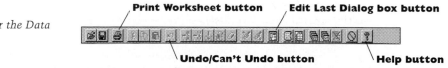

Print Worksheet button   Edit Last Dialog box button

Undo/Can't Undo button   Help button

Beneath the Data window is the *status bar*. The status bar indicates the name of the active data set, in this case, Worksheet.

To make a window active, you can either click it or select it from the list of windows on the Window menu:

- Click **Window** on the menu bar to open the Window menu, as shown in Figure 1-4

- Click **Worksheet 1** * * * on the Window menu

Cascade
Tile
Minimize All
Restore Icons
Arrange Icons
Refresh
Hide Toolbar
Hide Status Bar
Manage Graphs...
Close All Graphs
Set Graph Size/Location
Manage Worksheets...
1 Session   Ctrl+M
2 History   Ctrl+H
3 Info   Ctrl+I
✓ 4 Worksheet 1 ***   Ctrl+D

The Data window is now open and active (if it wasn't already). The Window menu is handy to use when windows are not visible on screen so that you cannot click on them.

▼ 1.2   Viewing the Data Window ▲

You will enter the yogurt data in the Data window. To see as many rows and columns as possible, maximize the window:

- Click the **Maximize** button on the Data window

    The Data window fills the screen, as shown in Figure 1-5.

FIGURE 1-5

*The Data window
maximized*

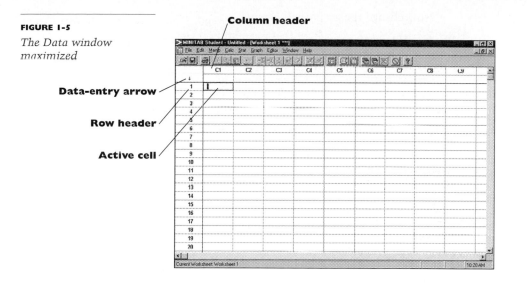

Column header

Data-entry arrow

Row header

Active cell

▼ **Note** Your screen may show fewer or more rows and columns than those shown in Figure 1-5, depending on your monitor. ▲

The grid, or *worksheet,* shown in the window consists of rows and columns. Each row contains the data from an individual case, while each column contains the data from a specific variable. The intersection of a row and a column is called a *cell.* Each cell is identified by its column (C1, C2, C3, and so on) and its row (1, 2, 3, and so on). For example, the cell in the upper-left corner of the worksheet corresponds to column 1, row 1; its *cell address* is C1 row 1.

Only one cell in the Data window is active at a given time. When you first start Minitab and open the Data window, the *active* cell is C1 row 1. The active cell appears *highlighted* — that is, shaded or with a thick border, depending on your monitor. Minitab enters the information you type at the keyboard in the active cell.

If C1 row 1 is not the active cell:

- Click **C1 row 1** to make it active

▼ 1.3   Moving Around the Data Worksheet ▲

You can easily make a different cell active in the worksheet by clicking it with the mouse. Or you can use the keyboard, which can be faster when entering data:

- Press the **right arrow key** [→] on your keyboard

    This action highlights C2 row 1.

Now change the active cell again:

■ Press and hold the **down arrow key** ⬇ on your keyboard until you reach row 10

The active cell is now C2 row 10.

The number of columns and rows you see at any time depends on the size of your screen. In the Student Edition of Minitab for Windows, the Data window has an upper limit of 1,000 columns and 5,000 cells. To see additional columns:

■ Click and hold the **right scroll arrow** ▶ at the bottom-right corner of your screen

The window scrolls horizontally to reveal more columns. It continues until you release the mouse button.

To scroll downwards in the worksheet:

■ Click and hold the **down scroll arrow** ▼ at the far right edge of your screen

The window scrolls down to show additional rows.

To return to the beginning of the worksheet:

■ Hold down ⟨Ctrl⟩ while you press ⟨Home⟩

You move directly to C1 row 1, and Minitab highlights the cell.

You also can move around the Data window using the commands on the Editor menu. Once there, you can use the Go To command to move to any cell you specify. Try using Go To to make cell C30 row 40 the active cell:

■ Click **Editor** to open the Editor menu

■ Click **Go To**

The Go To dialog box, shown in Figure 1-6, displays the column and row numbers of the active cell, in this case C1 row 1. The "Enter column number or name" text box shows a 1 highlighted.

FIGURE 1-6

The Go To dialog box

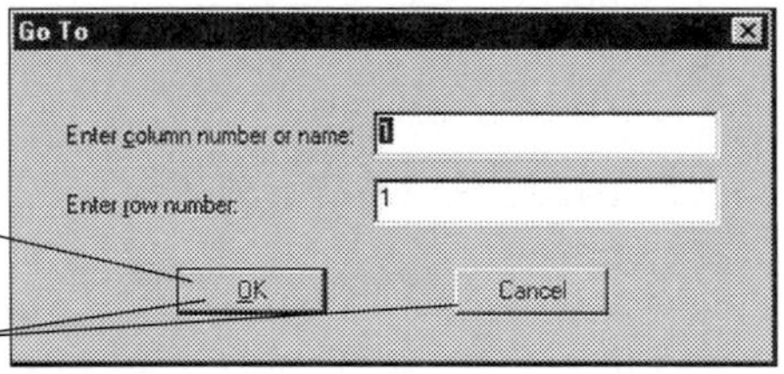

OK is highlighted ⸺

Command buttons ⸺

Whenever Minitab requires additional information from you, it almost always displays a *dialog box*. In a dialog box, you provide information by clicking *option buttons* and selecting or clearing *check boxes*. You also fill in *text boxes*. Whatever you type when the cursor is in the text box is entered in the box. For example:

- Type **30**

Note that in the Minitab tutorials, any text you are to type appears in boldface type in the instructions, for example, **30**.

Next, enter the row number:

- Press Tab

- Type **40**

Now that you've entered the desired cell location, column 30 and row 40, you are ready to tell Minitab to carry out the operation of going to that cell. Notice that the dialog box shows two *buttons*: OK and Cancel. Clicking OK tells Minitab to complete the function; clicking Cancel closes the dialog box without the operation's being performed.

Notice that the OK button has a thick border around it, unlike the Cancel button. This thick border indicates that the button is highlighted. Whenever a button is highlighted, pressing ⏎ (the Enter Key) has the same effect as clicking the button with the mouse; that is, the operation is carried out.

- Press ⏎ to accept the information in the dialog box

Minitab moves to C30 row 40.

This manual's tutorial directions may tell you to press ⏎ or to click OK to carry out an operation, depending on which is more convenient. If you're using the keyboard to complete the dialog box, the directions tell you to press ⏎. If you're using the mouse to select commands, the directions tell you to click OK.

▼ 1.4 Using Keyboard Shortcuts ▲

You also can use a *keyboard shortcut* to activate a different cell. Here a keyboard shortcut is a combination of two keys that, when pressed at the same time, cause an operation to be executed. For example:

- Click **Editor** in the menu bar to open the Editor menu

▼ **Note** The Editor menu is different from the Edit menu. ▲

Notice in the Editor menu that beside some commands are the names of two keys; these are the keyboard shortcuts for those commands. You use a keyboard shortcut to execute an operation without opening a menu by pressing both keys at the same time. As shown in Figure 1-7, the keyboard shortcut for Go To is Ctrl+G. From now on, directions in this manual will indicate keyboard shortcuts as two key names joined by a plus (+) sign, such as Ctrl+G.

FIGURE 1-7

*The Editor menu showing
four keyboard shortcuts*

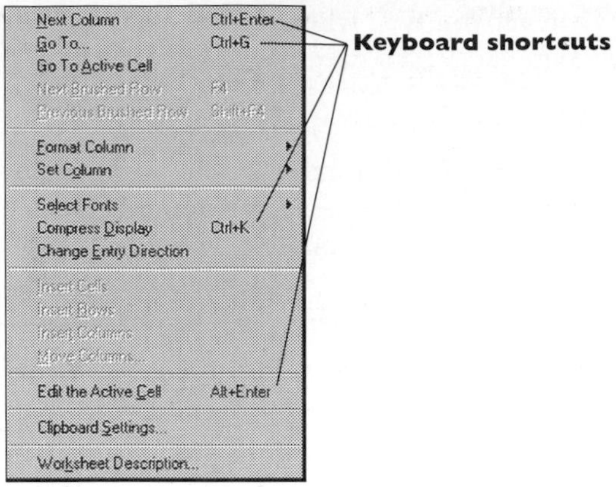

Use the Ctrl+G keyboard shortcut to return to C1 row 1:

■ Click in the **Data window** to close the Editor menu

■ Press Ctrl+G

Minitab displays the Go To dialog box.

■ Type **1** for the column number C1

■ Press Tab

■ Type **1** for the row number 1

■ Press ← to move to C1 row 1

Minitab returns you to the first cell in the worksheet.

▼ 1.5   Entering Data ▲

You are now ready to enter the yogurt data from Figure 1-1 into the Data window. Each row will contain data from one individual case — in this example, a certain brand of yogurt. Each column will record a different variable. You enter in a column the yogurt's nutritional rating in C1, its cost in cents per ounce in C2, and the calories per eight-ounce serving in C3. You do not have a Brand column because that column corresponds to the row number.

The value of the first case's rating is Excellent. Enter "Excellnt" (minus the "e" and no quotation marks) so that there are only eight letters in the coded value. With some output, Minitab truncates names of values and other labels within the worksheet if they are longer than eight characters; that is, character 9 on will not show. So it is good practice to use values that consist of eight or fewer characters. This tutorial uses coded values of eight or fewer characters for this reason.

- Type the first rating, **Excellnt**, in C1 row 1

  If you make a mistake, press the backspace key to delete a character.

- Press ⎡Tab⎤ or ⏎ to accept the data you just entered

▼ **Note** If you just typed a new value in a cell but have not pressed ⏎, you can restore the previous value of the cell by pressing ⎡Esc⎤. ▲

When you press ⎡Tab⎤ or ⏎, the cursor moves one cell either to the right or down, depending on the direction of the *data-entry arrow* in the upper-left corner of the Data window (see Figure 1-5). To change the direction of the data-entry arrow:

- Click the **data-entry arrow**

  The direction of the data-entry arrow changes. Click it again, if necessary, until the arrow is horizontal so that you can enter the yogurt data by rows:

- Click **cell C2 row 1**, if necessary, to make it active

- Type the first cost, **11**, in C2 row 1

- Press ⎡Tab⎤ to accept this entry and activate the cell to the right

- Type **120**

▼ **Note** If you are using the numeric keypad to enter numbers, be sure to press the ⎡NumLock⎤ key (so that the Num Lock light is lit on your keyboard). This will make the keys in the numeric keypad enter numbers instead of moving the active cell. ▲

Now you are ready to enter the data for the second brand of yogurt in row 2:

- Press ⎡Ctrl⎤+⏎ to move to the beginning of the second row

- Enter the next row of data by typing **Excellnt** and pressing ⎡Tab⎤

Continue in this manner until you have entered into the Data window all 14 rows of data shown in Figure 1-1, except the last value, 160. (Remember to enter VeryGood as one word.)

When you have entered all but the last value, 160, into C3 row 14, deliberately make a mistake so that you can see how to correct it:

- Type **660**

- Press ⏎ to accept it

▼ 1.6 Correcting Mistakes ▲

If you discover a typographical error after you enter data in a cell, you can easily fix it. To correct the last entry:

- Click cell **C3 row 14** to make it active

    Notice that when you click the cell, Minitab highlights the entire entry. If you type a new value and then press ↵, it replaces the original entry. You can also edit individual characters in the cell without retyping the entire entry.

    - Double-click the **active cell**

    When you double-click the cell, the highlight disappears and a vertical bar, or *insertion cursor*, appears. If you type new characters, Minitab inserts them at the location of the insertion cursor; any characters to the right of the insertion cursor move farther to the right.
    To delete characters:

- Use the arrow keys to move the insertion cursor to the right of the mistake

- Press the **backspace key** and then type the correct entry, **1**

- Press ↵ to accept the corrected entry

    You can also press ⌷Del⌷ to delete characters to the right of the cursor.

▼ 1.7 Identifying Text Data ▲

Notice from the data you have entered that C1 contains words, called *text data*, whereas C2 and C3 contain numbers. When you start typing in a column, Minitab classifies a column as text if it detects any alphabetic characters. Minitab also marks the column with a T suffix. So the first column heading in the Data window is now C1-T, not C1.

▼ **Note** You may encounter a third type of data — date/time — which Minitab designates with a D. You will not handle this type of data in this manual. ▲

A T suffix on a column of numeric data indicates that you have inadvertently entered text instead of a number. You can correct your mistake and change the data type of the column by choosing Manip > Change Data Type > Text to Numeric from the menu bar.
Note that for the remainder of this manual, instructions to choose menu commands are abbreviated in the format shown in the previous instruction, where the menu name (Manip, in this case) is followed by the menu commands you should choose, with all parts separated by > symbols. You may use the mouse, toolbar buttons, or keyboard shortcuts to invoke the operation.

▼ 1.8   Naming Columns ▲

It's easier to work with data if you assign a meaningful name to each column in your worksheet. Column or variable names may contain up to 31 characters. However, for presentation purposes, it is a good idea to limit names to eight characters. Like variable values, column names of more than eight characters may be truncated. When you name a column, avoid using an apostrophe ('), a pound sign (#), or an asterisk (*). Also, for now, do not include spaces within or on either side of a variable name. Minitab displays column names in the *name row* below the column labels (C1, C2, C3, and so on). To name C1:

- Click the **first cell in the name row** (the cell between the C1-T label and the first entry in the column) to highlight it

- Type **Rating** as the name for C1

- Press ← to accept the entry and move to the name cell for C2

- Type **Cents** as the name for C2

- Press ← to accept the entry and move to the name cell for C3

- Type **Cals** as the name for C3

- Press ←

Your Data window should look as shown in Figure 1-8.

FIGURE 1-8

Yogurt data with columns named

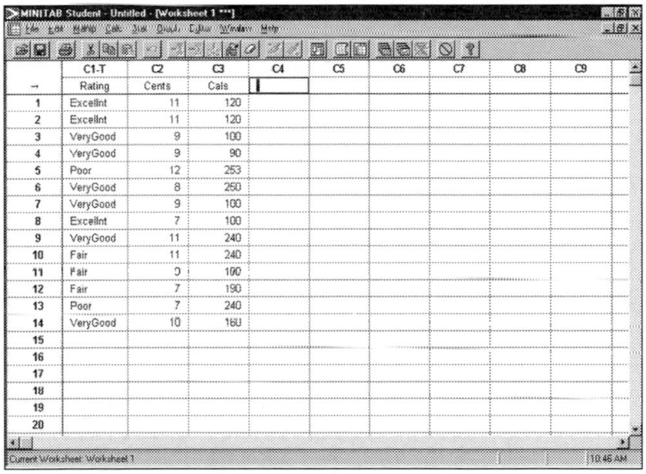

You can also name the columns before you enter the data.

▼ 1.9   Printing from the Data Window ▲

You have entered the yogurt data, and now you want to print out a copy of your worksheet on paper:

- Click the cell in the upper-left corner of the Data window, **C1-T**

- Press Shift+Ctrl+End to highlight the entire Data window containing the three columns

- Click the **Print Worksheet** button 🖨 on the toolbar (or choose **File > Print Worksheet** on the menu bar)

The Data window's Print Options dialog box is now active. Accept the defaults for the four check boxes and one command button. Also, include a title on your printout:

- Type **Yogurt Data** as the "Title"

- Click **OK** twice to print the selection you highlighted

Figure 1-9 shows the printed Data worksheet.

FIGURE 1-9

Printed 1Yogurt.mtw worksheet

	C1	C2	C3
1	Excellnt	11	120
2	Excellnt	11	120
3	VeryGood	9	100
4	VeryGood	9	90
5	Poor	12	253
6	VeryGood	8	250
7	VeryGood	9	100
8	Excellnt	7	100
9	VeryGood	11	240
10	Fair	11	240
11	Fair	9	190
12	Fair	7	190
13	Poor	7	240
14	VeryGood	10	160

▼ 1.10   Saving Data and Exiting Minitab ▲

Network
Drive
Apex.

Unsaved work exists temporarily in the computer's memory until you save it to a disk. It is good practice to save your work frequently to guard against losing it in the event of a mistake or a power failure.

When you save your worksheet, you do not save all of your work as with many other Windows applications. For example, a copy of your Session window is not saved. To save all of your work, you must save each window individually or save your work as a Minitab *project*. You will learn about projects in the third tutorial.

The following initial instructions presume you save your files to a disk. If your disk is in a drive other than A or you are saving your work to a different location, substitute the correct drive and directory name when you save your work. If you are using your own computer, you can save your work to your hard disk.

This manual also uses a file naming convention to help you remember which version of your work you are using at any given time. Each file you save on your disk has a prefix to indicate the tutorial number. For example, you will save the yogurt data you just entered as 1Yogurt. If you use this file again in Tutorial 5, for example, you will save it with a new name, 5Yogurt, so that you can easily distinguish which file you used in which tutorial.

To save your data:

■ Click **File**

■ Click **Save Current Worksheet As**

   The Save Current Worksheet As dialog box appears.
   To save the yogurt data as a Minitab worksheet for Release 12:

■ Insert your disk into drive A (or a different drive, if appropriate)

■ Click the "Save in:" **drop-down list arrow**

■ Click **3 1/2 Floppy (A:)** (you may have to scroll to find it). You may also use the Up One Level button to the right of the drop-down list arrow to find the drive or directory.

■ Click in the "File name" text box (highlight and delete any existing text)

■ Type **1Yogurt** in the text box

   The Save Worksheet As dialog box should look as shown in Figure 1-10.

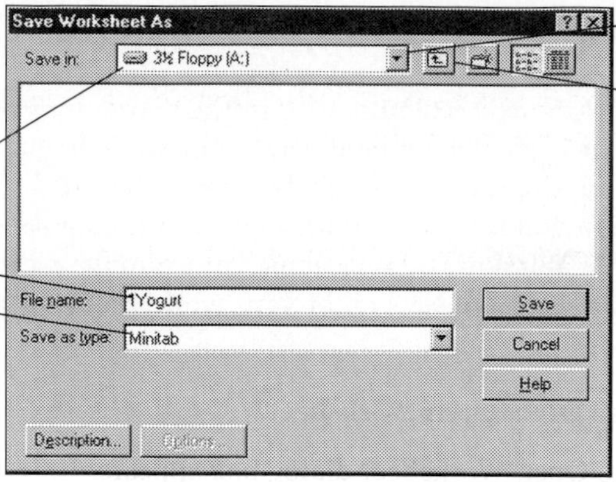

FIGURE 1-10

Save Worksheet As dialog box

Current drive or directory

File name text box

File type

Drop-down list arrow

Up One Level button

■ Press ⏎

▼ **Note** If an error message indicates that your disk is write-protected, click OK to acknowledge the message and then remove the disk. On a 3 1/2-inch disk, move the small tab in the disk's upper-right corner so that you can no longer see through the square hole. This unlocks the disk and lets you copy data to it. Then try again to save your yogurt data. ▲

After you save your data, the status window at the foot of the screen changes from Worksheet 1 *** to Current Worksheet 1Yogurt.mtw. Also, the Minitab title bar now reads MINITAB Student - Untitled - [1Yogurt.mtw ***]. "Untitled" refers to the name of the current project.

When you save the 1Yogurt file, Minitab automatically adds an *mtw file extension.* This three-letter suffix indicates the file type. File types make finding files easier.

As will be shown in later tutorials, you can create and use files of various types for different purposes in Minitab. Not all applications use the same file types. For example, Minitab can read files with an *mtw* extension, but other software programs, such as text editors, cannot.

▼ **Note** When you work with your own data, you should always save your data before you exit from Minitab and before you open a new worksheet. To help you remember, Minitab prompts you to save your work when you perform these actions. ▲

To exit Minitab:

■ Click **File** on the menu bar

■ Click **Exit**

■ In response to the "Save changes to this project before closing?" prompt, click **No**

This is a good time to take a break. Your data are secure in the directory in which your data files are located.

▼ 1.11   Retrieving Data ▲

Your yogurt data are stored in the directory in which your data files are located. To retrieve your data:

■ Start **Minitab**

■ Maximize the **Data** window (Worksheet 1 ***)

■ Insert the **disk** on which you stored your data files into drive A (or a different drive, if appropriate)

■ Choose **File > Open Worksheet**

   The Open Worksheet dialog box appears.

▼ **Note** You can use keyboard shortcuts to select the Open Worksheet dialog box. Notice that one letter in each menu name is underlined. Combine the underlined letter with the [Alt] key — in this case, [Alt]+F for File — and press W for the underlined letter in Open Worksheet on the File menu. ▲

■ Navigate to the location where your data files are located; for example, **3 1/2 Floppy (A:)**

■ Double-click **1Yogurt.mtw** in the "Open Worksheet" list box

■ Click OK

   A copy of the content of this file will be added to the current project. Recall that you will learn about projects in the third tutorial. The Data window now displays the yogurt data you saved. *1Yogurt.mtw* is the name of the active Data window.

▼ 1.12   Manipulating Data Using the Calculator Command ▲

In developing your yogurt budget, you must compute the total cost of feeding 200 patients. You can do this with the Calculator option on the Calc menu. Calculator lets you perform many mathematical operations on columns. Minitab uses the symbols +, -, *, /, and ** to add, subtract, multiply, divide, and raise to a power, respectively. In later tutorials, you will use Calculator to perform various algebraic and statistical operations.

   The following steps show you how to compute the total cost of feeding 200 patients:

■ Choose **Calc > Calculator**

   The Calculator dialog box appears, similar to the one shown in Figure 1-11.

FIGURE 1-11

The Calculator dialog box

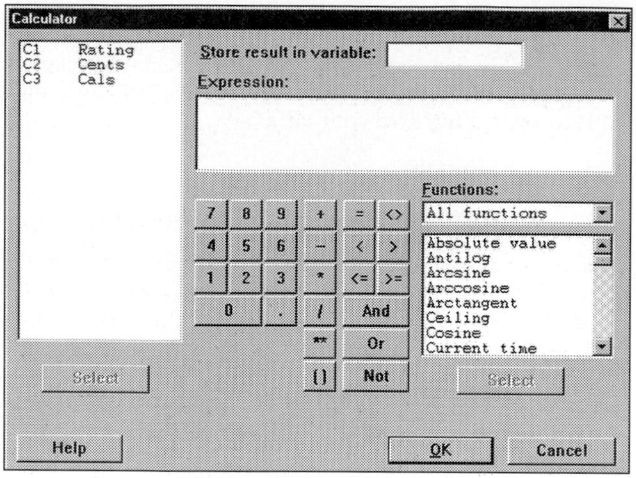

You want to compute the daily cost per ounce, in dollars, of serving each brand of yogurt to 200 patients and store the results in C4. First, name the new variable:

- Ensure your cursor is in the "Store result in variable" text box

- Type **Cost200**

  When you type in a name for a new variable, Minitab automatically assigns the entry you type as the name of the next available column after the last current column (C4, in this example). If you include spaces or other special characters in a name, you will have to enter single quotation marks around the column name in some situations. So don't use spaces in your variable names for this tutorial. (Remember, you cannot use the characters ' or # in a variable name.)

- To move the cursor to the "Expression" text box, press ⌃Tab⌄

  The cost, in dollars, of feeding 200 patients can be obtained by making C4 Cost200 equal to C2*200/100. (Recall that the original costs in C2 are in cents.) To enter this formula in the "Expression" text box either:

- Type **C2*200/100** (remember, the asterisk is Minitab's symbol for multiplication)

- Click **OK** to create the new variable

  or

- Double-click on **C2 Cents** in the variable selection box to the left of the keypad in the dialog box

- Click ***200/100** using the calculator keypad

■ Click **OK** to create the new variable

This formula tells Minitab to multiply each of the values in C2 by 200 and divide the product by 100. The Data window now contains a new column that shows the cost in dollars of providing yogurt to 200 patients.

▼ **Note** You can create expressions in the Calculator by any combination of typing, selecting variables from the variable list, using the keypad, and selecting functions from the functions list. You will select functions in later tutorials. If you introduced a wrong formula, and thus created an incorrect variable in the new column, you can correct the formula by using Calc > Calculator again. ▲

Next, add a column that shows the cost of feeding 300, rather than 200, patients. You can do this without retyping the entire expression, as follows:

■ Choose **Edit > Edit Last Dialog** (or click the **Edit Last Dialog** button ▦ on the toolbar)

Edit Last Dialog displays whichever dialog box you had open most recently.

To change Cost200 to Cost300, replace the 2 with a 3 in the Store result in variable text box

■ Click to the right of the 2 in Cost200

The arrow cursor turns into the insertion cursor (shaped like an I-bar), thereby indicating that you can enter text.

■ Drag the **I-bar** to the left to highlight just the number **2** and then release the mouse button

■ Type **3**

The entry in the "Store result in variable" text box now reads Cost300. Next, change the entry in the "Expression" text box to 300:

■ Highlight **2** in the Expression text box by dragging the **I-bar**

■ Type **3**

The "Expression" text box now reads either C2 * 300 / 100 or Cents * 300 / 100.

■ Click **OK** to create the new variable, Cost300

C4 and C5 display the costs of providing each brand of yogurt to 200 and 300 patients.

Many patients are on an 1800-calorie-per-day diet. For each brand, calculate how many calories remain for the day, presuming a patient on such a diet consumes one serving of yogurt for breakfast:

■ Click the **Edit Last Dialog** button ▦ on the toolbar

- Enter **CalLeft** in the "Store result in variable" text box and press ⊡Tab⊡

- Enter **1800-C3** in the "Expression" text box and click **OK**

C6 now lists the daily calories remaining after a patient has eaten an eight-ounce serving of each brand of plain yogurt. You can use this information to determine which brand gives you the most flexibility for planning patients' diets.

▼ **Note** ⊡Tab⊡ moves the cursor from one item to another in a dialog box. If you want to return to an item that appears above your present location, either press ⊡Tab⊡ until you return to it or press ⊡Shift⊡+⊡Tab⊡ to move the cursor backwards. If you are using a mouse, you can quickly move the cursor to any item by clicking the item (this action may also select the item, depending on the item). ▲

▼ **Note** You may have noticed that the Data window in Minitab is not a spreadsheet such as that in Microsoft Excel or Lotus 1-2-3. In those programs, the cells may contain formulas that are updated, based on the values in other cells. In Minitab, cells may contain values that you type or generate but not formulas. For example, in the yogurt case study you used the calculator to place the values for 200*C2 in C4. If you changed the values in C2, the values in C4 would not change until you use the calculator again or use some other command to change the contents of C4. ▲

▼ 1.13   Copying Columns ▲

You initially recorded the rating for each brand in C1. Now you want to repeat this information in C7 so that it is still visible when you use columns farther to the right in the worksheet. You can use Minitab's on-line Help system to find out how to copy a column:

- Choose **Help** > **Search for Help on**

The Help Topics: MINITAB Help window opens with the insertion cursor blinking in the text box.

This window is similar to an index in that you can look up a keyword to help you locate the information you need. Try entering the word "copy" as a keyword to find out more about duplicating a column:

- Type **copy** in the "Type the first few letters..." text box

As you type, the list box below the text box scrolls to show entries that begin with the letters you type. By the time you've typed the entire word, "copy" appears, highlighted in the list box, as Figure 1-12 shows. The lower list box in the window shows the alphabetical list of topics closest to the keyword "copy."

FIGURE 1-12

The Help Topics:
MINITAB Help window
showing on-line Help

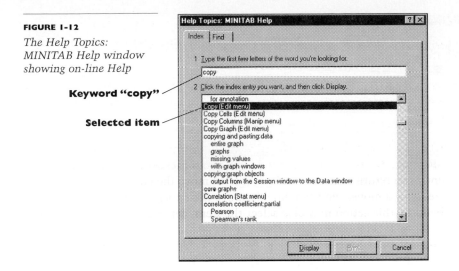

Keyword "copy"

Selected item

- Click **Copy Columns (Manip menu)**

- Click the **Display** button

- Under "Topics Found", click **Copy Columns (Manip menu)**

- Click the **Display** button

The Minitab Help window opens to the Copy Columns entry, as shown in Figure 1-13. The Help topic describes the Copy Columns command on the Manip menu.

FIGURE 1-13

*Copy Columns in the
Minitab Help window*

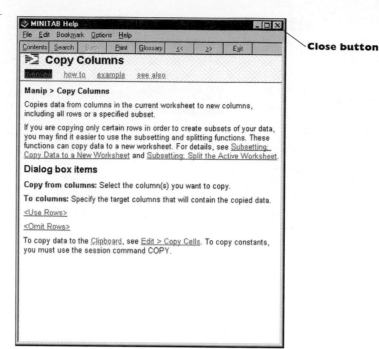

Close button

Close the Help window when you finish reading the information:

■ Click the Window's **Close** button and return to the Data window

There are other ways to access on-line Help in Minitab. For example, you can press F1 or the Help button on the toolbar to display the table of contents for the Help window. For more information getting started, refer to Chapter 3.

Next, use Minitab's Copy Columns command to copy the data from C1 Rating to C7:

■ Choose **Manip > Copy Columns** to open the Copy Columns dialog box, which is shown in Figure 1-14

Like the Calculator dialog box, the Copy Columns dialog box indicates the currently occupied columns (variables) in the Data window in a list box on the left side.

FIGURE 1-14

The Copy Columns dialog box

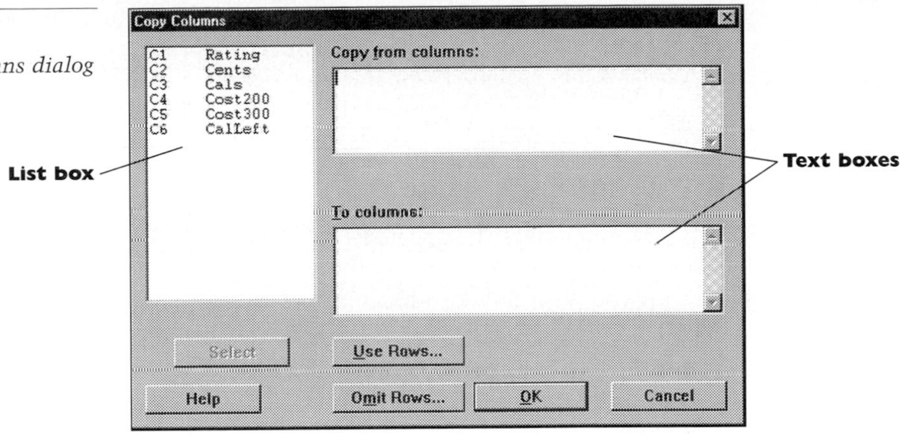

Be sure the cursor is blinking in the "Copy from columns" text box; if not, click the text box

- Double-click **C1 Rating** to enter it in the "Copy from columns" text box

- Press Tab to move to the "To columns" text box

- Type **Copy** and then press ↵

Minitab copies the ratings into C7; the ratings now appear in both C1 and C7 (you may have to scroll to see both columns). This is a good time to save your work again. You will do this in the next section.

▼ 1.14   Describing and Updating an Existing File ▲

Minitab allows you to attach a description to a data set. A description can serve to remind you, for instance, of when the data was saved, what the variables represent, and the reason for collecting and saving the data. To construct a description of the *1Yogurt.mtw* data set:

- Choose **Editor > Worksheet Description** to open the Worksheet Description dialog box

The Worksheet Description dialog box shows the name and location of the file. In the three text boxes, you can type the description, in this case, your name as the creator of the data set, the date, and comments about the data set.

- Enter a worksheet description

- Click **OK** to record the description

You have already saved your data once. Now you want to replace that saved file with this updated one and keep the same filename. To save a new version of an existing file under the same filename, click the Save Current Worksheet command (not the Save Current Worksheet As command). You will not be asked to specify a filename and location because the Save Current Worksheet command automatically saves the file to the previous location under the same name.

- Choose **File > Save Current Worksheet**

Minitab saves the updated *1Yogurt.mtw* file in the directory where your data files are located.

If you want to take a break before starting another case study, exit Minitab:

- Choose **File > Exit**

Minitab will ask if you want to save changes to the project before closing.

- Click **No**

If you want to begin the next case study right away:

- Choose **File > Close Worksheet** (you may also click the **Close** button ☒ in the upper right-hand corner of the Data window)

If you choose the menu Close command, Minitab will ask if you want to save the worksheet in a separate file (if you click the Close button it will not):

- Click **No**

▼ 1.15   Opening a Minitab Stored Data File ▲

The Student Edition of Minitab for Windows comes with a large selection of stored data sets. The following case study introduces you to one such data set.

CASE STUDY: MANAGEMENT — SALARY STRUCTURE

Temco, a midsize corporation, recently hired you as a managerial consultant. Your task is to analyze the salary structure of the Sales Department and then point out any inequities. Brett Reid, one of your coworkers, has already gathered data on the Sales Department personnel and entered it in a Minitab file named *Pay.mtw*. Brett informs you that some employees have left Temco since he entered the data and their records must be deleted. There also are some new employees whose records must be added.

- Start Minitab and maximize the Data window, if necessary

- Choose **File > Open Worksheet** to open the Open Worksheet dialog box

The Open Worksheet dialog box displays a list of files similar to the one shown in Figure 1-15. You need to navigate to the Student subdirectory of the Minitab directory to find the data files for this manual. If you cannot find these files, ask your instructor or technical resource person where on the computer the tutorial data files are located.

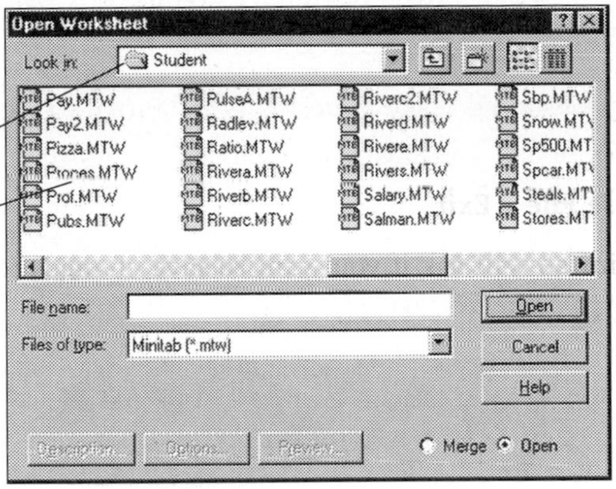

FIGURE 1-15

The Open Worksheet dialog box

Current directory

Files list box

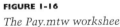

- Double-click **Pay.mtw** in the Open Worksheet dialog box (you may have to scroll to see the file)

- Click **OK**

The worksheet shown in Figure 1-16 appears on your screen.

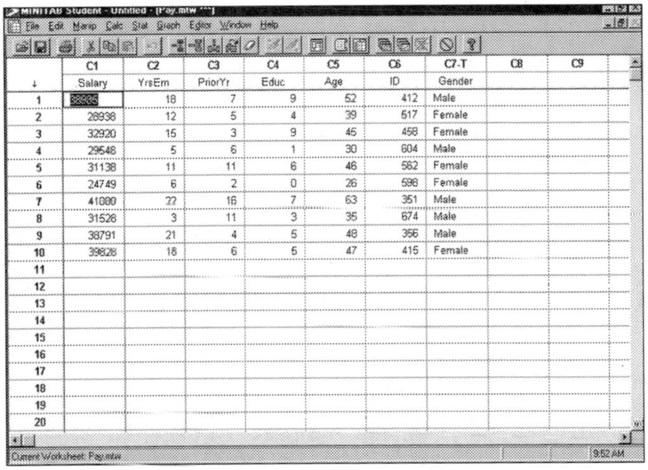

FIGURE 1-16

The Pay.mtw worksheet

Before you modify the data, you should save the file to your disk (or another directory if you are not using a disk) under a different filename using Save Current Worksheet As. Doing this will prevent you from accidentally overwriting the data file with Save Current Worksheet. To save the file:

- Choose **File** > **Save Current Worksheet As**

- Select the location where you are saving your work and type *1Pay* in the "File name" text box

- Press ⏎

Now, when you save your changes to the file, they will be written to *1Pay.mtw*, not *Pay.mtw*.

▼ 1.16   Deleting and Inserting Rows ▲

Brett measured seven variables for each employee:

C1	Salary of an employee in the Sales Department
C2	Number of years employed at Temco
C3	Number of prior years' experience
C4	Years of education after high school
C5	Current age
C6	Company identification number for the employee
C7-T	Gender of the employee (because this is a text variable, it is left-justified)

Start updating Brett's data by removing employee 562 (row 5), who has left Temco:

- Click the **row header** for row 5 to highlight the entire row, as shown in Figure 1-17

- Choose **Edit** > **Delete Cells** (or press the [Del] key)

Minitab moves rows 6 and beyond up one row (or level) to fill in the gap left by the deleted row 5. There are now only nine employees in the worksheet.

FIGURE 1-17

Pay.mtw with row 5 high-lighted

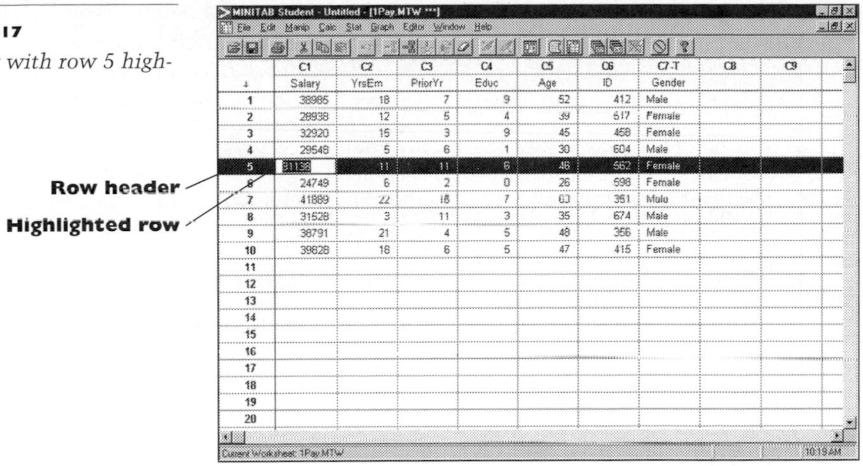

Row header

Highlighted row

If Temco hires a replacement, you might want to insert the new employee's data into the worksheet at a particular location. Try inserting a row above row 8:

- Click any cell in row 8

- Choose **Editor > Insert Rows**

Minitab inserts a blank row in this position and moves all of the rows below it down one row (or level). Minitab displays an asterisk (*) in each numerical cell and a blank ( ) in each text cell in row 8 to indicate that the information is missing. Since you don't want to insert data in this row, you should delete this empty row. You can delete it as you did before, or you can use the Undo Insert option:

- Choose **Edit > Undo Insert** or click the **Undo** button on the toolbar

Clicking Undo will undo the action of the previous command, which created the new row.

Your worksheet should now look like the one shown in Figure 1-18.

FIGURE 1-18

*The 1Pay.mtw worksheet
with one row deleted*

**Deleted row
was here**

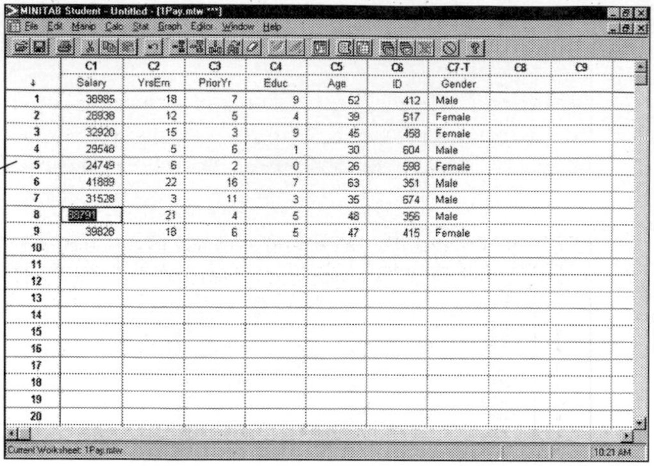

Brett tells you that the department is hiring two new employees. You want to enter the data for these employees in rows 10 and 11. As you enter the new data, remember that if the data-entry arrow (in the upper-left corner of the screen) points to the right, then pressing Tab or ← moves the cursor across the row.

■ If necessary, click the **data-entry arrow** so that it points to the right

The first new employee, whose data are to go in row 10, is a 23-year-old female who earns a salary of $28,985. She has one year's prior experience and four years' post-secondary education. Her employee number is 693. As a new employee, she has 0 years at Temco (the entry in C2 YrsEm). Enter her data:

■ Click **C1 row 10** (the cell address for the first cell in row 10)

■ Type the data in row 10, starting in C1 (press Tab between each value): **28985 0 1 4 23 693 Female**

■ Press Ctrl+← to accept the final value and move to the beginning of row 11

▼ **Note** If you notice a mistake after you press ←, correct the cell entry using the techniques discussed in Section 1.6. ▲

You have less information about the second new employee. He is male, his employee number is 694, and his salary is $32,782. Place an asterisk in each cell for which you're missing information.

■ Type the second employee's data in row 11: **32782 0 * * * 694 Male**

■ Press Ctrl+← to move to the beginning of row 12

The Data window should now resemble the window shown in Figure 1-19.

▼ **Note** An entry of 0 (zero) is different than an entry of *, which indicates a missing numeric value. Also note that when you entered the salaries, you didn't — and shouldn't — enter commas or dollar signs. ▲

FIGURE 1-19

The 1Pay.mtw worksheet with new employee information

New employee information

	C1	C2	C3	C4	C5	C6	C7-T	C8	C9
→	Salary	YrsEm	PriorYr	Educ	Age	ID	Gender		
1	38985	18	7	9	52	412	Male		
2	78938	12	5	4	39	517	Female		
3	32920	15	3	9	45	458	Female		
4	29548	5	6	1	30	604	Male		
5	24749	6	2	0	26	598	Female		
6	41889	22	16	7	63	351	Male		
7	31528	3	11	3	35	674	Male		
8	38791	21	4	5	48	356	Male		
9	39828	18	6	5	47	415	Female		
10	28985	0	1	4	23	693	Female		
11	32782	0	*	*	*	694	Male		
12									
13									
14									
15									
16									
17									
18									
19									
20									

Current Worksheet: 1Pay.MTW   10:22 AM

▼ 1.17 Deleting Columns ▲

Temco recently enacted a new policy against recording age, so you need to delete the age variable, as follows:

- Choose **Manip > Erase Variables**

- Double-click **C5 Age** in the list box to place it in the "Columns and constants to erase" text box

- Click **OK**

C5 is now blank. Check to ensure your *1Pay.mtw* worksheet contains only the information shown in Figure 1-20.

FIGURE 1-20

*The 1Pay.mtw worksheet
without the Age variable*

**Contents of
column C5
now erased**

	C1	C2	C3	C4	C5	C6	C7-T	C8	C9
→	Salary	YrsEm	PriorYr	Educ		ID	Gender		
1	38985	18	7	9		412	Male		
2	28938	12	5	4		517	Female		
3	32920	15	3	9		458	Female		
4	23548	5	6	1		604	Male		
5	24749	6	2	0		598	Female		
6	41889	22	16	7		351	Male		
7	31528	3	11	3		674	Male		
8	38791	21	4	5		356	Male		
9	38828	18	6	5		415	Female		
10	28985	0	1	4		693	Female		
11	32782	0	*	*		694	Male		
12									
13									
14									
15									
16									
17									
18									
19									
20									

▼ 1.18 Copying Parts of a Column ▲

Earlier in this tutorial, you copied a column in the yogurt worksheet. Now you will copy only part of a column.

One aspect of your salary structure investigation is examining the relationship between different variables, such as gender and salary. To do this, you need to list the male and female salaries in separate columns. First, copy only the male employees' salaries from C1 into C9:

- Choose **Manip > Copy Columns**

  Indicate the column from which you want to copy:

- Double-click **C1 Salary** to enter it in the "Copy from columns" text box

- Click the "To columns" text box and highlight the existing entry

- Type **SalMale** in the text box

  To select the salaries of only the male employees for this column:

- Click the **Use Rows** button

  The Copy Columns - Use Rows dialog box appears as shown in Figure 1-21.

FIGURE 1-21

The Copy Columns - Use Rows dialog box

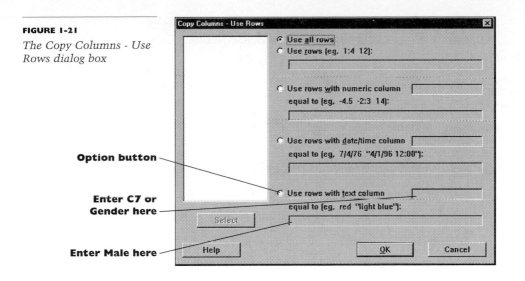

■ Click the **Use rows with text column** option button

■ Click in the text box to the right of the "Use rows with text column" option and enter **C7** or **gender**

■ Click in the text box beneath "equal to" and type **Male**

It is important to type the actual case of each letter in this column value because the "equal to" operation is case-sensitive. Typing "male" (lowercase "m") will not copy any columns.

■ Click **OK** to return to the Copy Columns dialog box

■ Click **OK**

The Data window now includes a list of male salaries in C8 (scroll to see it, if necessary).

Repeat this procedure to place the salaries of female employees in C9:

■ Choose **Manip > Copy Columns**

The Copy Columns dialog box reflects your most recent selections.

■ In the "To columns" text box, change SalMale to **SalFem**

■ Click **Use Rows** to open the Copy Columns - Use Rows dialog box

■ In the text box beneath "equal to," change Male to **Female**

■ Click **OK** twice to create the new variable

■ If necessary, scroll to the right to view columns C8 and C9

The two subsets of the Salary variable are side by side, as shown in Figure 1-22.

FIGURE 1-22

The 1Pay.mtw worksheet
showing male and female
salaries

**The two
subsets of the
Salary variable**

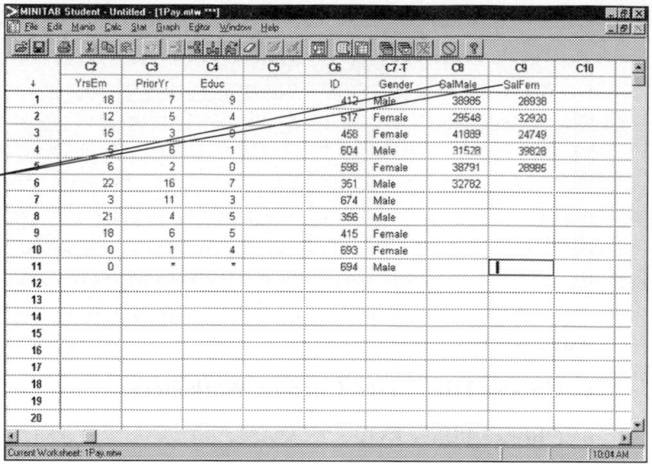

It appears that salaries of males and females are similar. In a later practice problem, you will examine the salary structure in more depth.

▼ 1.19 Viewing Data Set Information ▲

This is a good point to introduce the Info window. The Info window allows you to keep track, in summary form, of the contents of each column. To open the Info window:

■ Choose **Window > Info**

The current contents of the Info window are shown in Figure 1-23.

FIGURE 1-23

The Info window

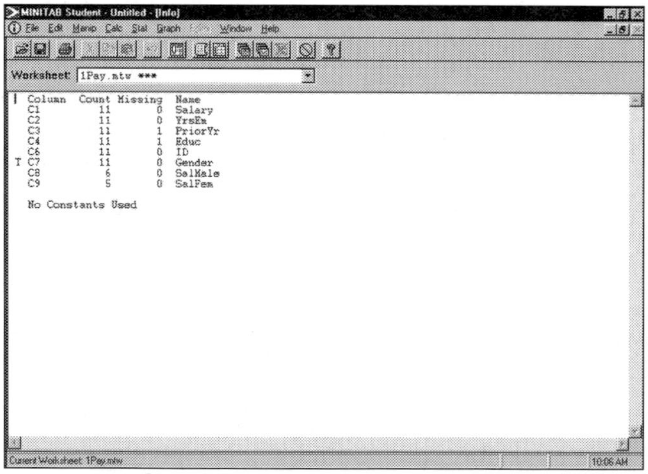

The figure shows that one value is missing for each of PriorYr and Educ, that C7 Gender is a text variable, and that in C8 and C9 are the salaries for the six male and five female employees, respectively. Lower in the Info window is the statement No Constants Used. You will learn about constants in Minitab in Tutorial 2.

With a small data set like the one shown in the Info window, all, or nearly all, of the data and the variable names can be viewed on the screen in the Data window. The Info window is more helpful when you are dealing with much larger data sets, when it often is difficult to keep track of data.

Next, save your file in the directory where your data files are located and leave Minitab:

■ Choose **File** > **Save Current Worksheet**

■ Choose **File** > **Exit**

■ In response to the "Save changes to this project before closing?" prompt, click **No**

Congratulations! You have finished the first tutorial. Now that you have seen some of the skills you need in order to prepare data for analysis, you are ready to take a closer look at how Minitab operates. In the second tutorial, you learn more ways to manipulate your data.

▼

Minitab Command Summary

▲

This section describes the menu commands introduced in, or related to, this tutorial. Use Minitab's on-line Help to find a complete explanation of all menus and commands.

Minitab Menu Commands

Menu	Command	Description
File		
	Open Worksheet	Retrieves a previously saved worksheet.
	Save Current Worksheet	Replaces a previously saved file with a copy of the current worksheet.
	Save Current Worksheet As	Saves a copy of the current worksheet to a file with a new filename and assigns that name to the current worksheet.
	Exit	Exits the Minitab application.

Menu	Command	Description
Edit		
	Undo	Undoes the most recent editing operation and returns the worksheet to its previous state.
	Delete Cells	Deletes the selected cells and moves all of the cells in each column up one level.
	Edit Last Dialog	Recalls the last dialog box that was open, retaining the previous information.
Manip		
	Delete Rows	Deletes the specified row(s) in the worksheet in the specified columns and moves all of the rows up one level.
	Erase Variables	Erases a column(s) in the worksheet.
	Copy Columns	Creates a duplicate of one or more columns or parts of one or more columns.
Calc		
	Calculator	Performs arithmetic using algebraic expressions, which may contain arithmetic operators, comparison operators, logical operators, and functions. Arguments may be columns, constants, or numbers.
Editor		
	Go To	Activates a given cell in a worksheet.
	Insert Rows	Inserts a row in the worksheet above the current one and moves down all the rows below it.
	Worksheet Description	Stores comments about your worksheet.
Window		
	Info	Makes the Info window active and displays summary information about the active worksheet.
	Data worksheet name	Makes the Data window active and displays the selected worksheet in a spreadsheet-like format.

Menu	Command	Description
Help		
	Contents	Displays the contents of the on-line Help system.
	Getting Started	Displays the Getting Started window, giving you access to on-line Help on basic Minitab procedures.
	Search for Help on	Displays Help Topics: MINITAB Help window, which lets you search for help on a single word. It is similar to an index.
	Session Command Help	Displays the Session Command Help window, which describes how to issue such commands and provides a list of them.
	How to Use Help	Opens the Microsoft Windows How to Use Help system, which describes the basics of using Windows Help systems.
	Minitab on the Web	Opens browser and links to the Minitab Website, http://www.minitab.com.
	About Minitab	Displays basic information about the current release of Minitab.

Matching

Match the following terms to their definitions by placing the correct letter next to the term it describes.

_____ Session window

_____ Text

_____ *

_____ 1,000

_____ Worksheet

_____ mtw

_____ Open Worksheet

_____ Variable

_____ Cell

_____ [F1]

a. A series of rows and columns in which Minitab displays data

b. The maximum number of columns in *The Student Edition of Minitab for Windows*

c. Minitab commands and output are displayed in this location

d. Minitab's default designation for a missing numeric value

e. The intersection of a row and column in a worksheet

f. The Minitab command to retrieve a previously saved worksheet

g. The default file extension added to Minitab files you create with Save Worksheet As

h. A data type that contains characters other than numbers

i. Another name Minitab uses for a column of data or text in a worksheet

j. The key you press to open the Help window for the current dialog box

True/False

Mark the following statements with a *T* or an *F*.

_____ You can assign a name to a column by typing the name in the name row of the Data window.

_____ The Insert Row command inserts a row of missing values immediately below the current one.

_____ The Minitab symbol for multiplication is x.

_____ You can use any popular word processor to edit Minitab worksheet files that are saved with the *mtw* extension.

_____ To save a worksheet to a floppy disk, select drive C.

_____ You choose Stop on the File menu to exit Minitab.

_____ The Minitab Help system is available on the File menu.

_____ Column or variable names must be eight characters or fewer.

_____ When you are entering data into the worksheet, pressing ⏎ always moves you to the next cell to the right in the same row.

Practice Problems

The practice problems instruct you to save your worksheets with a filename prefixed by P and followed by the tutorial number. In this tutorial, for example, you use P1 as the prefix. Use Minitab's on-line Help or Part III, Exploring Data, of this manual to review the contents of the data sets referenced in the problems below.

1. The following data represent the total snowfall (in inches) for a large city on the East Coast for the 36 years between 1962 and 1997:

   38.6 42.4 57.5 40.5 51.7 67.1 33.4 60.9 64.1 40.1 40.7 6.4 42.5 41.4 45.4 46.2 89.2
   19.5 18.7 31.9 49.7 29.8 44.1 27.2 20.7 52.1 39.8 22.5 29.7 23.6 26.5 85.2 86.3
   41.3 85.6 51.6

   a. Enter the 36 years into C1 and name the column Year.

   b. Enter the snowfall data into C2 and name that column Snow.

   c. Use Calc > Calculator to create a new column named Rainfall that represents the equivalent rainfall (1″ of rain equals approximately 10″ of snow).

   d. Save your worksheet as *P1Snow.mtw* in the directory where your data files are located.

2. Open the *Pulsea.mtw* data set. The data in this set are based on the following experiment. All of the 92 students in an introductory statistics course recorded their own pulse rates (Pulse1). Each student then flipped a coin. If the flip resulted in a head, the student ran in place for a minute; otherwise, the student did not run. All students then recorded their pulse rates for a second time (Pulse2). Those rates and related data are described in the following table.

C1	Pulse1	Initial pulse rate
C2	Pulse2	Second pulse rate
C3-T	Ran	Whether or not the student ran in place
C4-T	Smokes	Whether or not the student is a regular smoker
C5-T	Gender	Student's gender
C6	Height	Height in inches
C7	Weight	Weight in pounds
C8	Activity	Usual level of physical activity

   a. Use Calc > Calculator to compute the increase in pulse rate (C2–C1) and store the results in C9. Name this new column Increase.

   b. Save your worksheet as *P1Pulsea.mtw* in the directory in which your data files are located.

3. The following table summarizes the campus newspaper ratings for 13 pizza shops for two fall semesters.

Pizza Shop	Current Fall Rating	Last Fall Rating
A	6.7	6.73
B	5.4	7.29
C	4.9	5.77
D	4.8	6.69
E	3.9	4.33
F	3.2	*
G	3.2	*
H	3.1	5.01
I	2.8	2.58
J	2.8	6.88
K	2.6	5.08
L	2.2	7.50
M	1.5	*

a. Enter these data into C1, C4, and C5 in a new worksheet and name the columns Pizzeria, FallScor, and LFall, respectively. The asterisks represent missing values.

b. Compute the sum of the two ratings for the 13 pizza shops and store these values in C7. Which shop has the highest combined rating?

c. Compute the difference between the two ratings for each of the 13 pizza shops and store these values in C8. Which shop has the greatest difference in ratings?

d. How did the missing values affect your sum and difference computations?

e. Erase C7 and C8. Skipe.

f. Save your worksheet as *P1Pizza.mtw* in the directory where your data files are located.

4. Open the *Note98.mtw* data set, which contains information about a selection of notebook (portable) computers on the market in 1998.

   a. Use Go To activate the last cell in the last named column.

   b. After that cell, add the following information about a generic notebook computer to the worksheet by entering the following row of data in C1 through C8: 430TX 233 4 128 IDRAM TouchPad No 4400.

   c. Save the worksheet as *P1Note98.mtw* in the directory in which your data files are located.

TUTORIAL 2

Summarizing, Transforming, and Manipulating Data

Now that you know how to enter and save data in Minitab, you are ready to organize and manipulate it to perform various statistical analyses. Much of these analyses will be done in the Session window. You also print data from this window.

Objectives

In this tutorial, you learn how to:

- summarize the data for rows (individual cases) and for columns (variables)
- work with data in the Session window
- code, rank, and sort data
- standardize data for different variables in order to compare them
- obtain a subset of the worksheet
- combine and break down columns of data
- view and print data from the Session window

▼ 2.1   Computing the Mean and Median, and Rounding ▲

CASE STUDY: EDUCATION — CLASS EVALUATION

You have just completed your first marking period as a social studies teacher. You entered your students' grades for the first three tests into a Minitab worksheet. Your principal, Ms. Taylor, wants you to prepare a report about your students' progress.

Start Minitab and open the *Marks.mtw* worksheet from the Student data files (in the Student subdirectory of Minitab):

- Start **Minitab**

- Choose **File > Open Worksheet**

- Double-click ***Marks.mtw*** in the "Open Worksheet" list box (you may have to navigate to the Student subdirectory and then scroll to see the file)

- At the prompt, "A copy of the contents of this file will be added to the current project," click **OK**

- Maximize the **Data window**

Before analyzing the *Marks.mtw* data, save this data set under the name *2Marks.mtw*:

- Choose **File > Save Current Worksheet As**

- Click the "Save in" **drop-down list arrow** and select the location where you are saving your work

- Under "File name" type the name ***2Marks***

- Click **Save**

As you modify this data set, you should periodically save the modified worksheet.

You want to compute each student's average grade for the three tests. You can do this in either of two ways. The first involves using Calculator on the Calc menu to add each student's test grades in the third, fourth, and fifth columns of the appropriate row and then dividing each sum by 3:

- Choose **Calc > Calculator**

The Calculator dialog box appears.

- In the "Store result in the variable" text box, type **Averg** and then press ⎡Tab⎤

Minitab assigns the name to the column after the last column in the data set, in this case, C6.

Tell Minitab to average the three test scores. Do this by entering, in the "Expression" text box, (Test1 + Test2 + Test3)/3:

- Click ( ) (this symbol is just to the left of "Not" in the dialog box)

- Double-click **C3 Test1**

- Click **+**

- Double-click **C4 Test2**

- Click **+**

- Double-click **C5 Test3**

- Move the cursor to the right of the right-hand parenthesis

- Click **/**

- Click **3**

- Click **OK**

Minitab stores in C6 the results — the average score for each student.

The second way to compute each student's average grade for the three tests is to use Row Statistics on the Calc menu. This menu selection provides an even easier way to calculate the mean (or other statistic) of some or all of the data in a particular row and then save the results in a new column. It does it all for you — you don't even enter a formula. Try using Row Statistics:

- Choose **Calc > Row Statistics**

The Row Statistics dialog box appears as shown in Figure 2-1.

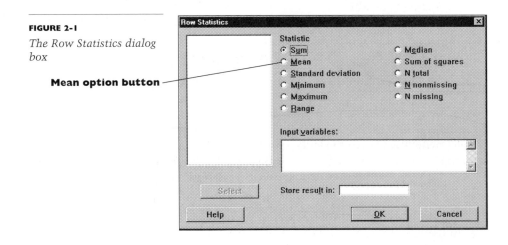

Row Statistics computes common statistics for each row. To compute the mean of the three grades recorded for each student in C3, C4, and C5:

- Click the **Mean** option button

- Press [Tab] to move the cursor to the "Input variables" text box

In the "Input variables" text box, you can enter the column names in any of three ways. First, you can type C3–C5 (a dash between columns designates a series of consecutive columns). Second, you can double-click each column individually in the list box on the left. Or third, you can use a shortcut technique to enter the three columns in the "Input variables" text box, as follows:

- Single-click **C3 Test1** in the list box on the left and hold down the left mouse button as you drag the highlight through **C4 Test2** and **C5 Test3**

- Click **Select**

The three columns now appear in the "Input variables" text box.

Dragging the highlight is usually the quickest way to select consecutive variables in a list box. Alternatively, you can click the first variable and then hold down [Shift] while clicking the last variable to highlight all of the variables in between the first and last. To select several nonconsecutive variables, hold down [Ctrl] while you click each one.

Tell Minitab where to display the resulting means:

- Press [Tab] to move to the "Store result in" text box

- Type **RMean** (for row mean) and press [↵]

If you compare the entries in C6 and C7 in Figure 2-2, you can see that the two methods produce the same results. You now have a test average for each student. Note that several students are performing extremely well (Jonathan Goldberg and Kathleen Sheppard, for example), while others (such as Jason Douglas and Mark McClure) are not performing well. (Again, depending on the size of your screen, you may have to scroll to see some of these data.)

FIGURE 2-2

The Data window, showing the mean calculated using two ways

The Data window, showing the mean calculated using two ways:

	C1-T	C2-T	C3	C4	C5	C6	C7	C8	C9
↓	LastName	First	Test1	Test2	Test3	Averg	RMean		
1	Adams	James	72	93	93	86.0000	86.0000		
2	Benson	Melissa	99	96	85	89.3333	89.3333		
3	Brown	Lamar	59	59	90	69.3333	69.3333		
4	Dougherty	Megan	79	69	80	69.3333	69.3333		
5	Douglas	Jason	48	77	25	50.0000	50.0000		
6	Gigliotti	Andrew	78	94	50	74.0000	74.0000		
7	Goldberg	Jonathan	98	98	94	96.6667	96.6667		
8	Green	Jennifer	92	91	99	94.0000	94.0000		
9	Kennedy	Kevin	71	78	62	70.3333	70.3333		
10	Lee	Sang	64	68	97	76.3333	76.3333		
11	McClure	Mark	49	79	43	57.0000	57.0000		
12	Messina	Steven	94	93	95	94.0000	94.0000		
13	Norman	Barbara	99	95	84	92.6667	92.6667		
14	Nowicki	Amy	91	81	79	83.6667	83.6667		
15	Patel	Hima	90	100	62	84.0000	84.0000		
16	Pierson	Richard	100	77	100	92.3333	92.3333		
17	Rojas	Luis	73	79	83	78.3333	78.3333		
18	Ryan	Matt	77	79	85	80.3333	80.3333		
19	Schmidt	Nancy	83	79	52	71.3333	71.3333		
20	Scott	Michael	81	75	100	85.3333	85.3333		

For additional practice, use Row Statistics to compute the median score for each student:

- Click the **Edit Last Dialog** button ▦ on the toolbar (it is the eighth button from the right) to reopen the Row Statistics dialog box

- Click the **Median** option button

    You want to use the same input variables as previously:

- Press ⟨Tab⟩ twice to move to the "Store result in" text box

- Type **RMedian** in the "Store result in" text box and press ⏎

    C8 RMedian, as shown in Figure 2-3, now contains the median of each student's test scores (you may have to scroll to see this column).

FIGURE 2-3

The Data window, showing median test scores

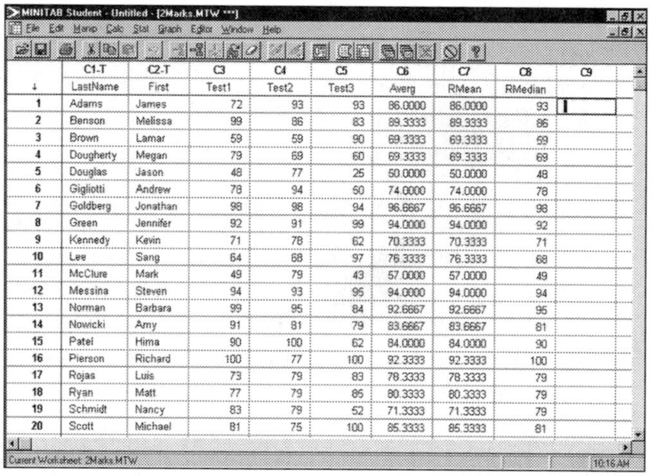

	C1-T	C2-T	C3	C4	C5	C6	C7	C8	C9
↓	LastName	First	Test1	Test2	Test3	Averg	RMean	RMedian	
1	Adams	James	72	93	93	86.0000	86.0000	93	
2	Benson	Melissa	99	86	83	89.3333	89.3333	86	
3	Brown	Lamar	59	59	90	69.3333	69.3333	59	
4	Dougherty	Megan	79	69	60	69.3333	69.3333	69	
5	Douglas	Jason	48	77	25	50.0000	50.0000	48	
6	Gigliotti	Andrew	78	94	50	74.0000	74.0000	78	
7	Goldberg	Jonathan	98	98	94	96.6667	96.6667	98	
8	Green	Jennifer	92	91	99	94.0000	94.0000	92	
9	Kennedy	Kevin	71	78	62	70.3333	70.3333	71	
10	Lee	Sang	64	68	97	76.3333	76.3333	68	
11	McClure	Mark	49	79	43	57.0000	57.0000	49	
12	Messina	Steven	94	93	95	94.0000	94.0000	94	
13	Norman	Barbara	99	95	84	92.6667	92.6667	95	
14	Nowicki	Amy	91	81	79	83.6667	83.6667	81	
15	Patel	Hima	90	100	62	84.0000	84.0000	90	
16	Pierson	Richard	100	77	100	92.3333	92.3333	100	
17	Rojas	Luis	73	79	83	78.3333	78.3333	79	
18	Ryan	Matt	77	79	85	80.3333	80.3333	79	
19	Schmidt	Nancy	83	79	52	71.3333	71.3333	79	
20	Scott	Michael	81	75	100	85.3333	85.3333	81	

Current Worksheet: 2Marks.MTW   10:16 AM

Next, you decide to compute a weighted average of the three tests in order to reward students who improved during the first marking period:

- Choose **Calc > Calculator**

- In the "Store result in variable" text box, type **W** in front of the **Averg** name and press ⟨Tab⟩

- Modify the "Expression" text box to create the formula **(1*Test1+2*Test2+3*Test3) / 6** and click **OK**

    Notice that the weighted averages, located in C9, do reward recent performance. For example, the weighted average for Lamar Brown (whose scores were 59, 59, and 90) is more than five points greater than his unweighted average.

    In your final grade report, you want each student's weighted average grade to appear as an integer. Minitab can round the scores for you:

[handwritten margin note: Formula for weighted Avg.]

- Click the **Edit Last Dialog** button ▦ on the toolbar to reopen the Calculator dialog box

  To tell Minitab in which column to store the rounded averages:

- Type **R** in front of the **WAverg** name in the "Store result in variable" text box

- Select and highlight the entire formula in the "Expression" text box

- In the "Functions" box, scroll down until you reach the Round command, click **Round**, and click **Select**

- Select and highlight **num_digits** in the "Expression" text box and type **0**

  The "num_digits" placeholder is where you specify the number of decimal places to which to round the number. When the value 0 is specified, the data is rounded to the nearest integer. (For example, had you wanted the scores rounded to two decimal places, you would have entered 2 instead of 0.) Each student's weighted average score, rounded to the nearest integer, appears in C10.

- Click **OK**

▼ **Note** Rounding is only one of the many *functions* (or *specific operations*) that Minitab provides in Calculator. You may be familiar with others, such as obtaining the absolute value, the log to the base 10, and the maximum. You will encounter a number of new and useful functions as you proceed through this manual. You may find information about such Calculator functions by referencing Minitab's on-line Help. ▲

▼ 2.2   Summarizing Columns ▲

Each row in a Minitab worksheet represents the data for an individual case, such as one particular student's test scores. When you perform a row operation, you calculate a statistic (for example, the mean for each case) and display the results in a designated column in the Data window. In contrast, Minitab's columns contain values of the same variable; for example, C3 contains all of the scores for Test1. When you want to compute statistics for a particular variable or column, you use a column operation.

Column operations frequently produce single numbers that appear in the Session window, not in the Data window. For example, the mean of the 24 Test1 scores will be a constant. Minitab can store such values in specific locations that you assign, such as K1, K2, and K3. You can also assign names to constants. If you plan to use a result again later, it's useful to store it as a constant. (Constants are stored as part of the worksheet but do not appear in the worksheet's Data window.)

Explore how Minitab operates on columns (variables) by finding the mean score for Test1. Remember, this is the mean of the whole class's performance on the first test, not the mean of a single student's performance. You do this by using Column Statistics on the Calc menu:

■ Choose **Calc > Column Statistics**

The Column Statistics dialog box appears as shown in Figure 2-4.

FIGURE 2-4

*The Column Statistics dia-
log box*

Column Statistics

Statistic
- ○ Sum
- ○ Mean
- ○ Standard deviation
- ○ Minimum
- ○ Maximum
- ○ Range
- ○ Median
- ○ Sum of squares
- ○ N total
- ○ N nonmissing
- ○ N missing

Input variable: _____

Store result in: _____ (Optional)

Select

Help   OK   Cancel

■ Click the **Mean** option button

■ Click in the "Input variables" text box

■ Double-click **C3 Test1** in the list box on the left to enter it in the "Input variable" text box

■ Click in the "Store result in" text box

■ Type **MeanC3** as the constant name in the "Store result in" text box and press ⏎

To see the column statistics in the Session window:

■ Choose **Window > Session**

The Session window appears as shown in Figure 2-5.

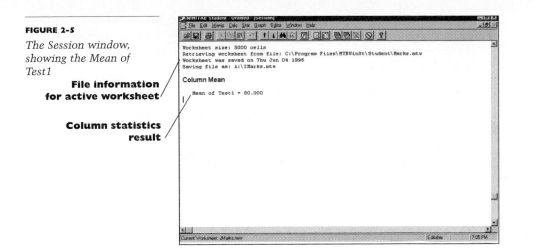

You can see the mean you requested — 80.000 — in the Session window. Your students performed relatively well on the first test.

▼ **Note** It is worth reviewing the column statistics that are listed in the Column Statistics dialog box. As well as the mean, you can obtain the median value, the range of values, and the standard deviation of the values. In Tutorial 5, you will learn how to obtain statistics, such as the quartiles, that are not included under Column Statistics. ▲

▼ 2.3 Using Session Commands ▲

Until now, you have primarily worked in the Data window and issued commands by choosing them from the Minitab menu bar. Every command you executed via the menu has a corresponding Session command that appears in the Session window in a special *Session command language.* To enable the Session command language:

■ Choose **Window > Session** (if this window is not already active)

■ Choose **Editor > Enable Command Language**

The Minitab prompt, "MTB >," appears at the bottom of the Session window. To see the impact of this change, ask again for the mean of Test1:

■ Choose **Edit > Edit Last Dialog** and repeat the previous command by clicking **OK**.

The output is shown in Figure 2-6.

Command entered by menu command

Minitab prompt ready for next command

Note that a command has appeared after the first Minitab prompt and before the second appearance of your mean output.

Minitab entered Mean 'Test1' 'MeanC3' when you requested a column mean. You could have typed this command directly in the Session window just as Minitab did and pressed ⏎ to issue the command.

Note the "MTB >" prompt at the bottom of the Session window. This prompt is Minitab's way of telling you that it is ready for you to type a command. To enter a command in this way, you need to know the correct words to type using Minitab's Session command language. For example, to obtain information about the worksheet, you type the info session command:

■ With your cursor at the "MTB >" prompt, type **info** and press ⏎ (Remember, always press ⏎ after typing a command.)

The contents of the Info window, which was introduced in the first tutorial, are displayed in the Session window. Notice that Minitab saved the mean for Test1 as the named constant K1.

▼ **Note** Here are three basic rules for typing session commands: 1. Type the main command, followed by any arguments. If you are going to use subcommands, end the main command line with a semicolon. 2. Type any subcommands and any subcommand arguments, ending each subcommand line with a semicolon, except the last subcommand line. 3. End the last subcommand line with a period. ▲

You can also display data in the Session window; this can sometimes be quicker than looking in the Data window. The print session command displays whatever values you specify in the Session window. In other words, it "prints" to the screen, not to paper. Suppose you want to see the names of your students and the students' rounded, weighted averages:

- With your cursor at the "MTB >" prompt, type **print C1 C2 C10** and press ⏎

Minitab lists the data in row and column format, along with the corresponding row numbers, as shown in Figure 2-7.

FIGURE 2-7

The Session window, showing students' names and their rounded, weighted average test grades

```
MTB > print c1 c2 c10
```

Data Display

Row	LastName	First	RWAverg
1	Adams	James	90
2	Benson	Melissa	87
3	Brown	Lamar	75
4	Dougherty	Megan	66
5	Douglas	Jason	46
6	Gigliotti	Andrew	69
7	Goldberg	Jonathan	96
8	Green	Jennifer	95
9	Kennedy	Kevin	69
10	Lee	Sang	82
11	McClure	Mark	56
12	Messina	Steven	94
13	Norman	Barbara	90
14	Nowicki	Amy	82
15	Patel	Hima	79
16	Pierson	Richard	92
17	Rojas	Luis	80
18	Ryan	Matt	82
19	Schmidt	Nancy	66
20	Scott	Michael	89
21	Sheppard	Kathleen	98
22	Smith	Holly	43
23	Thompson	Susan	72
24	Watson	Keisha	66

Notice that the Session window automatically scrolls to keep the last line of output and the current "MTB >" prompt visible. From now on, Session window output will be displayed in the format shown in Figure 2-7 so that you can see more than one screen of output. To see the beginning of the output and other areas of the Session window, you can scroll up and down or right and left using the scroll bars. Alternatively, you can use the direction keys to move quickly through one section at a time:

- Press `PageUp` to move to the previous screen

- Press `PageDown` to move to the next screen

- Press `Ctrl`+`Home` to move to the beginning of the Session window

- Press `Ctrl`+`End` to move to the end of the Session window

These key shortcuts also work in the Data windows.

▼ **Note** You will develop a preference on how to issue commands: using the menus or typing them at the Session window prompt. Usually, this manual directs you to use the menus, except in certain cases in which it's easier to type directly in the Session window. ▲

Now try printing the same three columns again using Display Data on the Manip menu. Display Data corresponds to the print session command that you used earlier in this section:

■ Choose **Manip > Display Data**

■ Press and hold down Ctrl while you click **C1**, **C2**, and **C10** in the list box that appears in the Display Data dialog box

■ Click **Select**

The three columns you selected appear in the "Columns and constants to display" text box.

■ Click **OK**

As Figure 2-8 shows, using Display Data produces the same result as using the print session command in the Session window.

FIGURE 2-8

Result of using the Data Display menu command

```
MTB > Print 'LastName' 'First' 'RWAverg'.
```

Data Display

Row	LastName	First	RWAverg
1	Adams	James	90
2	Benson	Melissa	87
3	Brown	Lamar	75
4	Dougherty	Megan	66
5	Douglas	Jason	46
6	Gigliotti	Andrew	69
7	Goldberg	Jonathan	96
8	Green	Jennifer	95
9	Kennedy	Kevin	69
10	Lee	Sang	82
11	McClure	Mark	56
12	Messina	Steven	94
13	Norman	Barbara	90
14	Nowicki	Amy	82
15	Patel	Hima	79
16	Pierson	Richard	92
17	Rojas	Luis	80
18	Ryan	Matt	82
19	Schmidt	Nancy	66
20	Scott	Michael	89
21	Sheppard	Kathleen	98
22	Smith	Holly	43
23	Thompson	Susan	72
24	Watson	Keisha	66

Notice that Minitab issued the command a little differently in the Session window; it used Print 'LastName' 'First' 'RWAverg'. You can specify columns by either number or name when you use Session commands.

Output in the Session window can be changed and edited. However, it is also easy to inadvertently change output that you didn't want to alter. To avoid this, it is recommended that newcomers to Minitab make the output *read-only*. When you make output read-only, you ensure that this display and other portions of the Session window are not altered in error. Make sure you are in the Session window:

■ Choose **Editor > Make Output Read-Only** (unless the Editor menu says Make Output Editable)

▼ **Note** This menu command is an example of a "toggle." When the Session window is set to read-only, the menu command changes to Make Output Editable, which you can select to edit the Session window again. The Make Output Editable and the Enable Command Language menu commands are available only when the Session window is active. ▲

At the beginning of each of the remaining tutorials, you will be asked to enable the Session command language and make the Session window read-only.

▼ 2.4   Coding Data ▲

The school district at which you work uses the letter grades A, B, C, D, and F. You want to code values for RWAverg that fall in the interval 90 to 100 as an A, values of 80 to 89 as a B, values of 70 to 79 as a C, values of 60 to 69 as a D, and values 59 and below as an F. You will store the letter grades corresponding to the numerical values in a new column.

To code the students' averages, you use Code on the Manip menu:

■ Choose **Manip > Code > Numeric to Text** to display the "Code - Numeric to Text" dialog box

■ Double-click **C10 RWAverg** to enter it in the "Code data from columns" text box

■ Press ⎡Tab⎤ and then type **Grade** in the "Into columns" text box

To specify the intervals, you can either list all of the values in the interval (separated by commas) or specify the first and last values in the range (separated by a colon):

- Press ⟨Tab⟩ to move to the first "Original values" text box

- Type **90:100** and then press ⟨Tab⟩ to move to the first "New" text box

    Minitab interprets the entry 90:100 as all of the rounded weighted averages between 90 and 100, inclusive.

- Type **A** in the first "New" text box and press ⟨Tab⟩

- Type **80:89**, press ⟨Tab⟩, type **B**, and then press ⟨Tab⟩ to enter data in the second "Original values" and "New" text boxes, respectively

- Type **70:79**, press ⟨Tab⟩, type **C**, and then press ⟨Tab⟩ to enter data in the third "Original values" and "New" text boxes, respectively

- Type **60:69**, press ⟨Tab⟩, type **D**, and then press ⟨Tab⟩

- Type **0:59**, press ⟨Tab⟩, and then type **F** to enter data in the fifth "Original values" and "New" text boxes, respectively

    The Code - Numeric to Text dialog box should appear as shown in Figure 2-9.

FIGURE 2-9

The completed Code - Numeric to Text dialog box

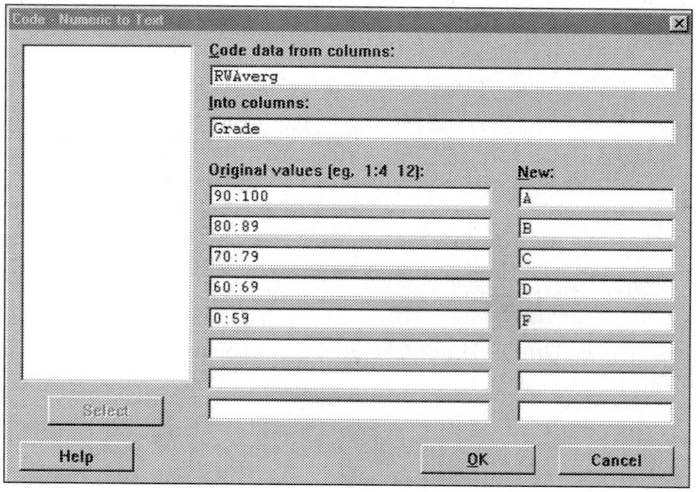

- Click **OK** to code the average grades with a number representing a letter grade

- Choose **Window > 2Marks.mtw***** to view the new column

- Scroll to the right to see C11-T Grade

    The resulting Data window is shown in Figure 2-10.

FIGURE 2-10

*Data window, showing
the variable Grade*

**The variable
Grade**

	C3	C4	C5	C6	C7	C8	C9	C10	C11-T
↓	Test1	Test2	Test3	Averg	RMean	RMedian	WAverg	RWAverg	Grade
1	72	93	93	86.0000	86.0000	93	89.5000	90	B
2	99	86	83	89.3333	89.3333	86	86.6667	87	B
3	59	59	90	69.3333	69.3333	59	74.5000	75	C
4	79	69	60	69.3333	69.3333	69	66.1667	66	D
5	48	77	25	50.0000	50.0000	48	46.1667	46	F
6	78	94	50	74.0000	74.0000	78	69.3333	69	D
7	98	98	94	96.6667	96.6667	98	96.0000	96	A
8	92	91	99	94.0000	94.0000	92	95.1667	95	A
9	71	78	62	70.3333	70.3333	71	68.8333	69	D
10	64	68	97	76.3333	76.3333	68	81.8333	82	B
11	49	79	43	57.0000	57.0000	49	56.0000	56	F
12	94	93	95	94.0000	94.0000	94	94.1667	94	A
13	99	95	84	92.6667	92.6667	95	90.1667	90	A
14	91	81	79	83.6667	83.6667	81	81.6667	82	B
15	90	100	62	84.0000	84.0000	90	79.3333	79	C
16	100	77	100	92.3333	92.3333	100	92.3333	92	A
17	73	79	83	78.3333	78.3333	79	80.0000	80	B
18	77	79	85	80.3333	80.3333	79	81.6667	82	B
19	83	79	52	71.3333	71.3333	79	66.1667	66	D
20	81	75	100	85.3333	85.3333	81	88.5000	89	B

Compare columns C10 and C11. Notice that each student whose rounded weighted average falls between 90 and 100, inclusive, is assigned a letter grade of A, each whose rounded weighted average falls between 80 and 89, inclusive, is assigned a B, and so on. By scanning this column, you can quickly determine which students are doing well and which ones need help.

▼ 2.5 Ranking Data ▲

Ms. Taylor has asked you to rank your students' average exam scores in numerical order so that she can see how each student's performance compares to the rest of the students' performances. Minitab ranks the data listed in any column by assigning a value of 1 to the lowest score, 2 to the second lowest, and so on. The top student is ranked number 24 because this is the total number of students in the class. To rank the weighted average exam scores, you use Rank on the Manip menu:

- Choose **Manip > Rank**

- Double-click **C10 RWAverg** to enter it in the "Rank data in" text box

- Type **Rank** in the "Store ranks in" text box

- Press ↵ and scroll to view C12 Rank

If two or more scores are tied, Minitab assigns them a rank equal to the average of the two separate ranks. For example, from the scores that placed seventh and eighth in C14, you can see that Minitab assigned each the rank of 7.5

(rows 6 and 19, Andrew Gigliotti and Kevin Kennedy). Verify that two students are tied for eighteenth place in your class. What are their names?

▼ 2.6   Sorting Data ▲

Ms. Taylor also wants you to create and print a list of the students ordered by their weighted mean scores. The student who had the highest weighted average should be listed first, the second highest should be listed next, and so on.

If you simply sort C10 RWAverg, Minitab rearranges the entries in that particular column but leaves the others intact. Sorting in this way usually creates unexpected and confusing results, such as one student's grade appearing next to another name. Usually, when you sort you want to "carry along" all of the columns in a worksheet that correspond to the data for an individual case. Here, you want to keep in a single row all of the data related to a given student. Note, for example, that before the sort, the test scores for Kathleen Sheppard are 94, 97, and 100.

Before you sort data, it's a good idea to save them just in case they get mixed up during the sort process:

- Choose **File > Save Current Worksheet**

Now you're ready to sort your data based on the values for RWAverg. You do this by using Sort on the Manip menu:

- Choose **Manip > Sort**

- Highlight all of the columns in the list box

- Click **Select** to display the columns in the "Sort column(s)" text box

You need to specify where you want Minitab to store the sorted data. In this case, put them in the same location they currently occupy:

- Click in the "Store sorted column(s) in" text box

- Highlight all of the columns (C1–C12) to enter them in the "Store sorted column(s) in" text box, then click **Select**

Next, tell Minitab to use C10 RWAverg — the student's rounded, weighted average on the three exams — as the sort criterion:

- Click in the first "Sort by column" text box

- Select **C10 RWAverg** to enter it in the first "Sort by column" text box

- Click the **Descending** check box to sort the students' weighted average grades in descending order (otherwise, the weighted average grades will be sorted in ascending order)

Your Sort dialog box should look like that shown in Figure 2-11.

FIGURE 2-11

The completed Sort dialog box

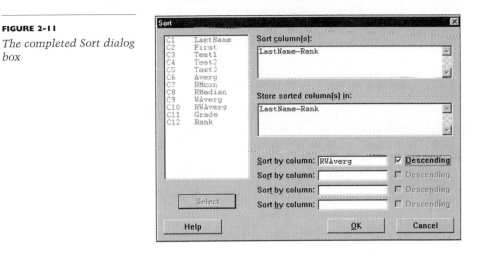

- Click **OK**

- Press Ctrl+Home to move to the beginning of the Data window

The students' data are ordered according to their RWAverg scores in C10, as shown in Figure 2-12. The scores for each student are carried along with them. For example, the student with the highest RWAverg score is Kathleen Sheppard, who had test scores of 94, 97, and 100.

FIGURE 2-12

The Data window after sorting

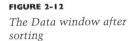

You also can sort rows by using a text variable. This is useful if you wish to place items in alphabetical order. You will do this later in this tutorial.

You now have a summary of your class's performance. Since your worksheet is sorted, you can quickly see which students are not doing well (those at the bottom of the list) and help them improve their grades.

In this example, you sorted the scores on the basis of the weighted averages. Minitab can use up to four columns as sorting criteria.

At this point, save your data again:

- Choose **File > Save Current Worksheet**

▼ 2.7   Standardizing Data ▲

In addition to submitting the grades, you want to report each student's progress during the marking period by comparing the grades from the three tests. Each test reflects a score based on 100 possible points. However, an 87 on an easy test might actually reflect less knowledge than a 75 on a more difficult test. If two scores come from two different samples, each with its own mean and standard deviation, you can compare them by *standardizing* them. You subtract from each the appropriate mean (this is called *centering*) and then divide the difference by the standard deviation.

To compute standardized scores for the various test grades, you use Standardize on the Calc menu:

- Choose **Calc > Standardize** to open the Standardize dialog box

- Select **C3 Test1**, **C4 Test2**, and **C5 Test3** to enter them in the "Input column(s)" text box

- Press Tab

- Type **Std1 Std2 Std3** in the "Store results in" text box

The completed Standardize dialog box should look as shown in Figure 2-13. Notice that the first option, "Subtract mean and divide by std. dev.," is already selected; it is the *default*, or preselected, option.

FIGURE 2-13

*The completed
Standardize dialog box*

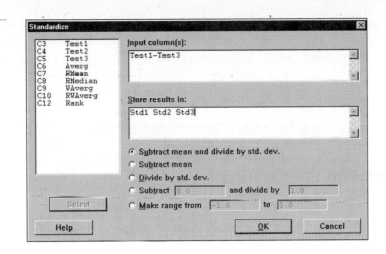

- Press ↵ to calculate the standardized scores
- Scroll to look at C13, C14, and C15, which contain the standardized scores

The standardized scores, the first few of which are shown in Figure 2-14, allow you to easily determine how each student performed on each test, relative to the class.

FIGURE 2-14

The Data window, showing standardized grades

	C7	C8	C9	C10	C11-T	C12	C13	C14	C15	
↓	RMean	RMedian	WAverg	RWAverg	Grade	Rank	Std1	Std2	Std3	
1	97.0000	97	98.0000	98	A	24.0	0.89626	1.18275	1.05442	
2	96.6667	98	96.0000	96	A	23.0	1.15233	1.25805	0.80713	
3	94.0000	92	95.1667	95	A	22.0	0.76822	0.73098	1.01321	
4	94.0000	94	94.1667	94	A	21.0	0.89626	0.88157	0.84835	
5	92.3333	100	92.3333	92	A	20.0	1.28037	-0.32314	1.05442	
6	86.0000	93	89.5000	90	A	18.5	-0.51215	0.88157	0.76592	
7	92.6667	95	90.1667	90	A	18.5	1.21635	1.03216	0.39498	
8	85.3333	81	88.5000	89	B	17.0	0.06402	-0.47373	1.05442	
9	89.3333	86	86.6667	87	B	16.0	1.21635	0.35451	0.35376	
10	76.3333	68	81.8333	82	B	14.0	-1.02430	-1.00079	0.93078	
11	83.6667	81	81.6667	82	B	14.0	0.70420	-0.02196	0.16890	
12	80.3333	79	81.6667	82	B	14.0	-0.19206	-0.17255	0.43619	
13	78.3333	79	80.0000	80	B	12.0	-0.44813	-0.17255	0.35376	
14	84.0000	90	79.3333	79	C	11.0	0.64018	1.40864	-0.51176	
15	69.3333	59	74.5000	75	C	10.0	-1.34439	-1.67044	0.64227	
16	67.6667	60	71.8333	72	C	9.0	-1.34439	-1.60315	0.39498	
17	74.0000	78	69.3333	69	D	7.5	-0.12804	0.95687	-1.00634	
18	70.3333	71	68.8333	69	D	7.5	-0.57617	-0.24784	-0.51176	
19	69.3333	69	66.1667	66	D	5.0	0.06402	-0.92550	-0.59419	
20	71.3333	79	66.1667	66	D	5.0	0.19206	-0.17255	-0.92391	

Current Worksheet: 2Marks.MTW

You can quickly spot trends in a student's performance. For example, relative to the class performance, the performance of the student in row 7 dropped on the last exam, while that of the student in row 3 improved.

▼ 2.8   Creating Subsets ▲

Your older colleagues have warned you to expect complaints and questions from those students who received an F for the class. As a handy reference, you want to store the various grades for these students separately from the original worksheet. Minitab's Subset Worksheet command in the Manip menu is perfect for this. It allows you to store a subset of the original data in a separate worksheet. To create a worksheet that contains the values in C1–C16 but only for those students with a grade of F:

- Choose **Manip > Subset Worksheet**

- Highlight the default "Name" and type **MarksF**

- Click **Condition**

- In the "Condition" text box, double-click **C11 Grade** and then type **="F"** (with the quotation marks) so that the text box contains Grade = "F"

- Click **OK** twice

The new worksheet, called *MarksF.mtw*, is shown in Figure 2-15. It contains the data for C1–C15 but only for the three F students. You will print scores for these students later.

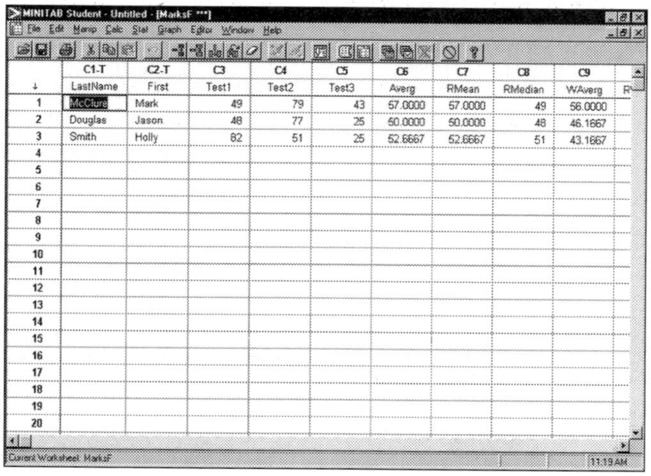

FIGURE 2-15

The MarksF. mtw Data window

Notice that when you specified the grade of F in the "Condition" text box, you enclosed the F within double quotation marks. Whenever you write an equation that includes the value for a text variable — such as Grade = "F" — you must enclose the value within quotation marks.

Return to the *2Marks. mtw* worksheet:

- Choose **Window > 2Marks. mtw** * * *

▼ **Note** Minitab has a Split Worksheet command that operates in much the same way as Subset Worksheet. It allows you to create several new worksheets based on the unique values in a column. For example, if you had classified each student according to gender, you could create separate worksheets for male students and for female students. However, one restriction on the use of both Subset Worksheet and Split Worksheet is that with the Student Edition of Minitab for Winows, a Minitab session can include only five worksheets. ▲

▼ 2.9   Combining Data Using the Stack Option ▲

Your principal, Ms. Taylor, has asked you to include statistical information based upon the three tests combined in your report. To obtain such information, you need to combine, or *stack*, the scores in Test1, Test2, and Test3 into a single column. Minitab does this with Stack on the Manip menu. Stack creates a new column that consists of data from all of the selected columns:

- Choose **Manip > Stack/Unstack > Stack Columns**

    The Stack Columns dialog box appears. To indicate the three columns you want to stack:

- Double-click **C3 Test1**, **C4 Test2**, and **C5 Test3** to enter them in the "Stack the following columns" text box and press Tab

- Type **Total** in the "Store the stacked data in" text box and press Tab

    When you stack data, you can tell Minitab to store a *subscript* variable that indicates the column from which the data originated. In this case, the subscript — 1, 2, or 3 — is simply a numerical label indicating to which test a score belongs:

- Type **Test** in the "Store subscripts in" text box

    Your Stack Columns dialog box should look as shown in Figure 2-16.

FIGURE 2-16

The Stack Columns dialog box

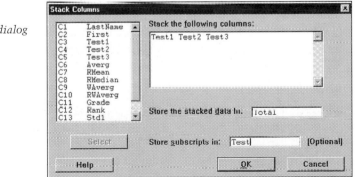

- Press ⏎ to stack the three test variables in the same column

- Scroll to the right so that you can see the stacked scores in C16 and the subscripts in C17

- Scroll down to view all of the data in these two columns

Notice how all of the grades are stacked on top of one another in the order in which you entered the tests; in other words, all three columns, C3, C4, and C5, are listed in a single column. Note, too, that C17 (the subscript) identifies the test from which each grade originated.

Calculate the mean of C16 and view it in the Session window:

- Choose **Calc > Column Statistics** to open the Column Statistics dialog box, which contains the selections you made the last time you used this command

- Double-click in the "Input variables" text box to highlight the variable you previously specified

- Double-click **C16 Total** to enter it in the "Input variables" text box

- Double-click in the "Store result in" text box to select it

- Type **MeanTest** in the "Store result in" text box and press ⏎

- Choose **Window > Session** to view the results, which are shown in Figure 2-17

FIGURE 2-17

Computing the Mean of Total score

```
MTB > Name K2 = 'MeanTest'
MTB > Mean 'Total' 'MeanTest'.
```

Column Mean

```
   Mean of Total = 78.569
```

The figure shows that Minitab created a new constant, K2, called 'MeanTest', which will contain the mean of all 72 (24 **X** 3) test scores. That mean is 78.569. You can report to Ms. Taylor that the average of test scores of all the tests is a respectable 78.569.

You moved from the Data window to the Session window by using a Window menu command. You can also use a keyboard shortcut to activate a different window:

- Press Ctrl+Tab

Note that the Data window is now the active window.
Try activating the other Minitab windows similarly:

- Press Ctrl+Tab several times

The title bar changes as you move from one window to another, identifying which is active.

- Continue to press Ctrl+Tab until the *2Marks.mtw* worksheet is active again

▼ 2.10   Separating Data Using the Unstack Option ▲

Ms. Taylor has requested a separate listing of all RWAverg scores that fall within each letter grade you specified earlier with Code (see Section 2.4). Just as you were able to combine several columns into a single column by using Stack, you can use Minitab's Unstack command to take a single column and break it into several new columns according to criteria you specify.

In this section, you will use Unstack on the Manip menu to *unstack* C10 RWAverg into five columns, C18–C22. You will put all of the grades within the range 90 to 100 (A's) in the first column (C18), all grades from 80 to 89 (B's) in the second column (C19), and so on, using the grade data that appears as the subscripts in C11. You will name these five new columns A, B, C, D, and F, respectively.

- Choose **Manip > Stack/Unstack > Unstack One Column** to open the Unstack One Column dialog box

- Double-click **C10 RWAverg** to enter it as the variable to unstack in the "Unstack the data in" text box

Starting with the highest category, specify the columns of data you want to unstack:

- Type the column names, **A B C D F** (leave a space between each name) in the "Store the unstacked data in" text box

- Click in the "Using subscripts in" text box and double-click **C11 Grade**, which contains the subscripts

The completed Unstack One Column dialog box should look as shown in Figure 2-18.

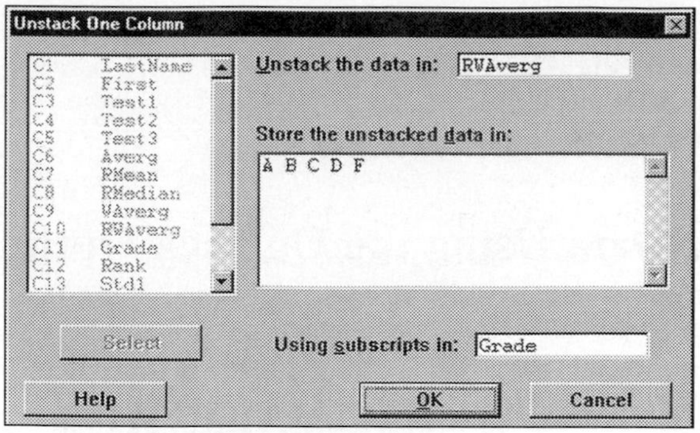

FIGURE 2-18

*The completed Unstack
One Column dialog box*

Unstack One Column dialog box

- Press ↵

- Scroll to the right to see the new columns, C18–C22

  The Data window shows the grades grouped by category, as shown in Figure 2-19.

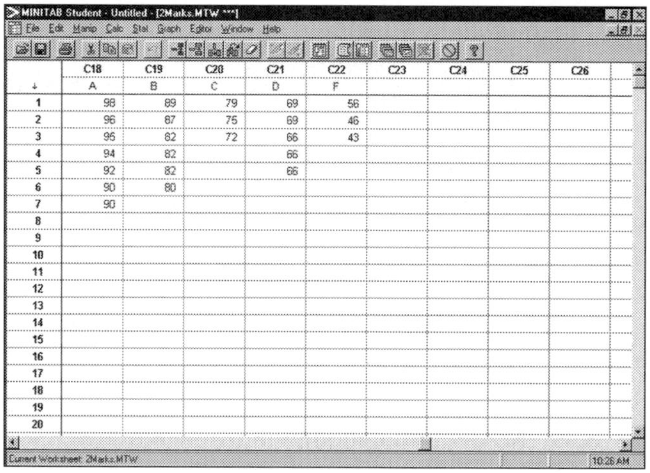

FIGURE 2-19

*The Data window, with
grades unstacked into
intervals*

At this point, you have 16 students earning grades of A, B, or C and only 8 earning Ds or Fs. Also, 2 of your 5 students with Ds are almost getting Cs. All in all, it appears your class is doing fairly well.

▼ **Note** In the Unstack One Column dialog box, you listed the names of five columns (A, B, C, D, and F), leaving a space between names. In general, when listing columns, whether by name or by number, you must, between the names or numbers, either leave one or more spaces or type a comma. Or, you may write a sequence of consecutive column names or numbers, inserting only a dash between the first and the last name or number in the sequence. For example, Minitab will interpret the list C3, C7, C9–C12, C14 as including the seven columns C3, C7, C9, C10, C11, C12, and C14. ▲

▼ 2.11   Printing the Results of Your Analysis ▲

Now that you have summarized your class's performance, you want to print your worksheet to paper for submission to Ms. Taylor.

First, save your data:

- Choose **File > Save Current Worksheet**

Then re-sort your grades in alphabetical order (excluding the columns that you created with Stack and Unstack):

- Choose **Manip > Sort**

- Double-click in the "Sort Column(s)" text box to highlight the previous entry, if needed

- Select **C1–C15** to enter it in the "Sort column(s)" text box (you do not want to include either the stacked or the unstacked data in this sort)

- Double-click in the "Store sorted column(s) in" text box to highlight the previous entry

- Select **C1–C15** again to enter it in the "Store sorted column(s) in" text box and then press [Tab]

- Double-click in the first "Sort by column" text box to highlight the previous entry

- Select **C1 LastName** to enter it in the "Sort by column" text box

- Click the first **Descending** check box to deselect it and press [Tab]

- Select **C2 First** to enter it in the second "Sort by column" text box, in case you have two students with the same last name

- Click **OK**

    Your worksheet is alphabetized again.
    Save the worksheet again:

- Choose **File > Save Current Worksheet**

Printing the Data

Now you are ready to print your grades data to paper. You could select File > Print Window to print the entire worksheet, but Ms. Taylor probably wants to see only your students' names, weighted averages, and grades. The easiest way to select only those columns that contain these data involves using the Session window:

- Choose **Window > Session**

- At the Minitab prompt, "MTB >", type **print C1 C2 C10 C11** and press ⏎

    Minitab displays the data you requested.

- Highlight the data by clicking the upper-left corner (just to the left of the row heading) and dragging the pointer to the lower-right corner (to the right of the final grade). Don't include any of the commands or prompts

    The Session window should look as shown in Figure 2-20, with the data highlighted.

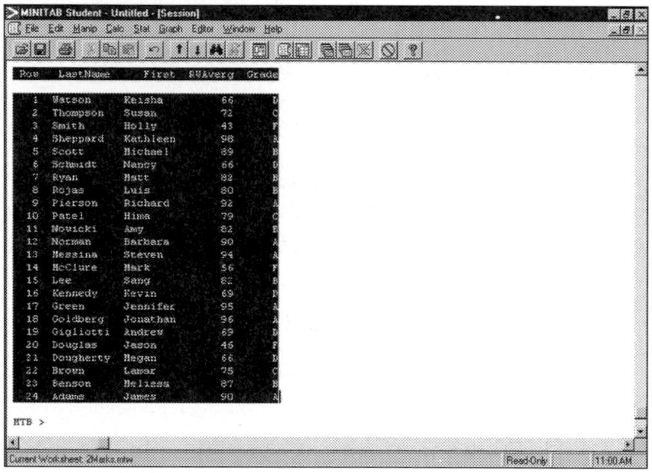

FIGURE 2-20

Session window, showing the grades data highlighted

- Choose **File > Print Session Window**

    The Print dialog box lets you specify how much of the window to print. The Selection option button is chosen by default, thereby indicating that Minitab will print only the highlighted data.

- Click **OK** to print the selection you highlighted

    Figure 2-21 shows the printed grade list.

FIGURE 2-21

Printout of alphabetical grade list

Row	LastName	First	RWAverg	Grade
1	Adams	James	90	A
2	Benson	Melissa	87	B
3	Brown	Lamar	75	C
4	Dougherty	Megan	66	D
5	Douglas	Jason	46	F
6	Gigliotti	Andrew	69	D
7	Goldberg	Jonathan	96	A
8	Green	Jennifer	95	A
9	Kennedy	Kevin	69	D
10	Lee	Sang	82	B
11	McClure	Mark	56	F
12	Messina	Steven	94	A
13	Norman	Barbara	90	A
14	Nowicki	Amy	82	B
15	Patel	Hima	79	C
16	Pierson	Richard	92	A
17	Rojas	Luis	80	B
18	Ryan	Matt	82	B
19	Schmidt	Nancy	66	D
20	Scott	Michael	89	B
21	Sheppard	Kathleen	98	A
22	Smith	Holly	43	F
23	Thompson	Susan	72	C
24	Watson	Keisha	66	D

At this point, you decide also to print, from the Session window, a paper copy of the names, the three test scores, and the rounded, weighted averages for the three students who failed the class. To review the data for these three students:

■ Choose **Window > MarksF**

You will print out columns C1, C2, C3, C4, C5, and C10. To return to the Session window and print out these columns:

■ Choose **Window > Session**

■ At the "MTB >" prompt, type **print C1–C5 C10** and press ⏎

■ Highlight the output in the Session window

■ Choose **File > Print Session Window**

■ Click **OK** to get a paper copy of the selected scores

Now that you have a paper copy of the test scores for the F students, you decide to close this new worksheet. To do this:

■ Choose **Window > Manage Worksheets**

■ Highlight **MarksF***

■ Click **Close**

- At the prompt "The worksheet 'MarksF.MTW' will be removed from the project 'Untitled.' This action cannot be undone. Would you like to save it in a separate file?", click **No**

- Click **Done** to return to the Session window

▼ **Note** If you disable the Session command language, Minitab will still provide output in the Session window, but without prompts and commands. This is helpful if you want to capture and print the results of several successive analyses. If the Session command language is not disabled, these analyses will be interrupted by prompts and commands. To disable the command language, you must be in the Session window. (If not, use Window > Session to make it active.) Then choose Editor > Disable Command Language. ▲

▼ 2.12   Creating a Text File ▲

Minitab printed the grades data in the Windows default fonts without any formatting. Ultimately, you want to format the report with boldface, italics, and borders before you present it to Ms. Taylor. To do so, you first save the grades data in the Session window as an ASCII (American Standard Code for Information Interchange) text file. You then can open this file in any text editor or word processor.

To save the highlighted data as an ASCII file called *Marks.txt*:

- Highlight the data for all 24 students as you did in Section 2.11, if it is not still selected

- Choose **File > Save Session Window As** to display the Save As dialog box (this menu selection saves the selected text from the Session window)

- Click the "Save in" **drop-down list arrow** and select the location where you are saving your work

- Click in the "File name" text box and type **Marks**

- Press ⏎ to save the text file

When you save all or part of the Session window with Save As, Minitab automatically adds the extension *txt*, which is a common extension for text files that makes them easy to find.

You can minimize Minitab and take a look at your text file in Notepad. Notepad is a Windows accessory that lets you open and work with text files; it's like a miniature word processor. (In Tutorial 16, you will place text into a word processor, such as Microsoft Word or Corel WordPerfect.)

To minimize Minitab:

- Click the Minitab symbol immediately to the left of "MINITAB Student" in the Minitab title bar

- Click **Minimize**

  To open Notepad from Windows:

- Choose **Start** > **Programs** > **Accessories**

  The Accessories folder contains several Windows accessories, including a calculator, a calendar, Notepad, and Wordpad (a slightly more sophisticated text editor).

  To open Notepad:

- Click **Notepad**

- Choose **File** > **Open** from the Notepad menu bar

- Click the "Look-in" **drop-down list arrow** and select the location where you saved the file *Marks.txt*

- Double-click ***Marks.txt*** in the "File" list box

  The Notepad window displays your grades data.
  Create a title for your grades listing:

- Press ⏎ twice to create two blank lines above the grades list and then press ↑ twice to move back to the top

- Type ***Your Name:*** **Grades Report for Ms. Taylor**

- The Notepad window should look as shown in Figure 2-22.

FIGURE 2-22

Marks.txt in Notepad

```
Marks.txt - Notepad
File  Edit  Search  Help
John McKenzie: Grades Report for Ms. Taylor

     1  Adams      James       90    A
     2  Benson     Melissa     87    B
     3  Brown      Lamar       75    C
     4  Dougherty  Megan       66    D
     5  Douglas    Jason       46    F
     6  Gigliotti  Andrew      69    D
     7  Goldberg   Jonathan    96    A
     8  Green      Jennifer    95    A
     9  Kennedy    Kevin       69    D
    10  Lee        Sang        82    B
    11  McClure    Mark        56    F
    12  Messina    Steven      94    A
    13  Norman     Barbara     90    A
    14  Nowicki    Amy         82    B
    15  Patel      Hima        79    C
    16  Pierson    Richard     92    A
    17  Rojas      Luis        80    B
    18  Ryan       Matt        82    B
    19  Schmidt    Nancy       66    D
    20  Scott      Michael     89    B
```

You can't do any formatting in Notepad. However, you can open the file in a more sophisticated word processor and work with it there. For now, print the file with your name on it:

- Choose **File** > **Print**

- Choose **File** > **Exit** to exit Notepad

- Click **Yes** to save the changes to *Marks.txt*

   You are returned to your desktop.

   You now have two paper copies of your grade report (one with a title) and a file that you can format in your word processor. At the end of the next marking period, it should be much easier for you to organize your grades. In the next two tutorials, you will learn how to produce graphical displays of your data. Meanwhile, save the file:

- Click the Minitab icon at the bottom of your screen to restore the Minitab window

- Choose **File** > **Save Current Worksheet**

   When you save a worksheet, you save all of the data — the columns and the constants associated with the data set. The contents of the Session window, the Info window, and other information, such as graphs you created, are not saved with the worksheet. These may be saved, however, as part of a *project*. In the next tutorial, you will learn to use and save projects.

   In this tutorial, you learned a variety of important methods for handling data. These methods include coding, ranking and sorting, creating subsets, and stacking and unstacking columns of data. Although these methods are not data analysis methods themselves, they will prove extremely valuable when you do analyze data in later tutorials.

   You have now completed Tutorial 2. As the last step, exit the program:

- Choose **File** > **Exit**

- In response to the prompt "Save changes to this project before closing?", click **No**

Minitab Command Summary

This section describes the menu and Session commands introduced in, or related to, this tutorial. Use Minitab's on-line Help to find a complete explanation of all menu commands.

Minitab Menu Commands

Menu	Command	Description
File		
	Close Worksheet	Closes the current worksheet from the Data window.
	Save Session Window As	Saves the contents of the Session window to a file. There is a corresponding command for the Data, Info, Graph, and History windows.
	Print Session Window	Prints the contents of the Session window. There is a corresponding command for the Data, Info, Graph, and History windows.
Manip		
	Subset Worksheet	Allows you to create a separate worksheet that is a subset of the original worksheet.
	Split Worksheet	Allows you to create several new work-sheets based on the unique values in a column.
	Sort	Sorts selected columns of the worksheet using up to four columns as the sorting criteria.
	Rank	Ranks the data in a column and stores the ranks (usually in another column).
	Stack/Unstack	Stacks the contents of two or more columns to form a new column. The number of cells in the stacked column equals the total number of cells in the columns selected for stacking. Unstacking creates several columns of data by splitting a given column.
	Code	Creates a new column whose values — numeric or text — are based on the values in another column. The command may also be used to modify the same column.
	Display Data	Displays one or more columns of data (or constants) in the Session window.

Menu	Command	Description
Calc		
	Column Statistics	Calculates various statistics for the selected column, displaying the results and, optionally, storing each result in a constant.
	Row Statistics	Computes a value for each row based upon a set of columns.
	Standardize	Creates new values by subtracting the mean and dividing by the standard deviation.
Editor		
	Disable/Enable Command Language	Hides or shows commands in Session window.
	Make Output Read-Only/ Editable	Controls whether or not the Session window can be edited.
Window		
	Manage Worksheet	Performs many actions on Data windows and their associated worksheets.
	Session	Moves you to the Session window, which contains a record of all commands issued in the current session and the resulting output. Lets you enter Session commands.

Minitab Session Commands

Session Command		Description
info		Displays worksheet information from the Info window, such as the columns and stored constants, in the Session window.
print		Displays one or more columns of data (or constants) in the Session window.

Review and Practice

Matching

Match the following terms to their definitions by placing the correct letter next to the term it describes.

_____ Display Data

_____ 1

_____ Functions

_____ Row operation

_____ Stack

_____ Unstack

_____ *txt*

_____ Subscripts

_____ N*

_____ MTB >

a. Value assigned to the lowest score by Rank

b. The Minitab command that creates a new column by placing several columns on top of each other

c. An optional indicator variable created when Minitab stacks several columns into one column

d. The Minitab command that creates several columns of data by splitting a given column

e. An arithmetic process performed on the entries in each row for a given set of columns in the worksheet

f. The default file extension given to files created with Save Window As

g. A Minitab command that prints one or many columns in the Session window

h. A summary statistic that reflects the number of missing values in a row or column

i. Standard, preprogrammed numeric operations stored in Minitab

j. Minitab prompt

True/False

Mark the following statements with a *T* or an *F*.

_____ Minitab will interpret C1–C5 as all of the columns C1, C2, C3, C4, and C5.

_____ Round rounds only to the nearest whole number.

_____ The info session command displays all columns that contain data in the current worksheet, the column names (if any), and the number of observations in the column.

_____ Sort automatically sorts all columns in the worksheet.

_____ You use Display Data to print to paper.

_____ The first quartile is one of the statistics available in the Column Statistics dialog box.

_____ The default operation of Standardize subtracts the mean of a variable and then divides by its standard deviation.

_____ Sort sorts only numeric variables or columns.

_____ Many of the statistics available in the Row Statistics dialog box are also available in the Column Statistics dialog box.

_____ Code Data Values interprets 10:20 as the numbers between 10 and 20, inclusive.

Practice Problems

Use Minitab's on-line Help or Part III, Exploring Data, of this manual to review the contents of the data sets referenced in the problems below.

1. Print a paper copy of the *Snow.mtw* worksheet from the Session window. Place a copy of this output into Notepad.

2. Open *Pulsea.mtw*, which contains the data you worked with in the Tutorial 1 Practice Problems.

    a. Compute the mean, median, and standard deviation of the initial pulse rates, the weights, and the heights.

    b. Compute the increase in pulse rate (C2–C1) and store the result in C9 (as you did in Tutorial 1). Unstack the increases into two columns, C10 and C11, based on whether the student ran in place. Name these two new columns.

    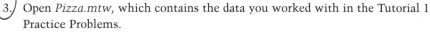c. Compute the mean, median, and standard deviation of the increase in pulse rate for both those who did and those who did not run in place. Do your results make sense?

    d. Unstack the weights and heights by gender and standardize each of the four new variables. Explain what information is gained by the standardization.

3. Open *Pizza.mtw*, which contains the data you worked with in the Tutorial 1 Practice Problems.

    a. Compute the mean, median, and standard deviation of the FallScor column.

    b. Rank the items in the FallScor column and place the results in C7. Name this variable FSRank1.

    c. Note that one way the computed ranks differ from the given ranks is that 1 does not indicate the greatest value. Transform C7 to conform to the newspaper ranks by subtracting each number from 14. Place the results in C8. Name this variable FSRank2.

    d. What is another difference between FallScor and FSRank2? Which column is most informative? Explain your answer.

     e. Print the worksheet.

    f. Use the Row statistics command to create a variable that is sum of FallScor and FSRank2? Name this variable ScoreSum. What additional insights do you gain from examining this variable?

    g. Use Subset Worksheet to create a new worksheet named *PizzaLoc.mtw* that is based only on those pizzerias that are local.

    h. Answer part a for this new subset of pizzerias. How do your results differ from those in a?

    i. Close the file *PizzaLoc.mtw*.

4. Open *Radlev.mtw.*

  a. Use the info command to determine the information that has been saved in this data set. Which columns are used? What names have been assigned to them? How many observations does the data set contain? Are there any missing data?

  b. Code the age variable so that new homes are those that are less than 2 years old. Assign newer homes a code value of 0 and older homes a code of 1.

  c. Save the worksheet as *P2Radlev.mtw* the location where you are saving your work.

  d. Sort the data set using the coded age variable.

  e. Delete the rows that correspond to older homes. You don't need to save your changes. Save to hand in

5. Open *Note98.mtw.*

  a. Use the info command to determine the information that was saved in this data set. Which columns are used? What names have been assigned to these columns? How many observations does the data set contain?

  b. Sort the worksheet using the ChipSet, Speed, and Price columns as the sorting criteria.

  c. Print the worksheet from the Session window. Which notebook computer with an SL chip is the least expensive? Most expensive? Which 2MHz notebook computer with an 430TX ChipSet is the least expensive? After how many minutes is a recharge needed for this notebook computer?

TUTORIAL
3

Graphical Methods for a Single Variable

Describing data graphically is an essential aspect of statistical analysis. In this tutorial, you will use Minitab's built-in graphing commands to depict the data you worked with in Tutorial 1. You will produce graphs that illustrate different characteristics of a single column of data—both quantitative and qualitative. You will also learn to create Minitab projects to organize the analyses you've done on a set of data and to store the graphs you create.

Objectives

In this tutorial, you learn how to:

- save your data, session, and graphs in a project
- graphically display any single variable using core, character, and specialty graphs
- graph single variables using histograms, stem-and-leaf plots, dotplots, and boxplots
- graph single qualitative variables using bar and pie charts
- create, rename, print, save, and close graphs

▼ 3.1   Creating a Project ▲

CASE STUDY: MANAGEMENT — SALARY STRUCTURE (CONTINUED)

In Tutorial 1, you updated the Temco employee worksheet. Senior management is concerned about the differences in the salaries paid to employees in the Sales Department and wants you to present a report on this matter at the next staff meeting. You will use Minitab's high-resolution graphs to explore the distribution of salaries and of variables related to salary. You will also save a set of graphs to use in your presentation.

In Tutorials 1 and 2, you saved a copy of your worksheet. In Tutorial 2, you learned to highlight text (your alphabetized grades listing) in the Session window and save it to a text file. Minitab provides a convenient method for saving a complete record of your entire session, including commands, output, and all open data sets. You simply tell Minitab to store all of this information in a *project*. A project also contains the session's History window, Info window, and graphs. Projects are particularly helpful when you wish to leave Minitab before finishing an assignment. If you save your work in a project, you can return to it at exactly the point at which you stopped.

In this and the following tutorials, you will save all of your work in (separate) projects. Be aware that projects require a great deal of disk space. Begin by starting Minitab:

- Start **Minitab**

- Maximize the **Session window**

Minitab opens a new, untitled project each time you start. You can work in this project or open a different one. You decide to work with this project, enable Session commands, and ensure that session output is not overwritten:

- Choose **Editor > Enable Command Language**

- Choose **Editor > Make Output Read-Only**

▼ **Note** Remember that these menu commands are "toggles." If you see "Disable Command Language" or "Make Output Editable," these commands have already been invoked. Also, notice that when you make the output read-only, the term "Read-Only" appears at the bottom right-hand corner of the screen. ▲

If you completed all of the steps in Tutorial 1, you saved the data you need in a file called *1Pay.mtw*. Whenever a tutorial uses a file from an earlier tutorial, this manual provides an updated file with a version suffix. Although you could use *1Pay.mtw* for this tutorial, use instead the updated version

(*Pay2.mtw*) provided with *The Student Edition of Minitab for Windows* to ensure that your results will match the results in the book.

Preview the file before opening it:

- Choose **File > Open Worksheet**

- Select **Pay2** in the "Open Worksheet" list box (you may have to navigate to the Student subdirectory and then scroll to see the file)

- Click **Preview** to examine the contents of the file

The Open Worksheet Preview dialog box displays the contents of the file with the names of the variables across the top. Use the scrollbar in the lower part of the box to observe that this file has eight variables in C1 – C4 and C6 – C9. (C5 is blank.)

- Click **OK** to return to the Open Worksheet dialog box and click **Open** to open the file

- At the prompt "A copy of the contents of this file will be added to the current project," click the message **Do not display this message again** and then click **OK**

This prompt will not appear again.

The worksheet opens, displaying information about 11 Temco employees, including salary, work history, and gender. When you open a worksheet in a project, Minitab makes a copy of it and adds it to the project. The original remains unchanged (unless you use the Save Worksheet command). The copy of the worksheet and any changes made to it will be stored with the new project file. Copies of a single worksheet file can be stored in several different projects.

Before proceeding, save this data set under the name *3Pay.mtw:*

- Choose **File > Save Current Worksheet As**

- Click the "Save in" **drop-down list arrow** and select the location where you are saving your work

- Replace the current name *Pay2* with the new name *3Pay*

- Click **Save**

Your worksheet is renamed *3Pay.mtw*

This is a good time to name and save the project that was begun when you started Minitab:

- Choose **File > Save Project As**

- Click the "Save in" **drop-down list arrow** and select the location where you are saving your work

- Under "File name," replace the default name Minitab with the name *T3*

- Click **Save**

Notice that Minitab saves a project in a file with an *mpj* suffix and that the name of the project precedes the name of the active file in the Minitab title bar. The result in this case is *T3.mpj*.

Minitab allows the creator of a data set to attach a description of the data to the file. To see a description for Pay2/3Pay:

- Choose **Editor > Worksheet Description**

    Notice that the authors of this manual created the worksheet on 22 April 1998 and you are referred to the manual for further information about the data set. You will find this description in the Exploring Data section, which follows the tutorials.

- Click **OK**

    Just as you can save a description of a data set, you also can attach a description to the project you are working on:

- Choose **File > Project Description**

- Type **your name** as the "Creator" of the project and enter the current "**Date**"

- Enter the following under "Comments": **This project, T3, contains numerous Minitab graphs that illustrate various aspects of the 3Pay data set**.

- Click **OK**

    Save the project again with the description, this time using the Save Project toolbar button

- Click the **Save Project** toolbar button ▣ (the second one from the left)

▼ 3.2   Introducing Types of Graphs ▲

The Student Edition of Minitab for Windows allows you to create graphs in two different modes: character (or text) and high-resolution.

A character graph is displayed in the Session window. It is constructed from keyboard characters such as *, +, -, and letters. *A high-resolution graph* is displayed in its own Graph window. Compared to a character graph, it uses more *pixels* (short for picture elements) per inch and produces clearer graphs. You probably will prefer to use high-resolution graphs in a presentation because they look more professional.

Many Minitab graphs can be created as character or high-resolution graphs. Although a high-resolution graph may look more impressive, a character graph generally provides the same kind of information. Figure 3-1 shows a character histogram of the variable Educ (years of education).

FIGURE 3-1

A character histogram for the variable Educ

```
MTB > GStd.
* NOTE  * Character graphs are obsolete.

MTB > Histogram 'Educ'.
```

Histogram

```
Histogram of Educ    N = 10    N = 1

Midpoint        Count
       0          1  *
       1          1  *
       2          0
       3          1  *
       4          2  **
       5          2  **
       6          0
       7          1  *
       8          0
       9          2  **
```

You can see from the comments above the histogram that Minitab views the character graph as out-of-date. Figure 3-2 shows a high-resolution histogram for the same data.

FIGURE 3-2

A high-resolution histogram for the variable Educ

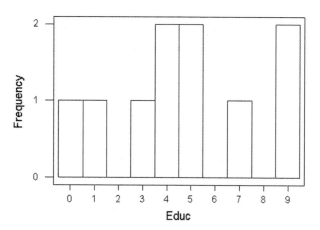

Histogram of the variable Educ

Later in this chapter, you will learn how to obtain such graphs. Not all graphs are available in each type, however. If a high-resolution version is available, Minitab will produce it as the default unless you specifically choose the character graph from the menu, as follows:

■ Click the **Graph** menu to see the list of graph types available

■ Click **Character Graphs** at the bottom of the menu

■ Click in the **Graph** window to close the menu

▼ **Note** The full version of Minitab can create a third type of graph, 3D. This type of graph is not available in *The Student Edition of Minitab for Windows.* ▲

Minitab offers two basic kinds of high-resolution graphs: *core* and *specialty*. Core graphs include most of the more common graphs such as histograms and scatter plots. They have a large number of options so that you can customize them to create many types of graphs. You will learn about these options in this tutorial and the next one.

By contrast, specialty graphs are precustomized graphs that combine elements from core graphs. They present several frequently used variations on core graphs so that you do not have to customize each one. Minitab also has built-in specialty graph options in many analysis commands, as you will see in future tutorials.

In this tutorial, you will work with character, core, and specialty graphs for one variable. In Tutorial 4, you produce high-resolution graphs for two or more variables.

Minitab offers four graphs that summarize information in a single column of *quantitative* data:

1. Histograms

2. Stem-and-leaf displays

3. Dotplots

4. Boxplots

Graphs that Minitab offers to summarize information in a single column of qualitative data include bar charts and pie charts. You will examine examples of each type of graph in the next six sections.

Before starting work on these graphs, examine the Graphs menu:

■ Choose **Graph**

The first seven graphs — from Plot to Draftsman Plot — are all core graphs. The next four — from Dotplot to Probability Plot — are specialty graphs. The Stem-and-Leaf display is a character plot.

▼ 3.3   Creating a High-Resolution Histogram ▲

For the Temco staff presentation, you want to show the salary distribution among employees in the Sales Department by describing the data in C1 Salary in a high-resolution histogram:

■ Choose **Graph > Histogram**

The Histogram dialog box opens, as shown in Figure 3-3.

The dialog boxes for histograms, stem-and-leaf displays, dotplots, box-plots, and bar charts are similar. Each has a section for defining variables (Graph variables), a section for defining how the data values look on the graph (Data display grid), and a set of buttons you click to specify further formatting and display options.

The Edit Attributes button lets you change the appearance (color, patterns, size, and so on) of the elements highlighted in the Display column of the Data display grid. Two arrow buttons display menus with further options: Annotation and Frame.

By clicking the Annotation arrow, you can annotate graphs with titles, footnotes, text, and lines. You can format these annotations in any number of ways. By clicking the Frame arrow, you can customize the axes and the minimum and maximum values on the axes. You also can control multiple graphs.

The Options button displays another dialog box that offers additional formatting choices specific to the type of graph with which you are currently working. First, specify the variable you want to graph and then add a title:

- Double-click **C1 Salary** to enter it in the first graph's "X" text box in the "Graph variables" list box

- Click the "Annotation" **arrow** to open the "Annotation" menu

- Click **Title** to display the Title dialog box

- Type **Salary Histogram I** in the "Title" text box

- Click **OK** twice to create the graph shown in Figure 3-4

FIGURE 3-4

First high-resolution histogram of the salary data

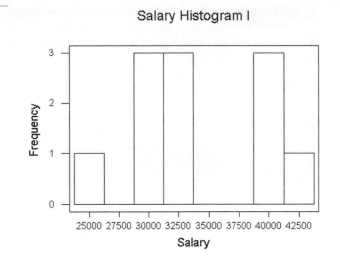

The histogram divides the data into *classes*, or *intervals*. The horizontal axis lists the midpoints of each salary class. The height of each bar indicates the frequency with which salaries fall in that particular class. For example, there were three employees with salaries in the interval with midpoint $30,000, that is, with salaries greater than or equal to $28,750 and up to but not including $31,250.

Generally speaking, the more bars your histogram contains, the more finely it divides up your data. After looking at the first histogram, you decide that having this many classes chops up the data too much. You think a histogram with five classes would make the data easier to understand.

You can determine the current class width by subtracting a midpoint from an adjacent one. In this case, you can subtract 27,500 from 25,000 to find a class width of 2,500 (27,500 – 25,000 = 2,500). To modify the histogram so that it contains approximately five classes, you can increase the class width to 4,000:

- Choose **Graph > Histogram**

- Click **Options**

The Histogram Options dialog box is shown in Figure 3-5. In this box, you can specify the type of histogram, the type of interval, and the definition of the intervals. You also can interchange (transpose) the variables defining the vertical and horizontal axes.

FIGURE 3-5

Histogram Options dialog box

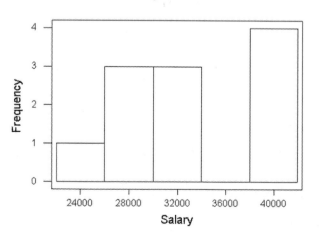

To specify 4,000 as the interval width, you must tell Minitab the range of the data, divided by the interval width. You can specify your five classes with the following expression: 24,000:42,000/4,000. The colon (:) indicates the range; the slash (/) indicates the width of each interval.

- Click **Midpoint/cutpoint positions** and click its text box

- Type **24000:42000/4000** and press ↵

- Click the "Annotation" **arrow**

- Click **Title**

- Type **Salary Histogram II** in the "Title" text box

- Click **OK** twice to create the graph, shown in Figure 3-6, that has five classes, each with a width of 4,000

FIGURE 3-6

Second high-resolution histogram of the salary data with five classes

Salary Histogram II

You are satisfied that this histogram shows your data better than the first one, so you decide to retain it and delete the first one you created. (If, instead, you wanted more classes, you could reduce the interval width in the same manner.)

When you plan to generate a considerable number of graphs — as you will in this tutorial — it is a good idea to name each one as you create it. Naming a graph is not the same as giving it a title. The title is internal to the graph, while the name is external to it and can be referenced by Minitab. You can use the Manage Graphs command to name and delete graphs:

- Choose **Window > Manage Graphs**

Notice that Minitab has assigned the same default name to your two histograms of Salary. Giving your graphs more descriptive names will make it easier to keep track of them and what they display. Do this:

- Click the *second* **3Pay.mtw: Histogram 'Salary'**

- Click **Rename**

- Type **Histogram of Salary** in the "Rename" text box

- Click **OK**

    You are returned to the Manage Graphs dialog box.
    To delete your first graph from the project:

- Click **3Pay.mtw Histogram: 'Salary'**

- Click **Close**

    Note that this graph disappears from the upper text box. It has been deleted from the project and cannot be reopened.

    The number of graphs that can be open at any time is limited only by the amount of free disk space you have available. To close some graphs but not delete them, you can save them to individual graph files via the Manage Graphs dialog box.

    To save the remaining histogram of Salary in a graph file:

- Click **Histogram of Salary**

- Click **Save As**

    You also can reach this dialog box by choosing "File > Save Graph As" from the menu:

- Click the "Save in" **drop-down list arrow** and select the location where you are saving your work

- Type **HistSal** in the "File name" text box (the *mgf* extension is added automatically)

- Click **Save**

Minitab saves the graph with an *mgf* (Minitab Graphics Format) file extension. This graph remains a part of the current project but is also stored as a separate graph file so it may be opened outside the project, for example, in a different project.

- Click **Done**

▼ **Note** You can close all of your project graphs by choosing Window > Close All Graphs. ▲

The histogram reveals that there are more Sales Department employees in the highest salary class than in any of the lower ones. Four have salaries in the upper level, and seven have salaries in the lower three intervals. Perhaps the employees in the top category have worked at Temco the longest. If so, it might be cost-effective to suggest a retirement incentive so as to reduce salary costs. The histogram also indicates a large gap between the highest salary level and lower ones — jumping from a midpoint of 40,000 to one of 32,000. In the next tutorial, you will explore whether these differences in salary can be explained by differences in years of experience or in years of education.

▼ 3.4   Creating a Character Stem-and-Leaf Display ▲

An important part of your report concerns the length of time employees have been at Temco. You will investigate this variable by constructing a *stem-and-leaf* display (or *stemplot*) of C2 YrsEm (years of employment at Temco). A stem-and-leaf display is similar to a histogram except that it uses the actual data values as the building blocks for the display. Further, it shows the data ordered from smallest to largest. Stem-and-leaf displays can be created only as character graphs.

To construct a stem-and-leaf display for C2 YrsEm:

- Choose **Graph > Stem-and-Leaf** (you can also reach this dialog box by choosing **Graph > Character Graphs > Stem-and-Leaf**)

- Double-click **C2 YrsEm** to enter it in the "Variables" text box

- Click **OK**

Figure 3-7 shows the resulting stem-and-leaf display in the Session window.

FIGURE 3-7

*Character Stem-and-Leaf
Display of years employed
at Temco*

```
MTB > Stem-and-Leaf 'YrsEm'.

Character Stem-and-Leaf Display

Stem-and-leaf of YrsEm    N = 11
Leaf Unit = 1.0

    3     0 003
    5     0 56
   (1)    1 2
    5     1 588
    2     2 12
```

▼ **Note** This graph does not appear in a Graph window because character graphs appear only in the Session window. ▲

For now, ignore the numbers in the left column. The column on the right contains the *leaves*, or rightmost digits, of the data values. The numbers in the center column represent the *stems*, or leftmost digits, of the data values. Because Minitab reports a leaf unit of 1 (Leaf Unit = 1.0), each leaf represents the one's digit of a data value and each stem represents the ten's digit of the data value. For example, the last line of the stem-and-leaf plot shown in Figure 3-7 indicates a stem of 2 followed by leaves of 1 and 2. You reconstruct these numbers into the data values 21 and 22.

Many stem-and-leaf displays use one line per stem, but in some cases, such as this one, Minitab uses two lines per stem. When the latter are used, the first line contains leaves with the first five digits (0, 1, 2, 3, and 4) and the second line contains leaves with the last five digits (5, 6, 7, 8, and 9). To break up the data even more finely, you could use five lines per stem corresponding to the leaf digits (0,1), (2,3), (4,5), (6,7), and (8,9).

The first (leftmost) column in the stem-and-leaf display indicates the *depths*, which are used to show cumulative frequencies. Starting at the top, the depths indicate the number of leaves that lie in the given row (or stem) plus any previous rows. For example, the 5 in the first column of the second line in Figure 3-7 indicates that there are five leaves (0, 0, 3, 5, and 6) in the first two rows (or stems). If the line containing the median has any entries, the number in the left column represents the number of leaves on that line and appears in parentheses. The median for this data set is 12 years. The 5 in the second line from the bottom indicates that there are a total of five leaves in the two bottom lines of the display.

Minitab uses the term *increment* to refer to the difference in value between any two lines of the display. In the display in Figure 3-7, Minitab uses an increment of 5. You can see this by noting that the smallest value possible for each line of the display is, respectively, 0 years, 5 years, 10 years, 15 years, and 20 years. In each case, the difference is 5 years. To see the effect of changing the increment to 10:

■ Choose **Edit > Edit Last Dialog** and press Tab three times

■ Type **10** in the "Increment" text box and press ⏎

Minitab records all values from the same stem on one line. Your new display should look like the one shown in Figure 3-8.

FIGURE 3-8

Character Stem-and-Leaf Display produced with an increment of 10

```
MTB > Stem-and-Leaf 'YrsEm';
SUBC>   Increment 10.
```

Character Stem-and-Leaf Display

```
Stem-and-leaf of YrsEm     N  = 11
Leaf Unit = 1.0

   5    0  00356
  (4)   1  2588
   2    2  12
```

A comparison of Figures 3-7 and 3-8 shows that Minitab's default graph with two lines per stem breaks up the data more finely and therefore gives the graph greater definition.

Now use Minitab's default settings to construct a stem-and-leaf display of the 11 salaries in C1 Salary:

■ Click the **Edit Last Dialog** toolbar button ▦ to reopen the Stem-and-Leaf dialog box

Notice that in any dialog box, Minitab retains your last entries. You want to examine a different variable, so you want to clear the previous settings that appear in the Stem-and-Leaf dialog box and restore them to the default settings.

To quickly restore the default settings:

■ Press the **F3** function key

The "Variables" box is now empty and the "Increment" setting is cleared. To create the stem-and-leaf plot of the salaries:

■ Double-click **C1 Salary** to enter it in the "Variables" text box

■ Click **OK**

The new plot appears in the Session window, as shown in Figure 3-9.

FIGURE 3-9

Character Stem-and-Leaf Display of the Sales Department salaries

```
MTB > Stem-and-Leaf 'Salary'.
```

Character Stem-and-Leaf Display

```
Stem-and-leaf of Salary    N  = 11
Leaf Unit = 1000

   1    2 4
   1    2
   4    2 889
   5    3 1
  (2)   3 22
   4    3
   4    3
   4    3 889
   1    4 1
```

Because Minitab reports a leaf unit of 1,000 (Leaf Unit = 1000), each leaf represents the thousand's digit of the data value and each stem represents the ten thousand's digit. For example, the first entry of 24 translates to a data value of 24,000 (20,000 for the stem and 4,000 for the leaf). This entry represents the actual salary value of 24,749. (To simplify the stem-and-leaf plot, Minitab truncates the value to show only the first two digits of a salary.)

In this display, Minitab has used an increment of 2,000. To see this, note that the smallest possible value for each line is, respectively, 24,000, 26,000, 28,000, 30,000, 32,000, and so on, and that in each case, the difference is 2,000. There are five lines per stem. To condense the salary stem-and-leaf display to two lines per stem, tell Minitab to use an increment of 5,000. (Recall that the leaf unit is 1,000 and there are 10 possible stems, so 10/2 × 1,000 = 5,000.)

- Choose **Edit > Edit Last Dialog**
- Click in the "Increment" text box, type **5000,** and press ↵

Minitab consolidates the display to show only two lines per stem.

When you are deciding whether to use any of these stem-and-leaf displays in a presentation, consider how much opportunity you will have to interpret them. As you can see, they require some careful explanation. However, if your audience is familiar with them, such plots can provide an excellent picture of your information.

This is a good time to save your project, *T3.mpj*.

- Choose **File > Save Project**

Because the stem-and-leaf displays you created are character plots, they will not appear in the Manage Graphs dialog box and you cannot save them as graphs. However, they are saved when you save the project, along with the rest of the output in the Session window.

▼ 3.5 Creating a High-Resolution Dotplot ▲

Next, you look at a *dotplot* representation of the data in C1 Salary. A dotplot is a specialty graph. The salary dotplot gives you an opportunity to compare the relative advantages of a dotplot versus a histogram. You then will be in a better position to decide which graph types you want to include in your presentation.

- Choose **Graph > Dotplot**
- Double-click **C1 Salary** to enter it in the "Variables" text box
- Type **Salary Dotplot** in the "Title" text box

The completed Dotplot dialog box should look like the one in Figure 3-10.

FIGURE 3-10

The Dotplot dialog box

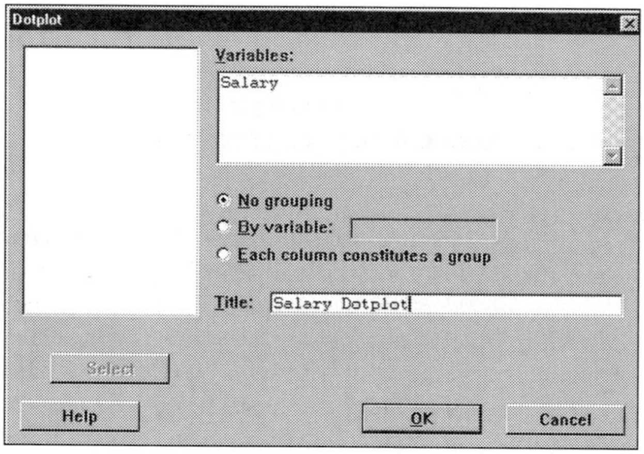

- Click **OK**

The dotplot appears as shown in Figure 3-11.

FIGURE 3-11

Salary dotplot

Salary Dotplot

Salary

If necessary, a dotplot displays each data value as a dot above a horizontal axis so that you can see exactly where each value falls. Similar to the histogram, the dotplot displays distribution characteristics for the data it describes. However, unlike the histogram it does so by showing individual points or small groups of points rather than summarizing the data in bars. The dotplot of the salary data tells the same story as the histogram. That is, salaries range from approximately $25,000 to $40,000, with a fairly large gap in the middle. You decide to keep this graph and name it Dotplot Salary.

- Select **Window > Manage Graphs**

- Click **3Pay.mtw: Dotplot for Salary**

- Click **Rename**

- Type **Dotplot Salary** in the "Rename" text box

- Click **OK**

- Click **Done**

Then return to the Session window:

- Choose **Window > Session**

Each time you make a menu selection, Minitab displays the corresponding command in the Session window. Look at the last two commands that appear in the Session window. The first is a command that instructs Minitab to construct a dotplot of the salary data. The second is a *subcommand*, as indicated by *SUBC* >. A subcommand provides additional information about the preceding command, in this case the command to add a title. They represent the options you select in dialog boxes.

In addition, you see the message "Macro is running...please wait." Recall that specialty graphs are customized versions of core graphs. When you select a specialty graph, Minitab activates a macro that contains all of the commands needed to produce the graph. The following table describes each entry in the Session window in more detail.

Entry	Represents
MTB	The Minitab prompt, which Minitab displays when it's ready for your next command.
%DotPlot 'Salary';	Your choice of dotplot from the menu. The semi-colon indicates that you made additional selections in the dialog box (if you did not, this command would be the only one that was in the Session window before the graph). The % prefix indicates that this is a specialty graph type.
SUBC	The Minitab prompt that indicates that a subcommand follows.
Title "Salary Dotplot".	Your selection of Salary Dotplot as the title of your graph. The period indicates the end of the command and subcommands.
Executing from file:...	The macro file being activated to create the specialty graph.

▼ **Note** Minitab uses a mixture of uppercase and lowercase characters when it records commands and dialog box choices. ▲

Most users find that choosing from the Minitab menus and selections in dialog boxes is the most straightforward and error-free method of issuing commands. However, more advanced users who use Minitab often, especially those who are proficient typists, may find that typing the Minitab command in the Session window is more efficient. (Chapter 2 and Minitab's on-line Help contain more information about the Minitab Session command language.) These tutorials, however, primarily use the menu commands. Regardless of which method you use, Minitab will provide a record of your activities by printing commands in the Session window.

▼ 3.6　Creating a High-Resolution Boxplot ▲

A boxplot (or box-and-whisker plot) provides you with a rather skeletal view of a data set. It highlights useful statistical information, such as quartiles and outliers. To obtain a boxplot of the salaries in C1:

- Choose **Graph > Boxplot**
- Double-click **C1 Salary** to enter it in the first "Y" "Graph variables" text box
- Click the "Annotation" **arrow**
- Click **Title**

- Type **Salary Boxplot** in the "Title" text box

- Click **OK**

The completed Boxplot dialog box looks like the one shown in Figure 3-12.

FIGURE 3-12

The Boxplot dialog box

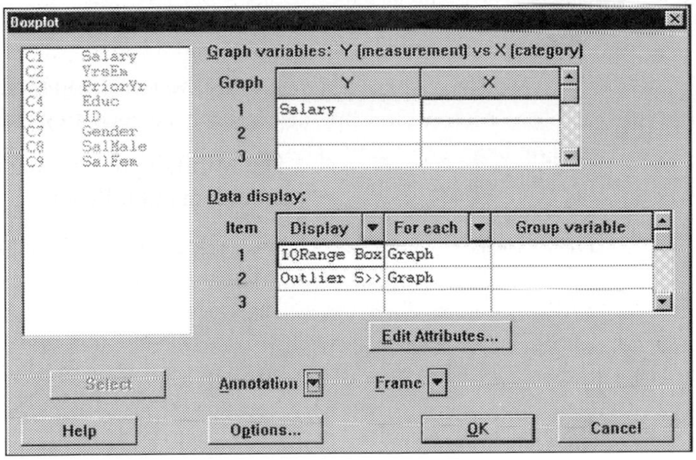

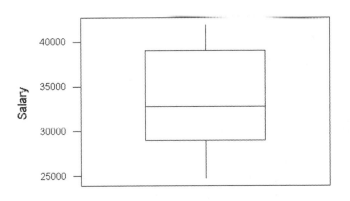

- Click **OK**

The boxplot appears as shown in Figure 3-13.

FIGURE 3-13

The boxplot of Sales Department salaries, shown vertically

Salary Boxplot

A boxplot uses five numbers to describe a set of data:

1. Minimum value

2. First quartile (25th percentile)

3. Median (50th percentile)

4. Third quartile (75th percentile)

5. Maximum value

Minitab constructs a rectangle between the lower and upper quartiles and displays a horizontal line at the location of the median. This box encloses the middle half of the data. The *whiskers* that extend in either direction indicate the nonoutlying data. If there are no outlying values, the whiskers extend to the smallest and largest values in the data set. If there are outlying values, Minitab identifies them with asterisks (*), as you'll see in Tutorial 4. (Minitab has an option to superimpose a confidence interval on the boxplot. See Tutorial 7.)

In this case, the boxplot clearly shows that the middle half of the salaries in the Sales Department fall between about $29,000 and $39,000. The median indicates that half of all salaries fall below $32,000 and half fall above.

You wonder whether it might not be better to transpose the axes so that the boxplot appears horizontally across the page rather than vertically. To find out:

- Click the **Edit Last Dialog** toolbar button ▣ to reopen the Boxplot dialog box

- Click **Options**

- Check the **Transpose X and Y** check box

- Click **OK** twice to produce the transposed graph, which is shown in Figure 3-14

FIGURE 3-14

The boxplot, shown horizontally

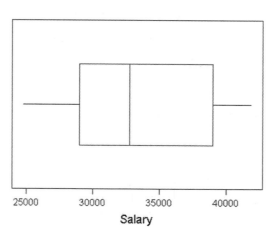

Salary Boxplot

You decide to name this graph and close your first boxplot:

- Choose **Window > Manage Graphs**
- Click the first **3Pay.mtw: Boxplot 'Salary'**
- Click **Close** to remove the graph from your project
- Click the remaining **3Pay.mtw: Boxplot 'Salary'**
- Click **Rename**
- Type **Boxplot Salary** in the "Rename" text box
- Click **OK** and **Done**

The Salary boxplot appears in its Graph window, as shown in Figure 3-14.

A boxplot does not show the level of detail as a histogram, a stem-and-leaf display, or a dotplot. For example, the boxplot in Figure 3-14 does not show the gap in salaries that is evident in the other types of graphs of these same data. However, in Tutorial 4 you will see that these graphs are excellent choices when you want to compare different distributions.

▼ 3.7 Creating a High-Resolution Bar Chart ▲

As a consultant to Temco, you want to examine qualitative variables such as gender in your salary analysis. You want to produce a bar chart showing the frequency of males and females in the Sales Department at Temco. Minitab's Chart command lets you do this. It produces many kinds of charts, including bar, line, symbol, and area. It also can incorporate a variety of summary statistics, such as sums, means, standard deviations, maximums, and minimums.

To create a bar chart of Gender:

- Choose **Graph > Chart**
- Click in the first "**X**" text box
- Double-click **C7 Gender** to enter it in the first "X" text box
- Click the "Annotation" **arrow** and click **Title**
- Type **Gender Bar Chart** in the "Title" text box
- Click **OK**

The Chart dialog box appears as shown in Figure 3-15.

FIGURE 3-15

The Chart dialog box

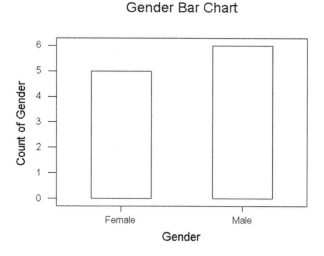

- Click **OK** to obtain the bar chart of Gender, as shown in Figure 3-16

FIGURE 3-16

Bar chart of Gender

Gender Bar Chart

The bar chart shows that there are slightly more males (6) than females (5) in the Sales Department.

In Tutorial 1, you added the data for a new employee in row 11. At this point in your analysis, you learn that he stayed with the company for only a week, so his data should be deleted from the Sales Department salary data. To delete the data for this person and to save the updated worksheet:

- Click the **Current Data Window** toolbar button ▦ (the sixth one from the right) to return to the *3Pay.mtw* worksheet

- Click the **row header for row 11** to select it (not the first cell, but the row number)

- Choose **Edit > Delete Cells**

- Choose **File > Save Current Worksheet** to save your updated worksheet

Creating a Grouping Variable

Gender is the only qualitative variable in the data set. However, you know that senior management considers years of education when making salary offers to new employees. In this case, they are concerned only with whether the person has either up to four years of post-secondary education or five or more years of post-secondary education. You intend to create a new variable called EdLevel, which will take only two values, Low or High, according to whether the employee has four or fewer or five or more years of post-secondary education. Most likely, an employee labeled Low has a bachelor's degree, whereas one labeled High has completed at least some graduate work. You will create a bar chart of this new variable.

You learned how to code data values in Tutorial 2. To assign codes based on the number of years of education after high school:

- Choose **Manip > Code > Numeric to Text**

- Double-click **C4 Educ** to enter it in the "Code data from columns" text box and press ⌶ab

- Type **EdLevel** in the "Into columns" text box and press ⌈Tab⌉

- Type **0:4** in the first "Original values" text box, press ⌈Tab⌉, type **Low** as the code in the first "New" text box, and press ⌈Tab⌉ again

- Type **5:10** in the second "Original values" text box, press ⌈Tab⌉, and type **High** as the second "New" code

The completed Code - Numeric to Text dialog box should look like the one shown in Figure 3-17.

FIGURE 3-17

The Code - Numeric to Text dialog box

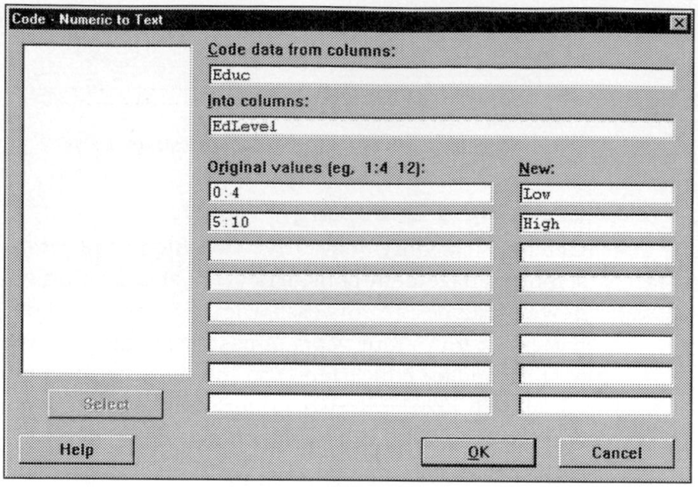

- Press ⏎

    By scrolling over to C10-T you can see the values for EdLevel.

Creating the Chart

To create a bar chart of EdLevel:

- Choose **Graph > Chart**

- Click in the first "**X**" text box

- Double-click **C10 EdLevel** to enter it in the first "X" text box

- Click the "Annotation" **arrow** and click **Title**

- Type **EdLevel Bar Chart** in the "Title" text box

- Click **OK** twice to obtain the bar chart of EdLevel as shown in Figure 3-18

    You can see that there are the same number of employees (5) at each level of education.

FIGURE 3-18

FIGURE 3-18

Bar chart of EdLevel showing the number of employees for two levels of education

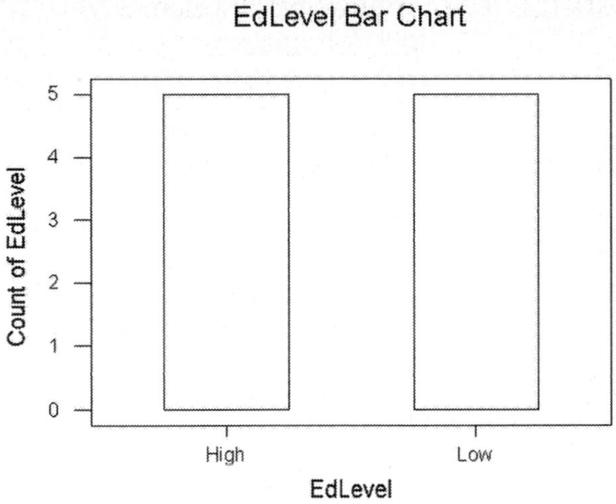

EdLevel Bar Chart

You have one problem with this graph — the bars are arranged in alphabetical order, High followed by Low. You believe that a better graph would result if the Low bar was placed before the High bar:

- Choose **Window > 3Pay.mtw*****

- Highlight the **C10 EdLevel** column

- Choose **Editor > Set Column > Value Order**

- Click the **User-specified order** check box

- Click **New Order** in the left text box

- Type **Low** followed by **High** in the "Define an order" text box (put one value on each line)

- Click **OK**

  To reproduce the bar chart with this ordering:

- Choose **Graph > Chart**

- Click **OK**

  Minitab has altered the chart, as shown in Figure 3-19.

FIGURE 3-19

Reordered bar chart of EdLevel showing Low before High

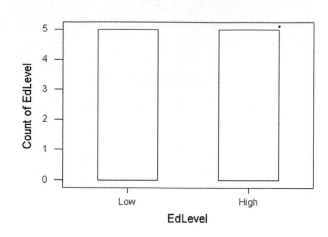

Next, you want to close the first bar chart and rename the second one. You can close a graph without entering the Graph Manager by clicking the Graph button in the upper left corner of its Graph window:

- Choose the **Window** menu

- Choose **More Windows**

- Click the first **3Pay.mtw: Chart 'EdLevel'** to make its window active

- Double-click the **Graph button** on the upper-left edge of the Graph window's title bar to close this graph

- Choose **Window > Manage Graphs**

- Click the remaining **3Pay.mtw: Chart 'EdLevel'**

- Click **Rename**

- Type **Bar Chart EdLevel** in the "Rename" text box

- Click **OK** and **Done**

Chart is a core graph that provides the user with a great number of display options. To see one, replace each bar in the bar chart of EdLevel with a vertical line:

- Choose **Graph > Chart**

- Click the "Display" **arrow** under "Data Display"

- Click **Project**

- Click **OK**

The resulting chart is shown in Figure 3-20. (The word "project" refers to the *projection* lines drawn in the chart.) The new chart replaces the two bars by vertical lines whose heights reflect the frequency of each educational level. Such a chart is often called a *line chart* or a *line plot*.

FIGURE 3-20

Bar chart of EdLevel, with vertical lines instead of bars

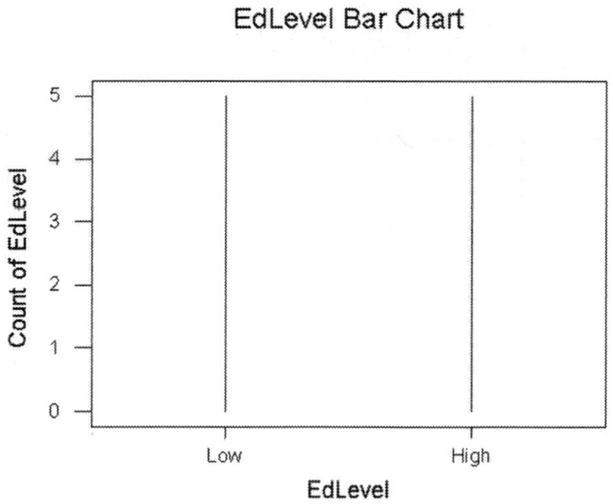

EdLevel Bar Chart

Close this graph.

- Double-click the **Graph** icon in the upper-left edge of the Graph window's title bar

- Save your project by clicking the **Save Project** toolbar button ▣

▼ 3.8   Creating a High-Resolution Pie Chart ▲

An alternative to the bar graph for displaying qualitative data is the pie chart. The pie chart is another example of a specialty graph. You decide to produce a pie chart of the same EdLevel data.

- Choose **Graph > Pie Chart**

- Click in the "Chart data in" text box

- Double-click **C10 EdLevel** in the "Chart data in" text box

- Click in the "Title" text box

- Type **EdLevel Pie Chart**

- Click **OK**

Minitab produces the pie chart depicted in Figure 3-21.

FIGURE 3-21

*Pie chart showing the
number of employees for
two levels of education*

EdLevel Pie Chart

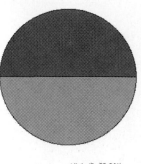

Low (5, 50.0%)

High (5, 50.0%)

The only additional information that this graph presents are the percentages of members of each category. There are equal percentages of employees of each education level (50%).

To print a copy of the pie chart in Figure 3-21:

■ Choose **File > Print Graph**

■ Click **OK** in the Print dialog box

Although the pie chart is in color on the screen, it will appear in color on paper only if your computer or terminal is connected to a color printer. A black-and-white printer renders the colors in shades of black, gray, and white.

To obtain multiple copies of the graph, type in the number you want in the "Number of copies" text box or click the up arrow. Then click OK.

To name the pie chart:

■ Choose **Window > Manage Graphs**

■ Click **3Pay.mtw: Pie**

■ Click **Rename**

■ Type **Pie Chart EdLevel** in the "Rename" text box

■ Click **OK** and **Done**

▼ 3.9   Opening and Printing a Graph ▲

You decide to print a copy of the histogram you saved at the beginning of this tutorial. First, you need to open the histogram graph file:

- Choose **File > Open Graph**
- Click the "Look in" **drop-down list arrow** and select the location where you are saving your work
- Double-click **HistSal** in the "Files" list box
- Click **OK** so that a copy of this file will be added to the current project

   Minitab displays the histogram.

- Choose **File > Print Graph**
- Click **OK** in the Print dialog box

   You now have a printed copy of the histogram that you can use during your presentation.

   Since you have saved this graph to a file, you can close the graph and return to the Session window:

- Double-click the **Graph button** on the top left edge of the Graph window's title bar
- Click the **Session window** toolbar button ▦ (the seventh one from the right)

   ▼ **Note** To print a high-resolution graph, you need to be in that graph's window. To print from the Session or Data window, that window needs to be active. For example, the Print option under the File menu for a Graph window is Print Graph; it's Print Session Window when the Session window is open. ▲

▼ 3.10   Saving and Reopening a Project ▲

To understand the function of a project more fully, you next will save the project *T3.mpj*, leave Minitab, return, and then open the project:

- Choose **File > Save Project**
- Choose **File > Exit**

   You have now saved your Tutorial 3 Session window (along with its History window), data worksheet, and one-variable graphs.

MINITAB AT WORK

FORESTRY: Foresters rely on easily obtained measurements to estimate how much timber a given forest contains. Researchers at Allegheny National Forest hoped to find a way to predict the volume of an individual tree by measuring only its base diameter.

The Allegheny team cut down 31 black cherry trees and measured the diameter and timber volume of each tree. They entered the resulting data into Minitab and created scatter plots of various combinations of the two variables. They found that plotting volume against the square of the diameter produced a strong linear relationship. If they wanted to estimate the volume of a tree with, say, a 1-foot diameter, they would mark 12^2, or 144 inches, on the x-axis and then find the corresponding volume on the y-axis — approximately 23 cubic feet of timber.

The foresters now had a tool that allowed them to estimate timber volume without having to cut down trees. Although they used other Minitab procedures that gave a more accurate estimate of volume, the plotting phase helped them single out the best variable transformation to use as a predictor.

▼ **Note** If you forget to save your project, Minitab will ask, at the "Exit" command, if you want to save the project before closing: "Save changes to this project before closing?" To save your project, click Yes. ▲

Now return to Minitab:

- Start **Minitab**

- Choose **File** > **Open Project**

- Click the "Look in" **drop-down list arrow** and select the location where you are saving your work

- Click the **T3 icon** in the "Project" list box

Minitab allows you preview the contents of a project. To preview the contents of *T3.mpj*:

- Click **Preview**

The list of items available in the project T3 includes all of the graphs you created and did not close and the worksheet *3Pay.mtw*. Not shown in the list are the Session window, the Info window, and the History window. (But they were saved!)

- Click **OK** to return to the Open Project dialog box

- Click **Open** to open *T3.mpj*

The graphs and the various windows open in rapid succession, and you are returned to exactly the point you were at when you exited Minitab. The Session window that was open when you left is still open. Open the Windows menu, and you will find all of the graphs that you named during this tutorial. Scroll back in the Session window, and you will discover all of the (character) stem-and-leaf displays that you created, as well as all of the commands you issued. Further, all of the settings you created at the beginning of the tutorial are still in effect. For example, the Session command language is enabled.

Now you can exit Minitab again:

■ Choose **File > Exit**

Congratulations. You've finished Tutorial 3!

▼

Minitab Command Summary

▲

This section describes the menu commands introduced in, or related to, this tutorial. To find a complete explanation of all menus and commands, refer to Minitab's on-line Help.

Minitab Menu Commands

Menu	Command	Description
File		
	Save Project As	Saves a project with a name to be specified.
	Project Description	Shows or creates a description of a project.
	Open Graph	Opens a high-resolution graph that has been saved in a graph file.
	Save Graph As	Saves a high-resolution graph (any graph in its own window).
	Print Graph	Prints a high-resolution graph.
Graph		
	Chart	Produces many kinds of charts, including bar, line, symbol, and area.
	Histogram	Produces a high-resolution histogram for each column of data indicated.
	Dotplot	Produces a high-resolution dotplot for each column of data indicated.
	Pie Chart	Produces a high-resolution pie chart.
	Boxplot	Produces a high-resolution boxplot for each column of data indicated.

Menu	Command	Description
Graph		
	Stem-and-Leaf	Produces a stem-and-leaf display for each column of data indicated.
	Character Graphs	Allows a choice of character graphs.
Editor		
	Worksheet Description	Shows or creates a description of a worksheet.
Window		
	Manage Graphs	Performs work on one or more high-resolution Graph windows.
	Close All Graphs	Removes all of the high-resolution graphs.

Matching

Match the following terms to their definitions by placing the correct letter next to the term it describes.

_____ Annotation

_____ Stem-and-leaf plot

_____ Close Graph

_____ Histogram

_____ Core and specialty graphs

_____ Project

_____ Dotplot

_____ Print Graph

_____ Save Graph As

_____ Boxplot

a. A Minitab command located in the Manage Graphs dialog box

b. A Minitab graph that is based on just five numbers

c. A graphical description of the frequency of a variable

d. A graphical description of the data in which some digits of the original data are evident

e. The Minitab command you use to save a high-resolution graph

f. The Minitab command that prints a high-resolution graph

g. A graph that has a horizontal axis and that represents each value by a black filled-in circle

h. File that includes an entire session's commands, output, and worksheets

i. High-resolution graphics

j. The button you use to add titles and footnotes to plots

True/False

Mark the following statements with a *T* or an *F*.

_____ High-resolution graphics in Minitab are viewed in the Session window.

_____ Minitab lets you annotate most graphical displays with titles and footnotes.

_____ Character plots are displayed in the Session window.

_____ All graphical displays in Minitab can be either high-resolution or character-based.

_____ High-resolution graphs are more appropriate for final reports.

_____ Save Window As is a command on the Window menu.

_____ Histograms, stem-and-leaf plots, dotplots, and boxplots are different types of one-variable displays.

_____ Minitab can interchange the variables on the axes of a high-resolution boxplot.

_____ For most displays (either high-resolution or character), you can change the scale, starting points, and increment values.

_____ You can produce bar plots and line plots with Minitab's Chart command.

Practice Problems

Use Help or Part III, Exploring Data, of the manual to review the contents of the data sets referenced in the problems below

1. Open *Marks.mtw*.

   a. Produce a histogram, dotplot, stem-and-leaf diagram, and boxplot of the first exam data. Compare the four graphs. Do all three provide the same information about the class's performance on the first exam?

   b. Compare the four graphs to identify extreme scores. What were the minimum and maximum scores, based on each graph?

   c. Compare the abilities of the four graphs to identify individual scores. How many students scored more than 75% on the first exam? What were their scores?

   d. Compare the abilities of the four graphs to identify median scores. What is the median score based on each graph?

   e. Briefly explain why you might use more than one of these graphs in a report.

2. Open *Ads.mtw*.

   a. Compute the ratio of full-page ads to pages. Name the new column C5 AdRatio.

   b. Save your worksheet as *P3Ads.mtw*.

   c. Produce a boxplot of the ads ratio data. Do the data appear symmetric? If not, in which direction is the ads ratio skewed?

d. Produce a boxplot of the ads ratio data for each magazine. How does the type of magazine affect the ads ratio?

3. Open *Ads2.mtw*.

   a. Produce a high-resolution histogram of the ad ratio data. Do the data appear symmetric? If not, in which direction is the ads ratio skewed? Interchange the histogram axes. Which histogram do you prefer? Why?

   b. Annotate your preferred histogram by adding the title "Ratio of Full Page Ad and Total Number of Pages Histogram."

   c. Print a hard copy of this histogram.

4. Open *PulseA.mtw*.

   a. Produce a dotplot of Weight. Name the dotplot Weight Dotplot. The dotplot is bimodal, with one peak at around 150 pounds and a smaller peak at about 115 pounds. Can you explain the shape of this plot?

   b. Produce a boxplot of Pulse1. From the plot, identify the approximate values for the smallest pulse rate, the first quartile, the median pulse rate, the third quartile, and the highest pulse rate.

   c. Produce for Smokes (i) a bar graph and (ii) a pie chart. Which graph gives you the best indication of how many of the students smoke? Which graph gives you the best indication of the percentage of students that smoke?

   d. The variable Activity has a missing value in row 54. Use the menu command Manip > Delete Rows to eliminate this row.

   e. Produce for the variable Activity (i) a bar chart and (ii) a pie chart. What are the advantages and disadvantages of each graph?

   f. Produce a stem-and-leaf graph of Weight. How much does the lightest person in the class weigh? How much does the heaviest person in the class weigh? Interpret the values 11 and 16 in the leftmost column of the display.

5. Open the data set *Snow.mtw*.

   a. Produce a histogram of both Rain and Snowfall. What do you notice about the shapes of the two graphs?

   b. Produce a stem-and-leaf graph of Snowfall. How much snow fell in the least-snowiest year in this data set? In which year did this occur?

TUTORIAL 4

Graphical Methods for Describing Two or More Variables

In this tutorial, you will construct graphs designed to uncover the relationship between two or more variables. You will examine situations in which both variables are quantitative, one is quantitative and the other qualitative, and both variables are qualitative. Two cases studies, one familiar and one new, will be used to illustrate theses graphs.

Objectives

In this tutorial, you learn how to:

- plot one quantitative variable against another, using scatter plots and marginal plots
- introduce a qualitative variable into a scatter plot
- use multiple boxplots and dotplots to compare distributions
- construct charts showing the relationship between two qualitative variables
- construct a chart that displays mean values for a quantitative variable
- use a scatter plot to plot a quantitative variable against time
- construct multiple plots on the same graph

▼ 4.1   Opening a Project ▲

CASE STUDY: MANAGEMENT — SALARY STRUCTURE (CONTINUED)

In Tutorial 3, you found considerable variation in the salaries of employees in the Sales Department at Temco. In this tutorial, you will use graphs to investigate how salary is related to length of employment with the company, to level of education, and, of particular concern, to gender.

Get started by opening Minitab:

- Open **Minitab** and maximize the Session window

  To enable the Session command language and make the output read-only:

- Choose **Editor > Enable Command Language** (unless the Editor menu says "Disable Command Language")

- Choose **Editor > Make Output Read-Only** (unless the Editor menu says "Make Output Editable")

  In this tutorial, you will add to the project begun in Tutorial 3 by creating graphs of two or more variables. If you completed all of the steps in the last tutorial, then you saved in a project called *T3.mpj* the original *Pay2* data set, all of the output in the Session window, the graphs you created, and the Info and History windows. (You are strongly urged to complete Tutorial 3 before beginning this tutorial.) Thus, instead of creating a new project, you will open and add to the project *T3.mpj*. Don't be concerned if you don't have — or think you don't have — a complete copy of this project file. A copy of it, as it looked at the end of Tutorial 3, is included in the Student subdirectory.

  Open the project *T3.mpj*:

- Choose **File > Open Project**

- Click the "Look in" **drop-down list arrow** and select the **Student** subdirectory

- Double-click **T3.mpj** in the "Open Project" list box to open the project

  The project will open at the point you left it in the last tutorial.

▼ 4.2   Scatter Plots ▲

In Tutorial 3, each graph you constructed described a single variable, such as C1 Salary. A natural question to ask is whether there is a relationship between salaries in the Sales Department at Temco and how long members of that department have been with the company. You can examine this question with the help of a *scatter plot*. A scatter plot is a graph used to display data for two quantitative variables. To plot C1 Salary against C2 YrsEm:

- Choose **Graph** > **Plot** to open the Plot dialog box
- Double-click **C1 Salary** to enter it into the first "Y" text box for Graph 1
- Double-click **C2 YrsEm** to enter it into the first "X" text box for Graph 1

The completed Plot dialog box looks like that shown in Figure 4-1.

FIGURE 4-1

Plot dialog box

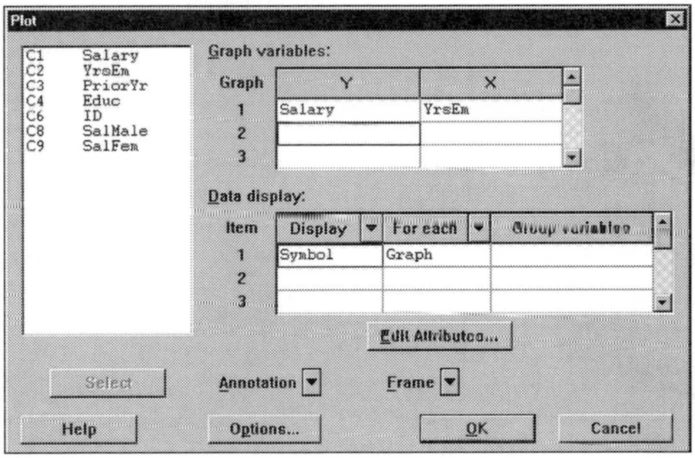

To add a title and obtain the plot:

- Click the "Annotation" **drop-down list arrow** and then click **Title**
- Type **Scatter Plot of Salary against Years Employed** in the first "Title" text box
- Click **OK** twice

The resulting scatter plot is shown in Figure 4-2.

FIGURE 4-2

*Scatter Plot of Salary
against Years Employed*

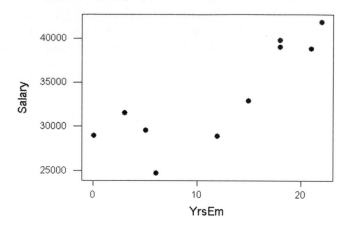

Scatter Plot of Salary against Years Employed

It appears from the scatter plot that Sales Department employees who have worked longer at Temco tend to have higher salaries. The relationship, however, is not perfect. For instance, the salesperson with the lowest salary has been with the company longer than three colleagues.

Notice that Minitab provides only three tick marks — 0, 10, and 20 — which represent the number of years employed. These are plotted on the horizontal axis (YrsEm, or *x*-axis). As a result, it is not easy to assess, for example, how long the employee with the lowest salary has been with the company. You decide that the default label on the *x*-axis, YrsEm, should be replaced with a clearer label, Years Employed.

You can close this graph and replace it with a scatter plot that has tick marks consisting of the values 0, 2, 4, 6, . . ., 22 on the *x*-axis and that has the new label. First, close the current graph:

- Double-click the **Graph icon** on the upper-left edge of the Graph window's title bar

You can adjust both the tick marks and the label for the *x*-axis by using options under the Frame drop-down list arrow in the Plot dialog box. This arrow, which is available on all Minitab's core graphs, allows you access to many options of the axes around the graph that you can adjust. To examine these options:

- Click the **Edit Last Dialog** toolbar button 🔳 to open the Plot dialog box

- Click the "Frame" **drop-down list arrow**

In this example, you will adjust the tick marks on the *x*-axis (horizontal axis) of the graph. Using Axis, you can, for example, specify names for each of the axes, as well as the size of the type. Grid and Reference allow you to draw different kinds of reference lines on the graph. As you might imagine, Min and Max allow you to specify the largest and smallest values for *x* and *y*. Later, you will use Multiple Graphs to superimpose one plot on another.

To adjust the tick marks and then the label:

- Click **Tick**

- Click in the **Positions** text box in the first (X) row and type **0:22/2**

This last command instructs Minitab to insert the values 0 to 22 at intervals of 2 along the *x*-axis.

- Click **OK**

Now change the name associated with the *x*-axis (horizontal axis):

- Click **Frame** and then **Axis**

Notice that under "Direction," Minitab views the first line in this dialog box as relating to the *x*-axis (horizontal) and the second as relating to the *y*-axis (vertical).

- Click in the first line beneath "Label" and type **Years Employed**

- Click **OK** twice

The resulting plot, shown in Figure 4-3, indicates that the sales employee with the lowest salary has worked at Temco for six years.

FIGURE 4-3

Scatter Plot of Salary against Years Employed with new tick marks and a new label on the x-axis

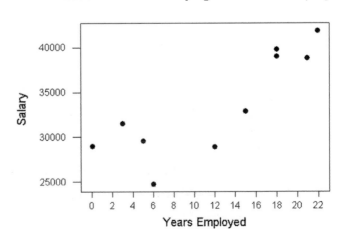

Scatter Plot of Salary against Years Employed

Following the practice adopted in the last tutorial, you will name this graph Plot Salary vs. Years:

- Click the **Manage Graphs** toolbar button 🖼 (the fourth one from the right) to open the Manage Graphs dialog box

- Click **3Pay.mtw: Plot 'Salary'*'YrsEm';** to activate this plot (you may have to scroll down to find it)

- Click **Rename** and type **Plot Salary versus Years** in the text box

- Click **OK** and then click **Done**

    Notice that the title bar now identifies this graph as Plot Salary vs. Years. To print the active graph:

- Click the **Print Graph** toolbar button 🖶

▼ 4.3   Adding a Grouping Variable to a Scatter Plot ▲

You wonder whether the general positive relationship between salary and years employed at Temco exists for both male and female members of the sales force. You can examine this question by labeling the data points on the Scatter Plot of Salary against Years Employed according to the gender of the individual:

- Choose **Graph > Plot** to open the Plot dialog box

- Under "Data display" for "Item 1," click the "For each" **drop-down list arrow** and select **Group**

- Click in the box immediately below "Group variables"

- In the variable list on the left of the dialog box, double-click the variable **C7 Gender** to enter Gender as the variable

    At this point, the Plot dialog box should look as shown in Figure 4-4.

FIGURE 4-4

The Plot dialog box for grouping by gender

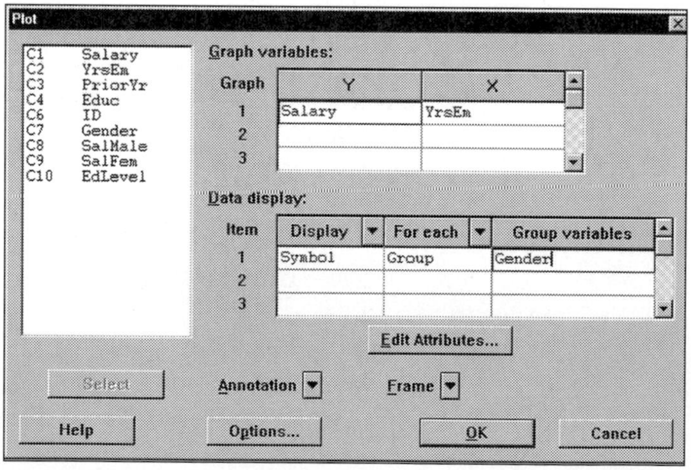

- Click the "Annotation" **drop-down list arrow** and then click **Title**
- Type **Scatter Plot of Salary by Years Employed with Gender** in the "Title" text box
- Click **OK** twice

The resulting plot is shown in Figure 4-5.

FIGURE 4-5

Scatter Plot of Salary by Years Employed with Gender

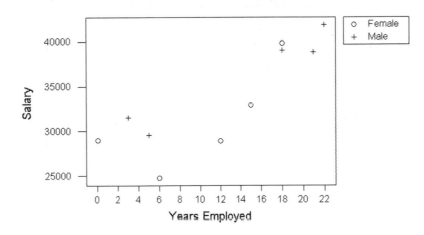

Scatter Plot of Salary by Years Employed with Gender

As the legend indicates, Minitab plots all female salaries with a circle (o) and all male salaries with a plus sign (+). The plot suggests that for both genders, there is indeed a positive relationship between salary and years employed. Moreover, the points in the upper-right corner of the graph show that males with higher salaries also have more experience with Temco. However, as before, there is one female with six years at Temco who has a lower salary than coworkers hired after her.

▼ **Note** In the commands used to construct the scatter plot in Figure 4-5, gender is referred to as a *grouping variable*. A grouping variable is a variable that is used to define different groups, in this case males and females. In this context, a grouping variable may be either text or numeric. Numeric variables must contain only integer values. ▲

To name this graph Plot Salary vs. Years with Gender:

- Choose **Window** > **Manage Graphs** to open the Manage Graphs dialog box
- Click **3Pay.mtw: Plot 'Salary'*'YrsEm';** to activate this plot (you may have to scroll down to find it)
- Click **Rename** and type **Plot Salary vs. Years with Gender** in the "Name" text box
- Click **OK** and then click **Done**

▼ 4.4   Marginal Plots ▲

A specialty Minitab graph called a *marginal plot* combines the features of a scatter plot with some of the one-variable graphs you generated in the Tutorial 3. That is, you can create a scatter plot that also has a histogram, boxplot, or dotplot on the axes. This specialty graph allows you to show the relationship between two variables while also viewing the distribution of each variable, all on the same plot.

To create a marginal plot of salary against years employed with boxplots on each margin:

- Choose **Graph > Marginal Plot** to open the Marginal Plot dialog box

- Double-click **C1 Salary** to make it the *"Y variable"*

- Double-click **C2 YrsEm** to make it the *"X variable"*

- Under "Type of marginal plot," click **Boxplot**

- Click in the "X axis label" text box and type **Years Employed**

- Click in the "Title" text box and type **Marginal Plot of Salary against Years Employed**

At this point, the Marginal Plot dialog box should look as shown in Figure 4-6.

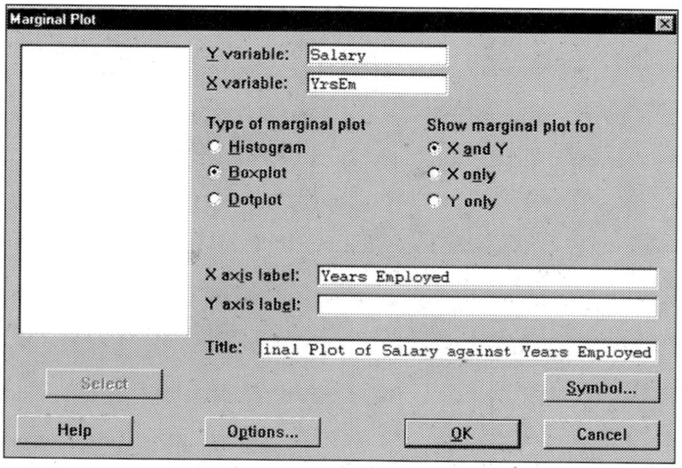

FIGURE 4-6

The Marginal Plot dialog box showing Marginal Plot of Salary against Years Employed

You can see from the dialog box in Figure 4-6 that marginal plots can be histograms, boxplots, or dotplots (but no combinations of these), and that they can appear on one or both margins. As a specialty graph, the marginal plot does not offer the wide range of options associated with core graphs, such as Plot or Chart.

■ Click **OK**

The resulting plot is shown in Figure 4-7.

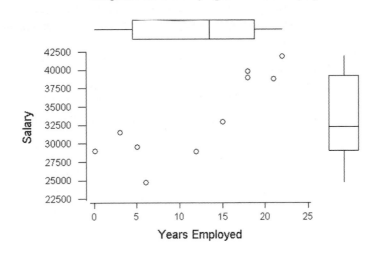

Each point is represented by a circle (o). In the top and right margins of the plot, Minitab places the boxplot of the x (YrsEm) values and the y (Salary) values, respectively. Notice that the tick marks in the marginal plot differ from the default tick marks you obtained with the scatter plot. In the Practice Problems at the end of this tutorial, you are asked to obtain a scatter plot with the tick marks that are present on this marginal plot.

To name this graph Marginal Plot Salary vs. Years Employed:

■ Choose **Window > Manage Graphs** to open the Manage Graphs dialog box

■ Click **3Pay.mtw: Marginal Distribution Plot** to activate this plot (you may have to scroll down to find it)

■ Click **Rename** and type in the "Name" text box **Marginal Plot Salary vs. Years Employed**

■ Click **OK** and then click **Done**

At this point, it would be a good idea to save the updated project with a new name, *T3&4*. To do this:

■ Choose **File > Save Project As**

■ Click the "Save in" **drop-down list arrow** and select the location where you are saving your work

■ Under "File name," replace the name *T3* with the name ***T3&4***

■ Click **Save**

▼ 4.5   Multiple Boxplots ▲

In Tutorial 3, you obtained for the Salary variable a histogram, a stem-and-leaf plot, a dotplot, and a boxplot. Minitab allows you to compare subgroups by obtaining any one of these graphs separately for each subgroup. For instance, you can compare a boxplot of salaries for male employees to a boxplot of salaries for female employees. The next example illustrates how to do this.

To obtain a graph showing separate boxplots of salaries for males and females:

- Choose **Graph** > **Boxplot** to open the Boxplot dialog box
- Double-click **C1 Salary** to select it as the "Y Graph variable"
- Double-click **C7 Gender** to select it as the "X Graph variable"
- Click **Options**
- If "Transpose X and Y" is checked, deselect it
- Click **OK**
- Click the "Annotation" **drop-down list arrow** and then click **Title**
- Type **Boxplots of Salary by Gender**
- Click **OK** twice

The resulting side-by-side boxplots are shown in Figure 4-8.

FIGURE 4-8

Side-by-side Boxplots of Salary by Gender

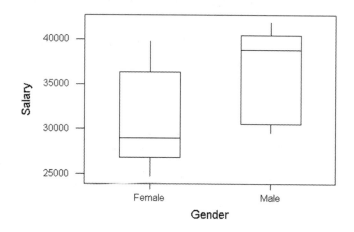

You can see that male salaries fall over a slightly narrower range and that their median is higher than that for females by about $7,000. However, the scatter plot shown in Figure 4-5 shows that the two longest-serving employees in the Sales Department were men. So this may, in part at least, explain this difference in median salary. As you can see, boxplots are an effective way to compare entire distributions.

- Use the Manage Graphs command to rename this graph **Boxplots of Salary by Gender**.

When you filled in the Boxplot dialog box, you selected Salary as the y-variable and Gender as the x-variable. When multiple boxplots are compared in this way, y is always a quantitative variable. Usually, but not always, x will be a qualitative or categorical variable, like Gender. If x is quantitative, it will typically take only a small number of values. For example, you could obtain a boxplot of salary for each number of degrees obtained (x), if you had the appropriate data.

▼ 4.6   Multiple Dotplots ▲

You can also use dotplots to easily compare distributions.
To obtain a dotplot of salary by gender:

- Choose **Graph > Dotplot** to open the Dotplot dialog box
- Double-click **C1 Salary** to enter it into the "Variables" text box
- Click **By variable** and then in the "By variable" text box
- Double-click **C7 Gender**
- Under "Title," type **Dotplots of Salary by Gender** and then press ⏎

The resulting dotplots are shown in Figure 4-9.

Dotplots of Salary by Gender

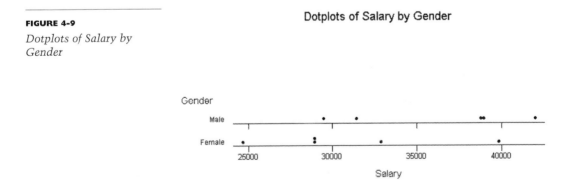

The dots help you to easily compare the two sets of salaries. You can see the generally higher salaries for males. Recall, though, that the males with the highest salaries have been with Temco for the longest time.

To name this graph Dotplots of Salary by Gender:

- Click the **Manage Graphs** toolbar button ▣
- Click **3Pay.mtw: Dotplot for Salary** to activate this plot (you may have to scroll down to find it)
- Click **Rename** and type **Dotplots of Salary by Gender** in the "Name" text box
- Click **OK** and then click **Done**

▼ 4.7 Examining the Relationship Between Two Qualitative Variables ▲

In Tutorial 3, you constructed a chart showing the percentage distribution of the variable EdLevel. Recall that the chart showed that exactly half of the sales staff had no more than a college degree (Low), while the other half had at least some graduate work (High). Next, you will use a chart to explore how, if at all, the distribution of EdLevel varies by gender. To generate this graph:

- Choose **Graph** > **Chart** to open the Chart dialog box
- Click in the first "**X**" text box and double-click **C7 Gender** in the variable list on the left to make Gender the x-variable
- Click the "Display" **drop-down list arrow** and click **Bar**
- Click the "For each" **drop-down list arrow** and then click **Group**
- Click in the text box beneath **Group variable** and double-click **C10 EdLevel** in the variable list on the left to make EdLevel the y-variable
- Click the "Annotation" **drop-down list arrow** and then click **Title**
- Type **Chart of Educational Level by Gender**
- Click **OK**

At this point, the Chart dialog box should look like that shown in Figure 4-10.

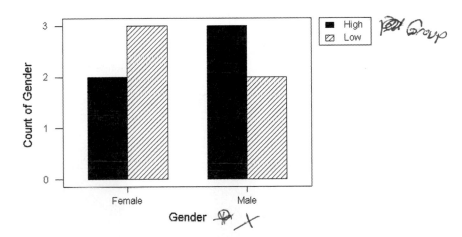

For each gender (X), you want to display the frequency of each EdLevel. You can do this in either of two ways. The first is to display two bars for each gender, one for those with a lower EdLevel and one for those with a higher EdLevel. To do this, you define EdLevel as a *cluster* variable:

- Click **Options** in the Chart dialog box
- Click the **Cluster** check box
- Press ⟨Tab⟩
- Double-click **C10 EdLevel**
- Click **OK** twice

FIGURE 4-11

Side-by-side Chart of Educational Level by Gender

Chart of Educational Level by Gender

You can see, with the help of the legend to the right of the chart, that two of the females have some graduate study and three do not. The numbers are exactly reversed for the males. Perhaps this difference in educational level accounts for the difference in salary levels you noted earlier. In the next section, you will explore this question by creating a more complex chart.

To name this graph Chart of EdLevel by Gender:

- Click the **Manage Graphs** toolbar button 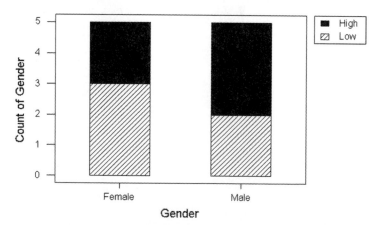 to open the Manage Graphs dialog box

- Click **3Pay.mtw: Chart 'Gender'** to activate this plot (you may have to scroll down to find it)

- Click **Rename** and type **Chart of EdLevel by Gender** in the "Name" text box

- Click **OK** and then click **Done**

In the context of charts, Minitab uses the term "clustering" in the same sense that it used "grouping variable" in the context of the core graphs, histograms, and boxplots. For each gender, you can view the distribution of EdLevel just as you viewed the distribution of salary in the earlier graph of multiple boxplots.

Another way to represent the distribution of EdLevel for each gender is to *stack* the bars for each EdLevel rather than show them side-by-side. To create this chart:

- Click **Graph > Chart** to open the Chart dialog box

- Click **Options**

- Deselect the **Cluster** option and click the **Stack** check box

- Click in the "Stack" text box and double-click **C10 EdLevel**

- Click **OK** twice

The resulting chart is shown in Figure 4-12.

FIGURE 4-12

Stacked Chart of Educational Level by Gender

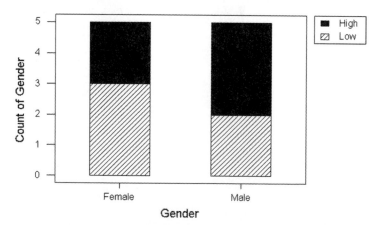

As you can see, the chart in Figure 4-12 shows exactly the same results as that in Figure 4-11. You decide to retain the chart in Figure 4-11 and close the current one. To close the current chart:

- Double-click the **Graph** icon on the upper-left edge of the Graph window's title bar

▼ 4.8   Using Charts to Display Means ▲

Minitab's Chart command produces many kinds of charts by using a variety of summary statistics, such as sums, means, maximums, and minimums. You want to chart the mean salary for males and females, grouped separately by educational level. To create this chart:

- Choose **Graph > Chart** to open the Chart dialog box

- Press **F3** to clear the previous selections

- Click the "Function" **drop-down list arrow** and then click **Mean** so that the chart will display the mean salary for each group

- Double-click **C1 Salary** in the variable list on the left to enter it into the first "Y" text box

- Double-click **C10 EdLevel** in the variable list on the left to enter it in the first "X" text box

    You want to display two bars in each of the two educational groupings, one for males and one for females. To achieve this effect, you define Gender as the clustering variable:

- Click the "For each" **drop-down list arrow** and then click **Group**

- Click in the first **Group variables** text box and then double-click **C7 Gender** in the variable list on the left to make it the variable

- Click **Options**

- Click the **Cluster** check box, click in the text box to its right, and then double-click **C7 Gender** to enter it as the cluster variable

- Click **OK**

    The Chart dialog box reappears as shown in Figure 4-13.

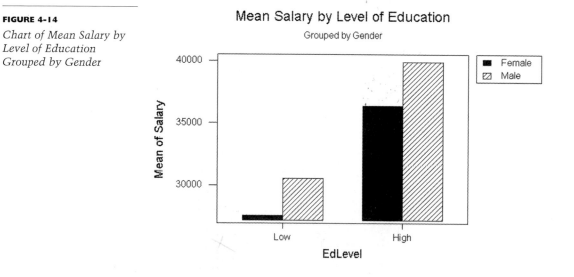

To add a title and a subtitle:

- Click the "Annotation" **drop-down list arrow** and then click **Title** to open the Title subdialog box

- Type **Mean Salary by Level of Education** in the first "Title" box and **Grouped by Gender** in the second

- To change the size of the subtitle text from the default 1.5 points to 1.0 points, type **1** in the second "Text Size" text box

- Click **OK** twice

Minitab creates the chart shown in Figure 4-14.

FIGURE 4-14

Chart of Mean Salary by Level of Education Grouped by Gender

The Title dialog box offers you great flexibility in creating titles. A long *title* may cover a number of lines. Alternatively, as in this case, you may create a *subtitle* by simply changing the font size on the corresponding line. You can also control the typeface of a font and whether a line is left-justified, right-justified, or centered.

Unlike in previous charts in which the bars represented frequencies, the bars in the chart shown in Figure 4-14 represent the mean salary for each gender at each educational level. The bars on the left show the mean salary for males and females who have a bachelor's degree or less. Those on the right show the mean salary for males and females who have completed at least some graduate work. In this example, clustering by Gender rather than by EdLevel enables you to compare the mean salary for each gender while EdLevel remains constant.

The chart suggests that Temco pays females less than males, regardless of educational level. Perhaps, however, the difference in the years of employment explains this difference in mean salary.

Notice that the bars in the chart in Figure 4-14 do not begin at $0. This is because, by default, Minitab selects a vertical scale so as to emphasize the variation in the data. However, this vertical scale creates the impression that those with a lower level of education receive only a small fraction of that earned by those with a higher level of education. You can re-create the previous chart, setting the vertical scale to start at $0 (that is, setting the *y*-axis based on the origin) as follows:

- Click the **Edit Last Dialog** toolbar button to open the Chart dialog box

- Click the "Frame" **drop-down list arrow** and then click **Min and Max**

- Click in the **Minimum for Y** text box and type **0**

- Click **OK** twice

The new chart is shown in Figure 4-15.

FIGURE 4-15

Chart of Mean Salary by Level of Education with the y-axis based at the origin

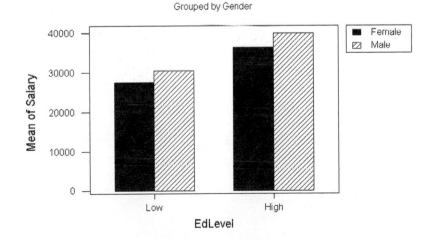

The chart in Figure 4-15 more accurately reflects the difference in mean salary levels for the four groups. It still shows that within each educational level, males earn roughly $2,000 more than females. You decide to keep and rename this graph and close the previous one:

- Choose **Window > Manage Graphs** to open the Manage Graphs dialog box

- Select the first **3Pay.mtw: Chart Mean (Salary) * 'EdLevel';** (you may have to scroll down to find it)

- Click **Close**

- Select the remaining **3Pay.mtw: Chart Mean (Salary) * 'EdLevel';**

- Click **Rename**, type **Chart of Mean Salary vs. EdLevel by Gender**, and click **OK**, then **Done**

The salary analysis completed thus far suggests that males do earn more than females in the Sales Department, even after control is exerted for level of education. However, you suspect that at least some of the difference may be explained by the fact that the male members of the department have been at Temco for a longer time than the females. You have done well relying only on graphs to guide you. You will work on this case study again as a practice problem in Tutorial 10.

Now save the project T3&4 again:

- Click the **Save Project** toolbar button ▣ (the second one from the left)

In the next case study, you revisit scatter plots but in the context in which the *x*-variable represents the passage of time.

▼ 4.9 Plots on Which X Represents Time ▲

CASE STUDY: DEMOCRATIC AND REPUBLICAN PARTY FORTUNES

Your final paper in the Introduction to American Politics course that you are taking will examine trends in the performance of the two major political parties over the 33 presidential elections between 1868 and 1996. You plan to use Minitab graphs to plot the percentage of the vote that each party received in each election so that you can explore and describe the patterns of change.

A special case of the scatter plot occurs in which the horizontal axis represents the passage of time in equally spaced intervals. In this case, the graph is called a *time series plot*. The data set *Election.mtw* contains three variables: C1, C2, and C3. C1 contains the dates of all 33 presidential elections from 1868 to 1996. C2 and C3 contain, respectively, the percentage of the popular vote won by the Republican and Democratic party candidates. To open the election data file:

- Choose **File > Open Worksheet**

- Select **Election** in the "Open Worksheet" list box (you may have to navigate to the Student subdirectory of Minitab and then scroll to see the file)

- Click **Open** to open *Election.mtw*

You want to examine the fortunes of the Democratic party by plotting Dem% against Year:

- Choose **Graph > Plot** to open the Plot dialog box

▼ **Note** If you did not leave Minitab before beginning this case study, the Plot dialog box will contain the selections you made when working with the *3Pay* data set. To return the dialog box — and all of its subdialog boxes — to their default positions, press the `F3` key. ▲

- Double-click **C3 Dem%** to enter it in the "Y" text box

- Double-click **C1 Year** to enter it in the "X" text box

- Click the "Annotation" **drop-down list arrow** and then click **Title**

- Type **Scatter Plot of Democratic Percentage of the Vote by Election Year**

- Click **OK** twice

The resulting plot is shown in Figure 4.16

FIGURE 4-16

Scatter plot of Dem% against Year

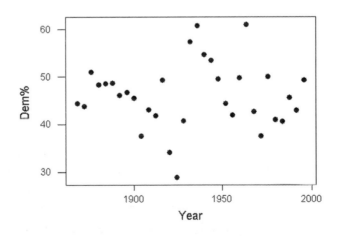

Scatter Plot of Democratic Percentage of the Vote by Election Year

Making sense of the relationship between these two variables is not easy because it is difficult to see how Dem% changes with the passage of time. The major reason for this is that the human eye has trouble picking up consecutive points. This can be remedied by connecting the points. To do this in this case, you will regraph Dem% against Year, setting tick marks at 20-year intervals from 1870 to 1990.

First, close the current graph:

- Double-click the **Graph** icon on the upper-left edge of the Graph window's title bar

Then, to make the specified modifications:

- Click the **Edit Last Dialog** toolbar button ⬚ to open the Plot dialog box

- Under "Data display," click the "Display" **drop-down list arrow** and click **Connect**

- Click **Frame** and then click **Tick**

- Under "Positions," for variable X, type **1870:1990/20**

- Click **OK** twice

The graph with the points connected is shown in Figure 4-17.

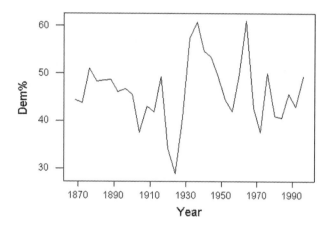

Scatter Plot of Democratic Percentage of the Vote by Election Year

Now you can see that the percentage of the popular vote won by the Democratic candidate follows a cyclical pattern. The lowest point is in 1924, when the Democrats won less than 29% of the popular vote. This is followed, however, by pcaks when the Democrats won almost 61% of the vote in 1936 and just over 61% in 1964.

Next, rename this graph Plot Dem% against Time:

- Click the **Manage Graphs** toolbar button ⬚ to open the Manage Graphs dialog box

- Click **Election.mtw: Plot 'Dem%'*'Year';** to activate this plot (you may have to scroll down to find it)

- Click **Rename** and type **Plot Dem% against Time** in the "Name" text box
- Click **OK** and then click **Done**

In the Plot dialog box under "Display," Connect is only one of the options. Area will shade in the area under the line that connects the points. Lowess will provide a "smoothed" version of the line connecting the points. Project will represent each point by a vertical line (projection). Symbol lets you choose your own plotting symbol.

In each plot in this case study, the x-axis, or Year axis, marked the passage of time in equal-sized increments (4-year periods). In fact, Minitab has a core graph called a Time Series Plot that is designed for precisely this kind of situation. You will encounter time series plots in more detail in Tutorials 11 and 15.

▼ 4.10   Overlaying Plots ▲

You could construct a graph similar to that created in Section 4.10 in order to examine the behavior of Rep%. However, Minitab lets you look at both graphs on the same plot. To do this:

- Choose **Graph > Plot** to open the Plot dialog box
- Click in the **Graph 2** box under "Y"
- Double-click **C2 Rep%** in the variable list on the left to make it the Variable
- Double-click **C1 Year** to enter it in the Graph 2 box under "X"
- Under "Data display," click in the **Item 2** box under "Display"
- Click the "Display" **drop-down list arrow** and click **Connect**
- Click in the **Item 2** box under "For each"
- Click the "For each" **drop-down list arrow** and click **Graph**
- Click the "Annotation" **drop-down list arrow**, click **Title**, and highlight the current entry
- Type **Scatter Plot of Dem% and Rep% by Election Year**
- Click **OK** to return to the Plot dialog box

Once the two sets of x- and y-variables have been entered, and assuming no further changes, Minitab will create two graphs, one showing Dem% plotted against Year and the other, Rep% plotted against Year. To get both plots on the same graph, you must *overlay* the second on top of the first:

- Click **Frame** and then **Multiple graphs**

- Click **Overlay graphs on the same page**

- Click **OK** twice

  A dialog box appears with the message that too many graphs are open. Close two of the graphs you constructed in Tutorial 3. Namely, the bar and pie charts showing the number of Temco employees for two levels of education.

- Choose **Window > Manage Graphs**

- Select **Bar Chart EdLevel** (you may have to scroll down to find it)

- Click **Close**

- Select **Pie Chart EdLevel**

- Click **Close** then click **Done**

  The dialog box with "Too many graphs are open" message reappears.

- Click **OK**

▼ **Note** If you are working with your own copy of Minitab, you can have more graphs open at once by choosing Edit > Preferences > Graphics and changing the default settings there. ▲

  The two graphs on the same plot are shown in Figure 4-18.

FIGURE 4-18

Scatter Plot of Dem% and Rep% by Election Year

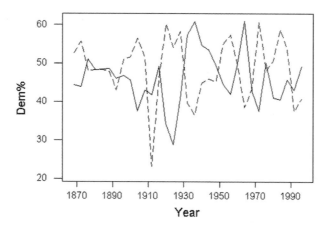

Scatter Plot of Dem% and Rep% by Election Year

  There are problems with this graph. One is that it shows both a solid line and a dashed line, but Minitab does not indicate which line represents the data for which party. The second is that Minitab erroneously places the name Dem% on the vertical axis; the name should be Percentage of Vote.

  To find out which line belongs to which party:

- Click the **Edit Last Dialog** toolbar button ▦ to open the Plot dialog box

- Click **Edit Attributes**

The Connect dialog box indicates that the first graph (Dem% against Year) is represented by a solid line and that the second graph (Rep% against Year) is represented by a dashed line. By using the Line Type arrow, you could change these choices. However, for now:

- Click **OK**

Next, you want to indicate which line is which by adding a footnote to the graph. You will use an underscore and a hyphen to indicate the line types in the graph.

- Click the "Annotation" **drop-down list arrow** and then **Footnote**
- On the first line, type **Dem% _____ Rep% - - - - -** and then press ⏎

Finally, change the name associated with the vertical axis:

- Click **Frame** and then **Axis**
- Click in the second line beneath "Label" and type **Percentage of Vote**
- Click **OK** twice

The new graph is shown in Figure 4-19. It has a corrected name for the vertical axis. The new footnote acts as a legend, identifying which line is for which party.

FIGURE 4-19

Plot of Dem% and Rep% by Election Year with a footnote legend

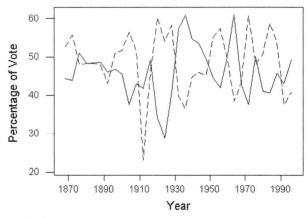

Notice that both parties show cyclical behavior, although the peak of the cycle for one party tends to correspond to the valley of the cycle for the other party. As could be expected, when one of the two major parties in the United States has a good election result, the other has a poor one. The

Republican low point was in 1912, when that party won less than 24% of the vote. The graphs indicate also that after 1950, both parties managed to avoid the large swings in popularity that was a feature of elections between 1910 and 1950.

▼ **Note** In some statistics classes in which many students generate similar graphs from the same printer, footnotes or subtitles can be used to add your name to a graph. You may want to explore this possibility with your instructor. ▲

With this graph in particular, you are ready to explore the reasons for these voting patterns. You decide to keep and rename this graph and close the previous one:

- Choose **Window > Manage Graphs** to open the Manage Graphs dialog box

- Select the first **Election.mtw: Plot 'Dem%' * 'Year' 'Rep%'*'Year';** (you may have to scroll down to find it)

- Click **Close**

- Select the remaining **Election.mtw: Plot 'Dem%' * 'Year 'Rep%'*'Year';**

- Click **Rename**, type **Plot of Dem% and Rep% against Election Year**, and click **OK** and then **Done**

For a last time, save your project:

- Choose **File > Save Project**

Minitab automatically replaces the old version of *T3&4* with all of the elements currently open: the *3Pay* and the election data sets; all graphs; and the new, updated Session, Info, and History windows.
Now you may exit Minitab:

- Choose **File > Exit**

Minitab Command Summary

This section describes the menu commands introduced in, or related to, this tutorial. To find a complete explanation of all menus and commands, refer to Minitab's on-line Help.

Minitab Menu Commands

Menu	Command	Description
File		
	New	Opens a new project or a new worksheet.
	Open Project	Opens the named project.
	Save Project As	Saves the current project under a name to be provided.
Graph		
	Plot	Provides a scatter plot of two quantitative variables.
	Time Series Plot	Produces a time series plot of one or more columns of data against time.
	Chart	Produces many kinds of charts, including bar charts, charts involving two qualitative variables, and charts displaying a variety of summary statistics.
	Boxplot	Can be used to produce multiple boxplots on the same graph.
	Dotplot	Can be used to produce multiple dotplots on the same graph.
	Marginal Plot	Creates a scatter plot in which one or two of the margins forms the base for a histogram, a boxplot, or a dotplot.

Review and Practice

Matching

Match the following terms to their definitions by placing the correct letter next to the term it describes.

_____ Grouping variable

_____ Plot

_____ Margins

_____ Multiple plots

_____ Transpose

_____ Min and Max

_____ Tick marks

_____ Close Graph

_____ Rename Graph

_____ Manage Graphs

a. The command to perform many Graph window functions

b. The command for changing the default name of a graph

c. Switches the position of the *x*- and *y*-axes

d. The numbered checkpoints along the axes of a graph

e. The command that produces a scatter plot for two variables

f. The option that overlays two or more graphs on the same plot

g. The option to delete a graph

h. The command that allows you to set the smallest and largest values for variables in a graph

i. The variable used to assign different symbols in a scatter plot

j. The top-right and right-top sides of a scatter plot

True/False

Mark the following statements with a *T* or an *F*.

_____ High-resolution graphs in Minitab are viewed in the Session window.

_____ Charts can represent means and medians as well as frequencies.

_____ Boxplots are useful for comparing subgroups.

_____ Charts are useful for relating two qualitative variables.

_____ Minitab can interchange the variables on the axes of some graphs.

_____ Stem-and-leaf displays can be obtained on the margins of a marginal plot.

_____ In a scatter plot, where the *x*-axis represents the passage of time, it is useful to connect the points.

_____ A marginal plot is a core Minitab graph.

_____ One graph cannot be superimposed on another.

_____ You can control the number and location of the tick marks for a plot.

Practice Problems

Use Help or Part III, Exploring Data, of the manual to review the contents of the data sets referenced in the problems below.

1. Open *Ads2.mtw*

   a. On one graph, produce a boxplot of the ads ratio data for each magazine. An ads ratio is the ratio of full-page ads to pages. How do the ads ratios differ by magazine?

   b. Add the title Boxplots of Ads Ratio by Magazine to the graph in part a.

   c. On one graph, produce a boxplot of the ads ratio data for each year. How do the ratios differ by year?

   d. Add the title Boxplots of Ads Ratio by Year to the graph in part c.

   e. In Practice Problem 2 in Tutorial 3, you produced boxplots of ads ratios for each magazine on separate graphs. Why is the approach in part a better than that in Tutorial 3?

2. Open *Homes.mtw*.

   a. Construct a scatter plot of Price against Area. What kind of relationship, if any, exists between these two variables? What is particularly striking about the behavior of Price as Area increases?

   b. Add the title Scatter Plot of Price against Area to the plot in part b.

   c. On one graph, produce a boxplot of Price for each number of rooms. Add the title Boxplots of Price by the Number of Rooms. Summarize the overall pattern exhibited by these boxplots.

3. Open *Pulsea.mtw*.

   a. Construct a scatter plot of Weight against Height. Add the title Scatter Plot of Weight against Height. What kind of relationship exists between these two variables?

   b. Construct the same plot as in part b, except make the tick marks for Height run from 60 to 76 at intervals of 2 inches.

   c. Construct a marginal plot for these same two variables, with boxplots on the margins. What extra piece of information does the boxplot of weights add to your understanding of the plot?

   d. Construct the same marginal plot as in (d), except use histograms on the margins instead of boxplots. Which marginal plot do you prefer? Explain your choice.

4. Open *MnWage.MTW.*

   a. Construct a scatter plot of the MinWage against Year. Give the plot the title Scatter Plot of Minimum Wage by Year, 1950–1997. How would you characterize the overall trend in the plot?

   b. Since 1950, what is the longest period of time without an increase in the minimum wage? What is the approximate minimum wage during this period?

5. Open *Pulsea.mtw*

   a. Plot Pulse1 against Weight. Give the graph an appropriate title. Summarize what the graph suggests about the relationship between these two variables. Add Gender as a grouping variable to the plot. Does the relationship between Pulse1 and Weight differ much for the two genders?

   b. Construct a chart showing the frequency of smokers and nonsmokers in the class. Give the graph the title Counts of Smokers and Nonsmokers. Are there more smokers or nonsmokers in the class? Approximately how many of each are there?

   c. Construct a chart showing the frequency of smokers and nonsmokers separately by gender. Give the chart the title Counts of Smokers and Nonsmokers by Gender. Does smoking appear to be more common among males or among females in the class?

6. Open *Election.mtw* again.

   a. Create a new variable: 100 – Dem% – Rep%. What does this new variable represent? Name this new variable Other.

   b. On the same graph, plot Dem%, Rep%, and Other. Create a suitable title, and use a footnote as a legend to identify the different plots. Use the tick marks 1868:1996/16. Create a footnote to identify the three plots. Write a brief explanation of the patterns suggested by the plots.

7. Open *Pay2.mtw.* and create a scatter plot of Salary against Years Employed. Use the tick marks on the two axes that are present on the marginal plot for the same variables in Figure 4.7.

TUTORIAL
5

Numerical Methods for Describing Data

Measures of central tendency and variation are the foundation of descriptive statistics, but most are quite tedious to compute, even with a calculator. Fortunately, Minitab lets you generate a number of commonly used descriptive statistics for as many columns as you designate, using just a single command. In this tutorial, you will use Minitab to produce various statistics and graphs to describe single variables and how they might relate to other variables in the data set.

Objectives

In this tutorial, you learn how to:

- produce descriptive statistics

- produce descriptive statistics with accompanying graphs

- describe data for one variable separately for each value or category of another variable

- calculate frequencies for classes of data

- compute the covariance and the correlation between two variables

▼ 5.1 Describing Quantitative Data ▲

CASE STUDY: SPORTS — BASEBALL STADIUMS

You've been asked to write an article about Major League Baseball ballparks and their effects on the success of the teams that play in them. You've gathered some basic data about the capacity of each of the 28 parks and when each was built, as well as the attendance at each for each event in 1997 and the team performance in 1997. You intend to start the article by comparing some of the basic data between leagues and looking for relationships, if any, between attendance and team performance. You also want to learn how these variables vary between the American and National Leagues.

To get started:

- Start **Minitab**
- Maximize the **Session window**
- If necessary, enable the Session command language and make the output read-only

You'll be working with the file, *Ballpark.mtw*, which is in the Student subdirectory:

- Open the worksheet ***Ballpark.mtw***
- Use **Help** to review the contents of the data set

The Help window in Figure 5-1 shows the information for these variables in the file: Team, League, ParkBlt (the year the park was built), Capacity, Attend (average attendance for the 1997 season), and Pct (percentage of games won in the 1997 season).

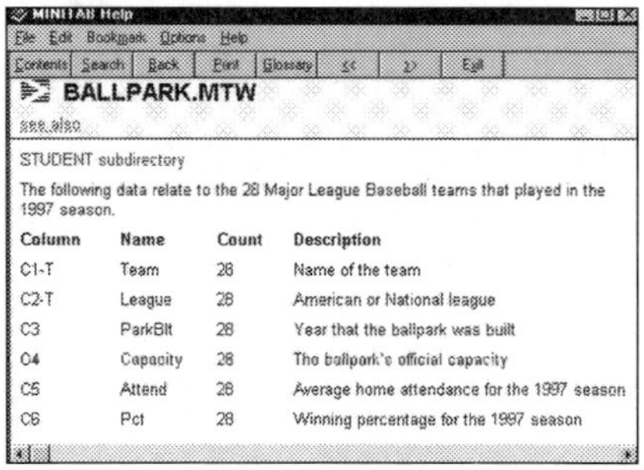

STUDENT subdirectory

The following data relate to the 28 Major League Baseball teams that played in the 1997 season.

Column	Name	Count	Description
C1-T	Team	28	Name of the team
C2-T	League	28	American or National league
C3	ParkBlt	28	Year that the ballpark was built
C4	Capacity	28	The ballpark's official capacity
C5	Attend	28	Average home attendance for the 1997 season
C6	Pct	28	Winning percentage for the 1997 season

FIGURE 5-1
The Help window showing information about Ballpark.mtw

Before analyzing the ballpark data, you should save the data in a file and this tutorial in a project:

- In the location where you are saving your work, save the worksheet as **5Ballprk.mtw**

- Save the work you have done thus far in this tutorial in a project named **T5.mpj**

You want to start the article with some descriptive statistics about the capacities and ages of the parks in both leagues. The age of each park is not in the data set, but you can calculate it (as of 1998) and store it as a new variable as follows:

- Choose **Calc > Calculator**

- Type **AgePark** as the new variable

- Enter, by clicking or typing, **1998 - ParkBlt** as the "Expression" and click **OK**

The ages of the 28 ballparks are stored in C7 AgePark. To obtain descriptive statistics for Capacity and AgePark:

- Choose **Stat > Basic Statistics > Display Descriptive Statistics**

- Double-click **C4 Capacity** and then **C7 AgePark** to enter them as the "Variables"

The completed Display Descriptive Statistics dialog box should look as shown in Figure 5-2.

FIGURE 5-2

The Display Descriptive Statistics dialog box

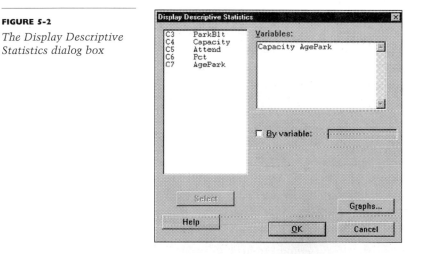

- Click **OK**

Minitab automatically displays in the Session window the statistics you requested, as shown in Figure 5-3.

FIGURE 5-3

*Basic statistics for
Capacity and AgePark*

```
MTB > Describe 'Capacity' 'AgePark'.
```

Descriptive Statistics

Variable	N	Mean	Median	TrMean	StDev	SE Mean
Capacity	28	50466	49695	50561	7549	1427
AgePark	28	30.64	28.00	29.62	24.87	4.70

Variable	Minimum	Maximum	Q1	Q3
Capacity	33871	64593	44866	55944
AgePark	2.00	86.00	9.50	35.50

The Display Descriptive Statistic command produces a variety of measures of central tendency and of variability for each variable you select. In particular, it produces the following statistics:

- N, the number of cases

- Mean, the mean

- Median, the median

- TrMean, the trimmed mean

- StDev, the sample standard deviation

- SE Mean, the standard error of the mean

- Minimum, the variable's smallest value

- Maximum, the variable's largest value

- Q1, the first quartile

- Q3, the third quartile

You have probably studied most of these statistics in class, but some may not be familiar to you. One you may not be familiar with is the *trimmed mean* (TrMean), which provides a more representative measure of central tendency. The sample mean can be distorted by extreme or outlying values. In such cases, it is often desirable to obtain a trimmed mean. Minitab calculates the trimmed mean by discarding the top 5% and the bottom 5% of the data. It then computes the mean of the central 90%. When no extreme values are present, the mean and the trimmed mean are relatively close in value, as they are in Figure 5-3 for both Capacity and AgePark.

▼ **Note** When the column you are describing contains missing values, the output for Display Descriptive Statistics includes a count of how many missing values there are. ▲

It is nearly always helpful to look at a graph as you study descriptive statistics. Minitab provides several graphical options when it computes descriptive statistics. Suppose you decide to obtain a histogram of both Capacity and

AgePark. So that you will be able to move between the two graphs easily, you should restore the split screen, with the Session window on top and the Data window on the bottom:

- Click the **Restore** button  on the title bar

  To obtain the histograms:

- Click the **Edit Last Dialog** toolbar button

- Click **Graphs** and select **Histogram of data**

- Click **OK** twice

Minitab produces, in addition to the output in the Session window, a histogram for each of these two variables, Capacity and AgePark. You can move easily from one to another by clicking in the graph you want to view. The two histograms are shown in Figure 5-4.

FIGURE 5-4

Histograms for Capacity and AgePark

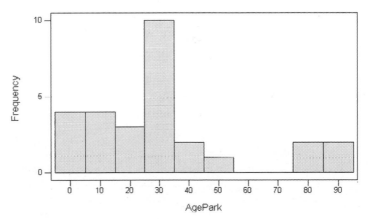

The distribution of Capacity is almost symmetrical, whereas that for AgePark is not. Indeed, the most distinctive feature of the latter histogram is that it shows clearly that the ages of the parks are divided into two distinct groups: those built within the past 50 years or so and the smaller number that were built before that. The histogram shows a peak of building between 35 and 45 years ago. During this peak period, a number of teams moved to new cities (and thus to new ballparks) and both leagues added new teams through expansion. The gap in the histogram occurs during the Great Depression and the Second World War.

You will see other examples of the graphical options that accompany Descriptive Statistics and other Minitab analysis commands later in this tutorial and in later tutorials.

▼ 5.2   Constructing Other Descriptive Statistics ▲

A measure of variation commonly used in business is the *Mean Absolute Deviation (MAD)*. The MAD is the average of the absolute values of the deviations of the data from the mean. This statistic is not directly available in Minitab, but it can be obtained using Minitab functions.

You need to create a new variable representing the absolute values of the differences between the values for Capacity and their mean. To obtain the MAD for the variable Capacity, which has mean 50,466:

- Click in the **Session window** and maximize that window

- Choose **Calc > Calculator**

- Type the name **AbsDiff** in the "Store result in variable" text box

- Enter, by clicking or typing, **ABSO(Capacity – 50466)** as the "Expression" and click **OK**

- Use the **Window menu** to move to the Data window to see that the column C8 AbsDiff contains the absolute values of the difference between Capacity and the average capacity

To obtain the mean of these absolute deviations:

- Choose **Calc > Column Statistics**

- Select **Mean**, choose **AbsDiff** as the "Input variable," and click **OK**

The Session window displays the value of the MAD statistic — 5947.2 — as shown in Figure 5-5. This value indicates that the 28 capacities vary from their mean — 50,466 — by an average of 5,947.2.

FIGURE 5-5

The value of the MAD statistic

```
MTB > Name C8 = 'AbsDiff'
MTB > Let 'AbsDiff' = ABSO(Capacity - 50466)
MTB > Mean 'AbsDiff'.
```

Column Mean

```
    Mean of AbsDiff = 5947.2
```

As a measure of variability, the MAD is comparable to the standard deviation. For the variable Capacity, the value for MAD is less than the standard deviation, StDev = 7549 from Figure 5-3. Because the standard deviation is a key component of so many statistical methods, it is much more widely known and used than the MAD.

▼ 5.3   Describing Quantitative Data Separately for Each Value of a Second Variable ▲

Earlier you obtained a description of the ballparks' capacities. The mean and median capacity of the 28 major league team ballparks are 50,466 and 49,695, respectively. The standard deviation is 7,549. How do these values change if you look at the American League and the National League separately? It is simple to obtain a description of Capacity for each league and to obtain a boxplot of Capacity for both leagues:

- Choose **Stat > Basic Statistics > Display Descriptive Statistics**

- Press **F3** to clear previous entries

- Select **C4 Capacity** as the variable

- Click **By variable** and enter **C2 League** in the "By variable" text box

- Click **Graphs** and select **Boxplot of data**

- Click **OK** twice

The boxplots of Capacity by League are shown in Figure 5-6.

FIGURE 5-6

Boxplots of Capacity by League

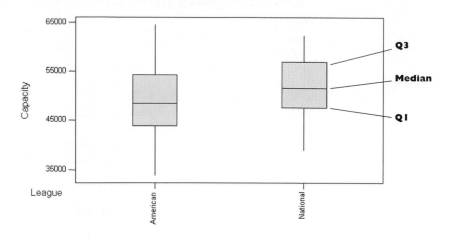

Boxplots of Capacity by League

The boxplots indicate that the range of capacities (the largest value to the smallest) is greater for the American League than for the National League. However, the median and the quartiles, Q1 and Q3, for the National League are greater than those for the American League.

The graph in Figure 5-6 comes as an option to the Display Descriptive Statistics command, and there are no other options available. To see the numerical output in this case, return to the Session window:

- Click the **Session window** toolbar button ▣

The output is shown in Figure 5-7.

FIGURE 5-7

Descriptive statistics of Capacity by League

```
MTB > Describe 'Capacity';
SUBC>   By 'League';
SUBC>   GBoxplot.
```

Descriptive Statistics

Variable	League	N	Mean	Median	TrMean	StDev
Capacity	American	14	48935	48470	48886	8012
	National	14	51996	51576	52225	7009

Variable	League	SE Mean	Minimum	Maximum	Q1	Q3
Capacity	American	2141	33871	64593	43813	54280
	National	1873	38884	62363	47604	56923

The output consists of all of the summary statistics referred to previously but for each league separately. The average capacity in the National League (51966) exceeds that in the American League by about 3,000. There is about the same difference in the median capacity for the two leagues. There is more variability among capacities in the American League (StDev = 8012) than in the National League (StDev = 7009). These values are consistent with the boxplots in Figure 5-6.

Figure 5-7 contains a "description" of the variable Capacity separately for (that is, "by") each value (American and National) of the variable League. In general, a description of a first variable by a second variable consists of a separate set of summary statistics for the first variable for the group defined by each value of the second variable. Usually the second variable, in this case, League, is either qualitative or quantitative with just a small number of values.

Two other variables you want to describe by League are average attendance and the percentage that average attendance is of capacity. You will calculate the latter rounded to the nearest whole number.

- Choose **Calc > Calculator**

- Type the name **Att/Cap** in the "Store result in variable" text box

- Enter, by clicking or typing, **ROUND(100*Attend/Capacity)** as the "Expression" and click **OK**

- Make the **Data window** active to see that, for each club, the column C9 Att/Cap contains the average attendance expressed as a percentage of capacity and rounded to the nearest whole number

To obtain a description of Attend and Att/Cap by League:

- Choose **Stat > Basic Statistics > Display Descriptive Statistics**

- Select **C5 Attend** and **C9 Att/Cap** to enter them as the "Variables"

- Click **Graphs**, deselect the option **Boxplot of data,** and click **OK** twice

The Session window output is shown in Figure 5-8.

FIGURE 5-8

Descriptive statistics of Attend and Att/Cap, by League

```
MTB > Describe 'Attend' 'Att/Cap';
SUBC>   By 'League'.
```

Descriptive Statistics

Variable	League	N	Mean	Median	TrMean	StDev
Attend	American	14	28013	25870	27533	10251
	National	14	28421	25693	27616	9394
Att/Cap	American	14	58.36	55.50	57.17	22.21
	National	14	56.00	45.00	54.75	20.64

Variable	League	SE Mean	Minimum	Maximum	Q1	Q3
Attend	American	2740	15965	45816	18240	37485
	National	2511	18489	48006	21030	34858
Att/Cap	American	5.94	34.00	97.00	36.75	76.75
	National	5.52	31.00	96.00	40.75	71.50

Mean attendance is slightly higher in the National League (28,421) than in the American League (28,013), although if you compare medians, that order is reversed. There is more variability in attendance in the American League (StDev = 10251) than in the National League (StDev = 9394).

The results are not as close when attendance as a percentage of capacity is considered. The mean value of Att/Cap for the American League (58.36%) is considerably higher than that for the National League (56.00%). The difference in the median values for Att/Cap is much greater — 55.50% for the American League and only 45.00% for the National League.

▼ **Note** Sometimes you need to be able to save the descriptive statistics, for example, for use in a later calculation. In this case, you can use Store Descriptive Statistics instead of Display Descriptive Statistics. The former command offers a more extensive list of statistics than the latter does. It also allows you to choose which statistics to display and save. ▲

■ At this point, in the location where you are saving your work, save the work you have done thus far in this tutorial in the project *T5.mpj*

▼ 5.4   Calculating Frequencies ▲

You want to include in your report information about the number of teams in each league. The Tally command counts the number of times each distinct value in a column/variable occurs. These counts are sometimes called *frequencies*. To count how many ballparks are in each league:

■ Choose **Stat > Tables > Tally**

■ Select **C2 League** to enter it as the variable

You also can ask for the corresponding percentages (100 times the counts divided by the total number), the cumulative counts, and the cumulative percents. In this example, you want to examine just the counts and percents:

■ Verify that **Counts**, the default, is selected and select **Percents**

The completed Tally dialog box should look as shown in Figure 5-9.

FIGURE 5-9

The Tally dialog box

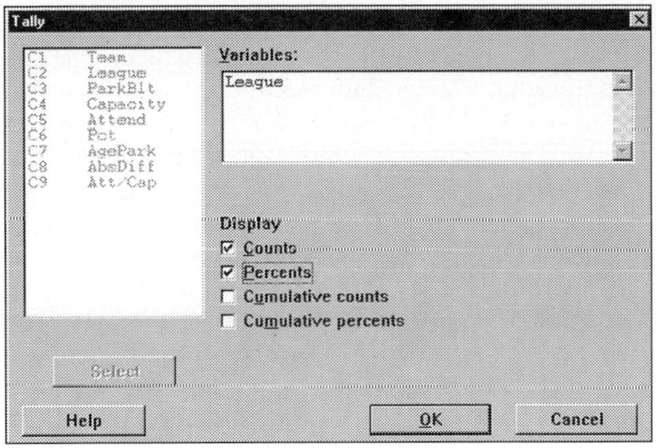

■ Click **OK**

Minitab produces a table showing the counts and percents you requested. Figure 5-10 shows the Session window with the tallies.

FIGURE 5-10

Tally results for League

```
MTB > Tally 'League';
SUBC>   Counts;
SUBC>   Percents.
```

Summary Statistics for Discrete Variables

League	Count	Percent
American	14	50.00
National	14	50.00
N =	28	

The table shows that there are 14 ballparks/teams in each league and, as a result, each league contains 50% of the ballparks. Next, you want to divide the 28 teams into four categories that indicate how full the ballparks were in 1997:

1. Those at least 80% full

2. Those between 60% and 79% full

3. Those between 40% and 59% full

4. Those less than 40% full

From the output in Figure 5-8, you can see that there are no values for Att/Cap below 20%, so you don't need a fifth interval.

You will use the Code command to create a new text variable, PerFull, whose values are based on the values for Att/Cap:

■ Choose **Manip > Code > Numeric to Text**

■ Select **C9 Att/Cap** to enter it in the "Code data from columns" text box

- Type **PerFull** in the "Into columns" text box

- Under "Original values," type, on successive lines, **80:100**, **60:79**, **40:59**, and **0:39**

- Under "New," type, on successive lines, **80% +**, **60-79%**, **40-59%**, and **0-39%**

The Code - Numeric to Text dialog box should look as shown in Figure 5-11.

- Click **OK**

To obtain a tally of the variable C10 PerFull with counts, percents, and cumulative percents:

- Choose **Stat > Tables > Tally**

- Double-click **C10 PerFull** to enter it as the variable

- Check **Counts, Percents, and Cumulative Percents** and then click **OK**

The resulting output is shown in Figure 5-12.

```
MTB > Tally 'PerFull';
SUBC>   Counts;
SUBC>   Percents;
SUBC>   CumPercents.
```

Summary Statistics for Discrete Variables

PerFull	Count	Percent	CumPct
20-39%	7	25.00	25.00
40-59%	9	32.14	57.14
60-79%	7	25.00	82.14
80% +	5	17.86	100.00
N=	28		

Only five of the ballparks were, on average, at least 80% full. This represented less than 18% of all ballparks. Conversely, just over 82% of ballparks were, on average, less than 80% full.

▼ **Note** In Figure 5-12, the categories of the text variable PerFull begin with numbers and are arranged in numerical order, which is what you want. By default, text variables are arranged in either alphabetical order or, as in this case, numerical order. Recall that you can select the order in which the categories for a text variable appear by using the Set Column command on the Editor menu. ▲

▼ 5.5   Computing Covariance ▲

So far in this tutorial, you have characterized the behavior of individual variables such as Att/Cap, the attendance as a percentage of capacity. You now want to examine the relationship between two variables, namely, Att/Cap (for 1997) and Pct, the percentage of games won in the 1997 season. You want to learn how success on the field relates to the ability to fill a ballpark.

First, produce a scatter plot of the relationship between these two variables:

- Choose **Graph > Plot**

- Select **C9 Att/Cap** as the "Y" variable and **C6 Pct** as the "X" variable

- Click **OK**

The scatter plot should look as shown in Figure 5-13.

FIGURE 5-13

Scatter plot of Att/Cap against Pct

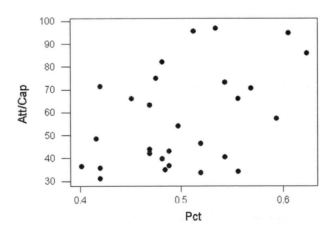

The scatter plot suggests only a weak, linear relationship between Att/Cap and Pct. Even the direction of the relationship is unclear. You decide to find the *covariance*, a numerical summary of the strength of the linear relationship between two variables:

- Choose **Stat > Basic Statistics > Covariance**

- Select **C9 Att/Cap** and **C6 Pct** to enter them as the "Variables" and click **OK**

The resulting Session window should resemble that shown in Figure 5-14.

FIGURE 5-14

Covariance between Att/Cap and Pct

```
MTB > Covariance 'Att/Cap' 'Pct'.
```

Covariances

```
           Att/Cap        Pct
Att/Cap   444.00397
Pct         0.54100    0.00351
```

The values 444.00397 and 0.00351 are, respectively, the variance of Att/Cap and the variance of Pct. (Recall that variance is the square of the standard deviation.) The *covariance* between the two variables is .54100. A *positive* covariance suggests that high values for one variable tend to be associated with high values for the other. However, because the value of the covariance depends on the units associated with the two variables, it is difficult to determine from the value .54100 the exact strength of the relationship. You need a way of measuring that strength that does not depend on the units.

▼ 5.6   Computing Correlation ▲

Pearson's correlation coefficient, or, simply, the correlation, measures the strength of the linear relationship between two quantitative variables. It is independent of the units of the two variables and is usually designated by r. The correlation always lies between −1 and 1. You want to obtain, in addition to the correlation between Pct and Att/Cap, the correlation between Pct and Attend and between Pct and Capacity.

- Choose **Stat > Basic Statistics > Correlation**

- Select **C6 Pct**, **C9 Att/Cap**, **C5 Attend**, and **C4 Capacity** to enter them as the "Variables"

- Deselect **Display p-values**

The completed Correlation dialog box should look as shown in Figure 5-15.

FIGURE 5-15

The Correlation dialog box

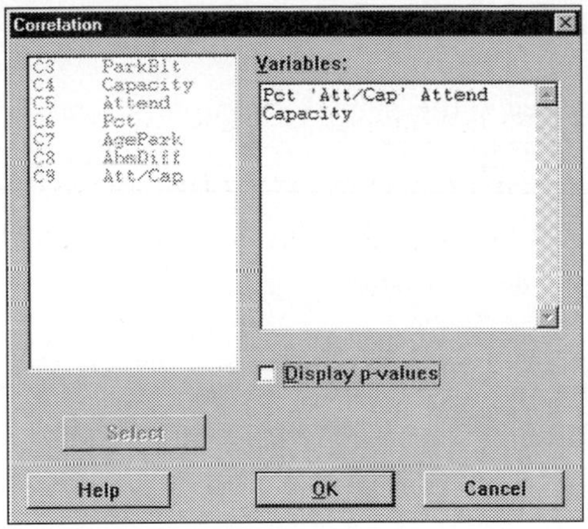

■ Click **OK**

The correlations appear as shown in Figure 5-16.

FIGURE 5-16

Correlation matrix for four quantitative variables

```
MTB > Correlation 'Pct' 'Att/Cap' 'Attend' 'Capacity';
SUBC>   NoPValues.
```

Correlations (Pearson)

```
             Pct   Att/Cap    Attend
Att/Cap    0.434
Attend     0.589     0.910
Capacity   0.270    -0.404    -0.012
```

The output consists of a triangle (half-matrix) consisting of six correlations. The ones you are most interested in are in the first column and consist of the correlation between Pct and, in turn, Att/Cap, Attend, and Capacity. All three are positive. Attend (attendance) is the variable most highly correlated ($r = .589$) with Pct. The correlation between Pct and Att/Cap is only .435. The middle column of correlations shows the high ($r = .910$) correlation between Att/Cap and Attend and the negative correlation ($r = -.402$) between Capacity and Att/Cap. The variables Attend and Capacity are almost independent ($r = -.012$). Not shown in Figure 5-16 is the fact that the correlation of a variable with itself is 1.

You will perform further analyses of these data in Tutorial 16.

▼ 5.7   Viewing the History Window ▲

You have looked at the ballpark data from several different perspectives. Because it's easy to forget what you have done previously with your data in a particular session, Minitab includes a History window that lists most of the commands you used in a session. To view this window:

■ Choose **Window > History**

Figure 5-17 shows a small part of the current History window.

FIGURE 5-17

Part of the History Window

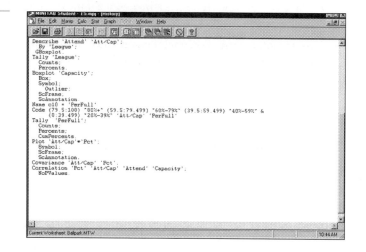

Whereas the Session window contains Minitab commands and plus the resulting output, the History window records only the commands that Minitab has processed; it does not show the output. For example, the History window displays the session command corresponding to the last command you issued, Correlation 'Pct' 'Att/Cap' 'Attend', 'Capacity'.

You can use the History window to retrace your analysis of a data set. You can also copy commands from either the Session or the History window and paste them into the Command Line Editor. There, you can modify these commands and submit the modified commands for execution.

For example, suppose you want the covariance of Attend and Pct — instead of Att/Cap and Pct — and then the correlation between Pct and (just) the two variables Att/Cap and Attend. You could use the menu commands but taking the following steps would be as quick, if not quicker:

■ In the History window, highlight the **last three lines** (the covariance and the correlation commands and subcommand)

■ Choose **Edit > Command Line Editor**

■ In the first line, change **Att/Cap** to **Attend**

■ In the second line, eliminate '**Capacity**' (but leave the semicolon)

■ Click **Submit Commands**

The new output appears in the Session window.

You feel that you have performed all of the analyses on the ballpark data that you need for the introductory section of your article. Now you can print the descriptive data that you want from the Session window. Remember that you don't need to print the entire window:

- Highlight only the section that you want to print

- Choose **File > Print Session Window**

  To finish this tutorial:

- Save the current project *T5.mpj* and then exit from Minitab

Minitab Command Summary

This section describes the menu commands introduced in, or related to, this tutorial. Use Minitab's on-line Help to find a complete explanation of all menu commands.

Minitab Menu Commands

Menu	Command	Description
Stat		
	Basic Statistics	
	Display Descriptive Statistics	Provides a numeric summary of central tendency and variability for one or more columns. Optionally, summarizes each level of a specified By variable.
	Store Descriptive Statistics	Computes and saves statistics selected by the user. Optionally, computes the selected statistics for each level of a specified By variable.
	Correlation	Computes the correlation between pairs of variables.
	Covariance	Determines the covariance between pairs of variables.
	Tables	
	Tally	Calculates a count (or frequency) of each value of a variable or variables.
Window		
	History	Displays a record of most commands issued during a session.

Matching

Match the following terms to their definitions by placing the correct letter next to
the term it describes.

_____ SE Mean

_____ Trimmed mean

_____ Correlation

_____ Counts

_____ MAD

_____ Second quartile

_____ Tally

_____ StDev

_____ By

_____ History window

a. A sample mean after deleting the top 5% and bottom
   5% of the data

b. Another name for the median

c. Minitab notation for the sample standard deviation

d. Minitab notation for the standard error of a sample
   mean

e. Another name for frequencies

f. A Minitab command to determine the frequencies for
   the data in a column

g. A statistic, other than the standard deviation, that
   measures the spread around the mean

h. A Minitab command that summarizes the linear relationship between two variables

i. The location of a record of commands issued during a
   session

j. The subcommand that provides for descriptions of
   subgroups

True/False

Mark the following statements with a _T_ or an _F_.

_____ The MAD is included as part of the descriptive statistics output.

_____ The Tally command can be used only with text data.

_____ The output from the Display Descriptive Statistics command is displayed
in the Session window.

_____ The Display Descriptive Statistics output includes the sample standard
deviation.

_____ The sample variance is part of the Display Descriptive Statistics output.

_____ The History window records the commands, subcommands, and output
generated in the Session window.

_____ A stem-and-leaf display is one of the optional graphs for the Display
Descriptive Statistics command.

_____ You can use the By subcommand with both the Tally and
the Correlation commands.

_____ Minitab designates the cumulative percentage of values greater than the given category with CumPercent.

_____ The output associated with the Covariance command does not include a p-value.

Practice Problems

If necessary, use Help to review the contents of the data sets referred to in the following problems.

1. Open *Crimes.mtw*.

   a. Summarize the rates for each division. Create boxplots of the rates as the graphical option. Explain how, if at all, crime rates differ by district.

   b. Repeat (a) for each region. Does there appear to be any differences in crime rates among regions?

2. Open *Ads2.mtw*.

   a. Describe the ratio data for the three years. Create dotplots of the ratios as the graphical option. Has the ratio increased over the years? If so, did it increase consistently?

   b. Unstack the ratio by Year. Place the data in C6–C8. Name these columns 1989, 1991, and 1993.

   Huh?

   c. Compute the correlation matrix for the yearly ratio data. Are the ratios for each year correlated with one another? If so, to what extent are they correlated?

   d. Determine the covariances between each year's data. What value is on the diagonal of the resulting matrix? Verify your answer using the results from (a). Is the covariance matrix as informative as the correlation matrix in (b)?

3. Open *Pulsea.mtw*.

   a. Use the Tally command to find out the number and percentage of students who ran in place.

   b. Obtain the increase (C2–C1) in pulse rate in C9. Name the variable Increase.

   c. Obtain a description of Increase for those who did and did not run in place. Obtain histograms and boxplots of the increases as the graphical option. Compare the means and the standard deviations for the two groups. Do these results make sense? Of the histograms or the boxplots, which best helps you compare the two sets of increases? Explain.

   d. Unstack the heights and the weights of the students using Gender as the subscript.

   e. Compute and compare the correlation between height and weight for the two groups.

4. Open *Prof.mtw.*

   a. Use the Tally command to summarize the frequency of the different levels of the courses surveyed (C9).

   b. How many questionnaires were filled out, on average, in the surveyed courses? Does the median differ much from the mean?

   c. Create a scatter plot of Instruct and Course ratings. Correlate these two variables, and interpret your findings.

5. Open *Mnwage.mtw.*

   a. Summarize the minimum wage variable. What is the most appropriate measure of central tendency? What is the most appropriate measure of spread?

   b. Create a scatter plot of minimum wage versus year. Describe its shape.

   c. Would you prefer to use the output from (a), (b), or both in a report? Briefly explain your answer.

TUTORIAL 6

Distributions and Random Data

Probability distributions are the foundation of inferential statistics. In this tutorial, you will use Minitab to compute probabilities and percentiles for various distributions, including the Normal distribution. You will also generate random samples from these distributions and learn how to check whether a data set comes from a normal population.

Objectives

In this tutorial, you learn how to:

- compute individual and cumulative binomial probabilities
- generate random samples from a discrete population with a specified probability distribution
- generate random samples from a normal population
- generate normal scores and produce normal probability plots
- use the inverse cumulative probability function to look up percentiles for a normal distribution
- sample from a column, with and without replacement

▼ 6.1   Calculating Binomial Probabilities ▲

CASE STUDY: BIOLOGY — BLOOD TYPES

You have been a Red Cross volunteer for the last few years. The volunteer coordinator, Paul Van Vleck, hears that you are learning how to use Minitab. Eager to put your skills to work, he tells you that the Type O blood supply is running dangerously low and that he anticipates needing from 10 to 12 additional pints for surgeries scheduled in the upcoming week. Paul has already recruited 25 unrelated potential donors. He wants to know if it is likely that next week's need for Type O blood can be met using these donors or if he will have to recruit more.

Individual Binomial Probabilities

Your reference books tell you that, on average, 45 out of 100 people have Type O blood, so the probability of a randomly selected individual having Type O blood is .45. To help Paul, you need to compute $P(X = K)$ — the probability of K people having Type O blood — for the values of K = 0, 1, 2, . . . , 25. In this case, $P(X = K)$ is a binomial probability function with n = 25 trials and p = .45. You could compute these probabilities using a calculator, but it would be very tedious. You also could obtain these probabilities from a table, but not all sets of probability tables cover all values of n and p. Instead, you decide to calculate the probabilities using Minitab.

To get started:

- Start **Minitab**

- Maximize the **Session window**

- If necessary, enable the **Session command language** and make the output read-only

- Choose **Window > Worksheet 1*****

- In the location where you are saving your work, save this project as **T6.mpj**

Minitab lets you compute at once all of the probabilities $P(X = 0)$, $P(X = 1)$, . . . , $P(X = 25)$. Begin by creating a column containing the integers 0, 1, 2, 3, . . . , 25 for K. Although you could type these numbers directly into the Data window, there is a much easier way to enter them:

- Choose **Calc > Make Patterned Data > Simple Set of Numbers**

- Type **K** in the "Store patterned data in" text box

- Type **0** (zero) in the "From first value" text box

- Type **25** in the "To last value" text box

The completed Simple Set of Numbers dialog box looks as shown in Figure 6-1.

FIGURE 6-1

The Simple Set of Numbers dialog box

The completed Simple Set of Numbers dialog box

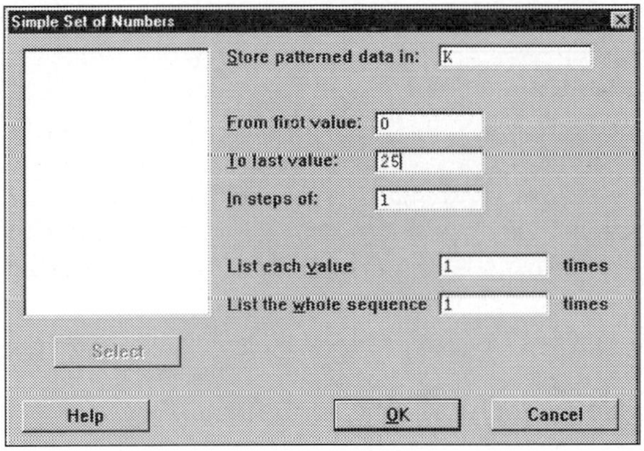

- Click **OK**

Minitab enters the integers 0–25 in the first column much more quickly than you could type them.

To obtain the binomial probabilities for each value of K in C1:

- Choose **Calc > Probability Distributions > Binomial**

- Type **25** as the "Number of trials" and **.45** as the "Probability of success"

- Select **C1 K** as the "Input column"

The completed Binomial Distribution dialog box looks as shown in Figure 6-2.

FIGURE 6-2

The Binomial Distribution dialog box

The Binomial Distribution dialog box

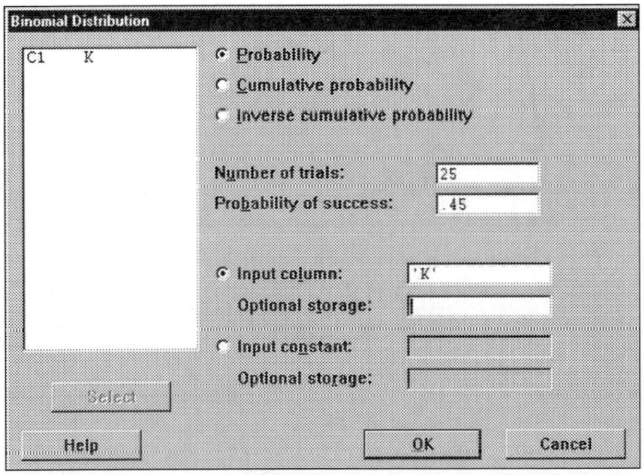

- Click **OK**

Minitab lists the complete binomial probability distribution for n = 25 and p = 0.45 in the Session window, as shown in Figure 6-3. Scroll the Session window to see the complete listing.

FIGURE 6-3

Binomial probability distribution in the Session window

```
MTB > PDF 'K';
SUBC>  Binomial 25 .45.
```

Probability Density Function

Binomial with n = 25 and p = 0.450000

x	P(X = x)
0.00	0.0000
1.00	0.0000
2.00	0.0001
3.00	0.0004
4.00	0.0018
5.00	0.0063
6.00	0.0172
7.00	0.0381
8.00	0.0701
9.00	0.1084
10.00	0.1419
11.00	0.1583
12.00	0.1511
13.00	0.1236
14.00	0.0867
15.00	0.0520
16.00	0.0266
17.00	0.0115
18.00	0.0042
19.00	0.0013
20.00	0.0003
21.00	0.0001
22.00	0.0000
23.00	0.0000
24.00	0.0000
25.00	0.0000

Minitab displays the probability distribution in two columns. The first column contains the values for the possible number of successes (people with Type O blood). The second lists the corresponding probability of obtaining exactly that number of successes. For example, the probability of having exactly 11 people in this sample with Type O blood is 0.1583.

These probability values are rounded to the nearest ten-thousandth, so probabilities less than 0.00005 are listed as 0.0000. For example, the probability of obtaining exactly one Type O individual in your sample isn't really 0.0000 — it's less than 0.00005.

▼ **Note** The menu under Probability Distributions lists three groups of probability distributions, many of which you will not have heard of. The first group consists of the most widely used continuous distributions. The second group, including the Binomial, consists of the most popular discrete distributions. The final group consists of less frequently used continuous distributions. ▲

The Probability Distributions command calculates probabilities, density function values, cumulative probabilities, and percentiles for the discrete and continuous random variables listed in the submenu. If you would like more information about these distributions or the terms used here, use Help to obtain information on probability distributions.

You can tell Minitab to save the probabilities in a column in the worksheet:

- Click the **Edit Last Dialog** toolbar button 🔲
- Click the first "Optional storage" text box
- Type **'P(X=K)'** (be sure to type the single quotation marks) and press ⏎
- Click the **Current Data window** toolbar button 🔲

Column C2, with the name P(X = K), lists the binomial probabilities, as shown in Figure 6-4. You will have to scroll down to see the entire distribution in the Data window.

FIGURE 6-4

Binomial probability distribution

K	P(X=K)
0	0.000000
1	0.000007
2	0.000065
3	0.000407
4	0.001830
5	0.006290
6	0.017155
7	0.038097
8	0.070133
9	0.108387
10	0.141889
11	0.158306
12	0.151110
13	0.123636
14	0.086705
15	0.052023
16	0.026603
17	0.011523
18	0.004190
19	0.001263
20	0.000310
21	0.000060
22	0.000009
23	0.000001
24	0.000000
25	0.000000

Minitab rounds probabilities to the nearest ten-thousandth in the Session window. In the worksheet, by default, Minitab displays results to the nearest one-millionth. As you can see, P(X = 11), which was rounded to 0.1583 in the Session window, takes the more accurate value 0.158306 in the worksheet. Also, the probability of exactly one person with Type O blood is not 0, but 0.000007.

According to the probabilities, you are most likely to obtain 10, 11, or 12 people with Type O blood in your sample of 25 (these are the values with the highest probabilities). However, these values will occur only 14.2%, 15.8%, and 15.1% of the time, respectively. Collectively, though, you have almost a 50% chance that the 25 donors will yield 10, 11, or 12 people with Type O blood (14.2 + 15.8 + 15.1 = 45.1%).

When you don't need all values of the probability distribution, you can compute the probability for only a single value:

- Click the **Edit Last Dialog** toolbar button ▣

- Click the **Input constant** option button and type **10** as the "Input constant"

- Press ⏎

The Session window shows that the probability that X = 10 is 0.1419. Verify that you obtained equivalent results in Figures 6-3 and 6-4.

To confirm that the most likely values (highest probabilities) are 10, 11, and 12, produce a plot of this binomial distribution:

- Choose **Graph > Plot**

- Select **C2 P(X=K)** as the "Y" variable and **C1 K** as the "X" variable

- Click the "Display" **drop-down list arrow** and select **Project**

- Click **OK**

The plot appears as shown in Figure 6-5.

FIGURE 6-5

Plot of binomial probabilities against the number of successes, K

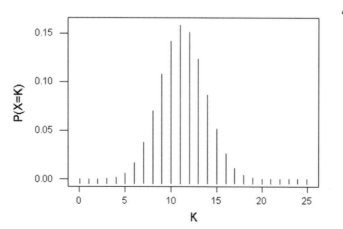

The heights of each line (projection) over each value for K correspond to the probability that K Type O blood donors will be found in the sample of 25. The peak of your plot occurs at K = 11; the next highest points are at K = 10 and K = 12. Indeed, the most likely numbers of Type O donors are 10, 11, and 12. Also, note that the shape of your plot is approximately bell-shaped.

To name this graph:

■ Use **Manage Graphs** to name this graph **Binomial (25, .45)**

■ Click the **Current Data window** toolbar button ▨

Cumulative Binomial Probabilities

In addition to calculating individual probabilities, Minitab can compute cumulative probabilities for either an entire column or an individual value. It does this by using the cumulative probability option in the Binomial Distribution dialog box (review Figure 6-2). After talking with the surgeons who will perform next week's surgery, Paul informs you that at least 13 pints of Type O blood will be needed. He needs to know the probability of getting 13 or more Type O donors in his sample of 25.

▼ **Note** For discrete random variables, individual probabilities are of the form $P(X = K)$, whereas cumulative probabilities are of the form $P(X \leq K)$. For binomial random variables, this is the probability of K or fewer successes. ▲

You can find the probability of 13 or more Type O donors by determining the probability of the complementary event: obtaining 12 or fewer individuals with Type O blood from the sample of 25. To do this:

■ Choose **Calc > Probability Distributions > Binomial**

■ Click the **Cumulative probability** option button

■ Verify that "Number of trials" is **25** and "Probability of success" is **.45**

■ Type **12** in the "Input constant" text box and press ⏎

The output appears in the Session window as shown in Figure 6-6.

FIGURE 6-6

Cumulative probability in the Session window

```
MTB > CDF 12;
SUBC>  Binomial 25 .45.
```

Cumulative Distribution Function

Binomial with n = 25 and p = 0.450000

```
        x      P( X <= x)
     12.00        0.6937
```

You tell Paul that there is a probability of .6937 (a 69% chance) that 12 or fewer people in this group of 25 will have Type O blood. Therefore, the likelihood of getting the 13 or more pints he needs is less than one-third (.3063 = a 31% chance).

Paul is concerned. The chances are quite good that he won't be able to provide enough Type O blood with only the current donors. He asks you to find the fewest number of unrelated donors he must have to be reasonably certain (probability $\geq$ .75) there will be at least 13 with Type O blood. You need to find the value of n so that $P(X \leq 12)$ is less than .25.

You must repeat the previous actions, substituting different values of n. To save time, start with a value of n = 33:

■ Click the **Edit Last Dialog** toolbar button 🔳

■ Type **33** as the "Number of trials" and press ↵

In the Session window, Minitab reports that a pool of 33 donors gives Paul a probability of .2062 of getting 12 or fewer Type O donors (and hence a probability of .7938 of getting 13 or more). This is fine. But to determine if you can get by with fewer donors, try n = 32:

■ Click the **Edit Last Dialog** toolbar button 🔳

■ Type **32** as the "Number of trials" and press ↵

When 32 donors are considered, the probability of 12 or fewer is .2512 (which means a probability of only .7488 of getting 13 or more). This doesn't quite meet Paul's requirements. You tell Paul that he will need at least 33 unrelated donors to obtain 13 or more pints of Type O blood with a probability of .75 or more. Minitab saved you quite a bit of calculation time.

Returning to the case in which Paul has only 25 volunteer donors, you can easily construct and display the complete set of cumulative probabilities for the values K = 0, 1, 2, . . . , 25.

■ Click the **Edit Last Dialog** toolbar button 🔳

■ Type **33** as the "Number of trials"

■ Click **Input column** and check that **K** appears in the corresponding text box

■ Type **'P(X<=K)'** in the first "Optional Storage" text box and press ↵

The complete set of cumulative probabilities should appear in C3 P(X<=K).

To plot these probabilities:

■ Choose **Graph > Plot**

■ Select **C3 P(X<=K)** as the "Y" variable, verify that **C1 K** is the "X" variable, and press ↵

The graph of cumulative probabilities is shown in Figure 6-7.

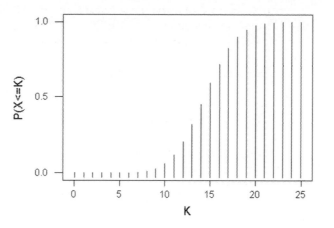

As the number of successes, K, increases, the cumulative probability of getting that number or fewer, $P(X \leq K)$, increases. Notice that the scale on the vertical axis (*y*-axis) of the cumulative probabilities runs from 0 to 1. By contrast, a review of the plot of individual binomial probabilities in Figure 6-5 shows that the vertical axis runs from 0 to .15. To name the plot of cumulative probabilities:

▪ Use Manage Graphs to name this graph **Cumulative Binomial (25, .45)**

You have completed your volunteer research on blood type samples. Before you turn your attention to the next case study:

▪ In the location where you are saving your work, save the work you have done thus far in this tutorial in the project **T6.mpj**

▼ 6.2   Generating Random Data from a Discrete Distribution ▲

CASE STUDY: MANAGEMENT — ENTREPRENEURIAL STUDIES

Your management professor, Dr. Michaels, has assigned a term paper in which you are to report on the pattern of sales for small-scale retail outlets for an industry of your choice. You select the music industry. As part of your research, you discover the fact that your neighborhood music outlet sells approximately 1,000 items of recorded music per week.

One of the references used in your Sales Management course, *The New York Times 1998 Almanac*, presents the percentages of recorded music sales for 1996 associated with different music genres. (The percentages are adjusted slightly from the original so that they sum to 100%.)

Genre	Percentage of Sales
1. Rock	33.7
2. Country	15.2
3. Urban-Contemporary	12.5
4. Pop	9.6
5. Rap	9.2
6. Gospel	4.4
7. Classical	3.5
8. Jazz	3.4
9. Other	8.5
	100.0

According to these data, the probability of a random music sale in 1996 being for rock music is .337. The corresponding probability for classical music is .035. You decide to use Minitab to generate a random sample of sales for one week. Specifically, you will *simulate* a week of music sales at the outlet and examine the differences between the population percentages and the sample percentages.

Minitab allows you to use your computer to obtain a random sample of data and simulate an experiment. This saves not only time but money.

In a new worksheet, you will enter three columns:

1. C1 contains the number (1 to 9) associated with each genre.

2. C2 contains the name of the genre.

3. C3 contains the theoretical probabilities for each genre.

The numbers in C1 for each genre are needed because the Minitab command you use to simulate the sales requires you to describe each genre with a numeric code.

Before entering this information, you need to create a new worksheet:

- Choose **File > New**

- In the New dialog box, double-click **Minitab Worksheet**

    Now, enter the data into C1–C3 using the case data as a guide:

- Assign the names **GenreN**, **Genre**, and **Prob** to columns C1, C2, and C3, respectively

- Type the values **1**, **2**, . . . , **8**, **9** in C1 GenreN to represent the nine genres numerically

- Type the names of the genre: **Rock**, **Country**, . . . , **Jazz**, **Other** in C2 Genre

- Type the values **.337**, **.152**, **.125**, **.096**, **.092**, **.044**, **.035**, **.034**, **.085** in C3 Prob to represent the corresponding probabilities

As part of your simulation, you will tell Minitab to produce a batch of random numbers. If you don't specify a *base*, or starting point, when generating random numbers, Minitab chooses its own. On the other hand, when you set a base, you can generate the same random data again simply by entering the same "seed" number. Specify 1996 as the base Minitab should use when generating the random numbers. (The choice of number for the base is arbitrary. However, it will determine the final sample, although not the randomness of the sample. The number 1996 was the year in which the data were recorded.)

- Choose **Calc > Set Base**

- Type **1996** in the "Set base of random data generator to" text box and press ⏎

You can now generate a random sample of 1,000 music sales using the theoretical (population) probabilities provided by the almanac that can be duplicated for future use:

- Choose **Calc > Random Data > Discrete**

- Type **1000** in the "Generate [ ] rows of data" text box and press (Tab)

- Type **Sample** in the "Store in column(s)" text box and press (Tab)

- Select **C1 GenreN** to enter it in the "Values in" text box

- Select **C3 Prob** to enter it in the "Probabilities in" text box

The completed Discrete Distribution dialog box should look as shown in Figure 6-8.

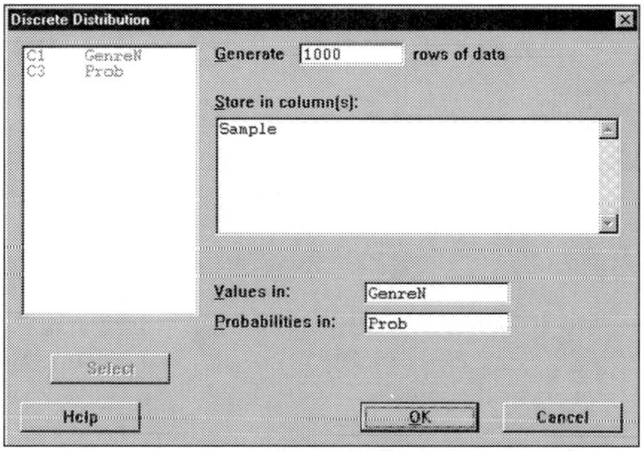

FIGURE 6-8

The Discrete Distribution dialog box

- Click **OK**

C4 Sample now lists 1,000 entries of the numbers 1, 2, 3, . . . , 8, 9 in random order and generated using the probabilities for each genre.

▼ **Note** If you think you'll want to regenerate these same data later, be sure to set the base to 1996. ▲

Presume these 1,000 values are the results of recording the genres for 1,000 sales of recorded music at your neighborhood music store. Before asking for the frequency for each genre, you can convert the 1,000 sales to text and determine the order in which the genres will be listed. To convert the values in C4 Sample to their original names:

- Choose **Manip > Code > Use Conversion Table**
- Select **C4 Sample** as the "Input Column"
- Type **TxSample** in the "Output Column" text box
- Select **C1 GenreN** as the "Column of original values"
- Select **C2 Genre** as the "Column of new values" and click **OK**

The original genre names will appear in C5 TxSample next to the corresponding numbers in C4 Sample. The "Use Conversion Table" option was used rather than the "Numeric to Text" option because the latter is limited to five values and you had nine.

To guarantee that, in later analysis, the nine genres will be listed in the order that they were provided in the almanac:

- Click anywhere in the **C5 TxSample** column
- Choose **Editor > Set Column > Value Order**
- Click **User-specified order**
- Arrange the nine genre names in the user-specified order text box in the following order: Rock, Country, Urban-Contemporary, Pop, Rap, Gospel, Classical, Jazz, Other
- Click **OK**

Nothing happens to the data in C5 TxSample, but when you obtain output involving this column the values will be ordered in the sequence you listed. (The default ordering is alphabetical.)

You can now use Tally to obtain the frequency with which each genre occurs in the sample:

- Choose **Stat > Tables > Tally**
- Select **C5 TxSample** to enter it as the "Variable"
- Verify that **Counts** is already checked
- Click the **Percents** check box and click **OK**

The frequency distribution for your sample appears in the Session window (Figure 6-9). (If you didn't set the base to 1996, your random sample Count and Percent values will differ slightly from those in Figure 6-9.)

FIGURE 6-9

Frequency distribution of genres in the sample

```
MTB > Tally 'TxSample';
SUBC>   Counts;
SUBC>   Percents.
```

Summary Statistics for Discrete Variable

TxSample	Count	Percent
Rock	338	33.80
Country	142	14.20
Urban-Co	138	13.80
Pop	96	9.60
Rap	102	10.20
Gospel	38	3.80
Classica	41	4.10
Jazz	29	2.90
Other	76	7.60
N=	1000	

Together, the music genres in C1 and C2 and the probabilities in C3 constitute the population of genres. Minitab selected 1,000 genres at random using the probabilities in C3. The percentages of music genres in this simulation are quite close to the percentages presented in the almanac. For example, in your simulated week of sales, 33.8% of sales were for rock music compared to 33.7% in the almanac. Similarly, in the sample 4.1% of sales were for classical music; the corresponding figure in the almanac was 3.5%. You can see that in a random sample of size n = 1,000, the percentages in the sample will not differ a great deal from those for the population. If you had selected a sample of only 100, the percentages in the sample would likely have deviated much more from the population percentages than in this sample.

You will return to this case study in Tutorial 12, so you should name and save this worksheet:

- In the location where you are saving your work, save the worksheet as **6Music.mtw**

- Save the work you have done thus far in this tutorial in the project **T6.mpj**

▼ 6.3   Generating Random Data from a Normal Distribution ▲

CASE STUDY: PHYSIOLOGY — HEIGHTS

Dr. Wei is a professor in the Physiology Department of the medical school on campus. She hopes that you can help her with a lecture she is preparing for her physiology class. She would like to explore with her class how to check whether physiological variables have a normal distribution. As one example, she would like to use the heights of college-age women which, she believes, have close to a normal distribution with a mean of 64 inches and a standard deviation of 3.1 inches. You suggest that she should illustrate methods for checking for normality by using both a random sample of heights from a population known to be normal and the actual heights for the 60 women students in her class. Dr. Wei will get the heights of her students from a questionnaire, while you agree to simulate the selection of a random sample of 60 heights from a normal population.

Your immediate task is to simulate the selection of a random sample of heights from the college-age women using the values μ = 64 inches and σ = 3.1 inches.

To obtain a new worksheet:

- Choose **File > New**

- Double-click **Minitab Worksheet** in the New dialog box

So that you can replicate the simulation, if necessary, you decide to set the base number. In this case, you choose the value 333 (Dr. Wei's office number is 333). To generate a sample of 60 observations from a normal population with a mean of 64 and a standard deviation of 3.1:

- Choose **Calc > Set Base**

- Type **333** in the "Set base of random data generator to" text box to enter it as the base and press ↵

- Choose **Calc > Random Data > Normal**

- Type **60** in the "Generate [ ] rows of data" text box and press ⏭Tab

- Type **'RanHts'** (you must include the single quotes) in the "Store in column(s)" text box and press ⏭Tab

- Type **64** as the "Mean" and **3.1** as the "Standard deviation"

The completed Normal Distribution dialog box should look as shown in Figure 6-10.

FIGURE 6-10

The Normal Distribution dialog box

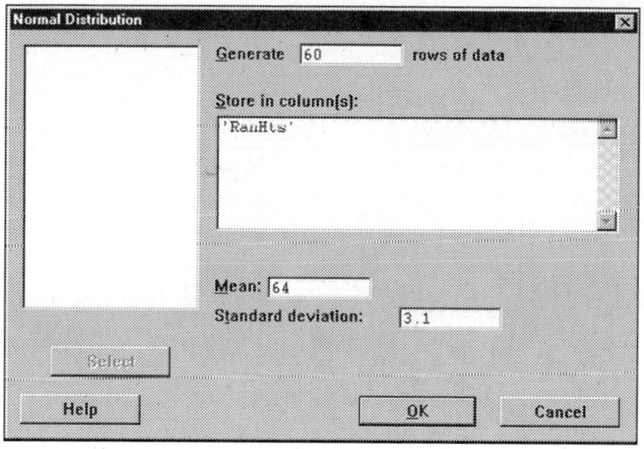

- Press ⏎

The worksheet contains 60 random values from a normal (μ = 64 and σ = 3.1) distribution.

Dr. Wei will present this data to her class as a random sample from the normal distribution of the heights of college-age women. She hopes to demonstrate that even though the population is normal, a randomly selected sample may well *not* be bell-shaped.

▼ 6.4 Checking Data for Normality ▲

You agree to help Dr. Wei compare the sample results to the normal population from which they were selected. Now, use Minitab to obtain the sample mean and standard deviation and a histogram of the sample heights with a superimposed normal curve:

- Choose **Stat > Basic Statistics > Display Descriptive Statistics**

- Select **C1 RanHts** to enter it as the "Variable"

- Click **Graphs** and then click **Histogram of data, with normal curve**

- Click **OK** twice

The histogram of the 60 heights, shown in Figure 6-11, are only approximately bell-shaped.

FIGURE 6-11

*Histogram of RanHts with
normal curve*

Histogram of RanHts, with Normal Curve

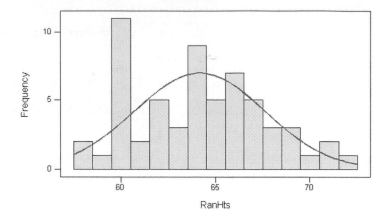

To view the numerical summaries, make the Session window active:

■ Click the **Session window** toolbar button

The results appear in Figure 6-12. The sample mean is 64.584 inches; the standard deviation is 2.931 inches. The normal curve that was superimposed on the histogram in Figure 6-12 has the mean of 64.584 inches and the standard deviation of 2.931 inches.

FIGURE 6-12

*Descriptive statistics for
RanHts*

```
MTB > Describe 'RanHts';
SUBC>   GNHist.
```

Descriptive Statistics

Variable	N	Mean	Median	TrMean	StDev	SE Mean
RanHts	60	64.584	64.523	64.635	2.931	0.378

Variable	Minimum	Maximum	Q1	Q3
RanHts	58.051	70.316	62.734	66.640

While the graph might be sufficient to convince Dr. Wei's class of the data's normality, you can use another Minitab feature to determine whether normality is a reasonable assumption. This is discussed next.

Obtaining the Normal Probability Plot Using Normal Scores

A common graphical technique for checking whether a sample comes from a normal population is to create a *normal probability plot (NPP)*.

▼ **Note** The normal scores associated with an ordered set of sample observations are the values you would expect to get if the observations followed the standard normal distribution. An NPP is a plot of the normal scores against the original values. The closer the points on the plot are to a straight line, the stronger the evidence that the data were drawn from a normal population. Ask your instructor for more information about this. ▲

You can easily generate an NPP in Minitab if you first generate normal scores for the data:

- Choose **Calc > Calculator**

- Type **NScores** in the "Store result in variable" text box (to create a column of normal scores)

- Enter, by clicking or typing, **NSCOR(RanHts)** as the "Expression"

The Calculator dialog box should look as shown in Figure 6-13.

FIGURE 6-13

The completed Calculator dialog box

- Click **OK**

- Click the **Current Data window** toolbar button 🔲

Minitab computes the normal scores and stores them in column C2 NScores.

To obtain the NPP:

- Choose **Graph > Plot**

- Select **C2 NScores** as the "Y" variable and **C1 RanHts** as the "X" variable

- Click the "Display" **drop-down list arrow** and select **Symbol**

- Click **OK**

The NPP is shown in Figure 6-14.

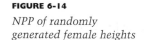

FIGURE 6-14

NPP of randomly generated female heights

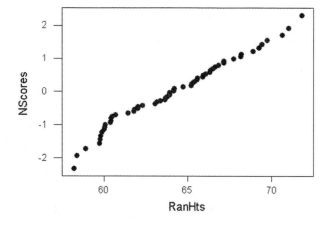

If an NPP approximates a straight line, you may reasonably conclude that the sample comes from a population that is approximately normal. Since the points on your scatter plot in Figure 6-14 do lie close to a straight line, this graph will make a good illustration for Dr. Wei's lecture on how to show that a variable is approximately normally distributed.

To name this graph:

- Use **Manage Graphs** to name this graph **NPP Random Heights**

Dr. Wei can produce a similar NPP for the self-reported heights she collected from her class. She stored the female students' heights and an ID variable in a Minitab file called *Height.mtw*. You would like to preview the results of plotting the data before Dr. Wei does so in class. The worksheet *Height.mtw* is in the Student subdirectory:

- Open the worksheet **Height.mtw**

- In the location where you are saving your work, save the worksheet as **6Height**

To produce the NPP, you need to obtain the normal scores for the heights in C2 Heights and then create the scatter plot:

- Choose **Calc > Calculator**

- Verify that **NScores** still appears in the "Store result in variable" text box

- Enter, by clicking or typing, **NSCOR(Heights)** as the "Expression"

- Click **OK**

  Minitab computes the normal scores.

- Choose **Graph > Plot**

- Verify that **NScores** is the "Y" variable and select **C2 Heights** as the "X" variable

- Click **OK**

  The NPP for the self-reported female heights appears in the Figure 6-15.

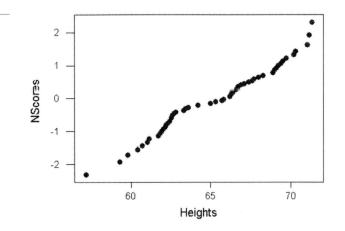

This plot isn't as straight as your simulation NPP. There is a bump in the middle, and the points at either end of the plot deviate from linear. You report to Dr. Wei that the NPP suggests that self-reported heights of college-age women may not be exactly normally distributed.

To name this graph:

- Use **Manage Graphs** to name this graph **NPP Actual Heights**

You decide to investigate the distribution of the self-reported heights further by constructing a stem-and-leaf display of C2 Heights:

- Choose **Graph > Stem-and-Leaf**

- Select **C2 Heights** to enter it as the variable

- Click **OK**

The resulting stem-and-leaf display is shown in Figure 6-16.

FIGURE 6-16

Stem-and-leaf display of the self-reported heights

```
MTB > Stem-and-Leaf 'Heights'.

Character Stem-and-Leaf Display

Stem-and-leaf of Heights   N = 60
Leaf Unit = 0.10

    1    57 2
    1    58
    3    59 38
    5    60 47
   10    61 01789
   21    62 01234555678
   24    63 346
   26    64 22
   30    65 0378
   30    66 2223466679
   20    67 1467
   16    68 0399
   12    69 012457
    6    70 23
    4    71 0013
```

The bump in the NPP in Figure 6-15 corresponds to the two peaks (bimodality) in the center of the display. The right-hand portion of the NNP corresponds to the "heavy" right-hand tail of the display. The isolated point on the left of the NNP corresponds to the outlying value on the left tail of the stem-and-leaf display.

▼ **Note** NPPs are frequently used in analysis of variance and regression. In fact, Minitab provides a number of slightly different, customized NPPs. You will encounter one of them in Tutorial 11. ▲

▼ 6.5   Determining Inverse Cumulative Functions for the Normal Distribution ▲

Impressed with your work, Dr. Wei returns a few weeks later to show you her follow-up work on self-reported heights. Using extensive information from all of her classes, she found that self-reported heights of college-age women appear to be approximately normally distributed with a mean of 64.25 inches and a standard deviation of 3.28 inches.

Dr. Wei is planning another study to investigate the relationship between bone structure and height. She wants to compare the bone structure distribution in four height groups. The height groups will be based on the quartiles of the population height distribution. She asks you to find the first and third quartiles.

To find the first quartile, Q1 (the 25th percentile), of the normal distribution with a mean of 64.25 and standard deviation of 3.28:

- Choose **Calc > Probability Distributions > Normal**

- Click the **Inverse cumulative probability** option button

- Type **64.25** as the "Mean" and **3.28** as the "Standard deviation"

- Click the **Input constant** option button and type **.25** as the "Input constant"

The completed Normal Distribution dialog box should look as shown in Figure 6-17.

FIGURE 6-17

The Normal Distribution dialog box

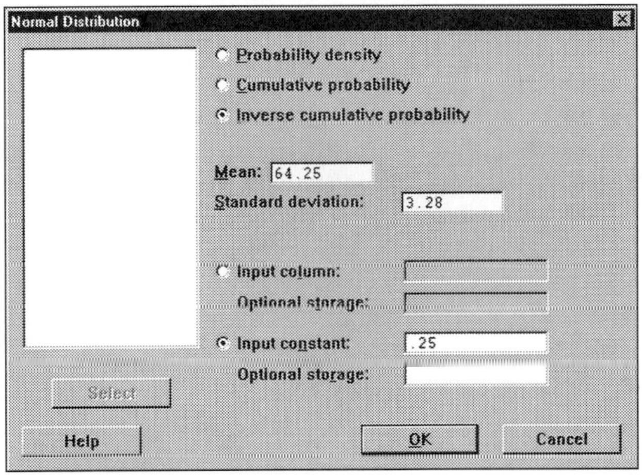

- Click **OK**

The Session window displays the results, as shown in Figure 6-18.

FIGURE 6-18

Inverse cumulative values

```
MTB > InvCDF .25;
SUBC>   Normal 64.25 3.28.
```

Inverse Cumulative Distribution Function

```
Normal with mean = 64.2500 and standard deviation = 3.28000


P( X <= x)          x
   0.2500      62.0377
```

The results indicate that 25% of the female heights are less than 62.04 inches. The first study group, therefore, consists of women who are less than 62.04 inches tall. The second group consists of women whose heights falls between 61.91 inches and the median of 64.25 inches. (Recall that for a normal distribution, the mean is equal to the median. So, in this case, the median is 64.25 inches.)

To obtain the third quartile, Q3 (75th percentile):

- Click the **Edit Last Dialog** toolbar button 🖫

- Type **.75** as the "Input constant" and press ↵

The output indicates that the 75th percentile of female heights is 66.4623 inches. So, the third group consists of women with heights between 64 and 66.46 inches. The last group contains those women who are taller than 66.46 inches.

Tutorial 7 introduces other uses for the cumulative and the inverse cumulative probability functions.

▼ 6.6   Sampling from a Column ▲

Dr. Wei will be presenting a paper at a convention in Chicago and wants eight students in the class to accompany her — four men and four women. To be fair, she asks you to use Minitab to select four female students at random from those whose heights are reported in C2 Heights. (She will then select the male students similarly.) Recall that Dr. Wei included a student ID number in C1 ID.

To randomly select the four female students who will travel to the Chicago convention:

- Choose **Calc > Set Base**

- Type **444** in the "Set base of random data generator to" text box to enter it as your base and then press ↵

- Choose **Calc > Random Data > Sample From Columns**

- Type **4** in the "Sample [ ] rows from column(s)" text box and press ⎣Tab⎦

- Select **C1 ID** as the column to sample and press ⎣Tab⎦

- Type **Chicago** in the "Store samples in" text box

The completed Sample From Columns dialog box resembles Figure 6-19.

FIGURE 6-19

*The Sample From
Columns dialog box*

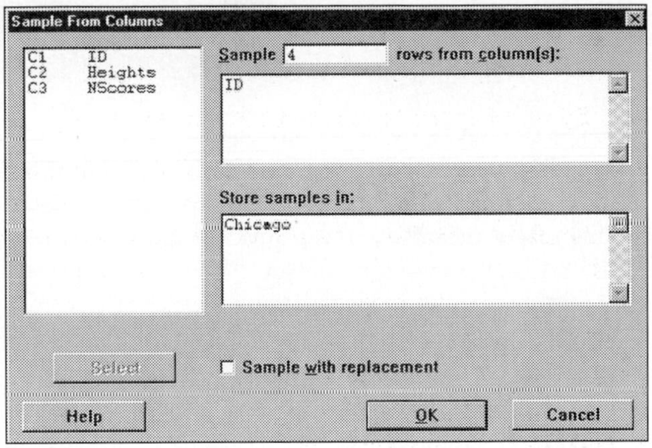

The default sampling option simulates an actual sample by eliminating data from the population as it is selected for the sample. To sample with replacement (so that the same population unit can be chosen more than once), you can select the "Sample with replacement" check box in the Sample From Columns dialog box.

- Press ⏎

- Click the **Current Data window** toolbar button 🔲

Minitab places the ID numbers of the four randomly selected students in C4 Chicago.

You want to give Dr. Wei the four ID numbers arranged from smallest to largest. To sort the column you just created:

- Choose **Manip > Sort**

- Select **Chicago** as the "Sort column(s)" and press ⏹Tab

- Type **SortChic** as the "Store sorted column(s) in" variable and press ⏹Tab

- Select **Chicago** as the first "Sort by column" variable and press ⏎

The ID numbers of the four lucky students are displayed in C5 SortChic (see Figure 6-20) in ascending order.

You can now inform Dr. Wei that the students with the following numbers were selected: 512, 639, 689, and 808. (Because this sample is random, your selections would be different if you used a different base.) Minitab also allows you to sample from a column containing text data, so if Dr. Wei had included names instead of ID numbers you could have selected a random sample of four names.

PUBLIC SAFETY: Six years after a rural university in Pennsylvania installed a nuclear reactor for educational purposes, concerned residents of the surrounding town claimed that the presence of the reactor was increasing infant mortality in the area. To support their contention, they presented data that compared infant mortality in their town to that in another town that was similar in size and character.

A statistician examined the data to help determine whether the infant mortality rate over the nine-year period was unusually high. The statistician focused on several aspects of the claim. One was whether the town's 1968 rate of 10 infant deaths was unusually high in a community in which the average yearly mortality rate was 6 deaths.

The statistician decided to see if randomly generated samples of similar data would contain any values as high as the 1968 value. He had Minitab randomly generate 100 Poisson distributions of nine-year spreads. He found that 58% of those randomly generated spreads contained one or more years with an infant mortality rate of at least 10. Since a majority of the spreads included a value as high as the 1968 rate, the statistician decided that the peak of 10 in 1968 was not uncommon in a situation with 6 deaths in an average year.

In the end, no dangerous environmental effects were linked to the presence of the reactor and it was allowed to remain. Although the causes of infant mortality remain a vital concern, it is important to recognize that peaks and valleys normally do occur in a nine-year period.

FIGURE 6-20

Subset of the Data window showing four randomly selected ID numbers

```
SortChic
512
639
689
808
```

In this tutorial, you worked with several of the most commonly used distributions. In later tutorials, you will use the Probability Distributions command to help solve other statistical problems.

- Save the current project **T6.mpj** and exit Minitab

Minitab Command Summary

This section describes the menu commands introduced in, or related to, this tutorial. Use Minitab's on-line Help for a complete explanation of all menu commands.

Minitab Menu Commands

Menu	Command	Description
Calc		
	Set Base	Allows the user to specify the "seed" number used to generate random data.
	Random Data	Produces random samples from specified columns or discrete and continuous distributions, given below.
	Sample From Columns	Takes random samples, with or without replacement, from a given column or columns.
	Chi-Square	
	Normal	
	F	
	t	
	Uniform	
	Bernoulli	
	Binomial	
	Discrete	Various discrete and continuous distributions from which random samples can be generated.
	Integer	
	Poisson	
	Beta	
	Cauchy	
	Exponential	
	Gamma	
	Laplace	
	Logistic	
	Lognormal	
	Weibull	

Menu	Command	Description
	Probability Distributions	Calculates probabilities, density function values, cumulative probabilities, and percentiles for the discrete and continuous random variables given below.
	Chi-Square	
	Normal	
	F	
	t	
	Uniform	
	Binomial	
	Discrete	Various discrete and continuous distributions on which probability calculations are based
	Integer	
	Poisson	
	Beta	
	Cauchy	
	Exponential	
	Gamma	
	Laplace	
	Logistic	
	Lognormal	
	Weibull	
Make Patterned Data		
	Simple Set of Numbers	Generates sequences or repetitive patterns of numbers and stores the results in a column.

Review and Practice

Matching

Match the following terms to their definitions by placing the correct letter next to the term it describes.

_____ From first value

_____ Make Patterned Data

_____ 0

_____ Random Data

_____ Sample From Columns

_____ Sample with replacement

_____ Inverse cumulative probability

_____ Normal scores

_____ Base

_____ 1

a. A Minitab command that allows you to enter sequences and/or repetitive patterns of data in the worksheet

b. The Minitab option in the Sample From Columns dialog box that can result in observations' being sampled more than once

c. The "seed" number used to generate random data

d. The Minitab option that can provide percentiles, quartiles, or deciles

e. The Minitab function used in NPPs

f. The text box in which you specify the beginning value for the Simple Set of Numbers command

g. The Minitab command that generates random data from a large number of discrete or continuous distributions

h. The Minitab command you use to obtain a subset of values from a variable, with or without replacement

i. The default value for a Normal distribution standard deviation

j. The default value for a Normal distribution mean

True/False

Mark the following statements with a *T* or an *F*.

_____ Minitab can compute probabilities for individual values and for whole columns of data, for both discrete and continuous random variables.

_____ Minitab can compute probability density function values for individual values and for whole columns of data for continuous random variables.

_____ Minitab can sample both with and without replacement from any column.

_____ Minitab can generate random data from over 20 continuous and discrete distributions.

_____ By default, the Simple Set of Numbers command uses an increment of 1.

_____ You use the Inverse cumulative probability option to determine percentiles for random variables.

_____ The output of the Probability Distributions command is always displayed in the Session window.

_____ For discrete random variables, Minitab can generate individual probabilities but not cumulative probabilities.

_____ The Random Data command allows you to simulate the outcomes of experiments without actually performing those experiments.

_____ Minitab calculates probabilities for the Bernoulli random variable.

Practice Problems

If necessary, use Help to review the contents of the data sets referred to in the following problems.

 1. A commuter airline flies 38-seat planes. The airline knows that, on average, 5% of passengers with reservations fail to show up for the flight. To compensate, the airline sells 40 tickets for each flight. Assume that whether or not one ticket-holder shows up is independent of whether or not any other ticket-holder shows up. Generate binomial probabilities for n = 40 and p = .05 and find the following:

a. The most likely number of passengers that will show up for a flight

b. The probability that all 40 ticket-holders will show up for a flight

c. The probability that all those who show up for a flight can be accommodated

d. Plot the individual binomial probabilities for the binomial distribution with n = 40 and p = .05. Comment on the shape of the distribution.

2. a. Use the Set Patterned Data > Simple Set of Data command to generate the values between 0 and 20 in increments of 0.2. Store your results in C1.

b. Obtain the cumulative probabilities for the values in C1 using a Normal distribution with a mean of 10 and a standard deviation of 2. Store your results in C2.

c. Obtain the cumulative probabilities for the values in C1 using a Normal distribution with a mean of 10 and a standard deviation of 8. Store your results in C3.

d. Obtain the cumulative probabilities for the values in C1 using a Normal distribution with a mean of 5 and a standard deviation of 2. Store your results in C4.

e. Construct three plots. Plot each cumulative distribution in C2, in C3, and in C4, in turn, against C1. Then use the Overlay option under Multiple Graphs to produce all three plots on the same graph. What happens to the cumulative distribution function if the standard deviation increases? What happens to the cumulative distribution function if the mean changes? What is the percentile of the mean for each distribution?

3. This problem explores the effect of degrees of freedom on the Chi-square distribution. Use the patterned data you generated in C1 in the previous problem to answer the following questions.

   a. Use the Probability Distributions command to store in C5 the Chi-square density values for a Chi-square distribution with 3 degrees of freedom.

   b. Plot the density values versus C1. Does your plot look like a Chi-square density? In which direction is the distribution skewed?

   c. Repeat (a) and (b) using a Chi-square distribution with 10 degrees of freedom. Is your curve more symmetrical? What appears to happen to the Chi-square distribution as the degrees of freedom increase?

4. Mr. Sims, the executive director of a professional organization, plans to contact 18 firms in hopes of recruiting five as members. He estimates that the probability of recruiting any firm is 0.6.

   a. What is the probability that he will recruit five or more firms? What is the most likely number of firms that he will recruit?

   b. Based on your analysis, has the executive director overestimated or underestimated his ability to recruit new members? Briefly explain your answer.

5. Open *Candyb.mtw.*

   a. Describe C6 NetWgt. What is its meaning? What is its standard deviation?

   b. Generate 57 observations from a normal distribution with the same mean and standard deviation. Place these data in C7. Name the column Rndnet.

   c. Obtain normal probability plots for C5 and C6. Which variable is more normal? Briefly explain your answer.

6. Open *Crimes.mtw.*

   a. Use the Sample From Columns command to obtain five 1991 violent crime rates.

   b. Which states (or districts) were selected? Explain how you determined the corresponding states.

   c. From which region(s) did your states come? Could they all come from one region? Briefly explain your answer.

TUTORIAL 7

Inference from One Sample

Normally, it is either impossible or impractical to conduct a study of an entire population to obtain the value of a parameter, such as a population mean. Statisticians have developed techniques that allow them to make inferences about parameters based on sample statistics. Two indispensable statistical inference tools for a single parameter are

1. *hypothesis tests* to investigate theories about parameters and

2. *confidence intervals* to estimate the value of a parameter.

In this tutorial, you will use Minitab to make inferences about the mean of a population and about the proportion of the population that has a particular characteristic. In the former case, you will examine situations in which the population variance is known and those in which they are not. You also will determine the sample size for estimating the population mean with a specified margin of error. Finally, you will compute the power of a test.

Objectives

In this tutorial, you learn how to:

- test a hypothesis about a *population mean*, μ, when the *population standard deviation*, σ, is known

- compute a confidence interval for μ when σ is known

- determine the sample size for estimating μ when σ is known

- test a hypothesis about μ when σ is unknown

- compute a confidence interval for μ when σ is unknown

- test a hypothesis about a *population proportion*, p

- compute the power of a test

- compute a confidence interval for p

▼ 7.1 Testing a Hypothesis about μ When σ Is Known ▲

CASE STUDY: SOCIOLOGY — AGE AT DEATH

A sociology professor, Dr. Ford, wants to test a claim that, on average, "famous" people — those whose obituaries appear in major newspapers — live to about the same age as that of the general public. Dr. Ford asks his class to randomly select 37 obituaries from the city's largest newspaper over the past two years. The sample includes 18 males and 19 females. The ages at death for the 18 males and 19 females are stored in separate columns in a file called *Age.mtw*.

Recent studies for the entire United States found that the mean age at death was 78.9 years for females and 72.5 years for males. The standard deviation was approximately 15 years for both females and males. Dr. Ford has asked your class to test, at the .05 significance level, the hypothesis that the mean age at death of famous women is less than 78.9 years. You are to assume that the standard deviation of age at death for all famous women is also 15 years.

To get started:

- Start **Minitab**

- Maximize the **Session window**

- If necessary, enable the **Session command language** and make the output read-only

You'll be working with the data worksheet *Age.mtw*, which is in the Student subdirectory:

- Open the worksheet **Age.mtw**

The worksheet shows female data in C1 DAgeF and male data in C2 DAgeM.

Before analyzing these data, save the worksheet in a new file and this tutorial in a project:

- In the location where you are saving your work, save the worksheet as **7Age.mtw**

- Save the work you have done thus far in a project named **T7.mpj**

To perform a hypothesis test on the value of μ, the population mean, when the value of σ (sigma), the population standard deviation, is known, you use the *Z-test*. As you can imagine, the population standard deviation is available only on rare occasions. In this case, since the sample size (n = 19) is quite small you must assume that the population of age at death for famous females is approximately normal.

You start by setting up the following hypotheses:

Null hypothesis, H_0: $\mu = 78.9$

Alternative hypothesis, H_1: $\mu < 78.9$

Here, μ is the true mean age at death for all famous women. You intend to use Minitab's 1-Sample Z procedure.

Now perform the test:

- Choose **Stat > Basic Statistics > 1-Sample Z**

- Select **C1 DAgeF** to enter it as the variable

- Click the **Test mean** option button and press ⌐Tab⌐

- Type **78.9** in the "Test mean" text box

- Click the "Alternative" **drop-down list arrow**, select **less than**, and press ⌐Tab⌐

- Type **15** for "Sigma"

The completed 1-Sample Z dialog box should look as shown in Figure 7-1.

FIGURE 7-1

The completed 1-Sample Z dialog box

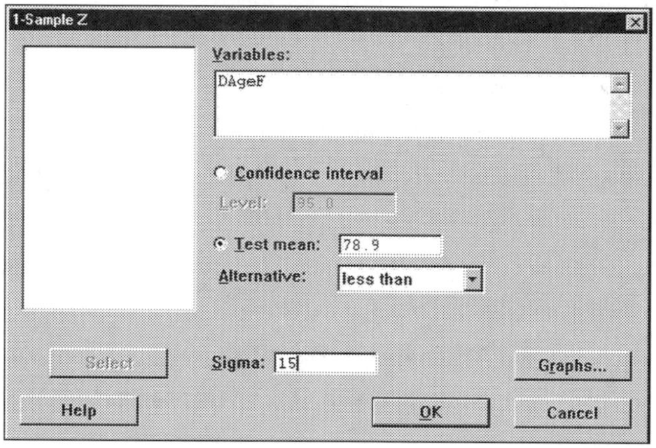

- Click **OK**

You are aware that you can test hypotheses in two (exactly equivalent) ways:

1. By comparing the value of the test statistic Z, with the critical value for Z corresponding to $\alpha = .05$

2. By comparing the p-value associated with the value of the test statistic to $\alpha = .05$

You will use both techniques.

In this case, the critical point will be the 5th percentile of the standard normal (Z) distribution. To determine this value:

- Choose **Calc > Probability Distributions > Normal**
- Click the **Inverse cumulative probability** option button

Notice that the default normal distribution is the standard normal with a mean of 0 and a standard standard deviation of 1, which is exactly what you want.

- Click the **Input constant** option button and press Tab
- Type **.05** as the "Input constant" and press ↵

The Session window shown in Figure 7-2 displays Minitab's commands and output corresponding to your previous menu choices.

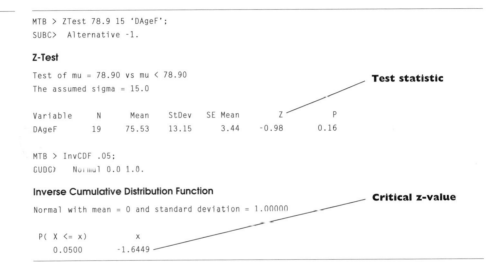

```
MTB > ZTest 78.9 15 'DAgeF';
SUBC>   Alternative -1.
```

Z-Test

```
Test of mu = 78.90 vs mu < 78.90
The assumed sigma = 15.0


Variable     N     Mean    StDev   SE Mean      Z        P
DAgeF        19    75.53   13.15    3.44      -0.98     0.16


MTB > InvCDF .05;
SUBC)   Normal 0.0 1.0.
```

Inverse Cumulative Distribution Function

```
Normal with mean = 0 and standard deviation = 1.00000


P( X <= x)            x
   0.0500        -1.6449
```

Test statistic

Critical z-value

The subcommand to ZTest, Alternative –1, designates the *left-tailed* (less-than or lower-tailed) alternative hypothesis. Correspondingly, +1 designates a *right-tailed* test and 0 indicates a *two-tailed* test.

The output includes the sample mean (75.53 years), the sample standard deviation (13.15 years), and $\sigma = \sqrt{n} = 3.44$. Minitab refers to this value as the *standard error of the mean* (SE Mean). The test statistic corresponding to the sample mean is

$$Z = \frac{75.53 - 78.9}{3.44} = -0.98.$$

You will reject H_0 only if the test statistic is less than the critical z-value, which is –1.6449. Since –0.98 does not fall in the rejection region, you cannot reject H_0 at the .05 level of significance. The data suggest that the mean age at death for famous women is not significantly less than 78.9 years.

You can also decide to reject or fail to reject the null hypothesis using the p-value in the Z-test output. The p-value is the probability of getting a result at least as extreme as that obtained in the sample, assuming the null hypothesis is true. You reject H_0 when the p-value is less than your chosen level of significance. In this case, the p-value of .16 is greater than .05, so your decision would be the same, as it should be: fail to reject H_0 at the .05 level. Many statisticians believe that reporting test results in terms of the p-value avoids confusion by letting readers use their own judgment as to whether the p-value is small enough.

In the Practice Problems at the end of this tutorial, you are asked to perform a similar Z-test for the mean age at death for all famous men.

▼ 7.2 Computing a Confidence Interval for μ When σ Is Known ▲

As part of your sociology project, Dr. Ford asks you to estimate the mean age at death for all famous women by forming a 90% confidence interval:

- Choose **Stat > Basic Statistics > 1-Sample Z**

- Verify that **DAgeF** is the "Variable"

- Click the **Confidence interval** option button and press ⌷Tab⌷

- Type **90** as the "Level"

    You can enter a confidence interval as a whole number (90) or as a decimal number (.90) in the "Level" text box. Minitab expects a value between 0 and 100 but will translate a decimal because it is so common to enter a percent in that format.

- Verify that "Sigma" is **15**

    The completed 1-Sample Z dialog box should look as shown in Figure 7-3.

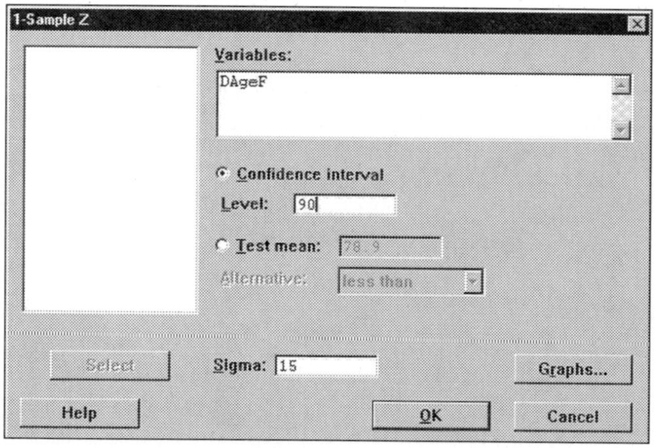

FIGURE 7-3

The completed 1-Sample Z dialog box for a confidence interval

- Press ⏎

Figure 7-4 shows the results in the Session window.

```
MTB > ZInterval 90.0 15 'DAgeF'

Z Confidence Intervals

The assumed sigma = 15.0
Variable     N     Mean    StDev   SE Mean      90.0 % CI
DAgeF       19    75.53    13.15     3.44  (  69.87,   81.19)
```

Based on these results, you can be 90% confident that μ, the population mean age at death for famous women, lies between 69.87 and 81.19 years.

▼ **Note** The 90% confidence interval takes this form:

$$\text{sample mean} \pm Z_{95} \, {}^{*}(\text{SE Mean}),$$

where the sample mean = 75.53 years, SE Mean = 3.44 years, and Z_{95} is the 95th percentile of the Z distribution. You can verify that Z_{95} = 1.6449 by using the sequence Calc > Probability Distribution > Normal and then selecting the Inverse cumulative probability option. Use .95 as the input constant. (Recall that in the last section, you obtained Z_5, the 5th percentile of Z, as –1.6449.) ▲

You have completed your inferences but are anxious about the normality assumption. You decide to examine this assumption by viewing a built-in graph that is an option with the 1-Sample Z procedure. You decide to select a histogram:

- Click the **Edit Last Dialog** toolbar button 🔲

- Click **Graphs**, click the **Histogram of data** check box, and click **OK** twice

The resulting histogram is shown in Figure 7-5.

FIGURE 7-5

Built-in histogram of DAgeF

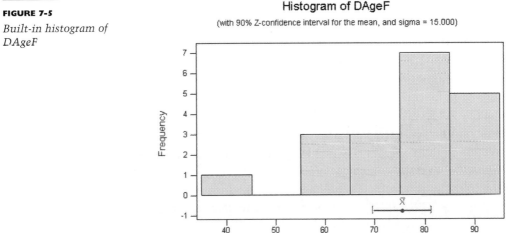

Histogram of DAgeF

(with 90% Z-confidence interval for the mean, and sigma = 15.000)

The graph shows the location of the sample mean = 75.53 years and the corresponding 90% confidence interval for the population mean. Most important, the histogram is skewed to the left with the suggestion of an outlier. This casts doubt on the assumption that the population is normal.

- Close the graph by clicking the **Close** button ⊠ in the top right-hand corner of the graph

▼ 7.3   Sample Size for Estimating μ When σ Is Known ▲

The half-width of a confidence interval is frequently called the *margin of error*. For instance, the margin of error when estimating the mean age at death for all famous women is (81.19 – 69.87)/2 = 5.66 years. You can be 90% confident that the population mean lies within 5.66 years of the sample mean, 75.53 years. You can improve (reduce) the margin of error by increasing the sample size, n.

As a footnote to your work for Dr. Ford, you decide to use Minitab to compute the sample sizes needed to be 90% confident of achieving the following possible margins of error: .5 year, 1.0 year, 1.5 years, . . . , 5.0 years. The formula for the sample size needed to achieve a margin of error of M with 90% confidence is

$$n = \frac{1.645^2 \sigma^2}{M^2} = \frac{(1.645)^2 (15)^2}{M^2} = \frac{608.856}{M^2}.$$

Begin by entering into C3 the values .5, 1.0, 1.5, . . . , 5.0:

- Choose **Calc > Make Patterned Data > Simple Set of Numbers**
- Type **MofE** in the "Store patterned data in" text box and press Tab
- Type **.5** in the "From first value" text box and press Tab
- Type **5.0** in the "To last value" text box and press Tab
- Type **.5** in the "In steps of" text box and press ⏎

You will compute the sample size needed to obtain each of these margins of error by having Minitab calculate the value for 608.856/ M^2 and *conservatively* rounding down to the next lowest integer. Minitab allows you to round down by using the Floor function:

- Choose **Calc > Calculator**
- Type **n** as the "Store result in variable"
- Enter, by clicking or typing, **FLOOR(608.856/MofE******2)** as the "Expression"
- Click **OK**
- Click the **Current Data window** toolbar button ▦

The values for C3 MofE and C4 n are shown in the Data window and in Figure 7-6.

	C1 DAgeF	C2 DAgeM	C3 MofE	C4 n	C5	C6	C7	C8	C9
1	76	55	0.5	2435					
2	77	60	1.0	608					
3	82	62	1.5	270					
4	74	71	2.0	152					
5	75	74	2.5	97					
6	89	79	3.0	67					
7	68	84	3.5	49					
8	60	90	4.0	38					
9	94	96	4.5	30					
10	91	61	5.0	24					
11	44	70							
12	90	58							
13	87	70							
14	57	93							
15	84	77							
16	79	62							
17	75	82							
18	74	90							
19	60								
20									

The more accurately you want to estimate the population mean — that is, the smaller you want the margin of error to be — the larger the sample size must be. For a margin of error of 4.5 years, for example, a sample size of n = 30 is sufficient. To obtain a margin of error of 1.0 year, however, a sample size of 608 women is necessary.

Next, you will work with another case study, in which you investigate changes in house prices. First, though.

- In the location where you are saving your work, save the work you have done thus far in the project *T7.mpj*

▼ 7.4   Testing a Hypothesis about μ When σ Is Unknown ▲

CASE STUDY: REAL ESTATE — HOUSING PRICES

As a newly hired real estate agent for Consolidated Properties, you want to investigate housing prices in a district. Several years ago, the mean house price was $143,000. You want to find out if this mean price is still valid. You formulate two hypotheses to test using 150 randomly selected houses:

Null hypothesis, H_0: μ – 143000

Alternative hypothesis, H_1: μ ≠143000

Here, μ is the current population mean selling price in the district.

In this case, because you do not know the population standard deviation of house prices, you cannot use a Z-test. You decide to use a t-test instead. Open the data file *Homes.mtw*, which is in the Student subdirectory:

- Open the worksheet **Homes.mtw**

- Use **Help** to review the contents of the data set

  Before analyzing these data, you should save the data:

- In the location where you are saving your work, save the worksheet as **7Homes**

  The variable you want to analyze is C1 Price. To test the previous hypotheses:

- Choose **Stat > Basic Statistics > 1-Sample t**

- Select **C1 Price** to enter it as the variable

- Click the **Test mean** option button and press Tab

- Type **143000** as the "Test mean"

  The default alternative is "not equal," which is what you wanted. The completed 1-Sample t dialog box should look as shown in Figure 7-7.

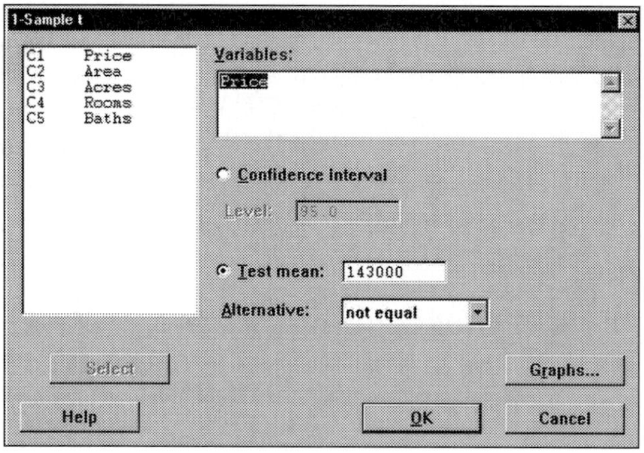

FIGURE 7-7

The completed 1-Sample t dialog box

- Press ↵

The Session window showing the t-test results is shown in Figure 7-8.

FIGURE 7-8

Results of t-test

```
MTB > T-Test 143000 'Price';
SUBC>    Alternative 0.
```

T-Test of the Mean

```
Test of mu = 143000 vs mu not = 143000

Variable    N      Mean    StDev   SE Mean       T        P
Price      150    153775   41611      3398    3.17   0.0018
```

In this case, the test statistic is

$$t = \frac{153775 - 14300}{3398} = 3.17.$$

The p-value corresponding to the t-value of 3.17 is 0.0018. Since the p-value is less than any reasonable level of significance, reject H_0 and conclude that there is significant evidence of a change — probably an increase — in house sales prices. This change probably reflects a broader trend in U.S. housing prices during recent years.

▼ **Note** The p-value (0.0018) in the previous two-sided t-test can be written as the sum of two equal probabilities: $P(t < -3.17)$ and $P(t > 3.17)$, where t has the t distribution with 149 degrees of freedom. You can confirm the fact that $P(t < -3.17)$ is $0.0018/2 = 0.0009$ by choosing the sequence Calc > Probability Distributions > t and then selecting the Cumulative probability option. Use 149 as the number of degrees of freedom and –3.17 as the input constant. ▲

You decide to obtain a histogram of the 150 selling prices using the built-in graph option that comes with the 1-Sample t procedure:

- Click the **Edit Last Dialog** toolbar button 🔲
- Click **Graphs**, click **Histogram of data**, and click **OK** twice

The resulting histogram is shown in Figure 7-9.

FIGURE 7-9

Built-in Histogram of Price

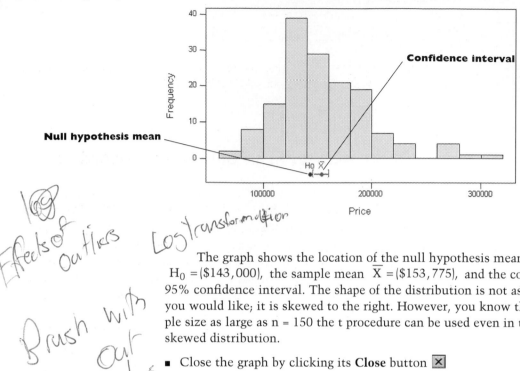

Histogram of Price

(with Ho and 95% t-confidence interval for the mean)

Confidence interval

Null hypothesis mean

Price

[handwritten notes in margin: 169, Effects of Outliers, Log transformation, Brush with Outliers]

The graph shows the location of the null hypothesis mean $H_0 = (\$143,000)$, the sample mean $\overline{X} = (\$153,775)$, and the corresponding 95% confidence interval. The shape of the distribution is not as bell-shaped as you would like; it is skewed to the right. However, you know that with a sample size as large as n = 150 the t procedure can be used even in the presence of a skewed distribution.

- Close the graph by clicking its **Close** button

▼ 7.5 Computing a Confidence Interval for μ When σ Is Unknown ▲

The t-test in the last section strongly suggested that μ, the population mean house-selling price, was greater than $143,000. Although this is helpful, you also want to answer this question: What is μ? To do this, compute a 95% confidence interval for the unknown current mean price of houses:

- Choose **Edit > Edit Last Dialog**

- Click the **Confidence interval** option button

    The default confidence level is 95%.

- Click **Graphs** and deselect **Histogram of data**

- Click **OK** twice

    The 95% confidence interval appears in the Session window, as shown in Figure 7-10.

FIGURE 7-10

*A 95% confidence interval
for the mean price*

```
MTB > TInterval 95.0 'Price'.
```

T Confidence Intervals

Variable	N	Mean	StDev	SE Mean	95.0 % CI
Price	150	153775	41611	3398	(147062, 160489)

You can report, with 95% confidence, that the current mean sale price of houses in this district falls between $147,062 and $160,489.

■ Save the project *T7.mpj*

▼ 7.6 Testing a Hypothesis Regarding a Population Proportion ▲

CASE STUDY: HEALTH CARE — WORK DAYS LOST TO PAIN

As a researcher at a large Health Maintenance Organization (HMO), you have been asked to select a sample of 300 patients who have reported low back pain in the past six months. Federal guidelines suggest that with the appropriate treatment, less than 60% of patients with low back pain need lose work days. You are to use the data to test whether this HMO has met this guideline. Because of incomplete records, you have a total sample size of 279.

The relevant data is in a file called *Backpain.mtw*, which is in the Student subdirectory:

■ Open the worksheet **Backpain.mtw**

■ Use **Help** to review the contents of the data set

Before analyzing these data, you should save the data:

■ In the location where you are saving your work, save the worksheet as **7Backpn**

For each of the 279 patients, the number of days lost as a result of low back pain is in C3 LostDays. The Minitab commands to obtain confidence intervals and hypothesis tests for a single proportion require that the sample values contain only numbers or text that stands for "successes" and "failures." If the column contains numbers, the larger of the two is considered a success. You decide to create a new variable that takes the value 0 if C3 LostDays is 0 and the value 1 if C3 LostDays takes any nonzero value. Such a variable is often called an *indicator* variable. You can use the Calc command to create such a variable, LostInd (short for LostDays Indicator):

■ Choose **Calc > Calculator**

■ Type **LostInd** in the "Store result in variable" text box and press Tab

■ Enter, by clicking or typing, **LostDays > 0** as the "Expression"

The Calculator dialog box should look as shown in Figure 7-11.

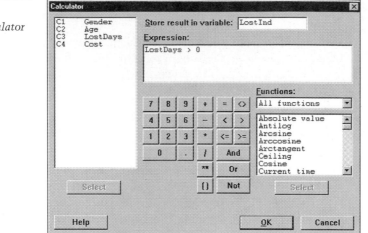

■ Click **OK**

The condition you entered in the "Expression" text box automatically creates an indicator variable in C5 LostInd, which takes the value 1 when the condition is met and 0 otherwise. The 1's in C5 LostInd represent those patients in the sample who lost at least one day of work as a result of low back pain; the 0's represent those patients who did not. You are ready to test a hypotheses about the proportion (p) of all patients at the HMO who missed at least one day's work.

Recall that federal guidelines suggest that, with appropriate treatment, less than 60% of patients with low back pain need lose work days. Do these data suggest that this HMO has met this guideline? Set up the following hypotheses:

Null hypothesis, H_0: p = .6

Alternative hypothesis, H_1: p < .6

To test H_0:

■ Choose **Stat > Basic Statistics > 1 Proportion**

■ Click in the "Samples in columns" text box and select **C5 LostInd**

■ Click **Options** and type **0.6** as the "Test proportion"

■ Click the "Alternative" **drop-down list arrow** and select **less than**

The 1 Proportion - Options dialog box should look as shown in Figure 7-12.

FIGURE 7-12

*The completed 1
Proportion - Options
dialog box*

■ Click **OK** twice

The resulting output is shown in Figure 7-13.

FIGURE 7-13

*Testing the hypothesis
p = 0.6 versus p<0.6*

```
MTB > POne 'LostInd';
SUBC>    Confidence 95.0;
SUBC>    Test 0.6;
SUBC>    Alternative -1.
```

Test and Confidence Interval for One Proportion

Test of p = 0.6 vs p < 0.6

Success = 1

Variable	X	N	Sample p	95.0 % CI	Exact P-Value
LostInd	154	279	0.551971	(0.491539, 0.611288)	0.058

According to the output, 154 patients, or approximately 55% of the 279 patients in the sample, lost at least one day's work. The p-value associated with the sample proportion, .551971, is 0.058. This is small, suggesting that the data provides little support for the null hypothesis that p = .6. However, if you insist on a level of significance of α = .05, you cannot quite reject H_0 at the .05 level.

Notice that, as well as the hypothesis test, Minitab automatically computes a 95% confidence interval for the p. You can be 95% confident that the unknown p lies between .492 and .611.

▼ **Note** By default, Minitab uses a procedure to compute confidence intervals and test hypotheses about a population proportion that differs from the normal approximation method used in most introductory texts. The procedure used by Minitab — called the *"Exact" Method* — does not require the usual stipulation that the products

(sample size)*(sample proportion) and

(sample size)*(1 – sample proportion)

should both exceed 5. As you can see in Figure 7-12, using the normal approximation method is an option. ▲

▼ 7.7   Computing the Power of a Test ▲

In the previous example, you could not quite reject the null hypothesis at the .05 level of significance. Thus you may have made what is known as a *Type II error*, that of failing to reject the null hypothesis (p = .60) when, in fact, the alternative hypothesis (p < .60) is true. What is the probability of such an error in this example? There is no single answer to this question, since your chance of failing to reject the null hypothesis depends on the value for the unknown p.

Suppose, for instance, p = .55; that is, 55% of all patients in the HMO who are suffering from low back pain lose work days. What is the probability that in this case, you would (incorrectly) fail to reject the null hypothesis? Minitab does not compute this probability, but it can compute the probability of the complementary event — that is, the probability of rejecting the null hypothesis correctly if p = .55. This probability is called the *power* of the test when p = .55.

To compute this probability:

- Choose **Stat > Power and Sample Size > 1 Proportion**

    You use the default option "Calculate power for each sample size."

- Type **279** as the "Sample sizes" and press Tab

- Type **.55** as the "Alternative p" and press Tab

- Type **0.6** as the "Hypothesized p"

- Click the **Options** button and click **less than** as the "Alternative Hypothesis"

- Keep α = .05 as the default "significance level.".

- Click **OK**

    The completed Power and Sample Size for 1 Proportion dialog box is shown in Figure 7-14.

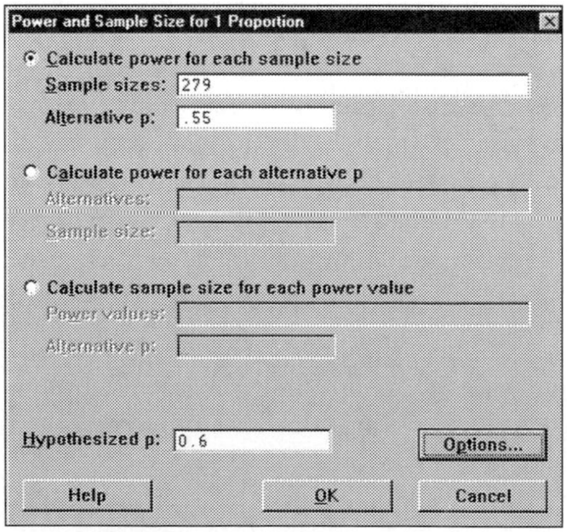

FIGURE 7-14

The completed Power and Sample Size for 1 Proportion dialog box

Power and Sample Size for 1 Proportion

○ **Calculate power for each sample size**
   Sample sizes: `279`
   Alternative p: `.55`

○ **Calculate power for each alternative p**
   Alternatives: ` `
   Sample size: ` `

○ **Calculate sample size for each power value**
   Power values: ` `
   Alternative p: ` `

Hypothesized p: `0.6`   [Options...]

[Help]   [OK]   [Cancel]

- Click **OK**

The Session window output is shown in Figure 7-15.

FIGURE 7-15

The computation of power

```
MTB > Power;
SUBC>   POne;
SUBC>     Sample 279;
SUBC>     PAlternative .55;
SUBC>     PNull 0.6;
SUBC>     Alternative -1.
```

Power and Sample Size

Test for One Proportion

Testing proportion = 0.6 (versus < 0.6)
Calculating power for proportion = 0.55
Alpha = 0.05   Difference = -0.05

Sample
  Size   Power   *Correctly Rejecting Hₒ*
  279   0.5235

The difference of –0.05 referred to in the output is the distance from the (assumed) true value for p (.55) and the hypothesized value for p (.60). This difference is often called the *effect size*. With a sample size of 279 patients, the test has a power of .5235. This is the probability of correctly rejecting the null hypothesis when p is, in fact, .55. This is not very encouraging. It means that if p is .55, your test is only slightly better than a coin toss at making the correct decision to reject the null hypothesis.

In this context, there is a close relationship between the power of the test, the sample size, and the alternative value for p. You can see from the dialog box in Figure 7-14 that Minitab allows you to compute the following:

- The power of the test for different sample sizes and a particular alternative value for p, as you did previously

- The power of the test for different alternative values for p and a specific sample size

- The sample sizes that will provide you with different powers for a specified alternative value for p

You are interested in examining how the power of your test varies with how far the true value for p is from the hypothesized value (p = .60). So you compute the power of the test against the alternatives p = .50, .51, . . . , .60:

- Click the **Edit Last Dialog** toolbar button 🖳

- Click the **Calculate power for each alternative p** option button and press ⎡Tab⎤

- Type **.50 .51 .52 .53 .54 .55 .56 .57 .58 .59 .60** as the "Alternatives" and press `Tab`

- Type **279** as the "Sample size"

- Click the **Options** button

- Type **Prop** in the "Store alternatives in" text box and press `Tab`

- Type **Power** in the "Store power values in" text box

- Click **OK** twice

The values for p and the corresponding values for the power of the test are reported in the Session window and are stored in the two new columns C6 Prop and C7 Power in the Data window. The output in the Session window is shown in Figure 7-16.

FIGURE 7-16

Power of the test for different values for p

```
MTB > Name c6 = 'Prop' c7 = 'Power'
MTB > Power;
SUBC>    POne;
SUBC>      PAlternative .50 .51 .52 .53 .54 .55 .56 .57 .58 .59 .60;
SUBC>      Sample 279;
SUBC>      PNull 0.6;
SUBC>      Alternative -1;
SUBC>      Store 'Prop' 'Power'.
```

Power and Sample Size

Test for One Proportion

Testing proportion = 0.6 (versus < 0.6)
Alpha = 0.05   Size of Each Sample = 279

Difference	Prop	Power
-0.10	0.50	0.9581
-0.09	0.51	0.9185
-0.08	0.52	0.8558
-0.07	0.53	0.7667
-0.06	0.54	0.6532
-0.05	0.55	0.5235
-0.04	0.56	0.3908
-0.03	0.57	0.2691
-0.02	0.58	0.1696
-0.01	0.59	0.0970
0.00	0.60	0.0500

The output consists of the difference between the assumed true value for p and the hypothesized value (this difference is the effect size), the assumed true value for p, and the corresponding power of the test. You notice that the power of the test increases how far the true p is from the hypothesized value for p — that is, the larger the effect size. If p is .5, the power of the test is 0.9581. However, if p is .59 the power of the test is only 0.0970. If the null hypothesis is true and p = .60, then the power of the test is precisely the level of significance, α = .05. Both are the probability of rejecting the null hypothesis.

Return to the Data window:

■ Click the **Current Data window** toolbar button

The values for Prop and for Power are stored in C6 and C7, respectively. The relationship between these two variables can be illustrated by a plot of C7 Power against C6 Prop:

■ Choose **Graph > Plot**

■ Select **C6 Prop** as the "X" and **C7 Power** as the "Y" variable

■ Click the "Display" **drop-down list arrow** and select **Connect**

■ Click the "Annotation" **drop-down list arrow** and select **Title**

■ Type **Plot of Power against the Value for p** and press ↵

■ Click **OK**

The resulting plot is shown in Figure 7-17.

FIGURE 7-17

Plot of power against p

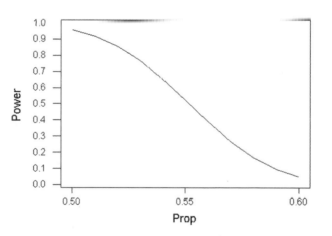

Plot of Power against the Value for p

The graph shows quite dramatically that the power of the test decreases the closer the value for the population proportion (p) is to the hypothesized value for p (0.6).

If you choose Stat > Power and Sample Size, you will see that Minitab can perform these kinds of power calculations for the 1-Sample Z, the 1-Sample t, the 2-Sample t, the 2 Proportions, and the One-way ANOVA procedures, as well as for the 1 Proportion procedure used previously. You will encounter the 2-Sample t and the 2 Proportions procedures in the next tutorial and the One-way ANOVA in Tutorial 9.

▼ 7.8   Computing a Confidence Interval for a Population Proportion ▲

Figure 7-13 showed that when you performed a hypothesis test for p, Minitab also reported a 95% confidence interval for p. In that case, the interval was 0.491539 to 0.611288. The 1 Proportion procedure can be used to compute confidence intervals with levels of confidence other than 95%. For example, to obtain an 80% confidence interval for p:

- Choose **Stats > Basic Statistics > 1 Proportion**

- Click the **Options** button

- Type **80** as the "Confidence level"

- Click **OK** twice

The output in the Session window is shown in Figure 7-18.

FIGURE 7-18

An 80% confidence interval for p

```
MTB > POne 'LostInd';
SUBC>    Confidence 80.0;
SUBC>    Test 0.6;
SUBC>    Alternative -1.
```

Test and Confidence Interval for One Proportion

Test of p = 0.6 vs p < 0.6

Success = 1

Variable	X	N	Sample p	80.0 % CI	Exact P-Value
LostInd	154	279	0.551971	(0.511844, 0.591539)	0.058

The output is not very different from that in Figure 7-13. However, here Minitab reports the 80% confidence interval for p, (0.511844, 0.591539). This interval is narrower than the corresponding 95% confidence interval, but you are less confident that p is in the interval.

You have successfully learned how to use Minitab to perform one-sample Z- and t-tests for means and proportions. In the next tutorial, you will cover two-sample techniques.

- Save the current project *T7.mpj* and exit Minitab

MINITAB AT WORK

RETAILING: Frozen foods — especially frozen pizzas — are a common staple in many American households. Pizza producers must carefully monitor how bacteria respond to prolonged refrigeration temperatures. Microbiologists used Minitab to help determine how long pizza can be refrigerated without becoming a threat to public health.

To examine the effect of freezing on specific bacteria, researchers inoculated the pizzas with measured amounts of *Escherichia coli (E. coli)* and other potential contaminants. They stored the pizzas at various temperatures, retrieving samples every other day for microbiological analysis. They counted colonies of bacteria at each testing and entered that data into Minitab. When they compared each day's count with the initial count, using a 1-sample t-test on the differences in counts, they found that the *E. coli* colonies increased significantly (p-value < 0.05).

This result suggests E. coli will grow when acceptable refrigeration temperatures are not maintained. Pizza producers could best safeguard public health by carefully monitoring bacteria levels before beginning the freezing process, while the vendors must ensure adequate refrigeration and must carefully monitor shelf dates.

▼

Minitab Command Summary

▲

This section describes the menu commands introduced in, or related to, this tutorial. To find a complete explanation of all menus and commands, use Minitab's on-line Help.

Minitab Menu Commands

Menu	Command	Description
Stat		
	Basic Statistics	
	1-Sample Z	Performs inferences (tests and confidence intervals) on a population mean when σ is known.
	1-Sample t	Performs inferences (tests and confidence intervals) on a population mean when σ is unknown.
	1 Proportion	Performs inferences (tests and confidence intervals) on a population proportion.

Menu	Command	Description
	Power and Sample Size	
	1 Proportion	Computes the power for different sample sizes or for different values for p. Also computes sample sizes for different power values.
	1-Sample Z	Computes the power for different sample sizes or for different values for μ based on the Z distribution. Also computes sample sizes for different power values.
	1-Sample t	Computes the power for different sample sizes or for different values for μ based on a t distribution. Also computes sample sizes for different power values.

▼

Review and Practice

▲

Matching

Match the following terms to their definitions by placing the correct letter next to the term it describes.

_____ Power

_____ 1-Sample t

_____ 1 Proportion

_____ Alternative

_____ Sigma

_____ Confidence level

_____ p-value

_____ 1-Sample Z

_____ σ

_____ p

a. The probability of getting a result at least as extreme as that obtained in the sample, assuming the null hypothesis is true

b. The Minitab command used to perform a 1-sample inference about a mean, assuming σ is unknown

c. The name Minitab uses for the population standard deviation

d. The probability of rejecting the null hypothesis correctly

e. The symbol Minitab uses for the unknown population proportion

f. The Minitab command you use to perform a 1 sample inference about a mean, assuming σ is known

g. The Minitab option that allows you to change the amount of confidence in an interval estimate

h. The Minitab command you use to perform a 1-sample inference about a population proportion

i. The Minitab option that enables you to specify the direction of the alternative hypothesis

j. The symbol used to represent the population standard deviation

True/False

Mark the following statements with a *T* or an *F*.

_____ Confidence intervals can be entered in Minitab as a percentage (99) or as a decimal (.99).

_____ The population standard deviation must be known to perform a 1-sample test of a mean in Minitab.

_____ Confidence intervals and 1-sample tests are performed using the same Minitab command on the Stat menu.

_____ Minitab's Power and Sample Size for 1 Proportion command will calculate the sample sizes corresponding to different power values.

_____ The confidence level for population confidence intervals can be set to any value you specify.

_____ Minitab allows you to specify a significance level for a hypothesis test.

_____ An upper-tailed test is designated Alternative 0.

_____ In Minitab's 1-sample confidence intervals, the default confidence level is 90%.

_____ Minitab selects the smaller of the two different values in a column to represent a success.

_____ Most of Minitab's 1-sample inference commands are found on the File menu.

Practice Problems

Use Help or Part III, "Exploring Data" to review the contents of the data sets referred to in the following problems.

1. Open *Candyb.mtw*. The mean net weight of a package of candy is advertised as 20.89 grams. Use the data in C6 NetWgt to determine if the mean net weight is less than the advertised value at a significance level of .05. Why is this one-sided alternative appropriate? Assume that the candy packages in the sample represent a random sample of all such packages.

2. Open *Prof.mtw*. Assume the sections in which the surveys were distributed are a random sample of sections from all of those at the college.

   a. Obtain 90% confidence intervals for the mean Course and Instrucr ratings at the university.

   b. Unstack the Course ratings into four columns using the Year variable. Obtain 90% confidence intervals for the mean course rating for each of the four years. Describe the results.

   c. Code the Instrucr ratings into two groups: a low group with ratings below 2 and a high group with ratings of 2 or above. Use the Tally command to determine the number of professors in each group. Using 90% confidence, estimate the percentage of professors that the students consider to be 2 or above.

3. Open *Wastes.mtw*.

   a. Stack the nine districts and obtain a 95% confidence interval for the mean number of hazardous waste sites in the entire country.

   b. Obtain 95% confidence intervals for the mean number of hazardous waste sites in each of the nine districts. How do these confidence intervals compare to the interval computed in (a)?

   c. Would you prefer to use the interval from (a) or those from (b) in a report? Briefly explain your answer.

   d. Is it reasonable to assume that these data are a ramdom sample? How does your answer affect your conclusions?

4. Open *Pay.mtw*.

   a. The industry average salary has been found to be approximately $35,000. Is this company's average salary comparable to the industry's average salary?

   b. Is it reasonable to assume that the members of the Sales Department are a random sample? How does your answer affect your conclusion in (a)?

5. Open *Prof.mtw*. Assume the surveys were distributed to a random sample from all sections at the college. Determine if the proportion of surveyed courses with senior numbers (400s) differs from 0.25 at a significance level of .05.

6. Open *Age.mtw*.

   a. Perform a Z-test of whether the mean age at death of famous males is less than the mean for all males, which is 72.5 years. Assume that $\sigma = 15$ years. Your output should include a histogram of the sample data.

   b. What does the shape of the histogram suggest about the normality assumption?

7. Open *Pulse.mtw*. Assume these 92 students can be considered a random sample of 18- to 21-year-olds in college.

   a. Some years ago it was believed that approximately one-quarter of such students smoked. There is some concern that the current proportion (p) who smoke is substantially higher. Perform the appropriate test at the .05 level of significance.

   b. How powerful is your test in (a) against the alternative that the true proportion of such students who smoke is .3?

   c. Answer (b) for the following alternative values: .25, .26, . . . ,.35. Produce a plot of power against the value for p and comment on what your plot shows.

   d. Answer (b) for the following levels of significance: .1, .05, .01, and .005. Explain how the power of the test varies with the level of significance.

8. Use Help to discover the exact methodology that Minitab uses to compute a confidence interval and test a hypothesis for a population proportion. You will want to consult your instructor for details.

TUTORIAL
8

Inferences from Two Samples

The one-sample procedures you used in Tutorial 7 are not used as frequently as two-sample procedures, which involve comparing two samples. The latter usually involve making inferences about differences between two population means or between two population proportions. In this tutorial, you will examine Minitab's various two-sample t-tests for comparing means and as well as Minitab's test for comparing two proportions. You will also explore the relationship between sample size and power when comparing two means and when comparing two proportions.

Objectives

In this tutorial, you learn how to:

- test for the significance of the difference between two population means when two independent samples are, first, recorded in separate columns and, second, stacked in a single column

- obtain a confidence interval for the difference between two population means when two independent samples are, first, recorded in separate columns and, second, stacked in a single column

- test for the significance of and obtain a confidence interval for the difference between two population means when the samples are paired (or dependent)

- compute power and sample size of the two-sample t-test for the difference between two population means when the two samples are independent

- test for the significance of and obtain a confidence interval for the difference between two population proportions when the two samples are independent

- compute power and sample size of the test for the difference between two population proportions when the two samples are independent

▼ 8.1   Comparing Population Means from Two Independent Samples ▲

CASE STUDY: SOCIOLOGY — AGE AT DEATH (CONTINUED)

When your sociology class was discussing the results of the mean age at death of "famous" females and males, the question arose whether there was a *difference* between the means of these two distinct populations. Actuarial studies predict that women will live longer than men, so the class was curious whether the same was true for the "famous" people from whom the sample was drawn. Dr. Ford, your professor, suggests that the class attempt to settle this question by performing a two-independent sample t-test.

To get started:

- Start **Minitab**

- Maximize the **Session window**

- If necessary, enable the **Session command language** and make the output read-only

You'll be working with the data file *Age.mtw*, which is in the Student subdirectory:

- Open the worksheet **Age.mtw**

Before analyzing these data, save them in a new file and this tutorial in a project:

- In the location where you are saving your work, save the worksheet as **8Age**

- Also save what you have done thus far in a project named **T8**

Using Unstacked Data

The worksheet shows data on 19 females in C1 DAgeF and data on 18 males in C2 DAgeM. In this data set, the values in the two samples are located in different columns.

First, examine the data by looking at numerical summaries:

- Choose **Stat > Basic Statistics > Display Descriptive Statistics**

- Select **C1 DAgeF** and **C2 DAgeM** to enter them as the "Variables"

- Click **OK**

The output is shown in the Session window and in Figure 8-1.

FIGURE 8-1

*Descriptive statistics for
DAgeF and DAgeM*

```
MTB > Describe 'DAgeF' 'DAgeM'.
```

Descriptive Statistics

Variable	N	Mean	Median	TrMean	StDev	SE Mean
DAgeF	19	75.53	75.00	76.29	13.15	3.02
DAgeM	18	74.22	72.50	73.94	13.19	3.11

Variable	Minimum	Maximum	Q1	Q3
DAgeF	44.00	94.00	68.00	87.00
DAgeM	55.00	98.00	61.75	85.50

The mean age of the 19 females (75.53 years) is about one and one-fourth years greater than that for males (74.22 years). The t-test will determine if this difference is statistically significant, but the difference does not seem to be of any practical importance. The standard deviations for the two samples of ages at death are very close (13.15 years for females and 13.19 for males).

Minitab offers several options for testing differences between two population means. Because the males and females were randomly and independently selected from the newspaper obituaries that were printed in a two-year period, you can use the test for independent samples. Pose the hypotheses to test for a difference between the population mean male and female ages at death, using a significance level of .05:

Null hypothesis, H_0: $\mu_F = \mu_M$

Alternative hypothesis, H_1: $\mu_F \neq \mu_M$

To obtain the test:

- Choose **Stat > Basic Statistics > 2-Sample t**

- Click the **Samples in different columns** option button, and press Tab

- Select **C1 DAgeF** in the "First" text box and **C2 DAgeM** in the "Second" text box

- Leave the default alternative hypothesis ("Alternative") set to **not equal**

- Click the **Assume equal variances** check box

In this case, the fact that the sample standard deviations for the two genders are so close supports the assumption of equal variances (remember, the variance is just the square of the standard deviation). In other cases, if there isn't a strong reason to make such an assumption, do not select the "Assume equal variances" check box.

The completed 2-Sample t dialog box should look as shown in Figure 8-2.

FIGURE 8-2

The completed 2-Sample dialog box for unstacked data

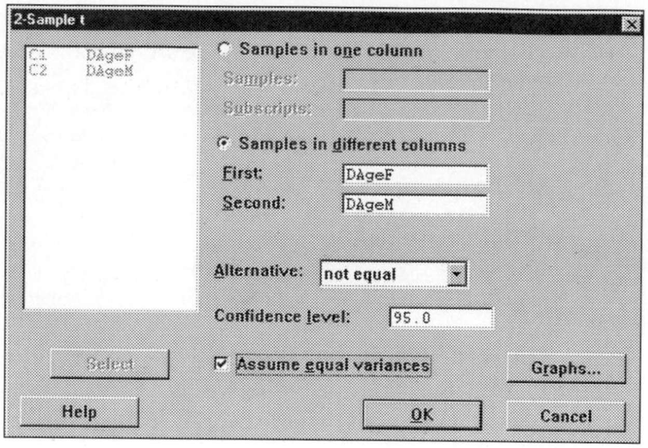

■ Click **OK**

The results appear in the Session window and in Figure 8-3.

FIGURE 8-3

Results of 2-Sample t-test comparing mean female and male ages at death

```
MTB > TwoSample 95.0 'DAgeF' 'DAgeM';
SUBC>    Alternative 0;
SUBC>    Pooled.
```

Two Sample T-Test and Confidence Interval

```
Two sample T for DAgeF vs DAgeM

           N     Mean    StDev   SE Mean
DAgeF     19     75.5    13.2      3.0
DAgeM     18     74.2    13.2      3.1

95% CI for mu DAgeF - mu DAgeM: ( -7.5,  10.1)
T-Test mu DAgeF = mu DAgeM (vs not =): T = 0.30   P = 0.77   DF = 35
Both use Pooled StDev = 13.2
```

Minitab presents summary information (sample size, mean, standard deviation, and standard error) for the females and males and then displays the t-statistic (T = 0.30), p-value (P = 0.77), and degrees of freedom for the t-statistic (DF = 35). Since the p-value of 0.77 exceeds the level of significance of .05, you fail to reject the null hypothesis that there is no significant evidence of a difference between the ages at death of all famous females and males. You can attribute the differences in the sample means to sampling variation.

Note that Minitab also provides a confidence interval for the difference in the population means. The 95% confidence interval for $\mu_F - \mu_M$ is (–7.5 years to 10.1 years). The fact that the 95% confidence interval includes the value 0 is consistent with the result of your test.

Two-sample t-tests, like their one-sample cousins you examined in Tutorial 7, assume that the samples come from normal populations. Graphical procedures are often the best ways to examine this assumption. Minitab offers two built-in graphics options — boxplots and dotplots — with the 2-Sample t-test. To see dotplots of the two samples of ages:

- Choose **Edit > Edit Last Dialog**

- Click the **Graphs** button, and click the **Dotplots of data** option button

- Click **OK** twice

The resulting graph is shown in Figure 8-4.

FIGURE 8-4

Built-in dotplots of DAgeF and DAgeM

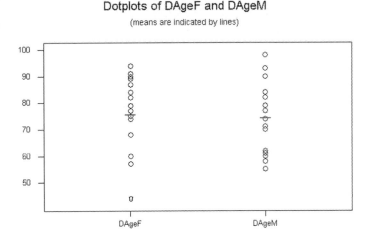

The dotplots are presented vertically with each age represented by a circle. The mean for each gender is indicated by a single line (–) through each dotplot. The only possible sign of non-normality is a low value for DAgeF that may be an outlier. This does not, however, seem to be a major problem. You may safely assume that the distribution of age at death is not substantially far from normality.

▼ **Note** Histograms and stem-and-leaf displays are generally considered better than dotplots or boxplots at representing the shape of the distribution of a data set. Minitab offers the latter two perhaps because they are easier to present on a single graph. A normal probability plot (NPP — discussed in Chapter 6) would be an even better technique for checking for normality. ▲

Before proceeding to the next case study:

- Save the project **T8.mpj**

CASE STUDY: REAL ESTATE — HOUSING PRICES (CONTINUED)

To continue the housing price study you started in Tutorial 7, you decide to test, at a significance level of .05, whether houses with 10 or more rooms have a statistically significantly higher selling price than do houses with nine or fewer rooms.

You've collected data on selling prices (C1 Price), living areas (C2 Area), lot sizes (C3 Acres), rooms (C4 Rooms), and number of baths (C5 Baths) in a file called *Homes.mtw*.

The data file *Homes.mtw* is in the Student subdirectory:

- Open the worksheet **Homes.mtw**

Before analyzing these data, you should save them:

- In the location where you are saving your work, save the worksheet as **8Homes**

Using Stacked Data

First, create a column that codes houses with 9 or fewer rooms as "small" and those with 10 or more rooms as "large":

- Choose **Manip > Code - Numeric to Text**

- Enter **C4 Rooms** as the "Code data from columns" variable, and press (Tab)

- Type **Size** as the "Into columns" variable, and press (Tab)

- Type **0:9** as the first "Original values," and press (Tab)

- Type **Small** as the first "New" value, and press (Tab)

- Type **10:100** as the second "Original values," and press (Tab)

- Type **Large** as the second "New" value

The Code - Numeric to Text dialog box should look as shown in Figure 8-5.

FIGURE 8-5

The completed Code - Numeric to Text dialog box

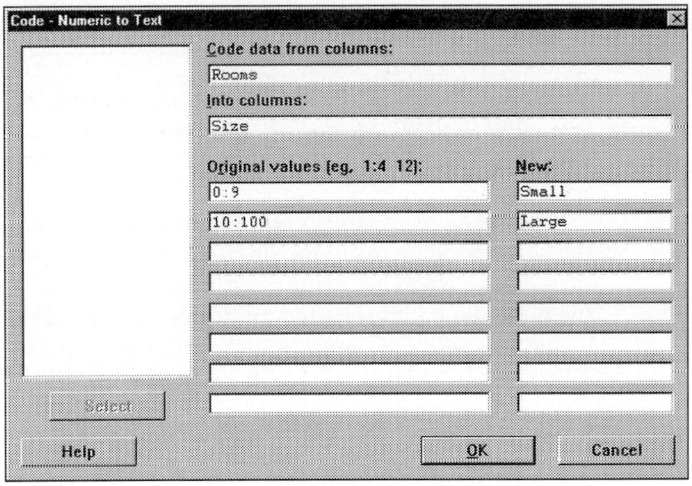

- Press ⏎

    Before performing the test, examine the data by looking at numerical summaries:

- Choose **Stat > Basic Statistics > Display Descriptive Statistics**

- Select **C1 Price** to enter it as the variable

- Click the **By variable** check box, and press `Tab`

- Select **C6 Size** as the "By variable"

- Click **OK**

    The output is shown in the Session window and in Figure 8-6.

FIGURE 8-6

Descriptive statistics for Price by Size

```
MTB > Describe 'Price';
SUBC>   By 'Size'.
```

Descriptive Statistics

Variable	Size	N	Mean	Median	TrMean	StDev
Price	Large	8	191769	198450	191769	38477
	Small	142	151635	142000	148827	40862

Variable	Size	SE Mean	Minimum	Maximum	Q1	Q3
Price	Large	13604	141000	235000	154125	228812
	Small	3429	72000	302000	125975	172750

There are only eight large houses; they have a mean price of $191,769. The 142 small houses have a mean price of $151,635, more than $40,000 less.

The sample standard deviations are of the same order of magnitude, but you decide that here you won't assume the population variances are the same.

Now formulate the hypotheses:

Null hypothesis, H_0: $\mu_L = \mu_S$

Alternative hypothesis, H_1: $\mu_L > \mu_S$

Here, μ_L is the mean selling price for all large houses in the area and μ_S is the corresponding mean for small houses in the area.

In the worksheet *Homes.mtw*, C1 Price lists selling prices and C6 Size, the column you just created, indicates the size of the houses. Perform the hypothesis test and obtain a 90% confidence interval for the difference between selling prices of large and small houses:

- Choose **Stat > Basic Statistics > 2-Sample t**

   In this example, the sample values are stacked in the same column, C1 Price. The code for the size of the houses are in C6 Size.

- Click the **Samples in one column** option button, and press (Tab)

- Select **C1 Price** as the "Samples" variable

- Select **C6 Size** as the "Subscripts" variable, and press (Tab)

- Select **greater than** as the "Alternative," and press (Tab)

- Type **90** as the "Confidence level"

- Deselect **Assume equal variances**

   In the last case study, you asked for a dotplot of the two samples. Since this option is still in force, you will get a dotplot of house prices, by size, with your output here. The completed 2-Sample t dialog box should look as shown in Figure 8-7.

FIGURE 8-7

The completed 2-Sample t dialog box for stacked data

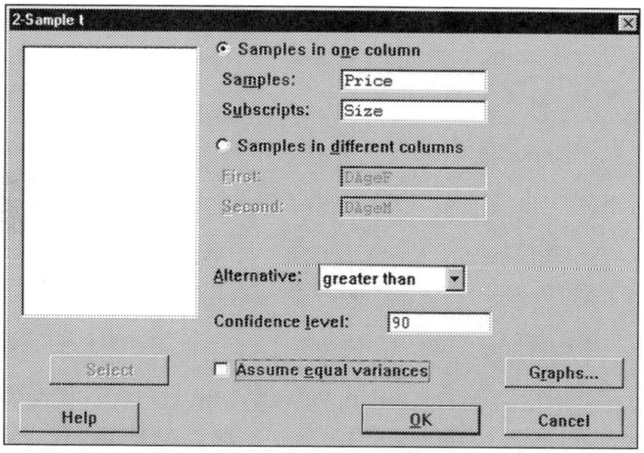

- Click **OK**

The dotplots will appear as shown in Figure 8-8.

FIGURE 8-8

Built-in Dotplots of Price by Size

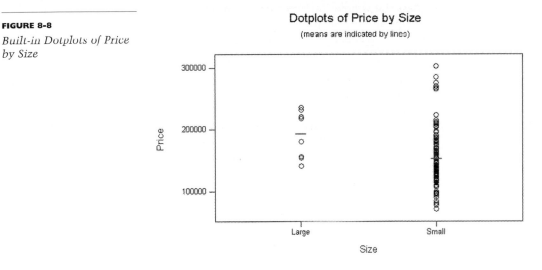

The dotplot of price for large houses is close to symmetric around the mean, but the distribution of prices for small houses is more skewed to the right. This is not a serious problem when the sample size is as large as it is here.

To examine the numerical outcome of the test:

- Click the **Session Window** toolbar button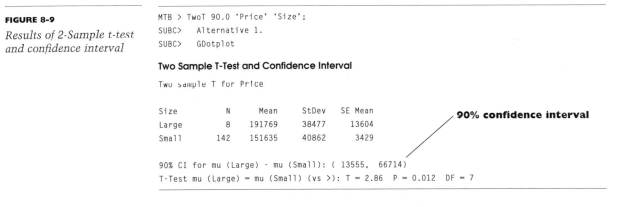

The output is shown in Figure 8-9.

FIGURE 8-9

Results of 2-Sample t-test and confidence interval

```
MTB > TwoT 90.0 'Price' 'Size';
SUBC>    Alternative 1.
SUBC>    GDotplot
```

Two Sample T-Test and Confidence Interval

Two sample T for Price

Size	N	Mean	StDev	SE Mean
Large	8	191769	38477	13604
Small	142	151635	40862	3429

90% confidence interval

```
90% CI for mu (Large) - mu (Small): ( 13555,  66714)
T-Test mu (Large) = mu (Small) (vs >): T = 2.86  P = 0.012  DF = 7
```

The difference in sample means, \$151,635 – \$191,769 = \$40,134, corresponds to a t-value with 7 DF, of 2.86. The p-value for this test is 0.012, which is less than .05. Therefore you reject H_0 and conclude that there is significant evidence that the population mean selling price of houses with 10 or more rooms is significantly higher than that for houses with 9 or fewer rooms. Minitab provides you with a 90% confidence interval ($13,555 to $66,714) for the unknown population difference in mean price.

Minitab uses the following notation for the two-sample t-test (where μ_1 is the mean for population 1, and μ_2 is the mean for population 2).

Hypothesis		Alternative Hypothesis in the Dialog Box
Null	$H_0: \mu_1 = \mu_2$	none
Alternative	$H_1: \mu_1 < \mu_2$	less than
	$H_1: \mu_1 \neq \mu_2$	not equal
	$H_1: \mu_1 > \mu_2$	greater than

When the samples are in separate columns, Minitab assumes that the data you entered in the "First" text box is the sample from population 1. When the samples are stacked and the column of subscripts is numerical, Minitab assumes that the smaller of the two numbers indicates the sample from population 1. When the column of subscripts is text with two names, Minitab assumes that the sample from population 1 corresponds to the name that begins with the letter that is closer to the beginning of the alphabet. Thus, in the case study on house prices, since L is closer to the beginning of the alphabet than S, Minitab assumes that Large houses are the sample from population 1 and Small houses are the sample from population 2.

Using Help to Find a Formula

You have performed the previous analysis as the newly hired real estate agent for Consolidated Properties. The appendix to your report on house prices in the area will include the formulas used for the various tests you have performed in this and the previous tutorial. The only formula you have not been able to locate is the one for the two-sample t-statistic when the population variances are not assumed equal. You decide to use Help to find this formula:

- Choose **Help > Search for Help on**

- Click the entry **2-Sample t (Stat Menu)**, and click **Display**

- Click the entry **calculations, 2-Sample t**, and click **Display**

- Scroll down until you see the material shown in Figure 8-10

  You can insert these formulas in your appendix.

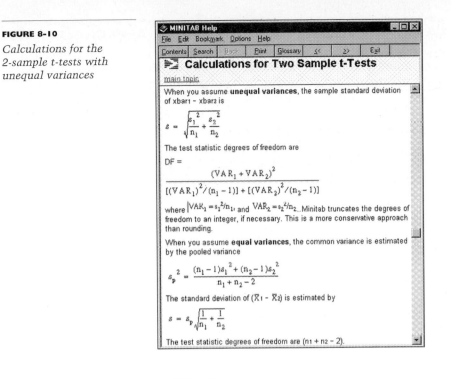

- Click **Exit**

  Before proceeding with the tutorial, save your work:

- Click the **Save Project** toolbar button ▣

▼ 8.2 Comparing Population Means from Two Paired (Dependent) Samples ▲

In the previous case studies in this tutorial, samples were drawn independently from each of two populations. Pairing subjects, such as identical twins or before-and-after measurements of a subject, can eliminate the effect of extraneous variables. Such data are called *paired*, or *dependent*, samples.

CASE STUDY: HEALTH CARE — CEREAL AND CHOLESTEROL

Recently 14 male patients suffering from high levels of cholesterol took part in an experiment to examine whether a diet that included oat bran would reduce cholesterol levels. Each was randomly assigned to a diet that included either corn flakes or oat bran. After two weeks, their low-density lipoprotein (LDL) cholesterol levels were recorded. Each man then repeated this process with the other cereal. The 14 pairs of LDL results are recorded in a data file called *Chol.mtw*. As a rookie analyst at the clinic where the research was conducted, you have been asked to analyze these data. (You may assume these men are a random sample of all men suffering from high levels of cholesterol.)

The data file *Chol.mtw* is in the Student subdirectory:

- Open the worksheet **Chol.mtw**

  Before analyzing these data, you should save them:

- In the location where you are saving your work, save the worksheet as **8Chol**

  In this data set, C1 CornFlke and C2 OatBran contain the LDL levels for each cereal, respectively, for each of the 14 patients in the study. Minitab enables you to obtain a paired t-test and confidence interval without computing the 14 (CornFlke – OatBran) differences. You form the hypotheses:

  Null hypothesis, H_0: $\mu_D = 0$

  Alternative hypothesis, H_1: $\mu_D > 0$

  Here, μ_D is the mean change in LDL that would result if every male with high cholesterol was included in the study. The alternative hypothesis is right-tailed, since your expectation is that if μ_D is not 0 it will be greater than 0. As a graphical check of the normality assumption, you decide also to ask for a histogram of the 14 differences.

- Choose **Stat > Basic Statistics > Paired t**

- Select **C1 CornFlke** as the "First sample" and **C2 OatBran** as the "Second sample"

- Click the **Options** button, and note that the default "Confidence level" is set at **95%** and that the default "Test mean" is set at **0**

- Select **greater than** as the "Alternative," and then click **OK**

- Click the **Graphs** button, click the **Histogram of differences** option button, and click **OK**

  The completed Paired t dialog box should look as shown in Figure 8-11.

FIGURE 8-11

The completed Paired t dialog box

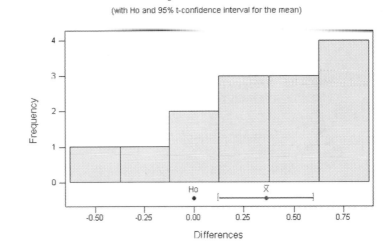

Notice that the Paired t dialog box shows that inferences are based on the First sample–Second sample differences.

■ Click **OK**

The built-in histogram of the 14 differences is shown in Figure 8-12.

FIGURE 8-12

Built-in Histogram of differences

Histogram of Differences

(with Ho and 95% t-confidence interval for the mean)

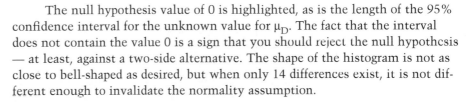

The null hypothesis value of 0 is highlighted, as is the length of the 95% confidence interval for the unknown value for μ_D. The fact that the interval does not contain the value 0 is a sign that you should reject the null hypothesis — at least, against a two-side alternative. The shape of the histogram is not as close to bell-shaped as desired, but when only 14 differences exist, it is not different enough to invalidate the normality assumption.

■ Click the **Session Window** toolbar button

The output in the Session window resembles Figure 8-13.

FIGURE 8-13

Results of the paired t-test

```
MTB > Paired 'CornFlke' 'OatBran';
SUBC>    Confidence 95.0;
SUBC>    Test 0.0;
SUBC>    Alternative 1;
SUBC>    GHistogram.
```

Paired T-Test and Confidence Interval

```
Paired T for CornFlke - OatBran

                N      Mean    StDev   SE Mean
CornFlke       14      4.444   0.969    0.259
OatBran        14      4.081   1.057    0.282
Difference     14      0.363   0.406    0.108


95% CI for mean difference: (0.128, 0.597)
T-Test of mean difference = 0 (vs > 0): T-Value = 3.34   P-Value = 0.003
```

The mean of the differences is 0.363, which corresponds to a t-value of 3.34. Since the p-value for this test is 0.003, you can reject H_0 at, for example, the 1% level of significance. Your test provides significant evidence that the use of oat bran significantly reduces the mean LDL cholesterol level.

■ Save the project *T8.mpj*

▼ 8.3 Sample Size and Power for Comparing Two Means ▲

CASE STUDY: WELFARE REFORM — ERRORS IN GRANT DETERMINATION

Errors in determining how much welfare a family is entitled to can be expensive for both the recipient (if the grant is smaller than it should be) and to the state (if the grant is larger than it should be). Part of the difficulty in determining the grant amount is that the standard procedure for determining the amount is by reference to a manual consisting of complex state and Federal regulations. To test a technique that might make this determination simpler, the Federal government is underwriting an experiment at two welfare offices that serve two similar populations.

At one (Control) office, the standard procedure for determining the grant amount will be used. At the other (Experimental) office, a new procedure using Decision Logic Table (DLT) will be tried for six months. DLTs are logical pathways through the regulations that should make it easier to determine the appropriate grant in each case. After six months, auditors will select a random sample of cases from each center and determine the error for each case. As the statistician working for the agency responsible for this experiment, your first job is to decide on the appropriate number of cases (n) to sample from each office.

First, create a new worksheet:

- Choose **File > New**

- In the New dialog box, double-click **Minitab Worksheet**

    You formulate the appropriate hypotheses as follows:

    Null hypothesis, H_0: $\mu_C - \mu_E = 0$

    Alternative hypothesis, H_1: $\mu_C - \mu_E > 0$

    Here, μ_C and μ_E are, respectively, the population mean dollar errors in the control and the experimental centers.

    You decide to use a level of significance of $\alpha = .05$. Previous studies of errors in grant determination suggest that the standard deviation of error is approximately $70. You have been informed that it is important to reject the null hypothesis if the true difference, $\mu_C - \mu_E$, is as small as $20. This is the effect size. Minitab allows you to investigate the sample size associated with different values for the power of the test. Specifically, you intend to obtain the sample sizes needed to provide power values from .5 to .95 at intervals of .05. You will represent this sequence in the form .5:.95/.05.

- Choose **Stat > Power and Sample Size > 2-Sample t**

- Click the **Calculate sample size for each power value** option button, and press Tab

- Type **.5:.95/.05** as the "Power values," and press Tab

- Type **20** as the "Difference," and press Tab

- Type **70** as "Sigma"

    The Power and Sample Size for 2-Sample t dialog box should look as in Figure 8-14.

FIGURE 8-14

The Power and Sample Size for 2-Sample t dialog box

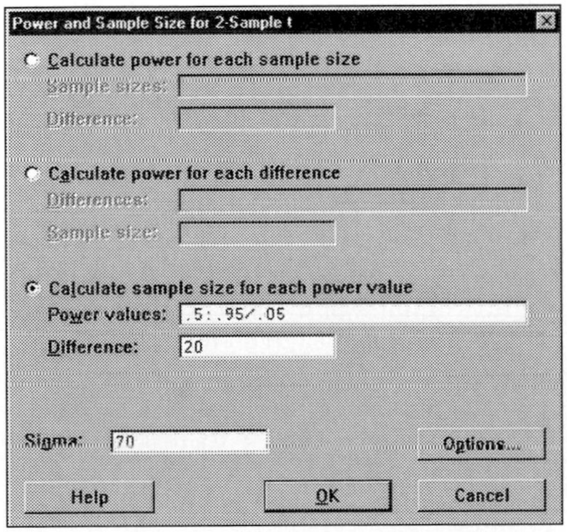

- Click the **Options** button, select **greater than** as the "Alternative," and press ⟨Tab⟩ twice

- Type **n** in the "Store sample sizes in" text box and press ⟨Tab⟩

- In the "Store power values in" text box, type **Power**

- Click **OK** twice

The output is shown in the Session window and in Figure 8-15.

FIGURE 8-15

Sample size and power calculations

```
MTB > Name c1 = 'n' c2 = 'Power'
MTB > Power;
SUBC>   TTwo;
SUBC>      Power .5:.95/.05;
SUBC>      Difference 20;
SUBC>      Sigma 70;
SUBC>      Alternative 1;
SUBC>      Store 'n' 'Power'.
```

Power and Sample Size

2-Sample t-Test

Testing mean 1 = mean 2 (versus >)
Calculating power for mean 1 = mean 2 + 20
Alpha = 0.05   Sigma = 70

Sample Size	Target Power	Actual Power
67	0.5000	0.5001
78	0.5500	0.5523
89	0.6000	0.6002
102	0.6500	0.6513
116	0.7000	0.7001
133	0.7500	0.7515
153	0.8000	0.8019
177	0.8500	0.8503
211	0.9000	0.9006
266	0.9500	0.9501

The sample sizes are given in the left column. The middle column contains the desired power values, which Minitab calls the "Target" power. The exact, or "Actual," power corresponding to the sample size is in the right-hand column. You note that the power of the test increases as the sample size increases. After consulting with your colleagues in the agency, you decide to recommend that samples of n = 211 cases be selected and audited in each office. This will guarantee a power of 0.9006.

You decide to plot the power of the test against the sample size:

- Click the **Current Data window** toolbar button ▦

The values for n are stored in C1 n and the corresponding power values in C2 Power.

To plot Power against n:

- Choose **Graph > Plot**

- Select **C2 Power** as the "Y" variable and then **C1 n** as the "X" variable

- Click **OK**

The resulting graph is shown in Figure 8-16.

FIGURE 8-16

*Plot of Power against
sample size n*

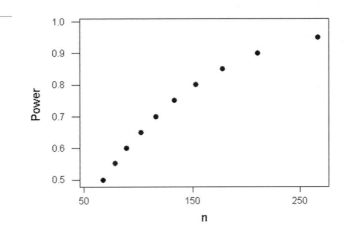

The plot shows that power increases with the value of n. It is also clear that because the power of the test cannot exceed 1, the graph begins to level off as n moves beyond 250 cases.

From Figure 8-14, note that the Power and Sample Size for 2-Sample t command offers three options:

1. Power for a variety of sample sizes for a specific difference (value for $\mu_1 - \mu_2$)

2. Power for a variety of differences (values for $\mu_1 - \mu_2$) for a specific sample size

3. Sample sizes needed to achieve a variety of power values for a specific difference (value for $\mu_1 - \mu_2$)

Before proceeding to the next case study:

- Save the project **T8.mpj**

▼ 8.4 Comparing Population Proportions from Two Independent Samples ▲

In the last tutorial, you tested whether the incidence of days lost to low back pain by patients at an HMO was significantly less than .6 As a follow-up to this, you decide to test whether there is any statistically significant difference in the proportion of males and females who miss work for this health problem.

You will be working with the data file *Backpain.mtw*, which is in the Student subdirectory:

- Open the worksheet **Backpain.mtw**

Before analyzing these data, you should save them:

- In the location where you are saving your work, save the worksheet as **8Backpn**

The gender of the patient is in C1 Gender and the number of days lost as a result of low back pain is in C3 LostDays. You will need to recreate the variable C5 LostInd, which takes the value 0 if C3 LostDays is 0 and the value 1 if C3 LostDays takes any nonzero value. You may want to review the procedure in Section 7.6.

- Choose **Calc > Calculator**

- Type **LostInd** in the "Store result in variable" text box and press ⌧Tab⌧

- Enter, by clicking or typing, **LostDays > 0** as the "Expression"

- Click **OK**

The 1's in C5 LostInd represent those patients in the sample who lost at least one day's work as a result of low back pain; the 0's represent those patients who did not. Minitab will assume that the larger of the two values (1) in C5 LostInd is the "success" and the smaller of the two (0) is the "failure."

Now formulate hypotheses to test whether the proportions of females and males (in the population) who miss work as a result of low back pain are statistically, significantly different:

Null hypothesis, H_0: $p_F = p_M$

Alternative hypothesis, H_1: $p_F \neq p_M$

To obtain the test at the 5% level of significance (and the default 95% confidence interval for $p_F - p_M$):

- Choose **Stat > Basic Statistics > 2 Proportions**

- Verify that the **Samples in one column** option button is checked, and press [Tab]

- Select **C5 LostInd** as the "Samples"

- Enter **C1 Gender** as the "Subscripts"

- Click the **Options** button and verify that the "Confidence level" is **95**

- Verify also that the default "Test difference" is **0** and that the default "Alternative" is **not equal**

- Click the **Use pooled estimates of p for test** check box

The 2 Proportions - Options dialog box should look as shown in Figure 8-17.

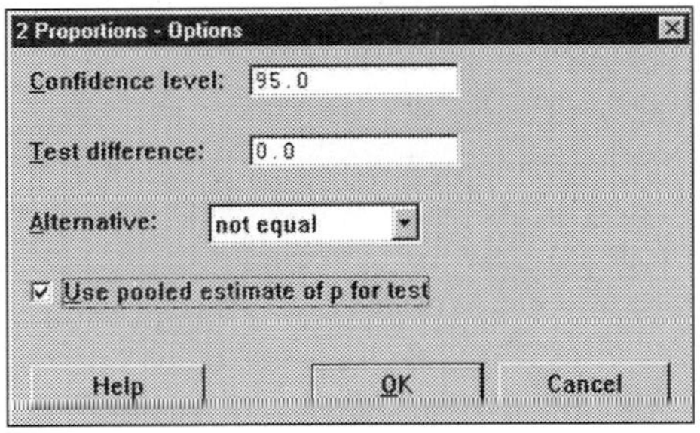

FIGURE 8-17

The completed 2 Proportions - Options dialog box

- Click **OK** twice

The output in the Session window is as shown in Figure 8-18.

FIGURE 8-18

The 2 Proportions output

```
MTB > PTwo 'LostInd' 'Gender';
SUBC>    Stacked;
SUBC>    Confidence 95.0;
SUBC>    Test 0.0;
SUBC>    Alternative 0;
SUBC>    Pooled.
```

Test and Confidence Interval for Two Proportions

Success = 1

Gender	X	N	Sample p
Female	61	106	0.575472
Male	93	173	0.537572

Estimate for p(Female) - p(Male): 0.0378994
95% CI for p(Female) - p(Male): (-0.0819902, 0.157789)
Test for p(Female) - p(Male) = 0 (vs not = 0): Z = 0.62 P-Value = 0.537

The sample proportions are quite close. Almost 58% of the 61 females and almost 54% of the 93 males lost work days. The difference in the sample proportions (0.0378994) translates into a Z value of only 0.62. The corresponding p-value is .537. Since this exceeds any standard level of significance, you cannot reject the null hypothesis. The data suggest that there is no significant difference between the proportion of females and the proportion of males who lose work time due to low back pain. This lack of statistical significance is reflected in the 95% confidence interval for $p_F - p_M$, which runs from approximately –.082 to .158 and contains 0.

▼ 8.5   Sample Size and Power for Comparing Two Proportions ▲

In the previous analysis, you could not reject the null hypothesis of no difference in the proportion of all male and all female sufferers of low back pain who miss work. You fear that this may be because the power of the test is inadequate to detect an important difference. Minitab does not allow you to compute the power of this test when the sample sizes are not the same. However, you can compute how many patients of each gender you would need to survey in order to detect a specified difference that has a specified power. For example, suppose you want to be 80% sure of detecting a difference between p_F and p_M (the effect size) of .10, where the level of significance is kept at the standard .05. To do this, you need to specify provisional values for p_F and p_M. From your statistics class, you know that sample sizes are likely to be conservatively high if you select values for these proportions that are close to .5, so you will use p_F = .6 and p_M = .5. The sample data you do have support these approximations.

To perform the power calculation:

■ Choose **Stat > Power and Sample Size > 2 Proportions**

■ Click the **Calculate sample size for each power value** option button, and press Tab

■ Type **.80** as the "Power values," and press Tab

■ Type **.60** as "Proportion 1"

■ Verify that the default for "Proportion 2" is **0.5**

■ Click the **Options** button, and verify that the default "Alternative" is **not equal** and that the default level of significance is **0.05**

■ Click **OK**

The Power and Sample Size for 2 Proportions dialog box should look as shown in Figure 8-19.

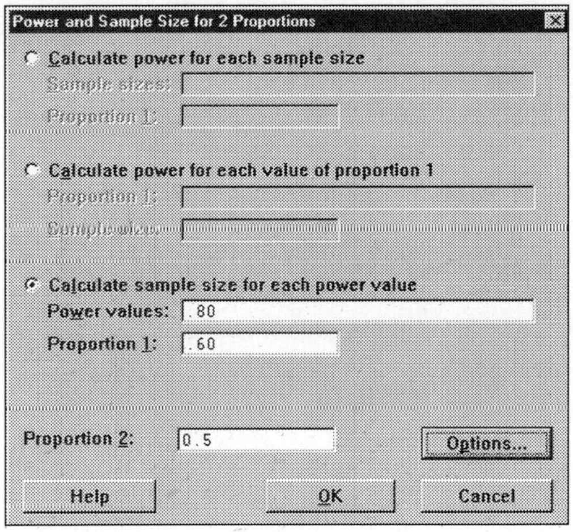

FIGURE 8-19

The competed Power and Sample Size for 2 Proportions dialog box

- Click **OK**

The calculations in the Session window are shown in Figure 8-20.

FIGURE 8-20

The 2-sample power calculations

```
MTB > Power;
SUBC>   PTwo;
SUBC>     Power .80;
SUBC>     PrOne .60;
SUBC>     PrTwo 0.5.
```

Power and Sample Size

```
Test for Two Proportions

Testing proportion 1 = proportion 2 (versus not =)
Calculating power for proportion 1 = 0.6 and proportion 2 = 0.5
Alpha = 0.05  Difference = 0.1

Sample   Target  Actual
  Size    Power   Power
   391   0.8000  0.8009
```

The output suggests that you would need to select 391 patients with low back pain of each gender in order to be 80% sure of rejecting the null hypothesis of no difference if, in fact, a difference of 0.1 exists.

- Save the current project ***T8.mpj***, and exit Minitab

SCIENTIFIC RESEARCH: A supernova, the explosion of a star, is a rarely observed phenomenon. Researchers often study it by examining the remnants it leaves behind. Astronomers have charted 29 supernova remnants (SNRs) in a nearby galaxy named the Large Magellanic Cloud. They predicted that SNRs produced by stars with relatively short lives would be close to areas of recent star formation, called H II regions. A physicist, a mathematician, and an undergraduate at a Colorado university teamed up to study the Large Magellanic Cloud supernovas by testing whether the remnants are indeed close to H II regions.

The team calculated the distance between each of the 29 known SNRs in the Cloud and its nearest H II region and then found the mean distance. They used Minitab to simulate what the mean distance would have been had the SNRs been randomly distributed throughout the galaxy. A 2-sample t-test showed that the actual mean distance was significantly less than Minitab's randomly generated SNR locations had led them to expect.

They concluded that supernova remnants in the Cloud are not randomly distributed. The SNRs cluster around areas of recent star formation and are likely to have resulted from the explosions of short-lived stars.

▼
**Minitab
Command
Summary**
▲

This section describes the menu commands introduced in, or related to, this tutorial. To find a complete explanation of all menus and commands, use Minitab's Help.

Minitab Menu Commands

Menu	Command	Description
Stat		
	Basic Statistics	
	2-Sample t	Performs inferences (tests and confidence intervals) on the differences between two population means using independent samples.
	Paired t	Performs inferences (tests and confidence intervals) on the differences between two population means using paired (dependent) data.
	2 Proportions	Performs inferences (tests and confidence intervals) on the differences between two population proportions using independent samples.

Menu	Command	Description
	Power and Sample Size	
	2-Sample t	Computes power for different sample sizes or for different values for $\mu_1 - \mu_2$ based on a t distribution. Also computes sample sizes for different power values.
	2 Proportions	Computes power for different sample sizes or for different values for $p_1 - p_2$. Also computes sample sizes for different power values.

▼

Review and Practice

▲

Matching

Match the following terms to their definitions by placing the correct letter next to the term it describes.

_____ Target

_____ Samples in one column

_____ Assume equal variances

_____ Samples in different columns

_____ Not equal to

_____ Subscript

_____ Basic Statistics

_____ 2-Sample t

_____ Actual

_____ Paired t

a. The default alternative hypothesis in Minitab commands

b. The Minitab option that lets you perform a 2-sample t-test, assuming the standard deviations of the populations are equal

c. The Minitab menu that includes all of the commands for 2-sample inferences about means and proportions

d. The Minitab command that performs inference on the differences between two population means using independent samples

e. The Minitab term for the column containing the codes identifying each sample in 2-sample inferences

f. The adjective describing the power of a test for the difference between two population proportions that you would like to achieve

g. The Minitab 2-sample test option that performs inference on means from two different populations using stacked data

h. The Minitab 2-sample test option that performs inference on means from two different populations using sample data stored in two different columns

i. The adjective describing the power of a test for the difference between two population proportions corresponding to a given sample size

j. The Minitab command that performs a t-test for two dependent samples

True/False

Mark the following statements with a *T* or an *F*.

_____ Minitab can perform a 2-sample t-test if the data from the populations are stored in either one or two columns.

_____ Minitab cannot obtain the power of a test for two proportions when the sample sizes are different.

_____ The 2-Sample t menu command performs a 2-sample test for the difference between two population proportions.

_____ The output of the test of the two population means includes a confidence interval for the difference between the two population means.

_____ Minitab can perform independent, 2-sample t-tests, assuming the population variances are equal or unequal.

_____ Minitab can perform only two-tailed, 2-sample tests.

_____ The default confidence level for 2-sample confidence intervals is 90%.

_____ In a 2-sample test, Minitab requires a subscripts column when the two sample data are stored in a single column.

_____ The subscript column used in the 2-sample t-test must be numeric.

_____ In a 2-sample test for proportions, Minitab assumes the smaller of the two values is the success.

Practice Problems

Use Help or Part III, "Exploring Data" to review the contents of the data sets referred to in the following problems.

1. Open *Prof.mtw*. Assume the sections in which the surveys were distributed are a random sample of all sections at the college.

   a. Test whether first-year courses have a different mean rating than fourth-year courses. (You can unstack the course rating data into four columns and then use the appropriate columns.)

   b. Repeat (a) using the Instrucr rating.

   c. Based on your results in (a) and (b), determine whether students' opinions about their instructors change over the course of their college careers? If so, in what direction?

2. Open *Ads2.mtw*. Assume the examined magazines are a random sample of the magazines in 1989, 1991, and 1993.

   a. Test whether the news magazine has a higher mean ad ratio than the sports magazine. Use a level of significance of .05. Perform this test twice, once with dotplots and once with boxplots of the sample data.

   b. Which of the two graphs in (a) best displays the results of your test in (a)? Explain your choice.

c. Are the graphs you obtained in (a) consistent with the normality assumptions? Explain.

3. Open *Rivers.mtw*.

  a. Determine if the mean temperature of the river is different at site 2, which is directly upriver from the power plant, or at site 3, which is directly down river from the cooling towers' discharge. To do so, create a new column using the code "1" for site 2 and "2" for site 3, with no code entered for all others. Use the Manip > Code > Numeric to Numeric command to code only the sites 2 and 3 values.

  b. Obtain a 95% confidence for the difference in the population means in (a).

4. Open *Backpain.mtw*.

  a. Create a new column that takes the value 0 when C3 LostDays is 0 and the value 1 otherwise.

  b. Create a new column that takes the name "younger" when the patient is 39 years old or younger and the name "older" otherwise.

  c. Test whether the proportion of older patients with lost work days is significantly greater than the corresponding proportion of younger patients.

  d. Obtain a 90% confidence interval for the difference in the population proportions referred to in (c).

5. Open *PulseA.mtw*. Assume these 92 students can be considered a random sample of 18- to 21-year olds in college.

  a. Test whether there is any significant difference between the proportions of males (p_M) and females (p_F) that smoke. Use a level of significance of .05.

  b. Obtain an 80% confidence interval for $p_M - p_F$.

  c. Create a new column that contains the increases in pulse rate (Pulse$_2$ – Pulse$_1$). Name this new column Increase.

  d. Use the command Manip > Copy Columns to create two new columns, SexRan and IncRan, which contain, respectively, the sex and the increase in pulse rate for just those students who ran in place (that is, for whom C3 Ran = 1).

  e. Test for any significant difference between the mean increase in pulse rates for males and for females who ran in place.

  f. For the test in (e), obtain graphs that help you determine whether the normality assumption is valid. What is your conclusion?

6. Open *Homes.mtw*. It contains data on 150 randomly selected homes. Create a new variable that takes the value 1 when a house has a single bathroom and 2 when more than one bathroom. Test the hypothesis that the mean price of houses with more than one bathroom is significantly greater than that for houses with just one bathroom.

7. Refer to the first case study in this tutorial.

   a. Compute power of the test that the mean age at death for famous men is the same as that for famous women against the alternative that famous women live .5, 1.0, 1.5, . . . , 7.0 years longer (the effect size). Assume samples of 100 men and 100 women and that the standard deviation of age at death is 15 years for both genders.

   b. Plot power against the effect size, and comment on what your plot shows.

TUTORIAL
9

Comparing Population Means: Analysis of Variance

In Tutorial 8, you used Minitab to perform t-tests to compare the means of two populations. You can extend this capability to compare the means of several populations by using a statistical tool called *Analysis of Variance (ANOVA)*. In this tutorial, you will perform *one-way* ANOVA, in which you test for the equality of population means when the populations are defined by the different values for a single (explanatory) variable. Then, in a *two-way* ANOVA, you will assess the effect of two explanatory variables on a response variable.

Objectives

In this tutorial, you learn how to:

- compare the means of several populations when the observations for all of the samples are in one column and all of the subscripts that identify the samples are in another

- generate residual and fitted values from a one-way ANOVA

- perform a Tukey multiple comparison test for significant differences between pairs of population means

- compare the means of several populations when the samples from each population are placed in different columns

- assess the effects of two factors on a response variable

▼ 9.1 Comparing the Means of Several Populations ▲

CASE STUDY: CHILD DEVELOPMENT — INFANT ATTENTION SPANS

You are a psychology student taking a course in child development. As part of your project for the course, you have been examining how different designs vary in their ability to capture an infant's attention. You devised an experiment to see whether an infant's attention span varies with the type of design on a mobile. You randomly divided a group of 30 three-month-old infants into five groups of six each. Each group was shown a mobile with one of five multicolored designs: A, B, C, D, or E. Because of time constraints, each infant could be shown only one design. You recorded the median time that the infant spent looking at the design. In a Minitab worksheet, you recorded the times in C1 Times and the designs that each infant saw in C2 Design. The worksheet is saved in the file *Baby.mtw*.

To get started:

- Start **Minitab**

- Maximize the **Session window**

- If necessary, enable the **Session command language** and make the output read-only

You'll be working with the data file *Baby.mtw*, which is in the Student subdirectory:

- Open the worksheet **Baby.mtw**

Before analyzing these data, save them as a worksheet and this tutorial in a project:

- In the location where you are saving your work, save the worksheet as **9Baby**

- Save what you have done thus far in this tutorial in a project named **T9**

One value in the data set was recorded by a friend in your class who admits to not paying close attention to the infant being studied. The value 5.6 for mobile E is the one your friend recorded. You are concerned about its accuracy, so you decide to replace it with an asterisk (*), the symbol Minitab uses to indicate a missing numeric value.

- In **row 27 of C1 Time**, replace the value 5.6 with an * (asterisk)

You are advised by the teaching assistant for the course that a one-way ANOVA should be used for these data. However, before doing an ANOVA you decide to examine numerical and graphical summaries of your data. You decide to obtain a description of the times for each design with boxplots:

- Choose **Stat > Basic Statistics > Display Descriptive Statistics**

- Select **C1 Time** as the "Variable"

- Click the **By variable** check box, and press Tab

- Select **C2 Design** as the "By variable"

- Click the **Graphs** button, and click the **Boxplot of data** check box

- Click **OK** twice

The boxplots are shown in Figure 9-1.

FIGURE 9-1

Boxplots of attention times by design

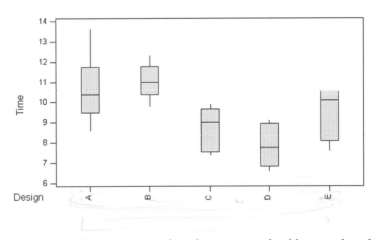

The boxplots suggest that there is considerable spread in the median attention times, with design B having the highest median and design D the lowest. The times for design A seem to be a little more variable than those for the other designs. The numerical summaries appear in the Session window as shown in Figure 9-2. To see them:

- Click the **Session window** toolbar button ▣

FIGURE 9-2

Descriptive statistics for Time by Design

```
MTB > Describe 'Time';
SUBC>   By 'Design';
SUBC>   GBoxplot.
```

Descriptive Statistics

Variable	Design	N	N*	Mean	Median	TrMean
Time	A	6	0	10.650	10.400	10.650
	B	6	0	11.050	11.000	11.050
	C	6	0	8.750	9.000	8.750
	D	6	0	7.833	7.750	7.833
	E	5	1	9.480	10.100	9.480

Variable	Design	StDev	SE Mean	Minimum	Maximum	Q1
Time	A	1.672	0.683	8.600	13.600	9.500
	B	0.855	0.349	9.800	12.300	10.400
	C	1.078	0.440	7.400	9.900	7.550
	D	1.019	0.416	6.600	9.100	6.825
	E	1.322	0.591	7.600	10.600	8.100

Variable	Design	Q3
Time	A	11.725
	B	11.775
	C	9.675
	D	8.950
	E	10.550

```
* NOTE * N missing = 1
```

You notice the missing value column in the output. The results are consistent with the findings from the boxplot. That is, design B has the highest mean and median times, while design D has the lowest of both. The standard deviations for designs C, D, and E are quite similar. However, the standard deviation for design A is higher than for these three, while that for design B is lower. You know that the one-way ANOVA assumes equal population variances. Although these five sample standard deviations differ, you judge that they do not differ enough to invalidate this assumption.

In this context, the *F-test* is a one-way ANOVA test that allows you to use the five sample means to test whether the population mean times associated with the five designs are significantly different statistically. There are two relevant hypotheses:

Null hypothesis, H_0: $\mu_A = \mu_B = \mu_C = \mu_D = \mu_E$

Alternative hypothesis, H_1: These means are not all equal.

Here, μ_A, μ_B, . . . , μ_E are the population mean attention times for the five designs.

You intend to use a level of significance (α) of .05. To perform the test:

■ Choose **Stat > ANOVA > One-way**

■ Select **C1 Time** as the "Response" variable and **C2 Design** as the "Factor"

In this context, the term *Factor* refers to the explanatory variable, Design. The completed dialog box should look as shown in Figure 9-3.

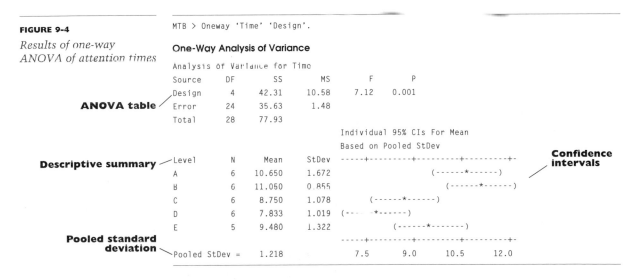

- Click **OK**

The Session window resembles Figure 9-4.

FIGURE 9-4

Results of one-way ANOVA of attention times

MTB > Oneway 'Time' 'Design'.

One-Way Analysis of Variance

Analysis of Variance for Time

ANOVA table

Source	DF	SS	MS	F	P
Design	4	42.31	10.58	7.12	0.001
Error	24	35.63	1.48		
Total	28	77.93			

Individual 95% CIs For Mean
Based on Pooled StDev

Descriptive summary

Confidence intervals

Level	N	Mean	StDev	
A	6	10.650	1.672	(------*------)
B	6	11.050	0.855	(------*------)
C	6	8.750	1.078	(------*------)
D	6	7.833	1.019	(------*------)
E	5	9.480	1.322	(------*-------)

```
                                        ----+---------+---------+---------+--
```

Pooled standard deviation

Pooled StDev =   1.218   7.5   9.0   10.5   12.0

The Session window display includes four components:

1. An ANOVA table that includes the value for F (7.12) and corresponding p-value 0.001 (since this p-value < α = 0.05, you would reject the null hypothesis at the 0.05 level of significance).

2. A descriptive summary of the attention times for each design that includes the sample size, the sample mean, and the sample standard deviation.

3. A diagram of the individual 95% confidence interval for the mean attention time for each design based on the pooled standard deviation (the asterisk represents the sample mean and the parentheses indicate the 95% confidence limits).

4. The pooled standard deviation used in the confidence intervals, in this case, 1.218 seconds.

The data suggest that the population mean attention times for the five designs are not all equal. From the diagram of the five individual confidence intervals, you notice that designs A and B together seem to elicit a longer mean attention span than do designs C, D, and E. You will look into this more closely in Section 9.3.

Although you covered the one-way ANOVA in your statistics course, you want a reminder of the role of the F-test in the analysis. Without a text available, you decide to check out the term F-test in Minitab's glossary:

- Choose **Help > Search for Help on**

- Type **glossary** in the text box

- When Glossary is highlighted, click the **Display** button

- Click on the letter **F** button in the Glossary and then on **F-test**

The resulting window is shown in Figure 9-5. The description in the window gives you the brief review of the F-test that you need.

> **F-test**
>
> An F-test is usually a ratio of two numbers, where each number estimates a variance. An F-test is used in the test of equality of two populations. An F-test is also used in analysis of variance, where it tests the hypothesis of equality of means for two or more groups. For instance, in an ANOVA test, the F statistic is usually a ratio of the Mean Square for the effect of interest and Mean Square error. The F-statistic is very large when MS for the factor is much larger than the MS for error. In such cases, reject the null hypothesis that group means are equal. The p-value helps to determine statistical significance of the F-statistic.

- Close the Help window

▼ 9.2   Checking the Assumptions for a One-Way ANOVA ▲

The ANOVA test requires three basic assumptions about the measurements in the study:

1. The observations must be randomly selected.

2. The populations from which the observations are taken must all be approximately normally distributed.

No Binomial or Categorical Responses

3. The values in each group must come from populations that have equal variances.

You are satisfied that the infants you included in the study can be regarded as a random sample of such children. You are ready to check the normality assumption using the residuals. In the One-way Analysis of Variance dialog box, clicking the "Store residuals" and "Store fits" check boxes stores the fitted values and the residual values in the next available columns:

- Choose **Stat > ANOVA > One-way**

- Click the **Store residuals** and the **Store fits** check boxes

- Click **OK**

- Click the **Current Data window** toolbar button ▦

The Data window displays columns containing the residuals and the fitted values.

You can use these values to examine whether the results satisfy the ANOVA assumptions. (In a one-way ANOVA, the *fitted value* associated with any actual value is simply the sample mean associated with that value. The *residual value* is the difference between the actual and fitted values; that is, actual value – fitted value.)

Compare the fitted values to the sample means shown in Figure 9-5. Note that the fitted values in C4 FITS1 — 10.65, 11.05, 8.75, 7.833, and 9.48 — are the sample means for each design. Minitab obtains the residuals, stored in C3 RESI1, by subtracting the corresponding fitted value (design mean) from each average time. The residuals can be used to check the normality of the pooled samples. They should "look" as though they come from a normal distribution. You could check for normality by, for example, examining a histogram of the residuals. However, you decide to construct a normal probability plot (NPP) which was introduced in Tutorial 6.

An NPP for the combined (pooled) samples can be used to determine if it is reasonable to assume that the attention times are normally distributed. First, compute the normal score for each residual:

- Choose **Calc > Calculator**

- Type **NS** in the "Store result in variable" text box, and press Tab

- Enter, by clicking or typing, **NSCOR(RESI1)** as the "Expression"

The completed Calculator dialog box should resemble that shown in Figure 9-6.

FIGURE 9-6

The completed Calculator dialog box

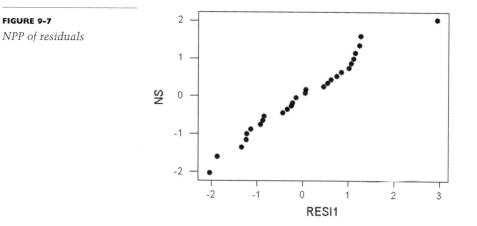

■ Click **OK**

   Minitab computes the normal scores and stores them in C5 NS. To obtain the NPP:

■ Choose **Graph > Plot**

■ Select **C5 NS** as the "Y" variable and **C3 RESI1** as the "X" variable

■ Click **OK**

   The NPP appears as shown in Figure 9-7.

FIGURE 9-7

NPP of residuals

Of the 29 residuals, 28 lie close to a straight line, but the NPP suggests one large outlier. This outlier corresponds to the largest value in the data set: 13.6 for Design A. In this case, the appropriate action is to remove this outlier and examine the impact that its removal has on the ANOVA. You are asked to do this in Problem 1 at the end of this tutorial. In fact, removing this value does not change the significant differences you discovered previously. After examining the boxplots of times in Figure 9-1 and the numerical summaries in Figure 9-2, you had decided earlier that the constant variance assumption was not violated.

▼ **Note** There are methods for testing for the equality of several population variances, but they are extremely sensitive to departures from the normality assumption and so are rarely used. Minitab offers a number of such tests via the menu sequence Stats > ANOVA > Homogeneity of Variance. ▲

▼ 9.3   Performing a Tukey Multiple Comparison Test ▲

Recall that you earlier rejected the null hypothesis of equality of attention time means at the 0.05 level. You can use Minitab's multiple comparison capabilities to determine which means differ from each other. Minitab provides four multiple comparison methods: Tukey, Fisher, Dunnett, and Hsu. You use the Tukey method in this tutorial. (Your instructor can provide more information about the other procedures, or you can read about them in Minitab's Help.)

For the Tukey multiple comparison test, you form 10 sets of hypotheses (one set for each pair of designs), given in the following chart.

$H_0: \mu_A = \mu_B$ $H_0: \mu_A = \mu_C$ $H_0: \mu_A = \mu_D$ $H_0: \mu_A = \mu_E$
$H_1: \mu_A \neq \mu_B$ $H_1: \mu_A \neq \mu_C$ $H_1: \mu_A \neq \mu_D$ $H_1: \mu_A \neq \mu_E$

$H_0: \mu_B = \mu_C$ $H_0: \mu_B = \mu_D$ $H_0: \mu_B = \mu_E$
$H_1: \mu_B \neq \mu_C$ $H_1: \mu_B \neq \mu_D$ $H_1: \mu_B \neq \mu_E$

$H_0: \mu_C = \mu_D$ $H_0: \mu_C = \mu_E$
$H_1: \mu_C \neq \mu_D$ $H_1: \mu_C \neq \mu_E$

$H_0: \mu_D = \mu_E$
$H_1: \mu_D \neq \mu_E$

The Tukey test forms confidence intervals for the differences between each pair of population means. To perform the Tukey multiple comparison:

- Choose **Stat > ANOVA > One-way**

- Verify that **C1 Time** appears as the "Response" and **C2 Design** as the "Factor"

- Click the **Store residuals** and the **Store fits** check boxes to deselect them

- Click the **Comparisons** button

- Click the **Tukey's, family error rate** check box

- Click **OK** twice

Figure 9-8 shows that part of the output in the Session window that includes the Tukey pairwise comparisons.

FIGURE 9-8

Results of Tukey multiple comparisons

```
Tukey's pairwise comparisons

    Family error rate = 0.0500
Individual error rate = 0.00701

Critical value = 4.17

Intervals for (column level mean) - (row level mean)

                 A          B          C          D

     B       -2.474
               1.674

     C       -0.174      0.226
               3.974      4.374

     D        0.743      1.143     -1.157
               4.891      5.291      2.991

     E       -1.005     -0.605     -2.905     -3.822
               3.345      3.745      1.445      0.529
```

According to Tukey's method, you should reject the null hypothesis that the two population means are equal whenever the confidence interval for the difference in the means does not contain 0. The *family error rate* (sometimes called the *overall error rate*) is the probability of making at least one Type I error (falsely rejecting H_0) in the ten tests. A summary of the results follows.

Difference Between	Confidence Interval 95% Family Confidence	Decision
Design A and Design B	−2.474 to 1.674	Cannot reject H_0: $\mu_A = \mu_B$
Design A and Design C	−0.174 to 3.974	Cannot reject H_0: $\mu_A = \mu_C$
Design A and Design D	0.743 to 4.891	Reject H_0: $\mu_A = \mu_D$
Design A and Design E	−1.005 to 3.345	Cannot reject H_0: $\mu_A = \mu_E$
Design B and Design C	0.226 to 4.374	Reject H_0: $\mu_B = \mu_C$
Design B and Design D	1.143 to 5.291	Reject H_0: $\mu_B = \mu_D$
Design B and Design E	−0.605 to 3.745	Cannot reject H_0: $\mu_B = \mu_E$
Design C and Design D	−1.157 to 2.991	Cannot reject H_0: $\mu_C = \mu_D$
Design C and Design E	−2.905 to 1.445	Cannot reject H_0: $\mu_C = \mu_E$
Design D and Design E	−3.822 to 0.529	Cannot reject H_0: $\mu_D = \mu_E$

From the results of the Tukey test, you determine that there is significant evidence of a difference in the population mean attention spans between designs A and D, between designs B and C, and between designs B and D. You conclude your psychology experiment with this result and include it in your report on other studies about infant perception.

■ In the location where you are saving your work, save the project **T9.mpj**

▼ 9.4 Comparing the Means of Several Populations with Responses in Separate Columns ▲

In your child development class, you observe that some students entered their data in separate columns and used a different Minitab menu sequence, Stat > ANOVA > One-way [Unstacked]. You decide to restructure your data by placing each of the five groups of attention spans for each design into separate columns:

- Design A into C6
- Design B into C7
- Design C into C8
- Design D into C9
- Design E into C10

To unstack your data in this way:

■ Choose **Manip > Stack/Unstack > Unstack one column**

■ Select **C1 Time** as the "Unstack the data in" column

■ Type **A B C D E** for the five columns in which the unstacked data will be stored (remember to type the spaces between the letters), and press Tab

■ Select **C2 Design** in the "Using subscripts in" text box

At this point, the Unstack One Column dialog box should look as shown in Figure 9-9.

FIGURE 9-9

The completed Unstack One Column dialog box

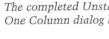

Unstack One Column

C1	Time
C2	Design
C3	RESI1
C4	FITS1
C5	NS
C6	RESI2
C7	FITS2

Unstack the data in: `Time`

Store the unstacked data in:

`A B C D E`

Using subscripts in: `Design`

Select   Help   OK   Cancel

- Click **OK**, then click the **Current Data window** toolbar button ▦

    You can see the unstacked data in C6 A, C7 B, C8 C, C9 D, and C10 E.
    Next, repeat the ANOVA test by using the One-way (Unstacked) command that is appropriate when the sample data are in different columns. The statistical results are the same, but they appear with slightly different labels.

- Choose **Stat > ANOVA > One-way [Unstacked]**

- Select **C6 A**, **C7 B**, **C8 C**, **C9 D**, and **C10 E** as the "Responses"

- Click **OK**

    The results appear in the Session window, as shown in Figure 9-10.

FIGURE 9-10

Results of one-way (unstacked) ANOVA of attention times

```
MTB > AOVOneway 'A' 'B' 'C' 'D' 'E'.
```

One-Way Analysis of Variance

```
Analysis of Variance
Source     DF        SS        MS        F        P
Factor      4     42.31     10.58     7.12    0.001
Error      24     35.63      1.48
Total      28     77.93
                                 Individual 95% CIs For Mean
                                 Based on Pooled StDev
Level       N      Mean     StDev   -----+---------+---------+---------+-
A           6    10.650     1.672                      (------*------)
B           6    11.050     0.855                        (------*------)
C           6     8.750     1.078            (------*------)
D           6     7.833     1.019   (------*------)
E           5     9.480     1.322             (------*------)
                                   -----+---------+---------+---------+-
Pooled StDev =    1.218             7.5       9.0      10.5      12.0
```

Minitab produces the same display in this case as it did for the one-way test in which all data were stacked in one column. There are only two differences in the labels: The analysis of variance table no longer identifies the response variable, and the levels now have names. However, there are some disadvantages to storing your data in separate columns. Not only does the data occupy more columns, but the Minitab dialog box associated with this data structure doesn't let you store fitted values and residuals or make pairwise comparisons. To accomplish these tasks for one-way ANOVA data stored in separate columns, you must stack your data and create a subscript column.

▼ **Note** For unstacked data, Minitab uses the session command AOVOneway. The exact appearance of this command in your session window will depend on whether you select the columns C6 A, C7 B, C8 C, C9 D, and C10 E one at a time or together. ▲

- In the location where you are saving your work, save the project **T9.mpj**

▼ 9.5 Performing a Two-Factor Analysis of Variance ▲

Earlier in this tutorial, you analyzed the effect of a single factor with five levels (the five mobile designs) on a response (infant attention times). However, many responses are affected by more than one factor. Statisticians frequently design studies to take this fact into account.

CASE STUDY: MARKETING — AD CAMPAIGN

A sports equipment company just hired you as a data analyst in the marketing department. Marketing manager Elaine Lasser is planning a new campaign and wants to place a full-page ad in one of two media: a news magazine or a sports magazine. She wants you to determine which magazine has the lowest ratio of full-page ads to the number of pages in the magazine and whether either magazine has experienced a change in this ratio in recent years.

For your study, you decide to examine the ad ratio for each publication in 1989, 1991, and 1993. You randomly select issues from each magazine for each of these three years. You determine the number of full-page ads and the number of pages in each issue. Then you calculate the ad ratio by dividing the number of full-page ads by the number of pages in each issue. You record the results in the table shown in Figure 9-11.

	Year	News Magazine	Sports Magazine
FIGURE 9-11			
Ad ratios for the two	1989	0.79	0.60
magazine types		0.80	0.46
		0.54	0.38
		0.72	0.42
	1991	0.49	0.39
		0.85	0.56
		0.50	0.57
		0.67	0.46
	1993	0.36	0.37
		0.65	0.64
		0.47	0.52
		0.68	0.41

A coworker has entered the ad ratio data in a Minitab worksheet called *Ratio.mtw*, which is in the Student subdirectory:

■ Open the worksheet **Ratio.mtw**

Before analyzing these data, you should save them:

■ In the location where you are saving your work, save the worksheet as **9Ratio**

Figure 9-12 shows the Data window with 20 of the 24 ad ratios (you may see more or fewer than 20 values, depending on your screen size). All 24 are stored in C1 AdRatio.

FIGURE 9-12

The Ratio.mtw data window

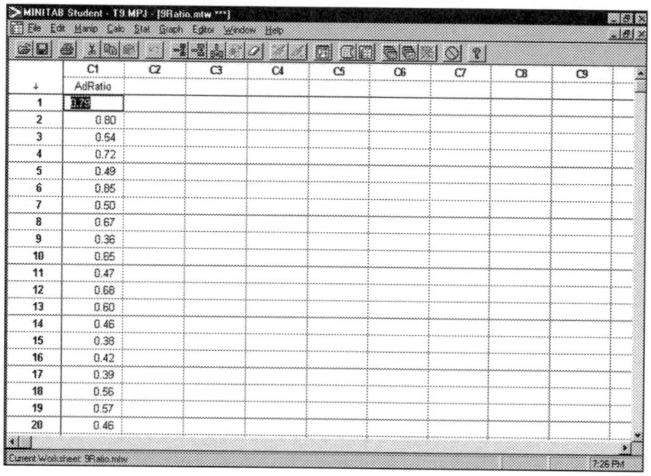

The first 12 values in C1 AdRatio correspond to the news magazine; the last 12 relate to the sports magazine. Values 1–4 and 13–16 correspond to 1989. The other values in C1 AdRatio correspond to the other years.

Creating Patterned Data

To perform the two-factor ANOVA, you need to add two columns that will identify each factor — year and magazine — for each row of C1 AdRatio.

To identify the year for each row in C1, you could enter in column C2 of the worksheet the sequence

1989 1989 1989 1989 1991 1991 1991 1991 1993 1993 1993 1993 1989 1989 . . . 1993.

For small data sets like this one, this might be the easiest method. However, for practice, use the Make Patterned Data command to enter this sequence of numbers. Note that the sequence consists of the values 1989, 1991, and 1993; the values start at 1989, end at 1993, and increase (increment) by 2. Each value is repeated four times and the whole list is repeated twice.

■ Choose **Calc > Make Patterned Data > Simple Set of Numbers**

- Type **Year** in the "Store patterned data" text box, and press `Tab`
- Type **1989** in the "From first value" text box, and press `Tab`
- Type **1993** in the "To last value" text box, and press `Tab`
- Type **2** in the "In steps of" text box, and press `Tab`
- Type **4** in the "List each value" text box, and press `Tab`
- Type **2** in the "List the whole sequence" text box

Figure 9-13 shows how the Simple Set of Numbers dialog box should look at this point.

- Click **OK**
- Verify that Minitab has entered the pattern of dates

Next, you need to store the values for the magazine. Identify the two magazines, one as "News" and the other as "Sports." The news magazine values are the first 12 values in C1 AdRatio; the next 12 values are for the sports magazine. Hence, you need to enter the label News 12 times followed by the label Sports 12 times. Use the Make Patterned Data command:

- Choose **Calc > Make Patterned Data > Text Values**
- Type **Magazine** in the "Store patterned data" text box, and press `Tab`
- Type **News Sports** as the "Text Values," and press `Tab`
- Type **12** in the "List each value" text box
- Verify that a **1** appears in the "List the whole sequence" text box
- Click **OK**

The Data window should now look as shown in Figure 9-14. You will probably have to scroll to see the entire window. If columns C2 and C3-T do not look exactly as shown in the figure, erase them and start over.

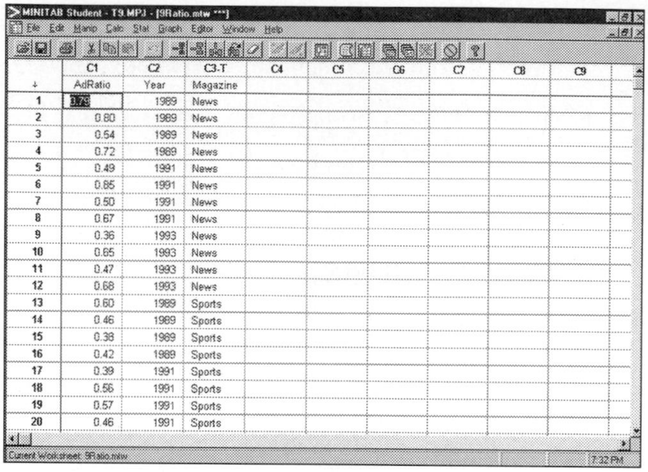

↓	C1 AdRatio	C2 Year	C3-T Magazine	C4	C5	C6	C7	C8	C9
1	0.79	1989	News						
2	0.80	1989	News						
3	0.54	1989	News						
4	0.72	1989	News						
5	0.49	1991	News						
6	0.85	1991	News						
7	0.50	1991	News						
8	0.67	1991	News						
9	0.36	1993	News						
10	0.65	1993	News						
11	0.47	1993	News						
12	0.68	1993	News						
13	0.60	1989	Sports						
14	0.46	1989	Sports						
15	0.38	1989	Sports						
16	0.42	1989	Sports						
17	0.39	1991	Sports						
18	0.56	1991	Sports						
19	0.57	1991	Sports						
20	0.46	1991	Sports						

FIGURE 9-14
The Ratio.mtw window with patterned data

▼ **Note** The two-way ANOVA command requires that the response and factor columns contain an identical number of rows. So you must ensure that all columns have exactly the same number of entries. You also must be sure to identify correctly the factor levels for each data point. Scroll to make sure that your window contains the correct data. ▲

You are interested in the impact of the factors Year and Magazine on the ad ratio. You know you must also consider the *interaction* between these two factors. Recall that two factors interact if the effect of one of the two factors on the response variable depends on the value for the other factor. In your case study, this might mean, for example, that the effect of type of magazine on the ad ratio differs by year. It is customary to test for significant interaction before testing for the effects of each of the two factors. The relevance of the results of testing for each factor depends on whether there is significant interaction between them.

The Two-Way ANOVA

For this two way ANOVA, you want to test three sets of hypotheses:

H_0: There is no interaction between year and magazine.

H_1: There is an interaction between year and magazine.

H_0: There is no difference in the average ad ratio for different years.

H_1: There is a difference in the average ad ratio for different years.

H_0: There is no difference in the average ad ratio when using different magazines.

H_1: There is a difference in the average ad ratio when using different magazines.

You perform a two-way ANOVA by using the Two-way ANOVA command. This command requires that there be an equal number of observations for all combinations of factor levels. That is, the data must be *balanced*. In your example, each combination of year and type of magazine has four values so that the data are balanced.

The ANOVA>Two-way command can produce not only the two-way ANOVA table, but also various residual and other helpful plots. You decide to ask for graphical displays of confidence intervals for both factors and for a normal probability plot of the residuals from the two-way ANOVA model. This latter plot is helpful because the F-tests in the two-way ANOVA assume that the observations are drawn from normal populations.

▼ **Note** Minitab calls the factors "Row factor" and "Column factor." These terms are derived from the traditional way of setting out the data. Figure 9-11 showed that the ad ratios are organized with the year as the Row factor and the type of magazine as the Column factor. ▲

To obtain the analyses:

- Choose **Stat > ANOVA > Two-way**
- Select **C1 AdRatio** as the "Response" variable, **C2 Year** as the "Row factor," and **C3 Magazine** as the "Column factor"
- Click the **Display means** check boxes to the right of the text window for each factor
- Click the **Graphs** button, and click the **Normal plot of residuals** check box
- Click **OK** twice

The built-in graph showing the NPP of the residuals is shown in Figure 9-15. The points on the plot lie close enough to a straight line so that you can be assured that the normality assumption has not been violated.

FIGURE 9-15

NPP of residuals

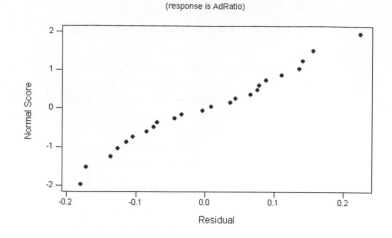

Normal Probability Plot of the Residuals

(response is AdRatio)

■ Click the **Session Window** toolbar button 🗔

The results in the Session window are shown in Figure 9-16. (You may need to scroll up to see them all.)

FIGURE 9-16

Results of ad ratios ANOVA

```
MTB > Two-way 'AdRatio' 'Year' 'Magazine';
SUBC>   Means 'Year' 'Magazine';
SUBC>   GNormalplot.
```

Two-Way Analysis of Variance

```
Analysis of Variance for AdRatio
Source        DF        SS        MS        F        P
Year           2    0.0239    0.0119     0.73    0.494
Magazine       1    0.1262    0.1262     7.76    0.012
Interaction    2    0.0375    0.0188     1.15    0.338
Error         18    0.2927    0.0163
Total         23    0.4802
```

```
                          Individual 95% CI
Year        Mean   -+---------+---------+---------+---------+
1989       0.589            (------------*-------------)
1991       0.561         (------------*-------------)
1993       0.512   (------------*-------------)
                   -+---------+---------+---------+---------+
                  0.420     0.490     0.560     0.630     0.700
```

```
                          Individual 95% CI
Magazine    Mean   ----------+---------+---------+---------+-
News       0.627             (--------*---------)
Sports     0.482   (--------*---------)
                   ----------+---------+---------+---------+-
                          0.480     0.560     0.640     0.720
```

The first table in the output is the standard ANOVA table. It lists the sources of variation (Year, Magazine, Interaction, and Error), the F-ratios for each test, and the corresponding p-values. The results of the three hypothesis tests are described in the following table.

Test	Effect	F-ratio	p-value	Decision
1	Year* Magazine (Interaction)	1.15	0.338	Do not reject H_0; the data suggest no significant interaction between year and magazine.
2	Year	0.73	0.494	Do not reject H_0; the data suggest that the mean ad ratios for the three years do not differ significantly.
3	Magazine	7.76	0.012	Reject H_0; the data suggest that the mean ad ratios are not the same for the two magazines.

Note that the order of the results here differs from Minitab's display. The test for the interaction effect is listed first in this manual because the main effect tests are usually performed only if you do not reject the null hypothesis of the interaction test.

The results indicate no significant interaction between year and magazine (p-value = 0.338). Further, you conclude that the mean ad ratios for the three years do not differ significantly (p-value = 0.494). However, the two magazines have significantly different ad ratios (p-value = 0.012).

The second part of the output consists of the (sample) mean ad ratios for each year and for each magazine and the graphical representations of the 95% confidence intervals for the corresponding population mean ad ratios. The sample mean ad ratio declines year-by-year but, as shown previously, the differences are not statistically significant. However, the mean ad ratio for the news magazine is clearly and statistically greater than that for the sports magazine. When you present your report, you plan to recommend advertising in the sports magazine so that the ads will have the greatest impact.

▼ **Note** The confidence intervals in Figure 9-16 are all based on the pooled standard deviation of AdRatio. This value is not shown in the output. It can be calculated as the square root of the MSE (0.0189) in the ANOVA table. ▲

When you have a balanced ANOVA with two or more factors, you can use the more general Minitab command, Balanced ANOVA. This command performs a multiway ANOVA and is more complex to use than the Two-way ANOVA command. If you need to use this command, you may want to ask your instructor for help or refer to the steps outlined in Minitab's Help.

- In the location where you are saving your work, save the current project *T9.mpj*, and exit Minitab

▼
Minitab Command Summary
▲

This section describes the menu commands introduced in, or related to, this tutorial. To find a complete explanation of all menus and commands, use Minitab's on-line Help.

Minitab Menu Commands

Menu	Command	Description
Calc		
	Make Patterned Data	
	Text Values	Generates sequences or repetitive patterns of text values and stores the results in a column
Stat		
	ANOVA	
	One-way	Performs a one-way analysis of variance when the response is stored in one column and the sample indicator or subscript is stored in another column.
	One-way [Unstacked]	Performs a one-way analysis of variance when the responses for each sample are stored in separate columns.
	Two-way	Performs a two-way analysis of variance when the response is stored in one column and the two-factor level indicators or subscripts are stored in two other columns; the data must be balanced.
	Balanced ANOVA	Performs a multiway analysis of variance when the response is stored in one column and the factor level indicators or subscripts are stored in other columns; the data must be balanced.

Matching

Match the following terms to their definitions by placing the correct letter next to the term it describes.

_____ Text Values

_____ Simple Set of Numbers

_____ Response variable

_____ Balanced Analysis of Variance

_____ Balanced

_____ Comparisons

_____ Factor

_____ Unstacked

_____ Two-way ANOVA

_____ Hsu's

a. The Minitab command that performs a multiway ANOVA

b. The Minitab command to create a text variable made up of patterned data

c. The Minitab command to create data that represent factors

d. A description of data that is taken from a single column and placed into two or more columns

e. A term that denotes that there are equal numbers of observations for each factor combination

f. The Minitab option that performs multiple comparisons of the means in a one-way ANOVA

g. The term used in ANOVA to denote a variable that affects a quantitative variable

h. The term used in ANOVA to denote the quantitative variable whose mean is affected by the factor(s)

i. A multiple comparison method

j. The Minitab command that performs a two-factor ANOVA

True/False

Mark the following statements with a *T* or an *F*.

_____ Minitab's Two-way ANOVA command allows unbalanced data, whereas the Balanced ANOVA command must have balanced data.

_____ You can use any of the ANOVA commands to store residuals and fitted values.

_____ Minitab can perform multiple comparisons only for stacked data.

_____ For the One-way ANOVA command, the fits can be saved without the residuals.

_____ The user specifies the columns in which the ANOVA commands store the residuals and/or fitted values.

_____ You can perform multiway ANOVA by using the Balanced ANOVA command.

_____ 95% confidence intervals for each population mean are part of the default output for the One-way ANOVA command.

_____ Three multiple comparison procedures are available via the One-way ANOVA command.

_____ Both one-way ANOVA procedures offer the option of obtaining a histogram of the responses for each sample.

_____ Minitab cannot perform an ANOVA if any of the factors are in text columns.

Practice Problems

Use Help or Part III, Exploring Data, to review the contents of the data sets referred to in the following problems.

1. Open _Baby.mtw_. Replace the value 5.6 and the outlier 13.6 with missing values. Show that removing this outlier has little impact on the result of the one way ANOVA of Times by Design. How does it change the normal probability plot?

2. Open _Yogurt.mtw_. Assume that these 14 yogurts can be considered a random sample of all yogurt.

    a. Replace the VeryGood values in rows 4,6,9 and 14 with Good values. What method did you use?

    b. Use the menu sequence Manip > Code > Text to Text to combine the Fair and Poor ratings into a new rating, NotGood.

    c. Determine if the population mean cost per ounce and the population mean calories per serving differ for different nutritional ratings.

3. Open _Temco.mtw_.

    a. Determine if the population average salary differs for the four departments at Temco. If there are significant differences between departments, explain which is the most highly paid and the least highly paid department.

    b. Is it reasonable to assume that the members of these departments are a random sample? How does your answer affect your conclusion in (a)?

4. Open _Crimeu.mtw_.

    a. Determine if the crime rates differ for different regions at a significance level of 0.10. If there are differences, provide a Tukey multiple comparison test to determine the pairwise differences.

    b. Is it reasonable to assume that these data are a random sample? How does your answer affect your conclusion in (a)?

5. Open _Age.mtw_.

    a. Perform a two-independent sample mean test for age at death, assuming equal variances. (Do a two-sided test.) What is the test's p-value?

b. Perform a one-way ANOVA on the same data. What is this test's p-value?

c. Since the tests are algebraically equivalent, your two p-values should be identical. If they are not, check your work in (a) and (b).

6. Open *Vpvh.mtw*.

a. Create two new columns: C6 Gender with men and women as the text values and C7 Age with 18to34 and 55Plus as the two text values.

b. Obtain an ANOVA table from a two-way ANOVA on C1 Movies with C6 Gender and C7 Age as the factors.

c. Test the following set of hypotheses:

H_0: There is no interaction between gender and age group.

H_1: There is an interaction between gender and age group.

d. Based on your answer to (b), should you test for any difference in average movie rating for gender or for age group? Briefly explain your answer.

e. Redo your two-way ANOVA, but this time display the Gender and Age mean movie ratings scores. What are the mean movie ratings for each gender? What are the mean movie ratings for each age group?

f. Is it reasonable to assume that these data are a random sample? How does this affect your conclusions?

7. Open *Nonprt.mtw*. Assume that these data represent a random sample. Use a one-way ANOVA on the response AveSize to examine if there are significant differences between the population average size of the nonprint displays by newspaper. If you obtain a significant result, use the Tukey multiple comparison test to determine which pairs of means are significantly different.

TUTORIAL 10

Fundamentals of Linear Regression

In this tutorial, you will use Minitab's basic regression commands. Regression allows you to investigate and model the relationship between a response (dependent) variable and one or more predictors (independent variables). A regression model can be used to estimate a future response based on the value of the predictor variables. You will begin with simple linear regression, building a model of the effect of a single variable and testing its predictive ability. Then you will examine how to build a multiple linear regression with three predictor (independent) variables. In each case, you will use Minitab's regression features to generate confidence intervals and perform t-tests to evaluate the model.

Objectives

In this tutorial, you learn how to:

- use simple linear regression to describe a linear relationship between two variables

- obtain a 95% confidence interval for the expected value of the response variable

- obtain a 95% prediction interval for an individual value of the response variable

- generate a quadratic regression model

- use multiple linear regression to investigate the form of the linear relationship between a response variable and several predictor variables

▼ 10.1   Fitting a Straight Line to Data: Simple Linear Regression ▲

CASE STUDY: INSTITUTIONAL RESEARCH — TUITION MODELING

In this and the next tutorial, you will play the role of a 1996 institutional researcher. You have been asked by the administration of the Massachusetts college at which you work to generate a model for out-of-state tuition based on data collected from other Massachusetts colleges. For each of 56 colleges, 10 variables were identified that could be related to the tuition charged there. These variables are stored in the worksheet *Masscoll.mtw*. You are to use this data to build a model that the administration can use to determine a reasonable tuition for the college's out-of-state students.

The variables in the data set are as follows:

C1	School	Name of the college
C2	PubPriv	Whether the school is public or private
C3	%Top10%	Percentage of the freshman class that was in the top 10% of their high school graduating class
C4	%Top25%	Percentage of the freshman class that was in the top 25% of their high school graduating class
C5	%WhoGrad	Percentage of the freshman class that graduated
C6	MSAT	Median math SAT score for the freshman class
C7	VSAT	Median verbal SAT score for the freshman class
C8	CSAT	Median combined Math and verbal SAT scores for the freshman class
C9	%Accept	Percentage of applicants that was accepted by the college
C10	%Enroll	Percentage of accepted applicants that enrolled
C11	SFRatio	Student-faculty ratio
C12	Tuition	Annual out-of-state tuition

To get started:

- Start **Minitab**

- Maximize the **Session window**

- If necessary, enable the **Session command language** and make the output read-only

You'll be working with the data file *Masscoll.mtw*, which is in the Student subdirectory:

- Open the worksheet **Masscoll.mtw**

Before analyzing these data, you should save them as a worksheet and this tutorial in a project:

- In the location where you are saving your work, save the worksheet as **10Massco**

- Also, save what you have done thus far in a project named **T10**

The Dean of Admissions is particularly interested in the relationship between tuition and verbal SAT scores for Massachusetts colleges. So, you begin your analysis of these data by investigating the relationship between these two variables. First, you examine a scatter plot of Tuition against verbal SAT:

- Choose **Graph > Plot**

- Select **C12 Tuition** as the "Y" variable and **C7 VSAT** as the "X" variable

- Click **OK**

The scatter plot should resemble Figure 10-1.

FIGURE 10-1

Scatter plot of Tuition against VSAT

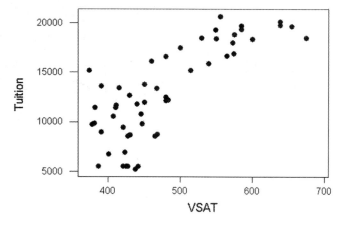

The scatter plot suggests a positive relationship between these two variables; that is, the higher the verbal SAT score, the higher the tuition. There is a slight curvature to the data, but the relationship is approximately linear. You can measure the strength of the linear relationship by computing the correlation coefficient:

- Choose **Stat > Basic Statistics > Correlation**

- Select **C12 Tuition** and **C7 VSAT** to enter them as the "Variables"

- Click **OK**

The Session window reports a correlation coefficient of 0.794. This value suggests a strong linear relationship between tuition and verbal SAT scores among Massachusetts colleges in 1995. This is verified by the corresponding p-value of 0.000. This p-value is less than any reasonable level of significance, so you reject the null hypothesis that the population correlation (ρ) between these two variables is 0. The small p-value supports the graphical evidence of a strong, positive, linear relationship. You are ready to obtain the linear equation that relates tuition to verbal SAT:

- Choose **Stat > Regression > Regression**

- Select **C12 Tuition** as the "Response" variable

- Select **C7 VSAT** as the "Predictors" variable

The completed Regression dialog box should look as shown in Figure 10-2.

FIGURE 10-2

The completed Regression dialog box

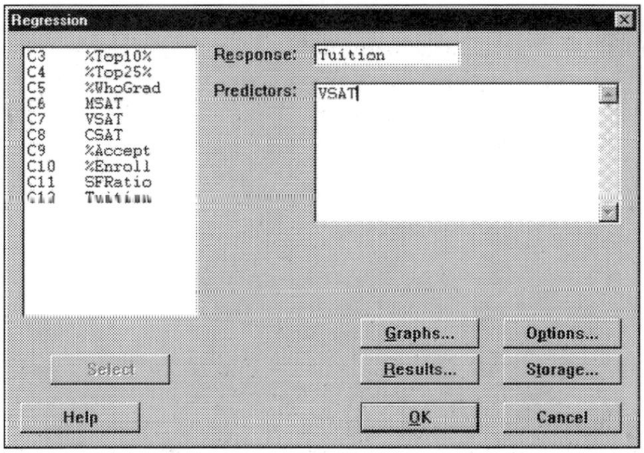

- Click **OK**

The Session window display resembles Figure 10-3. The regression equation is Tuition = –9215 + 46.4 VSAT.

FIGURE 10-3

*Results of tuition
regression analysis*

```
MTB > Regress 'Tuition' 1 'VSAT';
SUBC>    Constant;
SUBC>    Brief 2.
```

Regression Analysis

The regression equation is
Tuition = - 9215 + 46.4 VSAT ———————— **Regression equation**

53 cases used 3 cases contain missing values

Predictor table

```
Predictor         Coef       StDev          T        P
Constant         -9215        2422      -3.80    0.000
VSAT            46.435        4.982       9.32    0.000
```

Summary statistics

```
S = 2902          R-Sq = 63.0%      R-Sq(adj) = 62.3%
```

Analysis of Variance

ANOVA table

```
Source            DF          SS           MS         F        P
Regression         1   731793652    731793652     86.89    0.000
Residual Error    51   429538769      8422329
Total             52  1161332421
```

Unusual observations table

Unusual Observations

```
Obs      VSAT    Tuition        Fit  StDev Fit    Residual    St Resid
 21       437       5244      11077        452       -5833      -2.03R
 24       675      18485      22129       1052       -3644      -1.35 X
 34       373      15190       8106        664        7084       2.51R
```

R denotes an observation with a large standardized residual
X denotes an observation whose X value gives it large influence.

Predicted tuition is obtained by subtracting $9,215 from the product of 46.4 and the median verbal SAT score for the college. For example, the predicted tuition for a college with a median verbal SAT score of 450 is –9,215 + 46.4 * 450 = $11,665. The slope of the line, 46.4, indicates that for every one-point increase in median verbal SAT score, predicted tuition increases by $46.40.

The slope of the line is recorded with more decimal places (46.435) in the predictor table immediately beneath the equation. With this value, the predicted tuition for a college with median verbal SAT score of 450 is –9,215 + 46.435 * 450 = $11,681. Later in this tutorial, you will use Minitab to obtain this prediction.

The predictor table contains the sample regression coefficients (–9,215 and 46.435), their standard deviations, as well as the t-ratios and p-values for testing the hypothesis that a population coefficient is zero. The test of whether the slope of the population line is zero is of particular importance. The appropriate hypotheses for this test are as follows:

Null hypothesis, H_0: $\beta_1 = 0$

Alternative hypothesis, H_0: $\beta_1 \neq 0$

Here, β_1 is the slope of the population line.

The p-value of 0.000 for VSAT in the predictor table indicates that you should reject the null hypothesis. There is significant evidence of a nonzero population slope. This p-value is the same as the p-value you obtained when computing the sample correlation previously. In fact, the test for a nonzero slope is equivalent to the test that the population correlation, ρ, equals zero ($\rho = 0$).

The output shown in Figure 10-3 contains information that helps you assess the usefulness of the model, as described in the following paragraphs.

The summary statistics line includes S, the estimated standard deviation around the regression line. This statistic is often called the *standard error of the estimate*; in this case, its value is $2,902$. *R-sq*, the *coefficient of determination*, indicates that 63.0% of the variation in tuition can be explained by its linear relationship to the median verbal SAT scores at the Massachusetts colleges. Recall that the higher the R^2 value, the better the estimated regression equation fits the data. (*R-sq(adj)* is the R^2 value adjusted for the number of predictor variables in the regression — 1 in this case. It is not something that the beginning student needs to worry about.)

The F-test in the ANOVA table is exactly equivalent to the previous two-sided t-test. The hypotheses are the same and so are the p-values. The value F = 86.89 (sometimes called the *F-ratio*) is the square of the value t = 9.32. (In multiple linear regression, where there is more than one predictor variable in the model, the two tests are different.)

In the last table in the output, Minitab lists two types of unusual observations. The first is based on residuals. A residual is the difference between an observed value (in this case, Tuition) and a predicted value (shown in the Fit column) of an observation. Minitab lists outliers that have a *standardized residual* of more than 2 or less than –2. A standardized residual is the residual divided by an estimate of its variation. These values are marked with an "R." For example, Minitab reports that unusual standardized residuals exist for the colleges in rows 21 (Framingham State College with a verbal SAT of 437 and a tuition of $5,244) and 34 (Pine Manor College with a verbal SAT of 373 and a tuition of $15,190). Framingham State, with a standardized residual of –2.03, has a tuition rate unusually far below what would be predicted from its median verbal SAT. At the other extreme, Pine Manor, with a standardized residual of 2.51, has a tuition rate unusually far above what would be predicted from its median verbal SAT.

Minitab also lists in this table any values for the X variable (VSAT in this case) that differ substantially from the other predictor values in the data. These *influence* points are marked with an "X." Harvard University, with a verbal SAT of 675 and a tuition of $18,485, has a verbal SAT of 675 that has a large influence on the regression. You will look into such unusual observations in Tutorial 11.

A Confidence Interval for the Population Slope

As you can see from Figure 10-3, Minitab provides you with a lot of valuable information in the regression output. However, one thing that it does not provide are confidence intervals for the unknown population regression coefficients β_0 and β_1 — respectively, the intercept and the slope of the population line. You can, however, use a corresponding sample regression coefficient and its standard deviation to compute such an interval. For example, you could compute a 95% confidence interval for the population slope, β_1, by using the sample slope 46.435 — which is an estimate for β_1 — and the related standard deviation of 4.982 in the predictor table. The form of the confidence interval is

$$46.435 \pm t * 4.982,$$

where the value t is the 97.5th percentile of the t distribution with 51 DF (degrees of freedom). (You need the 97.5th percentile because 95% of the distribution lies between the 2.5th percentile and the 97.5th percentile.) You can find t by using Calc > Probability (as you did in Tutorial 6):

- Choose **Calc > Probability Distributions > t**

- Click the **Inverse cumulative probability** option button, and press $\boxed{\text{Tab}}$

- Type **51** as the "Degrees of freedom"

- Click the **Input constant** option button, and press $\boxed{\text{Tab}}$

- Type **.975** in the "Input constant" text box

- Click **OK**

The value for t is 2.0076, so the confidence interval for β_1 is 46.435 ± 2.0076 *(4.982), or (46.435 ± 10.0019), or ($36.43 to $56.44). You can be 95% confident that the slope of the population line lies in this interval. (For hypothesis tests and confidence intervals to be used, certain assumptions must be satisfied. These are discussed in Tutorial 11.)

Obtaining Residuals

Minitab can compute (and store for later use) the fitted values and residuals for each observation. You can use the fitted values and residuals to check assumptions and investigate possible tuition inequities. You also explore these matters in Tutorial 11.

To compute and then store the fitted and residual values in the worksheet:

- Choose **Stat > Regression > Regression**

- Click the **Storage** button

- Click the **Fits**, **Residuals**, and **Standardized residuals** check boxes in the Storage dialog box

- Click **OK** twice

- Click the **Current Data window** toolbar button 🖼
- Scroll right to display columns **C13**, **C14**, and **C15**, as shown in Figure 10-4

Minitab computes the fitted values, residuals, and standardized residuals for each observation in the data set. In addition, Minitab automatically names the columns. (Depending on the size of your screen, your Data window might differ slightly from that shown in Figure 10-4.) The new columns contain the information in the following chart.

FIGURE 10-4

Data window showing stored statistics

| | C7 | C8 | C9 | C10 | C11 | C12 | C13 | C14 | C15 |
	VSAT	CSAT	%Accept	%Enroll	SFRatio	Tuition	FITS1	RESI1	SRES1
1	430	875	76.9718	20.1261	14.7000	8700	10752.3	-2052.32	-0.71660
2	639	1324	23.0590	42.1371	8.4000	19760	20457.1	-697.15	-0.25234
3	445	900	80.8671	28.9753	11.7000	10800	11448.8	-648.84	-0.22612
4	450	930	79.6253	28.8624	13.8000	12000	11681.0	318.99	0.11111
5	480	1055	56.7514	35.7331	16.8000	16600	13074.0	3525.95	1.22858
6	450	990	67.2245	27.4678	17.5000	13800	11681.0	2118.99	0.73811
7	*	*	76.7595	46.9657	10.2000	11550	*	*	*
8	565	1210	47.1248	34.8600	16.6000	16640	17021.0	-380.99	-0.13401
9	560	1150	64.4166	29.2919	11.9000	18420	16324.5	2095.53	0.73447
10	*	*	74.4921	45.7576	10.2000	14080	*	*	*
11	585	1215	65.5280	26.9778	9.8000	19380	17949.7	1430.32	0.50608
12	441	923	67.9552	31.8563	17.1000	5542	11263.1	-5721.10	-1.99468
13	600	1066	71.3197	22.1952	10.5000	17500	14002.7	3497.26	1.21736
14	573	1200	56.4796	38.9710	11.3000	18000	17392.5	607.53	0.21417
15	390	810	76.4706	30.2350	8.7000	13600	8894.9	4705.07	1.65685
16	468	980	79.2636	48.8998	17.3000	8770	12516.8	-3746.83	-1.30368
17	440	890	84.8980	60.0962	11.3000	11800	11216.7	583.34	0.20341
18	515	1020	66.4143	40.0651	18.0000	15200	14699.3	500.74	0.17452
19	381	762	96.8000	37.1795	12.3000	11498	8477.0	2977.96	1.05141
20	424	891	73.1537	27.6077	14.7000	5542	10473.7	-4931.71	-1.72362

Column Name	Description
C13 FITS1	Lists each college's predicted tuition, as computed from the regression equation.
C14 RESI1	Records the residual for each college. This is the difference between each college's actual tuition and the predicted (fitted) tuition.
C15 SRES1	Records each residual divided by its standard deviation. Extreme standardized residuals (with an absolute value greater than 2) determine the unusual observations.

Notice the following for the college in row 4:

- Verbal SAT is 450.

- Tuition is $12,000.

- Predicted (fitted) tuition is, using the regression line, −9,215 + 46.435*450 = $11,681, which is the value for C13 FITS1.

- The residual, in C14 RESI1, is 12,000 − 11,681 = $318.99 (one or both of 12,000 or 11,681 is rounded, which is why the residual is not 12,000 − 11,681, or $319).

    At this point, save your work:

- In the location where you are saving your work, save the work you have done so far in the project *T10.mpj*

The Fitted Line Plot

Minitab provides a specialty graph called the *fitted-line plot* that draws the regression line with the data.

    To create a fitted-line plot:

- Choose **Stat > Regression > Fitted Line Plot**

- Select **C12 Tuition** as the "Response (Y)" variable

- Select **C7 VSAT** as the "Predictor (X)" variable

    The completed dialog box is shown in Figure 10-5.

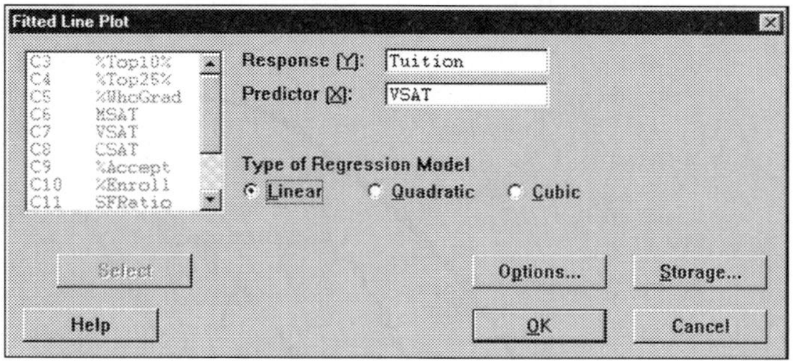

FIGURE 10-5

The completed Fitted Line Plot dialog box

- Click **OK**

    The plot of the fits against the predictor is shown in Figure 10-6.

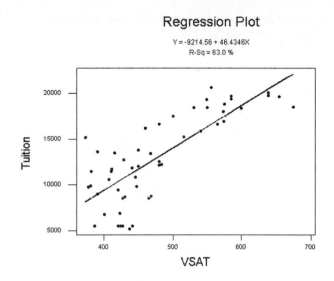

The plot in Figure 10-6 shows that there is quite a bit of variation around the regression line. Tuition at Massachusetts colleges is not based solely on their median verbal SAT scores — there are other factors at work. You plan to look into the relationship between tuition and additional predictor variables. Before you do, though, use Minitab to obtain point and interval estimates for Tuition for a given value of VSAT. You'll do this in the next section. But first, save the work you have done so far.

- In the location where you are saving your work, save the work you have done so far in the project **T10.mpj**

▼ 10.2   Computing Response Variable Estimates ▲

For a college with a median verbal SAT score of 450, the predicted tuition is, from the regression line, –9,215 + 46.435*450 = $11,681. This predicted value is a point estimate for two quantities:

1. The mean tuition for all colleges in the population with a median verbal SAT score of 450

2. The tuition for a specific college with a median verbal SAT score of 450

Minitab can not only obtain a point estimate for these two quantities, but also compute an interval estimate for each. When the mean tuition is being estimated, the interval is called, as usual, a *confidence interval*. But when the tuition at a specific college is being estimated, the interval is called a *prediction interval*. By default, Minitab computes confidence intervals and prediction intervals with confidence levels equal to 95%. However, you can ask Minitab to compute interval estimates with different percentage confidence levels.

Next, ask Minitab to compute the predicted tuition under the following conditions:

- A median verbal SAT of 450

- A 95% confidence interval for the mean tuition over all colleges with median verbal SAT scores of 450

- A 95% prediction interval for the tuition for a specific college with a median verbal SAT score of 450

Follow these steps:

■ Choose **Stat > Regression > Regression**

■ Press **F3** to clear the previous selections

■ Select **C12 Tuition** as the "Response" variable

■ Select **C7 VSAT** as the "Predictors" variable

■ Click the **Options** button

■ Click in the "Prediction intervals for new observations" text box

■ Type **450,** the value of the predictor variable

The completed Regression - Options dialog box should look as shown in Figure 10-7.

FIGURE 10-7

The completed Regression - Options dialog box

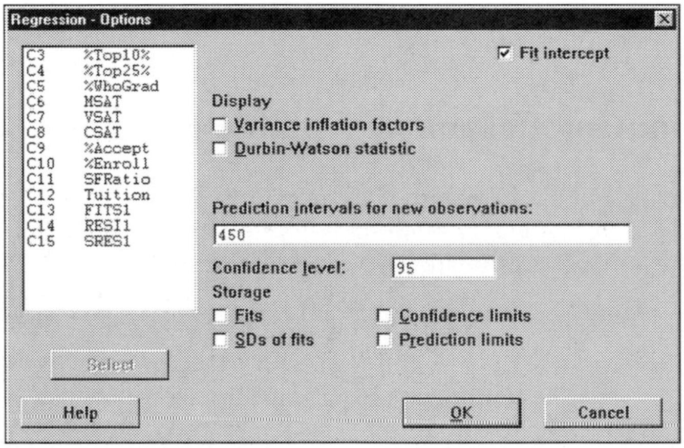

■ Click **OK** twice

When the analysis is complete, the bottom of the Session window display should resemble Figure 10-8.

FIGURE 10-8

Response variable estimate results

```
Predicted Values

   Fit  StDev Fit        95.0% CI            95.0% PI
  11681         425  (  10828,   12534) (   5793,   17569)
```

The predicted tuition for a Massachusetts college with a median verbal SAT score of 450 is $11,681. You are 95% confident that the mean tuition for all colleges with this score will be between $10,828 and $12,534. For an individual college with a score of 450, you can predict with 95% confidence that its tuition will be between $5,793 and $17,569.

You can display all possible fitted values, 95% confidence interval values, and 95% prediction interval values on a scatter plot of data for a simple linear regression:

- Choose **Stat > Regression > Fitted Line Plot**

- Click the **Options** button

- Click the **Display confidence bands** and the **Display prediction bands** check boxes

The completed Fitted Line Plot dialog box should look as shown in Figure 10-9.

FIGURE 10-9

The completed Fitted Line Plot - Options dialog box

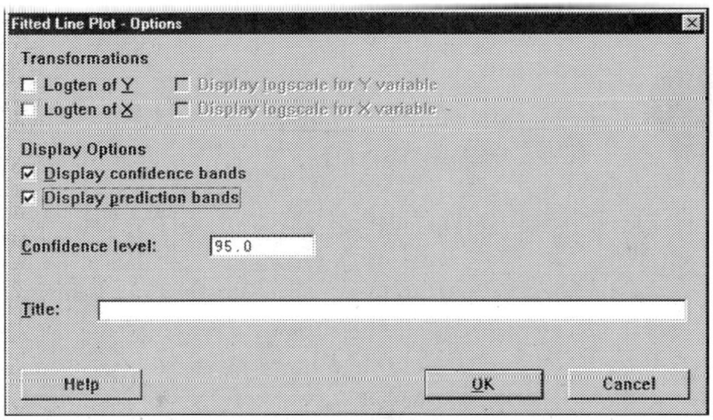

- Click **OK** twice

The resulting graph should resemble Figure 10-10.

FIGURE 10-10

Scatter plot of Tuition
against VSAT, with fitted
regression line, confidence
band, and prediction band

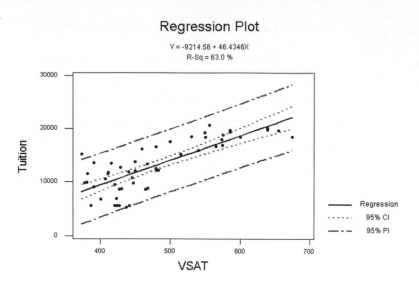

The scatter plot shows the fitted line. This is obtained by plotting the fitted values in C13 FITS1 against the median VSAT scores. In addition, the graph shows the 95% confidence bands and 95% prediction bands for values between the minimum and maximum values of VSAT. Note that one college is above the upper prediction interval band and another is on the lower prediction interval band. You suspect that these two values are the unusually large standardized residuals referred to previously.

■ Save the project **T10.mpj**

▼ 10.3 Performing a Quadratic Regression ▲

In the previous section, you examined the simplest case, that in which tuition is expressed as a linear function of the VSAT. Perhaps this relationship can be better described by a curve based on the slight curvilinear relationship observed in Figure 10-1. You can create a second-degree variable, such as $VSAT^2$, and use it to form a quadratic equation for Tuition. Note that a quadratic equation is an example of a polynomial equation.

First, use the Calculator command to create a second-degree variable, $(VSAT)^2$. (You will use the name VSAT**2. Recall that ** is the Minitab symbol for squaring a term.)

■ Choose **Calc > Calculator**

■ Type **VSAT**2** in the "Store result in variable" text box, and press ⎡Tab⎤

■ Enter, by clicking or typing, **VSAT**2** as the "Expression"

■ Click **OK**

Minitab records a new variable in C16 VSAT**2 the square of each term in C7 VSAT.

Next, try fitting a quadratic regression model for tuition using C7 and C16 as the predictor variables:

- Choose **Stat > Regression > Regression**

- Press **F3** to clear the previous selections

- Select **C12 Tuition** as the "Response" variable

- Select **C7 VSAT** and **C16 VSAT**2** as the "Predictors" variables

- Click **OK**

Figure 10-11 displays the new variable and the results of the regression.

FIGURE 10-11

Results of quadratic regression

```
MTB > Name C16 = 'VSAT**2'
MTB > Let 'VSAT**2' = VSAT**2
MTB > Regress 'Tuition' 2 'VSAT' 'VSAT**2';
SUBC>   Constant;
SUBC>   Brief 2.
```

Regression Analysis

```
The regression equation is
Tuition = - 12858 + 61.2 VSAT - 0.0145 VSAT**2


53 cases used 3 cases contain missing values


Predictor       Coef      StDev         T       P
Constant       -12858      16345     -0.79   0.435
VSAT            61.17      65.56      0.93   0.355
VSAT**2       -0.01449    0.06425    -0.23   0.823


S = 2930        R-Sq = 63.1%     R-Sq(adj) = 61.6%


Analysis of Variance


Source          DF          SS         MS         F       P
Regression       2    732229921   366114961    42.66   0.000
Residual Error  50    429102500     8582050
Total           52   1161332421


Source        DF      Seq SS
VSAT           1   731793652
VSAT**2        1      436269


Unusual Observations
Obs     VSAT   Tuition      Fit  StDev Fit   Residual   St Resid
 21      437      5244    11108        476      -5864      -2.03R
 24      675     18485    21833       1687      -3348      -1.40 X
 34      373     15190     7944        982       7246       2.63R
 54      655     19629    20995       1329      -1366      -0.52 X


R denotes an observation with a large standardized residual.
X denotes an observation whose X value gives it large influence.
```

The second-order equation, which appears at the top of the output, is

$$\text{Tuition} = -12858 + 61.2\ \text{VSAT} - 0.0145\ \text{VSAT**2}.$$

For a college with a median verbal SAT of 450, for example, predicted tuition is $-12,858 + 61.2 * (450) - 0.0145 * (450^2) = \$11,745.75$.

Minitab displays the t-ratio for testing that each of the population coefficients is 0 and the corresponding p-values. The table reports a p-value of 0.355 for the VSAT coefficient; this value is not significant in this model. The quadratic term, VSAT**2, has a p-value of 0.823, which also is not significant.

The standard error estimate of the quadratic regression equals $2,930. This value is greater than the simple linear regression value of $2,902. The regression explains 63.1% of the variation — this isn't much better than the simple linear regression model used previously.

The ANOVA table reports an F-ratio of 42.66. The corresponding p-value of 0.000 indicates that at least one of the coefficients in the model is not zero. The results imply that Tuition depends on VSAT, or the quadratic term VSAT**2. Note that this result appears to contradict the results of the t-tests in the predictor table that appeared to suggest that tuition was linearly unrelated to both VSAT and VSAT**2. In Tutorial 11, you will explore this contradiction further. Based on these results, you decide not to recommend the quadratic model to the administration.

▼ **Note** The content and interpretation of the Seq SS table following the ANOVA table is rather involved. See your instructor for details. ▲

Using Transformations

Minitab can include not only higher powers of a predictor variable, but also other transformations of both the response and predictor variables. Among the most common transformations of the response variables are square roots, logarithms, and negative reciprocals. You can use products of predictor variables like X1*X2 to create complex regression models. In addition, more advanced transformations are sometimes appropriate. For example, if a variable is cyclic in nature, you may consider including the cosine of that variable.

Next, save your work:

■ Save the project ***T10.mpj***

▼ 10.4 Performing Multiple Linear Regression ▲

You suspect that many factors other than the VSAT influenced tuition levels at Massachusetts colleges in 1995. You decide to add two variables to the model with median verbal SAT:

• %Top25% — the percentage of the freshman class that was in the top 25% of their high school graduating class

• SFRatio — the Student-faculty ratio

This model, with more than one predictor variable is called a *multiple linear regression* model.

- Choose **Stat > Regression > Regression**
- Press F3 to clear the selections
- Select **C12 Tuition** as the "Response" variable
- Select **C4 %Top25%**, **C7 VSAT**, and **C11 SFRatio** as the "Predictors" variables
- Click **OK**

The Session window shows the results as shown in Figure 10-12.

FIGURE 10-12

Multiple linear regression results with three predictors

```
MTB > Regress 'Tuition' 3 '%Top25%' 'VSAT' 'SFRatio';
SUBC>    Constant;
SUBC>    Brief 2.
```

Regression Analysis

The regression equation is
Tuition = 9545 + 109 %Top25% + 4.3 VSAT - 285 SFRatio

50 cases used 6 cases contain missing values

Predictor	Coef	StDev	T	P
Constant	9545	4733	2.02	0.050
%Top25%	109.38	34.58	3.16	0.003
VSAT	4.27	12.06	0.35	0.725
SFRatio	-285.22	91.15	-3.13	0.003

S = 2522   R-Sq = 72.8%   R-Sq(adj) = 71.0%

Analysis of Variance

Source	DF	SS	MS	F	P
Regression	3	783334935	261111645	41.05	0.000
Residual Error	46	292627676	6361471		
Total	49	1075962610			

Source	DF	Seq SS
%Top25%	1	715695271
VSAT	1	5350360
SFRatio	1	62289304

Unusual Observations

Obs	%Top25%	Tuition	Fit	StDev Fit	Residual	St Resid
23	56	20655	14792	809	5863	2.45R
26	33	11700	6979	1239	4721	2.15RX
34	10	15	9692	921	5498	2.34R

R denotes an observation with a large standardized residual.
X denotes an observation whose X value gives it large influence.

The multiple regression equation is

Tuition = 9545 + 109 %Top25% + 4.3 VSAT – 285 SFRatio.

Minitab displays the t-ratio for each population coefficient and the corresponding p-value. In multiple regression, the t-tests measure the benefit of adding that predictor variable, given the other variables in the model. A small p-value suggests that the corresponding population regression coefficient is not zero and that therefore the variable is significant in predicting the response variable.

The p-values for %Top25% (.003) and for SFRatio (.003) suggest that these two variables are significant in predicting tuition. The high p-value (.725) for VSAT suggest that, because of the other two variables, this variable is not significant in predicting tuition.

With a standard error of estimate of $2,522, this model explains 72.8% of the variation in tuition at Massachusetts colleges. The adjusted percentage of variation is only slightly less at 71.0%. The addition of other variables substantially improved your model over the linear and quadratic models considered previously.

The ANOVA table (which tests the hypothesis that all predictor population coefficients are zero) reports a p-value of 0.000. Therefore you can conclude that at least one of the population coefficients is different from zero at any reasonable level of significance.

▼ **Note** As with the corresponding section of the quadratic regression output, the content and interpretation of the Seq SS table following the ANOVA table is rather involved. See your instructor for details. ▲

Minitab has noted several unusual observations in the data set. There are two outliers (in rows 23 and 34) and one outlier/influence point (in row 26). You will investigate these values in Tutorial 11.

▼ **Note** The quadratic regression you developed in the last section is a special case of a multiple regression model with two (related) predictor variables. ▲

Next, save your work:

■ Save the project **T10.mpj**

▼ 10.5   Obtaining Multiple Linear Regression Response Variable Estimates ▲

Based on the output in Figure 10-12, you decide to obtain a regression equation without C7 VSAT. You also want to generate response estimates for this multiple linear regression. You will find tuition estimates for a college with 40% of its freshman class that were in the top 25% of their high school graduating class and with a student-faculty ratio of 13 (these are values that the college aspires to). You decide to generate 99% interval estimates, instead of the default 95% interval estimates.

- Choose **Stat > Regression > Regression**
- Highlight **VSAT** in the "Predictor" text box, and press (Delete)
- Click the **Options** button
- Click in the "Prediction intervals for new observations" text box
- Type **40 13** (be sure to put a space between them)
- Press (Tab)
- Type **99** in the "Confidence level" text box
- Click **OK** twice

Minitab reports a model of Tuition = 11314 + 119 %Top25% − 299 SFRatio, as shown in Figure 10-13.

```
MTB > Regress 'Tuition' 2 '%Top25%' 'SFRatio';
SUBC>    Constant;
SUBC>    Predict 40 13;
SUBC>      Confidence 99;
SUBC>    Brief 2.
```

Regression Analysis

```
The regression equation is
Tuition = 11314 + 119 %Top25% - 299 SFRatio


51 cases used 5 cases contain missing values
```

Predictor	Coef	StDev	T	P
Constant	11314	1627	6.95	0.000
%Top25%	119.44	13.77	8.68	0.000
SFRatio	-299.47	87.26	-3.43	0.001

```
S = 2483      R-Sq = 72.5%    R-Sq(adj) = 71.4%
```

Analysis of Variance

Source	DF	SS	MS	F	P
Regression	2	780868588	390434294	63.35	0.000
Residual Error	48	295852445	6163593		
Total	50	1076721033			

Source	DF	Seq SS
%Top25%	1	708277276
SFRatio	1	72591312

Unusual Observations

Obs	%Top25%	Tuition	Fit	StDev Fit	Residual	St Resid
23	56	20655	14589	395	6066	2.47R
26	33	11700	6931	1213	4769	2.20RX
31	21	9744	5527	1186	4217	1.93 X
34	10	15190	9844	882	5346	2.30R

```
R denotes an observation with a large standardized residual.
X denotes an observation whose X value gives it large influence.
```

Predicted Values

Fit	StDev Fit	99.0% CI	99.0% PI
12199	389	(11155, 13243)	(5459, 18939)

The predicted tuition for a college with %Top25% = 40 and SFRatio = 13 is $12,199. A 99% confidence interval for the mean tuition for colleges with this combination of values is $11,155 to $13,243. You are pleased with this model. With just two predictor variables, it explains 72.5% of the variability in tuition, only slightly less than the 72.8% for the model with three variables that you investigated previously.

MINITAB AT WORK

Human Resources: A faculty member, as a member of its College Compensation Committee, was asked to analyze the current salaries of faculty members with the aim of uncovering any inequities. A different multiple regression model was used to predict salaries for professors, associate professors, and assistant professors.

For professors, almost 80% of the variability in salary from one individual to another could be explained by a linear model consisting of just three variables: years at that rank, whether the individual held an endowed chair, and the length, in months, of their annual contract. A similar linear model based on these same three variables explained 70% of the variability in the salaries of associate professors. There were no endowed chairs among the assistant professors, but the other two variables explained almost 60% of the variability in their salaries. Surprisingly, neither gender nor department was a significant predictor of salary at any rank.

When these three models were used, it was possible to obtain a predicted salary and a corresponding residual for each instructor, based on their values for these variables. When the data set for each rank was ordered according to the magnitude of the residual, it was simple to identify those instructors earning substantially less than their predicted salaries (i.e., those with large negative residuals). These faculty members were given salary equity adjustments before receiving the basic annual increase enjoyed by every faculty member.

You have completed your initial regression analysis of tuition at Massachusetts colleges and are ready to submit your preliminary recommendations. At this point, you will recommend to the administration the model that relates tuition to the percentage of the college's freshman class that were in the top 25% of their high school graduating class and to the student-faculty ratio. You will also show how the regression can provide tuition estimates for different types of colleges and thereby assist the administration in setting future tuition levels.

In the next tutorial, you will continue your analysis of the Massco data using some of Minitab's advanced regression features to obtain a better model to explain variation in tuition. Next, however, save your data.

- In the location where you are saving your work, save the current project *T10.mpj*, and exit Minitab

Minitab Command Summary

This section describes the menu and Session commands introduced in, or related to, this tutorial. To find a complete explanation of all menus and commands, use Minitab's Help.

Minitab Menu Commands

Menu	Command	Description
Stat		
Basic Statistics		
	Correlation	Provides the correlation, and, optionally, the corresponding p-value, between pairs of variables.
Regression		
	Regression	Performs simple or multiple linear regression.
	Fitted Line Plot	Graphs a regression line and a scatter plot of the regression data and, optionally, confidence bands and prediction bands around the line.

Review and Practice

Matching

Match the following terms to their definitions by placing the correct letter next to the term it describes.

_____ SRES1

_____ FITS1

_____ X**2

_____ X

_____ R

_____ X1*X2

_____ Predictor

_____ S

_____ Response

_____ R-Sq

a. The Minitab symbol that denotes an influential point

b. A variable in a quadratic model

c. A name given to the column of standardized residuals

d. A name assigned to the column of predicted values

e. Minitab's notation for the standard error of the estimate

f. Minitab's name for an independent variable

g. An example of a complex multiple linear regression variable

h. Minitab's notation for the coefficient of determination

i. Minitab's name for a dependent variable

j. The symbol that Minitab uses to identify an unusual observation that shows a large standardized residual

True/False

Mark the following statements with a *T* or an *F*.

_____ You use the Regression command to perform simple linear regression and multiple linear regression.

_____ The Fitted Line Plot command can graph 90% confidence bands and prediction bands for a simple linear regression line.

_____ The number of entries in the "Prediction intervals for new observations" text box is equal to the number of predictors plus one.

_____ Among the most used transformations of the response variable are cube roots, logarithms, and negative reciprocals.

_____ Minitab regression output includes an ANOVA table.

_____ A quadratic model is an example of a polynomial model.

_____ The Regression command can print a 95% confidence interval for the slope of a simple linear regression.

_____ You can place fitted values in the worksheet only if you also place the residual values.

_____ Even if you don't place the residual and fitted values in the worksheet, Minitab displays these values for unusual observations.

_____ Minitab uses "s" to denote the standard deviation of the response variable in its regression output.

Practice Problems

Use Help or Part III, Exploring Data, to review the contents of the data sets referred to in the following problems.

1. Open *Homes.mtw*. Perform a simple linear regression with C1 Price as the response variable and C2 Area as the predictor variable, as follows.

   a. Construct a scatter plot with C1 Price on the vertical axis and C2 Area on the horizontal axis. Based on this plot, do you believe there is a linear relationship between these two variables?

   b. Compute the correlation coefficient between these two variables and the corresponding p-value. Do these values surprise you? Explain.

   c. What is the regression equation for this simple linear regression?

   d. Interpret the slope of the line in this case.

   e. What are the values of the standard error of estimate and the coefficient of determination?

   f. Test the hypothesis that the population slope is equal to 0 against the alternative hypothesis that it is not equal to 0.

   g. Construct a 95% confidence interval for the population slope.

2. Open *Pulsea.mtw.*

   a. Plot C7 Weight against C6 Height. Based on this plot, do you believe there is a linear relationship between these two variables?

   b. What is the regression line relating Weight to Height?

   c. Interpret the slope of this line.

   d. What are the values of the standard error of estimate and the coefficient of determination?

   e. Test the hypothesis that the population slope is equal to 0 against the alternative hypothesis that it is not equal to 0.

   f. Construct a 95% confidence interval for the population slope.

   g. For the mean height, construct a point estimate for the weight based upon this model and corresponding 95% confidence and prediction intervals. Identify these intervals on a Fitted Line Plot that displays 95% confidence and prediction bands.

3. Open *Temco.mtw* (the data file *Pay.mtw* is a subset of this data set).

   a. Perform a simple linear regression to explain salary based on the number of years employed, YrsEm. Does the output support this model? Explain in a concise fashion.

   b. Perform a quadratic regression to explain the salary based on YrsEm and YrsEm**2. Does the output support this model? Explain concisely.

   c. Which of the two regression models do you consider to be the best? Explain your answer by referring to the regression output.

4. Open *Mnwage.mtw.*

   a. Plot minimum wage against year. Perform a related simple linear regression relating minimum wage to year.

   b. Compute the square root of minimum wage. Plot this new variable against year. Perform a related simple linear regression relating the square root of minimum wage to year.

   c. Compute the natural logarithm of minimum wage. Plot this new variable against year. Perform a related simple linear regression relating the natural logarithm of minimum wage to year.

   d. Compute the negative reciprocal of minimum wage. Plot this new variable against year. Perform a related simple linear regression relating the negative reciprocal of minimum wage to year.

   e. Which is the best model? Explain your answer using the plots and the regression output.

5. Open *Temco.mtw*.

    a. Perform a multiple linear regression with C1 Salary as a response variable and the other four quantitative variables as predictors.

    b. Based on your analysis in part a, do you believe that any predictor(s) should be dropped from the model? Briefly explain your answer. If you believe any predictor(s) should be dropped, perform a multiple or simple linear regression analysis with the appropriate subset of predictors.

TUTORIAL 11

Advanced Linear Regression

In this tutorial, you will use some of Minitab's advanced regression commands. First, you will see an excellent example of why it is important to use graphs in regression analysis. Then, you will examine the problems caused by predictor variables that are highly correlated and check the validity of the assumptions underlying regression analysis. You will check for the existence of unusual observations and examine a technique that allows you to include qualitative variables in a regression model. In addition, you will use a technique for selecting an optimal subset of predictor variables from a large number of possible predictors. Finally, you will be introduced to binary logistic regression, an increasingly popular technique for modeling dichotomous variables.

Objectives

In this tutorial, you learn how to:

- appreciate the importance of graphs in a regression analysis

- identify the presence of collinearity in a multiple linear regression

- perform a residual analysis to check the assumptions of a linear regression

- examine unusual observations (outlying points and points of influence) in a linear regression

- create indicator (dummy) variables so that you can use qualitative variables as predictors in a linear regression

- use best subsets regression to explore the relative importance of predictor variables

- use binary logistic regression to model a dichotomous response variable

▼ 11.1   The Importance of Graphs in Regression ▲

CASE STUDY: DATA ANALYSIS — IMPORTANCE OF GRAPHS

The statistician Frank J. Anscombe created a data set to illustrate the importance of inspecting scatter plots before examining the standard computer regression output. Four pairs of variables with very different relationships all result in the same basic regression output. These data are saved in the file *Fja.mtw*. There are 11 values for each of the following six variables: C1 X, C2 Y1, C3 Y2, C4 Y3, C5 X4, and C6 Y4. (X represents predictors, and Y represents response variables.) The instructor in your introductory statistics class gives these data to your group and asks you to summarize the output from four simple linear regressions: Y1 on X, Y2 on X, Y3 on X, and Y4 on X4.

This tutorial is a continuation of Tutorial 10. Thus, instead of creating a new project, you will open and add to the project *T10.mpj*. Don't worry if you don't have — or think you may not have — a complete copy of this project file. A copy of it, as it looked at the end of Tutorial 10, is included in the Student subdirectory. The following directions assume that you open this project.

To get started:

- Choose **File > Open Project**

- In the Student subdirectory, double-click on **T10**

Minitab will take a few seconds to open the project. The Session command language will be enabled, and the output will be read-only.

- Maximize the **Session window**

Rename the project *T11.mpj*:

- Choose **File > Save Project As**

- In the location where you are saving your work, save the project as *T11*

You'll be working with the data file *Fja.mtw*, which is in the Student subdirectory:

- Open the worksheet **Fja.mtw**

Before analyzing the Anscombe data, you should save them under the name *11Fja*:

- In the location where you are saving your work, save the worksheet as *11Fja*

Your group is skeptical about doing a regression analysis before examining plots of the data, but you proceed as you did in the last tutorial:

- Choose **Stat > Regression > Regression**

- Select **C2 Y1** as the "Response" variable and **C1 X** as the "Predictors" variable

To focus on the essential aspects of the output, limit the amount of regression output:

- Click the **Results** button

- Click the second option button, **Regression equation, table of coefficients, s, R-squared, and basic analysis of variance**

In the Results dialog box, Minitab allows you some control over the amount of output produced with the Regression command. In this example, with one predictor variable, your choice will eliminate the printing of unusual observations.

- Click **OK** twice

Minitab produces the first regression. Notice that your selection in the Results dialog box is equivalent to entering a Brief 1 Session subcommand. (Brief 1 produces minimal output, Brief 2 is the default, and Brief 3 produces the most output).

- Choose **Stat > Regression > Regression** three more times, and enter the pairs in the following chart

Response	Predictor
C3 Y2	C1 X
C4 Y3	C1 X
C6 Y4	C5 X4

When you have finished the four regressions, the Session window contains the output shown in Figure 11-1 (you may have to scroll to see all of this output).

FIGURE 11-1

*Results of four Brief 1
regression analyses*

```
MTB > Regress 'Y1' 1 'X';
SUBC>   Constant;
SUBC>   Brief 1.
```

Regression Analysis

```
The regression equation is
```

**First regression
equation** ⟋Y1 = 3.00 + 0.500 X

```
Predictor      Coef      StDev         I        P
Constant      3.000      1.125      2.67    0.026
X            0.5001     0.1179      4.24    0.002


S = 1.237      R-Sq = 66.7%     R-Sq(adj) = 62.9%


Analysis of Variance

Source         DF        SS         MS        F        P
Regression      1      27.510     27.510    17.99    0.002
Residual Error  9      13.763      1.529
Total          10      41.273
```

```
MTB > Regress 'Y2' 1 'X';
SUBC>   Constant;
SUBC>   Brief 1.
```

Regression Analysis

```
The regression equation is
```

**Second regression
equation** ⟋Y2 = 3.00 + 0.500 X

```
Predictor      Coef      StDev         T        P
Constant      3.001      1.125      2.67    0.026
X            0.5000     0.1180      4.24    0.002


S = 1.237      R-Sq = 66.6%     R-Sq(adj) - 62.9%


Analysis of Variance

Source         DF        SS         MS        F        P
Regression      1      27.500     27.500    17.97    0.002
Residual Error  9      13.776      1.531
Total          10      41.276
```

FIGURE 11-1 (CONTINUED)

```
MTB > Regress 'Y3' 1 'X';
SUBC>    Constant;
SUBC>    Brief 1.
```

Regression Analysis

Third regression equation —

```
The regression equation is
Y3 = 3.00 + 0.500 X
```

Predictor	Coef	StDev	T	P
Constant	3.002	1.124	2.67	0.026
X	0.4997	0.1179	4.24	0.002

```
S = 1.236     R-Sq = 66.6%     R-Sq(adj) = 62.9%
```

Analysis of Variance

Source	DF	SS	MS	F	P
Regression	1	27.470	27.470	17.97	0.002
Residual Error	9	13.756	1.528		
Total	10	41.226			

```
MTB > Regress 'Y4' 1  'X4';
SUBC>    Constant;
SUBC>    Brief 1.
```

Regression Analysis

Fourth regression equation —

```
The regression equation is
Y4 = 3.00 + 0.500 X4
```

Predictor	Coef	StDev	T	P
Constant	3.002	1.124	2.67	0.026
X4	0.4999	0.1178	4.24	0.002

```
S = 1.236     R-Sq = 66.7%     R-Sq(adj) = 63.0%
```

Analysis of Variance

Source	DF	SS	MS	F	P
Regression	1	27.490	27.490	18.00	0.002
Residual Error	9	13.742	1.527		
Total	10	41.232			

Note that the four regression equations are alike. They also all have a t-statistic of 4.24, with a corresponding p-value of 0.002, which Minitab uses to test whether the population slope is zero. Except for rounding, the standard error of estimates and the coefficients of determinations are the same. It's tempting to assume that the response and predictor variables are the same. But if you return to the Data window, you will see that this is not true. The data are shown in Figure 11-2.

- Click the **Current Data window** toolbar button 🖳

FIGURE 11-2

*The Data window showing
the Anscombe data set*

	C1	C2	C3	C4	C5	C6	C7	C8	C9	
↓	X	Y1	Y2	Y3	X4	Y4				
1	10	8.04	9.14	7.46	8	6.58				
2	8	6.95	8.14	6.77	8	5.76				
3	13	7.58	8.74	12.74	8	7.71				
4	9	8.81	8.77	7.11	8	8.84				
5	11	8.33	9.26	7.81	8	8.47				
6	14	9.96	8.10	8.84	8	7.04				
7	6	7.24	6.13	6.08	8	5.25				
8	4	4.26	3.10	5.39	19	12.50				
9	12	10.84	9.13	8.15	8	5.56				
10	7	4.82	7.26	6.42	8	7.91				
11	5	5.68	4.74	5.73	8	6.89				
12										
13										
14										
15										
16										
17										
18										
19										
20										

The four pairs of variables are very different. Your group decides to produce scatter plots for each pair of variables:

■ Choose **Graph > Plot**

■ Select **C2 Y1** as the "Y variable" and **C1 X** as the "X variable"

■ Click the "Annotation" **drop-down list arrow** and select **Title**

■ Type **Scatter Plot of Y1 against X** as the "Title"

■ Click **OK** twice

■ After the plot appears, use the **Edit Last Dialog** toolbar button [icon] to repeat these steps to produce three more scatter plots (titled: **Scatter Plot of Y2 against X**, **Scatter Plot of Y3 against X**, and **Scatter Plot of Y4 against X4**)

The four resulting scatter plots are shown in Figure 11-3 (you may want to use the Graph Manager to see each of these graphs).

FIGURE 11-3

*Four Anscombe data set
scatter plots*

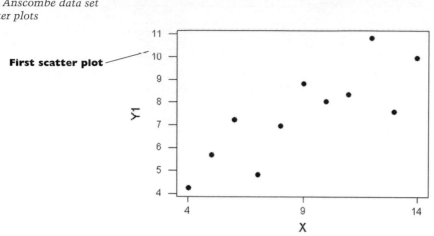

First scatter plot

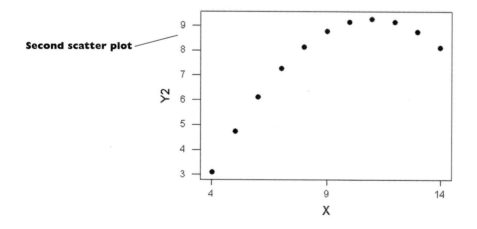

Second scatter plot

FIGURE 11-3 (CONTINUED)

Scatter Plot of Y3 against X

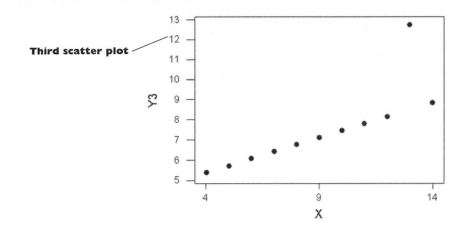

Third scatter plot

Scatter Plot of Y4 against X4

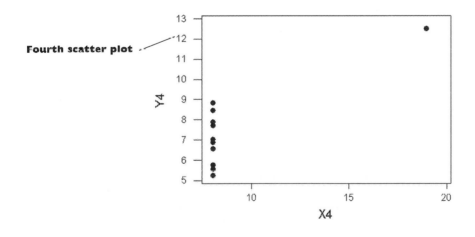

Fourth scatter plot

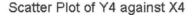

   These plots demonstrate why Anscombe constructed this data set. The first scatter plot resembles the type of plot you see in most textbooks. The second clearly calls for a quadratic model to describe the relationship. An outlying observation – the third observation with coordinates (13, 12.74) – is apparent in the third scatter plot. Finally, the fourth scatter plot shows an unusual variable: 10 out of the 11 observations have an X4 value of 8, while X4 is 19 for the other observation. This eighth observation greatly influences the regression analysis.

Your group reports on these four very different situations. Your instructor asks you to repeat the four regressions with the amount of output restored to the default level. You will do this by copying your previous commands from the History window to the Command Line Editor and then editing the four Brief subcommands. This time, Minitab will produce more output.

- Choose **Window > History**
- Highlight the **12 regression command lines**
- Choose **Edit > Command Line Editor**
- Change each Brief 1 to a **Brief 2**

The Command Line Editor dialog box should resemble Figure 11-4.

- Click **Submit Commands**

The Session window displays the output shown in Figure 11-5. Minitab notes the unusual observations you saw in the last two scatter plots. In the third plot, it flags the third observation with an R; in the fourth, it marks the eighth observation with an X. Notice that Minitab doesn't notify you of the need for a quadratic model for the second data set. Although Minitab's unusual observation regression output block is valuable, you should still plot your data whenever you perform a regression.

FIGURE 11-5

*Results of four Brief 2
regression analyses*

```
MTB > Regress 'Y1' 1  'X';
SUBC>    Constant;
SUBC>    Brief 2.
```

Regression Analysis

```
The regression equation is
Y1 = 3.00 + 0.500 X
```

Predictor	Coef	StDev	T	P
Constant	3.000	1.125	2.67	0.026
X	0.5001	0.1179	4.24	0.002

$S = 1.237$ R-Sq = 66.7%   R-Sq(adj) = 62.9%

Analysis of Variance

Source	DF	SS	MS	F	P
Regression	1	27.510	27.510	17.99	0.002
Residual Error	9	13.763	1.529		
Total	10	41.273			

```
MTB > Regress 'Y2' 1  'X';
SUBC>    Constant;
SUBC>    Brief 2.
```

Regression Analysis

```
The regression equation is
Y2 = 3.00 + 0.500 X
```

Predictor	Coef	StDev	T	P
Constant	3.001	1.125	2.67	0.026
X	0.5000	0.1180	4.24	0.002

$S = 1.237$ R-Sq = 66.6%   R-Sq(adj) = 62.9%

Analysis of Variance

Source	DF	SS	MS	F	P
Regression	1	27.500	27.500	17.97	0.002
Residual Error	9	13.776	1.531		
Total	10	41.276			

FIGURE 11-5 (CONTINUED)

```
MTB > Regress 'Y3' 1 'X';
SUBC>   Constant;
SUBC>   Brief 2.
```

Regression Analysis

The regression equation is
Y3 = 3.00 + 0.500 X

Predictor	Coef	StDev	T	P
Constant	3.002	1.124	2.67	0.026
X	0.4997	0.1179	4.24	0.002

S = 1.236   R-Sq = 66.6%   R-Sq(adj) = 62.9%

Analysis of Variance

Source	DF	SS	MS	F	P
Regression	1	27.470	27.470	17.97	0.002
Residual Error	9	13.756	1.528		
Total	10	41.226			

Unusual Observations

Obs	X	Y3	Fit	StDev Fit	Residual	St Resid
3	13.0	12.740	9.499	0.601	3.241	3.00R

R denotes an observation with a large standardized residual

```
MTB > Regress 'Y4' 1 'X4';
SUBC>   Constant;
SUBC>   Brief 2.
```

Regression Analysis

The regression equation is
Y4 = 3.00 + 0.500 X4

Predictor	Coef	StDev	T	P
Constant	3.002	1.124	2.67	0.026
X4	0.4999	0.1178	4.24	0.002

S = 1.236   R-Sq = 66.7%   R-Sq(adj) = 63.0%

Analysis of Variance

Source	DF	SS	MS	F	P
Regression	1	27.490	27.490	18.00	0.002
Residual Error	9	13.742	1.527		
Total	10	41.232			

Unusual Observations

Obs	X4	Y4	Fit	StDev Fit	Residual	St Resid
8	19.0	12.500	12.500	1.236	0.000	* X

X denotes an observation whose X value gives it large influence.

Before moving on to the next case study, save your work:

■ In the location where you are saving your work, save the project **T11.mpj**

▼ 11.2 Identifying Collinearity ▲

CASE STUDY: INSTITUTIONAL RESEARCH – TUITION MODELING (CONTINUED)

As an institutional researcher for a Massachusetts college, you have been asked by the administration to refine the model for out-of-state tuition that you generated in Tutorial 10. The college is constructing a strategic plan to attract better qualified students. A major component of the plan is an understanding of how tuition is related to measures of student quality and other key measures.

The data you will use for this research, *10Massco.mtw*, were stored along with the rest of *T10.mpj* and can be accessed through the Window menu:

■ Choose **Window > 10Massco.MTW**

10Massco.mtw contains the original data from all 56 four-year colleges in Massachusetts, plus the variables created in Tutorial 10. In all, there are 16 variables for the 56 colleges. An explanation of the contents of C13 FITS1, C14 RESI1, and C15 SRES1 can be found in Section 10.1. The variable C16 VSAT**2 contains the square of values in C7 VSAT.

Before analyzing these data, you should save them as the worksheet *11Massco*:

■ In the location where you are saving your work, save the worksheet as **11Massco**

In Tutorial 10, you performed a quadratic regression analysis, that is, a multiple linear regression analysis with C12 Tuition as the response variable and C7 VSAT and C16 VSAT**2 as the predictor variables. If you look back at Figure 10-11, you can see the regression equation of Tuition = –12,858 + 61.2 VSAT – 0.0145 VSAT**2. According to the predictor table, each coefficient is not significant at reasonable levels of significance, in the presence of the other. (The p-value is 0.355 for the VSAT coefficient and 0.823 for the VSAT**2 coefficient.) However, the ANOVA table reports that at least one of the two coefficients is not zero because the p-value is 0.000.

This contradiction is due to the high degree of linear association between the two predictors. The value of their correlation coefficient is 0.997. (You could use Stat > Basic Statistics > Correlation to verify this value.) This is an example of collinearity (or multicollinearity) that occurs in multiple linear regression when there is a high correlation among the predictors.

Minitab's Variance inflation factors option helps identify collinearity. The variance inflation factor (VIF) is a measure of how much the variance of an estimated regression coefficient increases if your predictors are correlated (collinear). The higher the VIF value, the greater the degree of collinearity. VIF values above 10 are considered strong evidence that collinearity is affecting the regression coefficients.

▼ **Note** If there are k predictor variables, the VIF for the jth predictor is $1/(1 - R\text{-sqj})$, where R-sqj is the R-sq from regressing the jth predictor on the remaining $k - 1$ predictors. ▲

You decide to redo the quadratic regression analysis from Tutorial 10 using this option:

- Choose **Stat > Regression > Regression**
- Press **F3** to clear the previous selections
- Select **C12 Tuition** as the "Response" variable
- Select **C7 VSAT** and **C16 VSAT**2** as the "Predictors" variables
- Click the **Options** button
- Click the **Variance inflation factors** check box
- Click **OK** twice

Figure 11-6 displays the results of the quadratic regression with the VIFs.

FIGURE 11-6

Results of quadratic regression with VIFs

```
MTB > Regress 'Tuition' 2 'VSAT' 'VSAT**2';
SUBC>    Constant;
SUBC>    VIF;
SUBC>    Brief 2.
```

Regression Analysis

```
The regression equation is
Tuition = - 12858 + 61.2 VSAT - 0.0145 VSAT**2
```

```
53 cases used 3 cases contain missing values
```

Variance inflation factors

Predictor	Coef	StDev	T	P	VIF
Constant	-12858	16345	-0.79	0.435	
VSAT	61.17	65.56	0.93	0.355	170.0
VSAT**2	-0.01449	0.06425	-0.23	0.823	170.0

```
S = 2930        R-Sq = 63.1%     R-Sq(adj) = 61.6%
```

Analysis of Variance

Source	DF	SS	MS	F	P
Regression	2	732229921	366114961	42.66	0.000
Residual Error	50	429102500	8582050		
Total	52	1161332421			

Source	DF	Seq SS
VSAT	1	731793652
VSAT**2	1	436269

Unusual Observations

Obs	VSAT	Tuition	Fit	StDev Fit	Residual	St Resid
21	437	5244	11108	476	-5864	-2.03R
24	675	18485	21833	1687	-3348	-1.40 X
34	373	15190	7944	982	7246	2.63R
54	655	1962	20995	1329	-136	-0.52 X

```
R denotes an observation with a large standardized residual.
X denotes an observation whose X value gives it large influence.
```

The predictor table contains the VIFs. Each coefficient's VIF is 170.0 — with only two predictor variables, the VIFs are always the same. Since these values indicate a high degree of collinearity, there may be statistical and computational difficulties with this model.

Now that you have identified a problem with this quadratic regression, try to remedy it by creating and using two new, less correlated predictor variables. First, subtract the *mean* of VSAT from VSAT and then square the resulting variable, which is called a *centered* variable:

- Choose **Calc > Standardize**

- Select **C7 VSAT** as the "Input Column(s)," and press [Tab]

- Type **VSATSM** in the "Store results in" text box

- Click the **Subtract mean** option button

The completed Standardize dialog box should look as shown in Figure 11-7.

FIGURE 11-7

The completed
Standardize dialog box

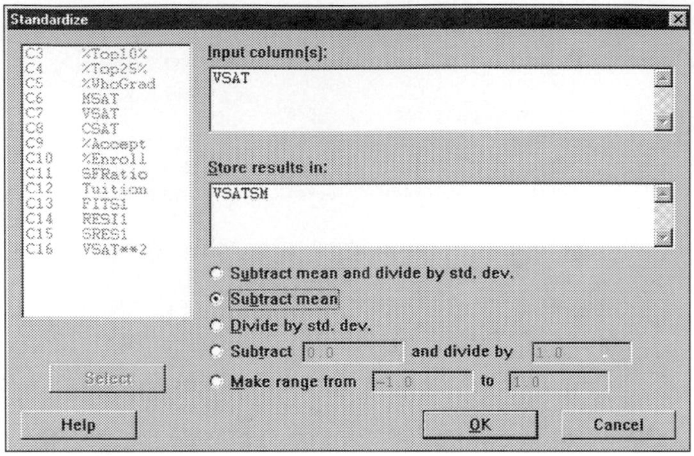

- Click **OK**

Next, create the square of this new variable:

- Choose **Calc > Calculator**

- Type **VSSM**2** as the "Store result in variable," and press ⟨Tab⟩

- Enter, by either clicking or typing, **VSATSM**2** as the "Expression," and click **OK**

The new variables C17 VSATSM and C18 VSSM**2 do not have a correlation coefficient close to 1; it equals 0.597. (This can be verified by using Stat > Basic Statistics > Correlation.)

Now, as your solution to collinearity in polynomial regression, regress tuition on these two new variables:

- Choose **Stat > Regression > Regression**

- Verify that **C12 Tuition** is the entry in the "Response" text box

- Press ⟨Tab⟩, and select **C17 VSATSM** and **C18 VSSM**2** to replace the previous contents of the "Predictors" text box

- Click **OK**

Figure 11-8 displays the results of this new regression. Note that the VIF column now contains VIFs of 1.6. You no longer have a problem with collinearity.

FIGURE 11-8

Results of quadratic regression with centered predictors

```
MTB > Regress 'Tuition' 2  'VSATSM' 'VSSM**2';
SUBC>    Constant;
SUBC>    VIF;
SUBC>    Brief 2.
```

Regression Analysis

```
The regression equation is
Tuition = 13148 + 47.3 VSATSM - 0.0145 VSSM**2


53 cases used 3 cases contain missing values


Predictor        Coef       StDev         T        P       VIF
Constant      13147.5       575.5     22.84    0.000
VSATSM         47.278       6.268      7.54    0.000       1.6
VSSM**2       -0.01449     0.06425     -0.23    0.823       1.6


S = 2930       R-Sq = 63.1%      R-Sq(adj) = 61.6%

Analysis of Variance


Source          DF          SS          MS        F        P
Regression       2    732229921   366114961    42.66    0.000
Residual Error  50    429102500     8582050
Total           52   1161332421


Source          DF      Seq SS
VSATSM           1    731793652
VSSM**2          1       436269


Unusual Observations
Obs    VSATSM    Tuition       Fit   StDev Fit    Residual   St Resid
 21       -43       5244     11108        476       -5864      -2.03R
 24       195      18485     21833       1687       -3348      -1.40 X
 34      -107      15190      7944        982        7246       2.63R
 54       175      19629     20995       1329       -1366      -0.52 X


R denotes an observation with a large standardized residual.
X denotes an observation whose X value gives it large influence.
```

Note, also, that there are many similarities between the outputs in Figures 11-6 and 11-8. The values of S, R-sq, and F and the p-value for F are identical. In addition, Minitab flags the same unusual observations. However, there is a difference in the predictor table: The first predictor coefficient changed. Minitab indicates that this coefficient is significant by its p-value of 0.000. You no longer have a contradiction between the t-test and F-test. Because the quadratic term is not significant, you decide to forgo inclusion of this term based on VSAT in developing your tuition model for Massachusetts colleges.

Before continuing, save your work:

■ In the location where you are saving your work, save the project *T11.mpj*

▼ 11.3 Verifying Linear Regression Assumptions ▲

To use the t-test, F-tests, and interval estimates introduced in Tutorial 10, you assumed that the data met certain conditions. Most of those conditions concerned the error component, or unexplained portion, in a model. Here are the three major assumptions of linear regression:

1. Normality: The error component is normally distributed.

2. Constant variation (homoscedasity): The error component has a constant standard deviation.

3. Independence: The error components for two observations are independently distributed.

Serious departures from these assumptions affect the results of the inference associated with simple and multiple linear regression. You can check the validity of these assumptions by using the residuals and measures related to the residuals.

Storing the Residuals

The differences between the response variable and its fitted values are called *residuals*. In fact, residuals are estimates of the error terms in a linear regression model. When you perform a linear regression, Minitab allows you to store many columns of useful information. For example, in Tutorial 10 you stored the fitted values, the residuals, and the standardized residuals for a simple linear regression.

Next, you will store this same information, along with two other statistics related to the residuals, for the multiple linear regression model you recommended to the administration at the end of Tutorial 10 (with C12 Tuition as the response and C4 %Top25% and C11 SFRatio as the predictors). You will use the results to check the three major assumptions of linear regression.

- Choose **Stat > Regression > Regression**

- Verify that **C12 Tuition** is the "Response" variable, and press Tab

- Select **C4 %Top25%** and **C11 SFRatio** as the "Predictors" variables

- Click the **Storage** option button, and click the **Fits**, **Residuals**, **Standardized residuals**, **Hi (leverages)**, and **Cook's distance** check boxes in the Storage dialog box

- Click **OK** twice

Figure 11-9 shows the results.

FIGURE 11-9

*Results of multiple linear
regression with storage*

```
MTB > Name c19 = 'FITS2' c20 = 'RESI2' c21 = 'SRES2' c22 = 'HI2' &
CONT>       c23 = 'COOK2'
MTB > Regress 'Tuition' 2 '%Top25%' 'SFRatio';
SUBC>    Fits 'FITS2';
SUBC>    Residuals 'RESI2';
SUBC>    SResiduals 'SRES2';
SUBC>    Hi 'HI2';
SUBC>    Cookd 'COOK2';
SUBC>    Constant;
SUBC>    VIF;
SUBC>    Brief 2.
```

Regression Analysis

```
The regression equation is
Tuition = 11314 + 119 %Top25% - 299 SFRatio


51 cases used 5 cases contain missing values

Predictor        Coef       StDev          T       P       VIF
Constant        11314        1627       6.95   0.000
%Top25%        119.44       13.77       8.68   0.000       1.2
SFRatio       -299.47       87.26      -3.43   0.001       1.2


S = 2483       R-Sq = 72.5%     R-Sq(adj) = 71.4%

Analysis of Variance

Source           DF          SS          MS       F       P
Regression        2   780868588   390434294   63.35   0.000
Residual Error   48   295852445     6163593
Total            50  1076721033


Source       DF      Seq SS
%Top25%       1   708277276
SFRatio       1    72591312


Unusual Observations
Obs    %Top25%    Tuition        Fit   StDev Fit   Residual   St Resid
 23         56      20655      14589         395       6066      2.47R
 26         33      11700       6931        1213       4769     2.20RX
 31         21       9744       5527        1186       4217      1.93 X
 34         10      15190       9844         882       5346      2.30R


R denotes an observation with a large standardized residual.
X denotes an observation whose X value gives it large influence.
```

Notice that Minitab has created five new variables in the Name command line. Also observe that there doesn't appear to be a problem with
collinearity based on the two VIF values. The rest of the output is identical to
Figure 10-13.

You can use either the residuals or the standardized residuals for a residual analysis. Some statisticians prefer residuals (with a mean of 0); others prefer

standardized residuals (with most values between −3 and 3). You decide to use standardized residuals.

Before continuing, save the project:

■ In the location where you are saving your work, save the current project *T11.mpj*

Checking the Normality Assumption

To check the normality assumption, you decide to let Minitab construct a normal probability plot (NPP) rather than constructing it yourself, as you did in previous tutorials. You will obtain an NPP of the standardized residuals. You can choose one of three tests in the Normality Test dialog box to verify normality:

■ Choose **Stat > Basic Statistics > Normality Test**

■ Select **C21 SRES2** as the "Variable"

Use the default test for normality (Anderson-Darling). The completed Normality Test dialog box looks as shown in Figure 11-10.

FIGURE 11-10

The completed Normality Test dialog box

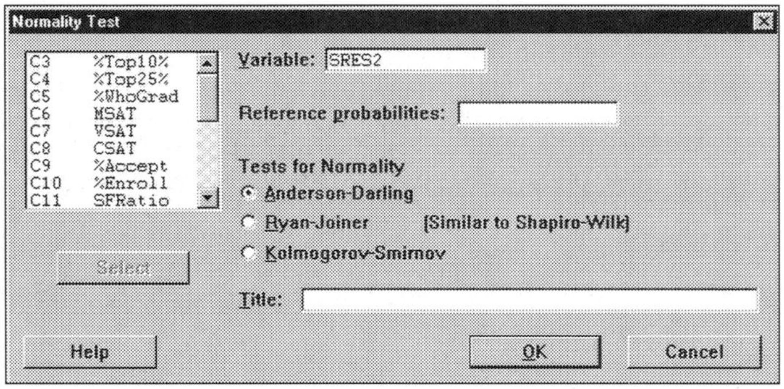

■ Click **OK**

The NPP appears as shown in Figure 11-11. The vertical axis is a probability scale; the horizontal axis is a data scale. Minitab has fitted and drawn a least-squares line for the points that estimate the cumulative distribution function from which the data are drawn. Note that there are a number of points away from the line. Most of them are associated with extremely low and high values of standardized residuals at the end of the line. The average, standard deviation, and sample size appear in the lower-left corner. The results of the Anderson-Darling normality test are in the lower-right corner. The test's p-value is 0.232, so you do not reject the null hypothesis that the standardized residuals are normally distributed at a significance level of .05. This is probably due to the highly linear pattern present for the standardized residual values between −1 and 1.

FIGURE 11-11

NPP of standardized
residuals using the
Anderson-Darling
normality test

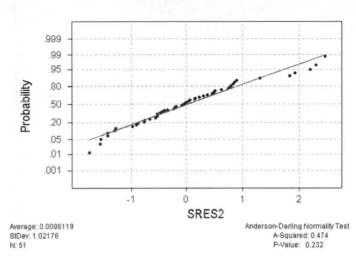

Normal Probability Plot

Average: 0.0096119
StDev: 1.02176
N: 51

Anderson-Darling Normality Test
A-Squared: 0.474
P-Value: 0.232

Using Scatter Plots to Verify the Constant Variation Assumption

The best single check for constant variance is a scatter plot with the standardized residuals on the vertical axis and the fitted values on the horizontal axis. In addition, you should construct two scatter plots with the standardized residuals on the vertical axis and each predictor variable on the horizontal axis. There should be approximately the same amount of variation in the standardized residuals over the range of the horizontal variable in each plot; otherwise, the assumption is violated. Begin by plotting the SRES2 versus FITS2:

- Choose **Graph > Plot**

- Press F3 to clear the previous selections

- Select **C21 SRES2** as the "Y" variable and **C19 FITS2** as the "X" variable, and click **OK**

The scatter plot appears as shown in Figure 11-12. There appears to be more variation for the fitted values between $10,000 and $15,000 than for the other fitted values. This may be a concern if you decide to use this as your final model.

FIGURE 11-12

*Scatter plot of standard-
ized residuals against fits*

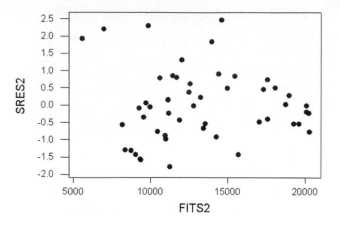

You also observe that there are three outlying standardized residuals with values greater than 2. Minitab allows you to identify the observations corresponding to these points by *brushing* the scatter plot. Brushing allows you to highlight points on a graph to learn more about them. It is especially well-suited for showing the characteristics of outliers and for determining whether points that lie in a brushing region share other characteristics. You decide to brush these outlying values. First, you must go into brushing mode:

- Choose **Editor**

Notice the black dot on the menu next to View. This indicates that you are in viewing mode.

- Choose **Brush**

- Choose **Editor** again, and notice that the black dot now indicates that you are in brushing mode (this mode is available in the Graph window only)

- Click anywhere in the **Graph window** to close the menu

Your cursor has changed from its standard form to a brushing tool (it looks like a small pointing hand). In addition, notice the small window that appears in the upper-left corner of the plot. This is the brushing palette. It presents information about the points you select. The word Row that appears is the default piece of information that always appears.

You decide to have the brushing palette identify a college's name and standardized residual in addition to its row number:

- Choose **Editor > Set ID Variables**

- Select the **Use columns** check box, and type **c1** and **c21**, the columns containing the two variables you want to display

The completed Set ID Variables dialog box is shown in Figure 11-13.

FIGURE 11-13

The completed Set ID Variables dialog box

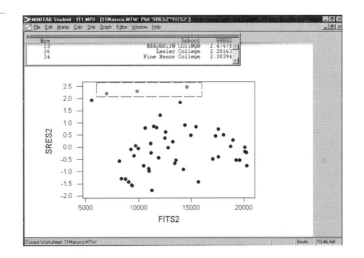

■ Click **OK**

The brushing palette has changed. It is now much wider in order to accommodate the two requested variables.

■ Use your brushing tool to draw a box around the three outlying points

Note the row numbers, school names, and standardized residual values for each of these points that now show in the brushing palette, as shown in Figure 11-14. Note, too, that each of these three colleges have standardized residual values greater than 2.

From an examination of boxplots (not shown) of the two predictors, you discover the presence of outliers in the student faculty ratio. Thus you decide to construct one more plot: SRES2 against SFRatio, shown in Figure 11-15. This is based on the outlying values in SFRatio.

■ Choose **Graph > Plot**

■ Verify that **SRES2** is the "Y" variable, and press Tab

■ Select **C11 SFRatio** as the "X" variable, and click **OK**

FIGURE 11-15

Scatter plot of
standardized residuals
against SFRatio

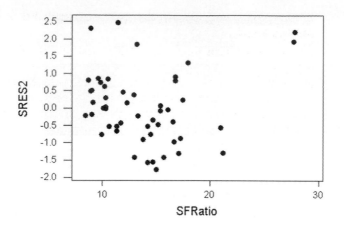

This plot reveals constant SRES2 variation for SFRatios of less than 20. You also observe that there are two outlying SFRatio values. You decide to identify these colleges by brushing, as shown in Figure 11-16:

- Choose **Editor > Brush**, and drag a box around the two values

FIGURE 11-16

Brushed scatter plot of
standardized residuals
against SFRatio

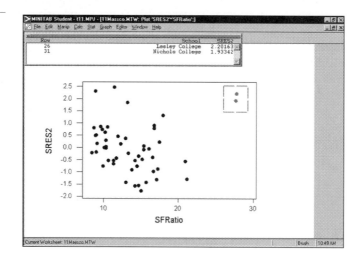

Looking back at the previously brushed scatter plot in Figure 11-14, you identify one of these same colleges as a potential unusual observation. In the next section, you will examine all four of these colleges in more detail before constructing your final model.

Although you construct scatter plots such as these to check the constant variation assumption, they are also useful in detecting other problems with the model. You should study any unusual pattern in a residual analysis because it may indicate an underlying weakness in the model.

Checking the Independence Assumption with a Time Series Plot

Usually, you check the independence assumption when you know the order in which the data were collected. Even though this isn't the case in this instance, you decide to practice the technique with a time series plot of the standardized residuals in C21 SRES2. This approach is appropriate if the values are arranged in the order in which they were collected. Such plots are similar to the one you constructed in Tutorial 4 for the election data.

To obtain the plot:

- Choose **Graph > Time Series Plot**

- Select **C21 SRES2** as the first "Y variable"

The completed Time Series Plot dialog box is shown in Figure 11-17.

FIGURE 11-17

The completed Time Series Plot dialog box

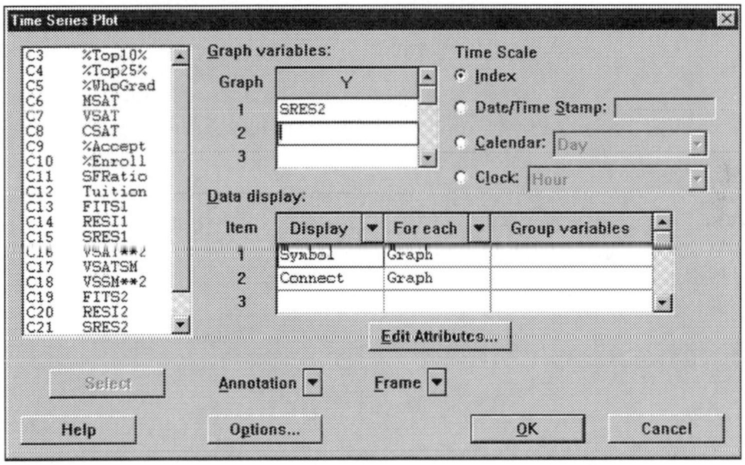

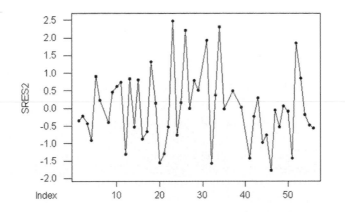

- Click **OK**

The time series plot appears as shown in Figure 11-18.

FIGURE 11-18

Time series plot of standardized residuals

Time series plots plot measurement data (in this case SRES2) on the y-axis against the passage of time or the sequence order on the x-axis. By default, points on the graph are displayed as symbols connected by lines.

You discover no unusual patterns in this plot (for example, long runs of values with the same sign). However, you again notice that there are three colleges that have large, positive, standardized residuals. You will want to examine the data for these three colleges in more detail before you submit your final model.

A convenient way of getting plots suitable for checking the various assumptions in regression is to use the Residual Plots command on the Stat > Regression menu. This produces four residual model diagnostics plots:

1. A normal score plot of residuals to check for normality

2. A histogram of the residuals to check for normality

3. A residual versus fits scatter plot to check the constant variation assumption

4. A time series plot of the residuals to check the independence assumption

(This final plot type, which is discussed more fully in Tutorial 14, is often called an I chart.) A Tutorial 11 practice problem allows you to examine these four residual plots. An additional way to check the independence assumption is by using the Durbin-Watson statistic, which is available in the Regression Options dialog box. You will find an explanation of this statistic under Regression - Options in Help.

▼ 11.4   Examining Unusual Observations ▲

Now turn your attention to the four unusual observations identified at the bottom of the output in Figure 11-9 and shown again in Figure 11-19.

FIGURE 11-19

Unusual observations table from Figure 11-9

Unusual Observations

Obs	%Top25%	Tuition	Fit	StDev Fit	Residual	St Resid
23	56	20655	14589	395	6066	2.47R
26	33	11700	6931	1213	4769	2.20RX
31	21	9744	5527	1186	4217	1.93 X
34	10	15190	9844	882	5346	2.30R

R denotes an observation with a large standardized residual.
X denotes an observation whose X value gives it large influence.

The three unusual observations flagged with an R identify Massachusetts colleges whose standardized residuals have absolute values that exceed 2. The tuition at Hampshire College (Obs 23) is $20,655, but the regression equation predicts a value of $14,589, thus leaving a residual of $6,066. At $4,769 and $5,346, the residuals of Lesley (Obs 26) and Pine Manor Colleges (Obs 34) are slightly smaller. These are the same three colleges identified in the brushed scatter plot of standardized residuals against fits shown in Figure 11-14.

The two unusual observations flagged with an X identify Massachusetts colleges that have large *HI*, or *"leverage," values*. The HI value for an observation is a measure of the potential influence of that observation on the regression equation. Those observations with HI values that exceed the smaller of .99 and $3(p + 1)/n$ are marked with an X and should receive special attention from the analyst. Here, p is the number of predictor variables and n is the sample size. From the results in Figure 11-9, p = 2 and n = 51, so the smaller of .99 and $3(3)/51 = .1765$ is .1765.

To check for observations that have a substantial influence, take a look at the HI2 column:

■ Choose **Manip > Display Data**

■ Select **C12 Tuition**, **C4 %Top25%**, **C11 SFRatio**, **C19 FITS2**, and **C22 HI2** as the "Columns and constants to display" variables, and click **OK**

The printed data appear in the Session window and in Figure 11-20 (you may have to scroll to see all of this output).

FIGURE 11-20

Data display containing HI values and four other variables

MTB > Print 'Tuition' '%Top25%' 'SFRatio' 'FITS2' 'HI2'.

Data Display

Row	Tuition	%Top25%	SFRatio	FITS2	HI2
1	8700	22	14.7000	9539.9	0.041414
2	19760	96	8.4000	20265.2	0.083481
3	10800	34	11.7000	11871.6	0.037550
4	12000	59	13.8000	14228.8	0.022049
5	16600	68	16.8000	14405.4	0.048928
6	13800	60	17.5000	13240.2	0.045542
7	11550	*	10.2000	*	*
8	16640	94	16.6000	17570.7	0.106900
9	18420	80	11.9000	17306.0	0.042971
10	14080	36	10.2000	12559.7	0.048431
11	19380	77	9.8000	17576.6	0.045283
12	5542	21	17.1000	8701.8	0.045821
13	17500	61	10.5000	15455.9	0.030889
14	18000	95	11.3000	19277.3	0.072586
15	13600	25	8.7000	11695.1	0.088737
16	8770	40	17.3000	10911.3	0.033421
17	11800	46	11.3000	13424.7	0.028874
18	15200	51	18.0000	12015.5	0.042767
19	11455	29	12.3000	11094.7	0.040403
20	5542	20	14.7000	9301.1	0.044734
21	5244	28	21.2000	8310.1	0.079974
22	12200	54	14.2000	13511.8	0.020581
23	20655	56	11.4000	14589.2	0.025299
24	18485	100	9.9000	20293.8	0.086031
25	11475	21	9.1000	11097.5	0.091908

FIGURE 11-20 (CONTINUED)

26	11700	33	27.8000	6930.8	0.238672
27	20100	99	10.1000	20114.5	0.083135
28	12500	36	16.8000	10583.2	0.031284
29	19300	79	9.0000	18055.0	0.052751
30	9810	*	13.5000	*	*
31	9744	21	27.7000	5527.4	0.228330
32	5542	19	14.2000	9331.3	0.047844
33	13380	42	12.9000	12467.8	0.023526
34	15190	10	8.9000	9843.6	0.126314
35	12700	38	10.3000	12768.6	0.044741
36	5542	*	21.0000	*	*
37	16160	53	8.9000	14979.5	0.046560
38	16900	*	8.2000	*	*
39	18820	88	10.3000	18740.7	0.059031
40	9438	*	12.8000	*	*
41	12170	69	13.0000	15662.8	0.029045
42	10584	32	13.3000	11153.6	0.031226
43	19701	90	10.3000	18979.6	0.062801
44	8566	39	16.7000	10971.5	0.029676
45	8568	29	14.5000	10435.9	0.031912
46	6919	37	15.0000	11241.7	0.024623
47	9838	29	16.1000	9956.8	0.033247
48	18345	96	10.6000	19606.4	0.075157
49	9850	25	15.4000	9688.6	0.036642
50	8994	21	15.4000	9210.9	0.042383
51	5542	20	15.7000	9001.6	0.044017
52	18460	55	13.2000	13930.7	0.020259
53	13472	25	9.6000	11425.5	0.075290
54	19629	96	9.0000	20085.5	0.080025
55	15884	86	15.2000	17034.4	0.069210
56	6797	26	21.0000	8131.1	0.077725

This display verifies that colleges 26 and 31, Lesley and Nichols, are the only ones with HI2 values greater than 0.1765. You observe that these two colleges have extremely high student-faculty ratios, at 27.8 and 27.7, respectively. You are not surprised that these colleges are classified as unusual observations. Their predictor values greatly influence your regression equation. If you removed them from the analysis, you might obtain a strikingly different equation. Note that these are the same two colleges identified in the brushed scatter plot of SRES2 against SFRatio in Figure 11-16.

Cook's Distance

Cook's distance is a function of the standardized residuals and the HI values. Check Minitab's Help for its equation. It is an overall measure of how unusual the predictor values and response are for each observation. Large values signify unusual observations. You are interested in observations with Cook's distances that are greater than the 50th percentile of an F distribution. These observations usually have either large standardized residuals or a large HI value and hence a substantial impact on the regression equation. You can check the Data window to compare the Cook's distance values to 0.8002 (the 50th percentile of the F distribution with 3 numerator DF (degrees of freedom) and 47 denominator DF). There are no such observations.

▼ 11.5 Incorporating an Indicator (Dummy) Variable into a Model ▲

You are concerned about the results of both your residual analysis and your examination of unusual observations. You need to construct a better model. Thus far, you have considered only quantitative variables in your modeling. But there is also one qualitative variable, C2 PubPriv, that you could include as a predictor in your regression equation. Recall that C2 PubPriv is a text variable with the codes of Private and Public. Before you can include this variable, however, you must convert it to the appropriate form.

Qualitative variables must be transformed into dummy or indicator variables in order to use them as predictors. An *indicator* (or *dummy*) variable is a variable that takes two values – typically 0 and 1.

The Make Indicator Variable command can be used to transform C2 PubPriv into two indicator variables:

- Choose **Calc > Make Indicator Variables**

- Select **C2 PubPriv** to enter it in the "Indicator variables for" text box

- Type **PP1** and **PP2** in the "Store results in" text box

The completed Make Indicator Variables dialog box should look as shown in Figure 11-21.

FIGURE 11-21

The completed Make Indicator Variables dialog box

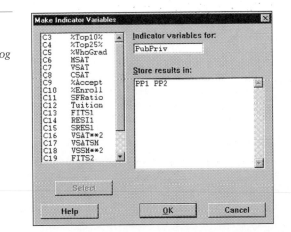

- Press

Then print out C2 PubPriv and the two corresponding indicator (dummy) variables:

- Choose **Manip > Display Data**

- Select **C2 PubPriv**, **C24 PP1**, and **C25 PP2** as the "Columns and constants to display" variables, and click **OK**

The printed data appear in the Session window as shown in Figure 11-22. (you may have to scroll to see all of this output). Observe that the private Massachusetts colleges (coded Private in C2 PubPriv) have a 1 in C24 PP1 and a 0 in C25 PP2. Public colleges are coded with a 0 in C24 PP1 and a 1 in C25 PP2.

FIGURE 11-22

Session window displaying qualitative variable PubPriv and its two indicator (dummy) variables

```
MTB > Name c24 = 'PP1' c25 = 'PP2'
MTB > Indicator 'PubPriv' 'PP1' 'PP2'.
MTB > Print 'PubPriv' 'PP1' 'PP2'.
```

Data Display

Row	PubPriv	PP1	PP2
1	Private	1	0
2	Private	1	0
3	Private	1	0
4	Private	1	0
5	Private	1	0
6	Private	1	0
7	Private	1	0
8	Private	1	0
9	Private	1	0
10	Private	1	0
11	Private	1	0
12	Public	0	1
13	Private	1	0
14	Private	1	0
15	Private	1	0
16	Private	1	0
17	Private	1	0
18	Private	1	0
19	Private	1	0
20	Public	0	1
21	Public	0	1
22	Private	1	0
23	Private	1	0
24	Private	1	0
25	Private	1	0
26	Private	1	0
27	Private	1	0
28	Private	1	0
29	Private	1	0
30	Private	1	0
31	Private	1	0
32	Public	0	1
33	Private	1	0

FIGURE 11-22 (CONTINUED)

34	Private	1	0
35	Private	1	0
36	Public	0	1
37	Private	1	0
38	Private	1	0
39	Private	1	0
40	Private	1	0
41	Private	1	0
42	Private	1	0
43	Private	1	0
44	Public	0	1
45	Public	0	1
46	Public	0	1
47	Public	0	1
48	Private	1	0
49	Private	1	0
50	Private	1	0
51	Public	0	1
52	Private	1	0
53	Private	1	0
54	Private	1	0
55	Private	1	0
56	Public	0	1

You are ready to include C2 PubPriv in your regression analysis. You will model tuition as a function of eight of the nine quantitative variables (there is a problem with collinearity if you include CSAT because it is the sum of VSAT and MSAT) and one of the two indicator variables (there is a problem with collinearity if you include both of these variables, because PP1 and PP2 always add up to 1).

To fit a multiple linear regression:

■ Choose **Stat > Regression > Regression**

■ Verify that **C12 Tuition** is the entry in the "Response" text box, and press Tab

■ Select **C3 %Top10%**, **C4 %Top25%**, **C5 %WhoGrad**, **C6 MSAT**, **C7 VSAT**, **C9 %Accept**, **C10 %Enroll**, **C11 SFRatio**, and **C24 PP1** as the "Predictors" variables

■ Click the **Storage** button, and deselect all of the check boxes in that section

■ Click **OK** twice

The Session window shows the regression output as shown in Figure 11-23.

FIGURE 11-23

*Results of multiple linear
regression with the eight
quantitative and one indicator variables*

```
MTB > Regress 'Tuition' 9 '%Top10%'-'VSAT' '%Accept'-'SFRatio' 'PP1';
SUBC>    Constant;
SUBC>    VIF;
SUBC>    Brief 2.
```

Regression Analysis

```
The regression equation is
Tuition = - 512 - 55.5 %Top10% + 123 %Top25% - 74.0 %WhoGrad - 4.7 MSAT
            + 33.2 VSAT + 5.3 %Accept - 23.9 %Enroll - 185 SFRatio + 4661 PP1


44 cases used 12 cases contain missing values
```

Predictor	Coef	StDev	T	P	VIF
Constant	-512	6667	-0.08	0.939	
%Top10%	-55.49	46.67	-1.19	0.243	24.6
%Top25%	122.73	37.45	3.28	0.002	16.3
%WhoGrad	-73.98	28.54	-2.59	0.014	3.6
MSAT	-4.75	12.07	-0.39	0.697	17.2
VSAT	33.19	12.26	2.71	0.011	14.7
%Accept	5.29	29.88	0.18	0.861	4.3
%Enroll	-23.93	31.31	-0.76	0.450	1.6
SFRatio	-184.87	84.73	-2.18	0.036	1.6
PP1	4660.7	894.6	5.21	0.000	2.1

```
S = 1656      R-Sq = 90.6%     R-Sq(adj) = 88.1%
```

Analysis of Variance

Source	DF	SS	MS	F	P
Regression	9	893821550	99313506	36.23	0.000
Residual Error	34	93211614	2741518		
Total	43	987033164			

Source	DF	Seq SS
%Top10%	1	626607304
%Top25%	1	116741486
%WhoGrad	1	982400
MSAT	1	514804
VSAT	1	36881830
%Accept	1	17205470
%Enroll	1	8802255
SFRatio	1	11683330
PP1	1	74402672

Unusual Observations

Obs	%Top10%	Tuition	Fit	StDev Fit	Residual	St Resid
5	30.0	16600	13420	936	3180	2.33R
16	17.0	8770	12092	718	-3322	-2.23R
26	12.0	11700	9120	1222	2580	2.31R

```
R denotes an observation with a large standardized residual.
```

You are encouraged by the introduction of the indicator variable. There is a smaller S and a higher R-sq than with your previous model. Still there remains a collinearity problem. Four of the variables have a VIF over 10. Also, four population coefficients are individually insignificant, as indicated by p-values greater than .2. You decide to obtain a regression equation without the predictors associated with these insignificant coefficients. You might simplify your model without decreasing its predictive ability by omitting these insignificant variables. If you do this on your own, the resulting equation still has a major problem in that the variable %Top25% has a VIF of 10.5 (this output is not shown here):

$$\text{Tuition} = 4,906 + 69.8 \text{ \%Top25\%} - 72.1 \text{ \%WhoGrad} + 19.5 \text{ VSAT} - 264$$
$$\text{SFRatio} + 5,364 \text{ PP1}$$

You do not believe that there should be collinearity associated with your model. Thus you decide to omit the %Top25% variable from the model. The new equation of this multiple linear regression is

$$\text{Tuition} = -3,945 - 42.2 \text{ \%WhoGrad} + 38.3 \text{ VSAT} - 198 \text{ SFRatio} + 5,588 \text{ PP1}$$

Its associated output doesn't indicate any collinearity problems, but it does contain a troublesomely large p-value of 0.140 for the variable %WhoGrad. Hence you decide to remove %WhoGrad from the model. The Session window shows the regression results for this reduced model. The results are also shown in Figure 11-24.

FIGURE 11-24

Results of multiple linear regression with VSAT, SFRatio, and PP1 as the predictor variables

```
MTB > Regress 'Tuition' 3 'VSAT' 'SFRatio' 'PP1';
SUBC>    Constant;
SUBC>    VIF;
SUBC>    Brief 2.
```

Regression Analysis

The regression equation is
Tuition = - 5322 + 34.0 VSAT - 147 SFRatio + 5168 PP1

53 cases used 3 cases contain missing values

Predictor	Coef	StDev	T	P	VIF
Constant	-5322	2348	-2.27	0.028	
VSAT	34.020	3.683	9.24	0.000	1.3
SFRatio	-147.45	68.64	-2.15	0.037	1.3
PP1	5168.5	701.7	7.37	0.000	1.2

S = 1879   R-Sq = 85.1%   R-Sq(adj) = 84.2%

Analysis of Variance

Source	DF	SS	MS	F	P
Regression	3	988370324	329456775	93.33	0.000
Residual Error	49	172962098	3529839		
Total	52	1161332421			

Source	DF	Seq SS
VSAT	1	731793652
SFRatio	1	65075538
PP1	1	191501134

Unusual Observations

Obs	VSAT	Tuition	Fit	StDev Fit	Residual	St Resid
16	468	8770	13216	402	-4446	-2.42R
26	411	11700	9729	994	1971	1.24 X
31	377	9744	8587	987	1157	0.72 X
34	373	15190	11223	670	3967	2.26R

R denotes an observation with a large standardized residual.
X denotes an observation whose X value gives it large influence.

Interpreting the Regression Equation

You are pleased with this output. There is still a big improvement in S and R-sq compared to your previous model with two predictors. There are statistically significant results for all three t-tests and the F-test. In addition, there are now still only four unusual observations and no problem with collinearity. Note that the college in row 16, Eastern Nazarene, has replaced the college in row 23, Hampshire, as being classified as an unusual observation. (Normally, you would perform a residual analysis as well; in this case, you would find no obvious problems.)

Now take a look at the regression equation:

$$\text{Tuition} = -5{,}322 + 34.0\ \text{VSAT} - 147\ \text{SFRatio} + 5{,}168\ \text{PP1}$$

The sample coefficient associated with the indicator variable PP1 has an interesting interpretation. The predicted base tuition for a private Massachusetts college is $5,168 more than that for a public college in the same state, even if they have the same VSAT and student-faculty ratio.

▼ **Note** In general, if the original qualitative variable takes k different values or labels, the Make Indicator Variables command will create k indicator variables. For each value or label associated with the original variable, one of the indicator variables will take the value 1 when that value or label occurs and 0 otherwise. However, since these k new variables will add to 1, only k – 1 of them need be included in the regression model ▲

Before continuing, save your work:

- In the location where you are saving your work, save the current project **T11.mpj**

▼ 11.6   Performing Best Subsets Regression ▲

You are concerned that you obtained the previous regression model by trial and error. You decide to take a more systematic approach and begin by constructing a matrix plot for the ten variables under consideration:

- Choose **Graph > Matrix Plot**

- Select **C3 %Top10%, C4 %Top25%, C5 %WhoGrad, C6 MSAT, C7 VSAT, C9 %Accept, C10 %Enroll, C11 SFRatio, C24 PP1**, and **C12 Tuition** as the "Graph variables"

▼ **Note** Selecting Tuition as the last variable makes it easier for you to see the relationship of this response variable to the eight possible predictor variables. ▲

- Click the **Options** button and then the **Lower left** option button under "Matrix Display"

■ Click **OK** twice

The matrix plot appears as shown in Figure 11-25.

▼ **Note** Depending on your computer speed, it may take several minutes to create this plot. ▲

FIGURE 11-25

Matrix plot with response variable and nine possible predictor variables

Scatter plots of possible predictors against Tuition ⟶

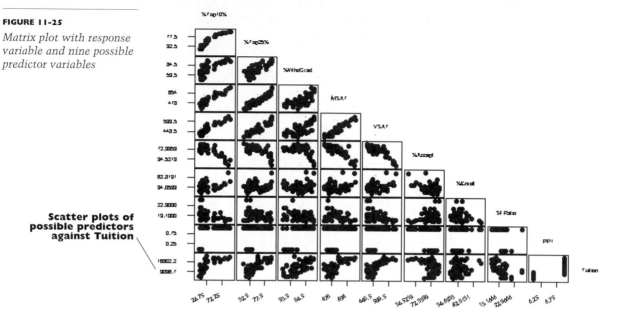

The graph contains a scatter plot for each pair of variables listed in the "Graph variables" text box. You are most interested in the bottom row of plots; in each, Tuition is the variable on the vertical axis. These plots indicate that many of the predictors are linearly related to Tuition. Further, in the bottom-right plot you can see that tuition tends to be much lower at public colleges (where PP1 = 0) than at private colleges (where PP1 = 1). This bottom row of plots gives you some insight into which possible predictor variables you should include in the regression model. However, the relationship between the response variable and possible predictor variables can change depending on the variables already in the model. So, you decide to use a popular variable-selection procedure, *best subsets regression*.

▼ **Note** Another possible variable selection procedure is *stepwise regression*. Minitab allows the user to perform three stepwise regression techniques: stepwise selection, forward selection, and backward elimination. Currently, most statisticians prefer to use best subsets regression except when the number of predictors is too large to be accommodated by best subsets regression. Check Minitab's Help or your instructor for further information. ▲

Best subsets regression generates regression models using the maximum R-squared criterion by first examining all one-predictor regression models and selecting the two models giving the largest R-sq. Then Minitab displays information on these models. It next examines all two-predictor models, selects the two models with the largest R-sq, and displays information on these two models. This process continues until the model contains all predictors. The technique includes only colleges that have no missing values for the response and predictor variables.

Best Subsets Regression is an efficient way to select a group of "best subsets" for further analysis by selecting the smallest subset that fulfills certain statistical criteria. You use this output to select a reasonable small set of predictors that is associated with a reasonable large value of R-sq.

You decide to use Best Subsets Regression to identify predictors for Tuition from the nine predictors considered previously:

- Choose **Stat** > **Regression** > **Best Subsets**

- Select **C12 Tuition** as the "Response" variable

- Select the nine variables **C3 %Top10%**, **C4 %Top25%**, **C5 %WhoGrad**, **C6 MSAT**, **C7 VSAT**, **C9 %Accept**, **C10 %Enroll**, **C11 SFRatio**, and **C24 PP1** as the "Free Predictors"

The completed Best Subsets Regression dialog box is shown in Figure 11-26. (The appearance of the variable list in the "Free predictors" text box may differ from that shown in Figure 11-27 depending on how you select the variables.)

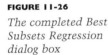

FIGURE 11-26

The completed Best Subsets Regression dialog box

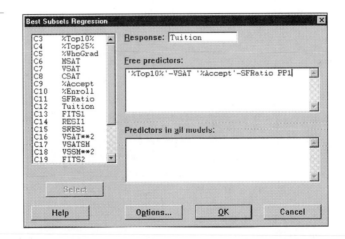

- Click **OK**

FIGURE 11-27

Results of Best Subsets Regression

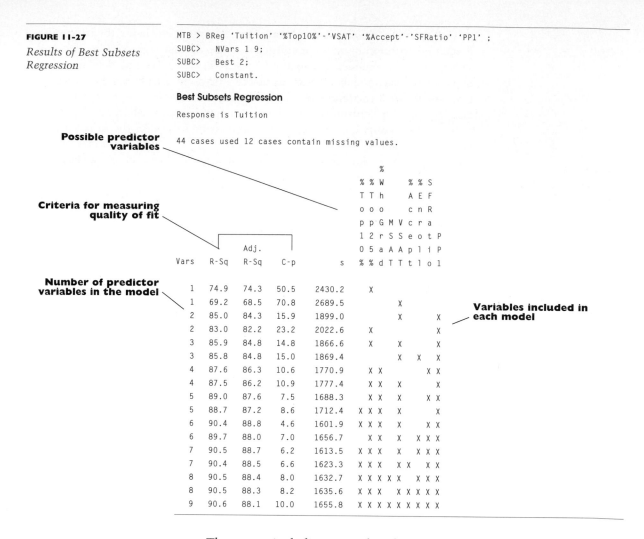

```
MTB > BReg 'Tuition' '%Top10%'-'VSAT' '%Accept'-'SFRatio' 'PP1' ;
SUBC>   NVars 1 9;
SUBC>   Best 2;
SUBC>   Constant.
```

Best Subsets Regression

Response is Tuition

Possible predictor variables

44 cases used 12 cases contain missing values.

Criteria for measuring quality of fit

Number of predictor variables in the model

Variables included in each model

```
                                        %
                               % % W        % % S
                               T T h      A E F
                               o o o      c n R
                               p p G M V  c r a
                               1 2 r S S  e o t P
                    Adj.       0 5 a A A  p l i P
Vars  R-Sq  R-Sq  C-p     s    % % d T T  t l o 1

  1   74.9  74.3  50.5  2430.2  X
  1   69.2  68.5  70.8  2689.5            X
  2   85.0  84.3  15.9  1899.0            X       X
  2   83.0  82.2  23.2  2022.6  X                 X
  3   85.9  84.8  14.8  1866.6  X         X       X
  3   85.8  84.8  15.0  1869.4            X   X   X
  4   87.6  86.3  10.6  1770.9    X X         X X
  4   87.5  86.2  10.9  1777.4    X X   X       X
  5   89.0  87.6   7.5  1688.3    X X   X     X X
  5   88.7  87.2   8.6  1712.4  X X X   X       X
  6   90.4  88.8   4.6  1601.9  X X X   X     X X
  6   89.7  88.0   7.0  1656.7    X X   X   X X X
  7   90.5  88.7   6.2  1613.5  X X X   X   X X X
  7   90.4  88.5   6.6  1623.3  X X X   X X   X X
  8   90.5  88.4   8.0  1632.7  X X X X X   X X X
  8   90.5  88.3   8.2  1635.6  X X X   X X X X X
  9   90.6  88.1  10.0  1655.8  X X X X X X X X X
```

The output includes a note that the analysis was based on only the 44 of the 56 colleges that had complete data for Tuition and the nine possible predictor variables. These nine variables are listed vertically on the top-right section of the output. The first column on the left gives the number of predictor variables in each model listed. For each model, the values for four criteria are given: R-sq, Adjusted R-sq, C-p, and the standard error of estimate (s). Ask your instructor for more information about the criterion C-p. The Xs to the right of the output indicate which of the predictor variables are included in the "best" models.

With its relatively high R-sq value of 85.0 with only two predictors, this Best Subsets output suggests a tuition model with VSAT and PP1 as the predictors. You can see this choice by the two Xs in the third row and the VSAT and PP1 columns. You decide to examine this model:

- Choose **Stat > Regression > Regression**
- Verify that **C12 Tuition** is in the "Response" text box
- Press ⎡Tab⎤, and select **C7 VSAT** and **C24 PP1** to replace the previous contents of the "Predictors" text box
- Click **OK**

FIGURE 11-28

Regression suggested by Best Subsets Regression

```
MTB > Regress 'Tuition' 2 'VSAT' 'PP1';
SUBC>   Constant;
SUBC>   VIF;
SUBC>   Brief 2.
```

Regression Analysis

```
The regression equation is
Tuition = - 9076 + 36.9 VSAT + 5575 PP1

53 cases used 3 cases contain missing values

Predictor       Coef       StDev         T       P      VIF
Constant       -9076        1624     -5.59   0.000
VSAT          36.933       3.546     10.42   0.000      1.1
PP1           5575.0       699.7      7.97   0.000      1.1

S = 1946     R-Sq = 83.7%     R-Sq(adj) = 83.1%

Analysis of Variance

Source         DF          SS          MS          F       P
Regression      2   972082611   486041305     128.41   0.000
Residual Error 50   189249810     3784996
Total          52  1161332421

Source         DF     Seq SS
VSAT            1   731793652
PP1             1   240288959

Unusual Observations
Obs     VSAT    Tuition       Fit   StDev Fit    Residual    St Resid
 16      468       8770     13784         313       -5014       -2.61R
 34      373      15190     10275         522        4915        2.62R

R denotes an observation with a large standardized residual.
```

This equation looks like a winner. With only two predictor variables, it has an R-sq of 83.7% and an S of $1,946.

▼ **Note** The R-sq value is slightly lower than the value found in Figure 11-27. This is due to nine more cases being used in the regression. ▲

Both predictor values have p-values of 0.000. This suggests that at any reasonable level of significance, both variables belong in the model. In addition, there is no problem with collinearity and there are only two unusual observations. (There also are no difficulties with regression assumptions based on a residual analysis that is not shown here.)

You have completed your regression analysis on the tuition at Massachusetts colleges and are ready to submit your recommendations. Best Subsets Regression helped you to determine the best variables to use as predictors. You will recommend a model that uses median verbal SAT and that indicates whether a college is private to predict the out-of-state tuition structure for the colleges. You will review the tuitions of those colleges whose standardized residuals fall above 2 and below –2 to determine why they differ greatly from the estimated average. Your results will be valuable to the administration as it develops a strategic plan for attracting students and deciding tuition rates.

▼ 11.7   Performing an Elementary Binary Logistic Regression ▲

The administration is so pleased with your multiple linear regression model for out-of-state tuition that it immediately asks you to obtain a preliminary model for predicting type of college (public or private). You accept the assignment but realize that you cannot use multiple linear regression because the response variable is not *quantitative*. PubPriv is a *qualitative* variable with two possible values. To obtain a model for this dichotomous variable, you decide to employ Minitab's Binary Logistic Regression command. Binary logistic regression performs logistic regression on a binary response variable. A binary variable has only two possible values, such as, in this case, Public or Private.

▼ **Note** As you saw in Section 11.5, qualitative variables can be included as predictor variables when they are transformed into indicator variables. However, a number of the assumptions associated with the standard regression model will be violated if such a variable is used as the response. Both the normality and the constant variance assumption are violated in this case. ▲

Binary logistic regression is used to classify observations into one of the two categories. It is also used to identify which variables best explain these classifications. More information about binary logistic regression is available in Minitab's Help. The first part of the overview Help screen is shown in Figure 11-29.

FIGURE 11-29

Binary Logistic Regression Help

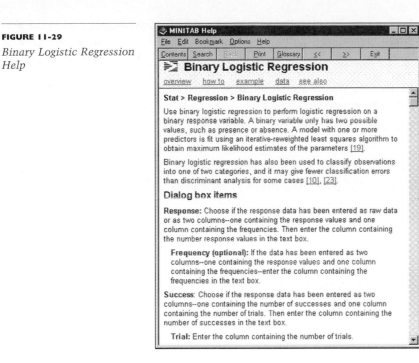

For this assignment, you decide to focus on which of the three quantitative variables C4 %Top25%, C7 VSAT, and C11 SFRatio are best at distinguishing between the two types of colleges. In addition, you decide to use all of Minitab's default options:

- Choose **Stat > Regression > Binary Logistic Regression**

- Select **C2 PubPriv** as the "Response" variable and **C4 %Top25%**, **C7 VSAT**, and **C11 SFRatio** as the "Model" variables

The completed dialog box is shown in Figure 11-30.

FIGURE 11-30

The completed Binary Logistic Regression dialog box

To focus on the essential aspects, you decide to print only part of the possible output:

- Click the **Results** button

- Click the **Response information, regression table, log-likelihood, and test that all slopes equal 0** check box

This completed dialog box is shown in Figure 11-31. The results of this Brief 1 output are shown in Figure 11-32.

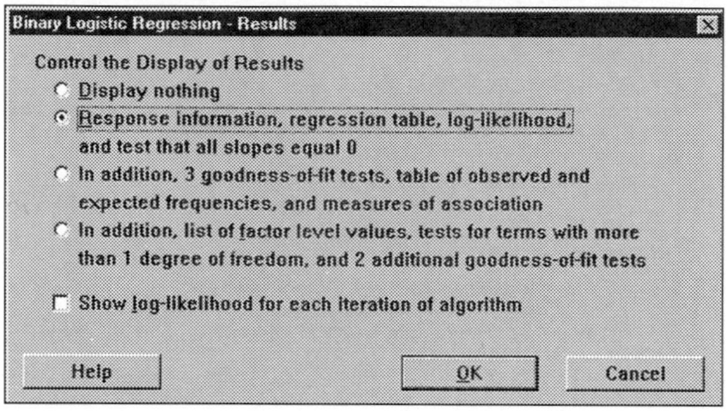

Binary Logistic Regression - Results

Control the Display of Results
- ○ Display nothing
- ● Response information, regression table, log-likelihood, and test that all slopes equal 0
- ○ In addition, 3 goodness-of-fit tests, table of observed and expected frequencies, and measures of association
- ○ In addition, list of factor level values, tests for terms with more than 1 degree of freedom, and 2 additional goodness-of-fit tests

☐ Show log-likelihood for each iteration of algorithm

Help   OK   Cancel

- Click **OK** twice

FIGURE 11-32

Results of binary logistic regression

```
MTB > BLogistic 'PubPriv' = '%Top25%' VSAT SFRatio;
SUBC>    Logit;
SUBC>    Brief 1.
```

Binary Logistic Regression

Link Function: Logit

Response Information

Variable	Value	Count	
PubPriv	Public	10	(Event)
	Private	40	
	Total	50	

   50 cases were used
    6 cases contained missing values

Logistic Regression Table

Predictor	Coef	StDev	Z	P	Odds Ratio	95% CI Lower	95% CI Upper
Constant	-15.147	8.109	-1.87	0.062			
%Top25%	-0.19983	0.08146	-2.45	0.014	0.82	0.70	0.96
VSAT	0.04155	0.02187	1.90	0.057	1.04	1.00	1.09
SFRatio	0.15355	0.09557	1.61	0.108	1.17	0.97	1.41

Log-Likelihood = -15.150
Test that all slopes are zero: G = 19.741, DF = 3, P-Value = 0.000

The G-statistic of 19.741 is used to test the null hypothesis that all three population slopes are zero. It is similar to the F-statistic used in multiple linear regression. Its associated p-value of 0.000 indicates that at least one of the three quantitative variables belongs in the model.

In binary logistic regression, the Z-test plays the same role as the t-test for determining the significance of individual variables in multiple linear regression. When the level of significance is .05, only the variable %Top25% with a Z-statistic of –2.45 and associated p-value of 0.014 is a statistically significant predictor of whether a college is public or private.

You report to the administration that the percentage of the freshman class that were in the top 25% of their high school graduating class predicts whether a school is public or private. Also, you mention that, if the administration wishes, you may perform a more complete analysis of this model.

To finish this tutorial:

■ In the place where you are saving your work, save the current project *T11.mpj*, and exit from Minitab

Minitab Command Summary

This section describes the menu and Session commands introduced in, or related to, this tutorial. To find a complete explanation of all menus and commands, use Minitab's on-line Help.

Minitab Menu Commands

Menu	Command	Description
Calc		
	Make Indicator Variables	Creates indicator (dummy) variables that you can use in a regression analysis.
	Standardize	Centers and scales columns of data.
Stat		
	Basic Statistics	
	Normality Test	Generates a normal probability plot (NPP) with a grid on the graph that resembles the grids found on normal probability paper and output that enables you to test whether the data come from a normal population.

Menu	Command	Description
Stat		
	Regression	
	Regression	Performs simple or multiple linear regression.
	Stepwise	Performs stepwise regression using backward elimination, forward selection, or both.
	Best Subsets	Performs an all-possible subsets regression using the R-squared criterion.
	Residual Plots	Provides four residual plots: a normal plot, a histogram, a plot of residuals versus fits, and an I chart.
	Binary Logistic Regression	Performs logistic regression on a two-possible-value (dichotomous) response variable.
Graph		
	Time Series Plot	Produces a high-resolution time series plot for one or more columns of data against time on the same axes.
	Matrix Plot	Produces a scatter plot matrix of up to 20 variables at once.
	Probability Plot	Draws an NPP or other distribution plot that resembles the usual form of probability paper.
Editor		
	View (Graph window only)	Puts the graph in View mode.
	Brush (Graph window only)	Puts the graph in Brush mode.
	Set ID Variables (Brush mode only)	Adds more information to the brushing palette for each brushed point.

Minitab Session Command

brief k		Controls the amount of output from Regression and other commands displayed in the Session window. For regression, $k = 0$ produces no output and $k = 3$ displays the most, with $k = 2$ being the default.

Matching

Match the following terms to their definitions by placing the correct letter next to the term it describes.

_____ Time Series Plot

_____ SRES against FITS plot

_____ HI

_____ Best Subsets

_____ Binary Logistic Regression

_____ Brushing

_____ Make Indicator Variable

_____ brief

_____ 3

_____ 2

a. The number of major linear regression assumptions

b. A display you can use to check the independence assumption

c. The number of dummy variables that Minitab includes in a regression model when a qualitative variable has three levels

d. Minitab notation for a command that allows you to highlight points on a graph to learn more about them

e. The Minitab Session command that you use to control the amount of output produced by the Regression command

f. Minitab notation for the leverage associated with an observation

g. The Minitab command that examines all possible combinations of predictor variables

h. The Minitab command that allows one to model a dichotomous response variable

i. The Minitab command for creating dummy variables

j. A display you can use to check constant variation assumption

True/False

Mark the following statements with a *T* or an *F*.

_____ High VIF values indicate the presence of collinearity.

_____ Make Indicator Variables is the Minitab command that creates dummy variables you can use in a regression analysis.

_____ The Normality Test command provides a choice of two tests: the Anderson-Darling normality test and the Ryan-Joiner W test.

_____ Residuals are estimates of the error component in a regression model.

_____ To perform a Best Subsets regression in Minitab, you should choose Stat > Regression > Regression.

_____ You create indicator variables so that you can use a qualitative variable as a response variable in a linear regression.

_____ You create indicator variables so that you can use a dichotomous variable as the response variable in a Binary Logistic Regression.

_____ Minitab identifies an observation that has an unusual standardized residual with an R and prints out the value of its standardized residual.

_____ Minitab identifies an observation that has high leverage with an X and prints out its HI value.

_____ An NPP is an excellent way to check one of the major linear regression assumptions.

Practice Problems

Use Help or Part III, Exploring Data, of the manual to review the contents of the data sets referenced in the following problems.

1. Open *Mnwage.mtw.*

   a. Perform a simple linear regression to explain the minimum wage based on year.

   b. Perform a quadratic regression to explain the minimum wage based on year and year squared. There are problems with this analysis due to extreme collinearity. Verify this fact by computing the regression's VIFs and the correlation coefficient between these two variables.

   c. Perform a quadratic regression to explain the minimum wage based on a centered year variable and a centered year squared variable. Is there any problem with collinearity in this model? Briefly explain your answer.

   d. Is the quadratic term worth adding?

2. Open *Homes.mtw.*

   a. Perform a simple linear regression with C1 Price as the response variable and C2 Area as the predictor variable.

   b. Is there collinearity present in this model?

   c. Discuss any unusual observations. In particular, brush a plot of Price against Area to identify the observations with large influence.

   d. Perform a complete residual analysis using the techniques introduced in this tutorial. Are you comfortable with constructing interval estimates and performing hypotheses based on this model?

   e. Perform a residual analysis using the Residual Plots command. Compare this analysis with the analysis in (d).

3. Open *Crimes.mtw.*

   a. Create four indicator variables for the qualitative variable C3 Region. Name your indicator variables Region1, Region2, Region3, and Region4.

   b. Perform a multiple linear regression to explain CrimeRte based on Region1, Region2, and Region3.

   c. What are this model's F-statistic value and corresponding p value?

   d. Perform a one-way ANOVA with CrimeRte as the response variable and Region as the factor. (Choose Stat > ANOVA > Oneway.)

   e. What are this model's F-statistic value and corresponding p-value? They should equal the values you reported in (c) because regression and ANOVA are related analyses.

4. Open *Homes.mtw.*

   a. Perform a best ~~subsets~~ *Stepwise* regression to determine a model to estimate C1 Price based on the other variables.

   b. Perform a complete regression analysis on this model. Would you use the best subsets regression model based on your examination of unusual observations, assumptions, and so on? Briefly explain your answer.

5. Open *Tomoo.mtw.*

   a. Use best subsets regression and linear regression to determine which of the variables in the data set affect Salary. Remember to transform each text variable into indicator variables. Be sure to consider the unusual observations and to perform a complete residual analysis.

   b. Use binary logistic regression to obtain a model for predicting Gender based on Salary.

TUTORIAL 12

Analyzing Categorical Data

Most of the data you worked with in previous tutorials were quantitative. In this tutorial, you will use Minitab to make statistical decisions about categorical/qualitative data. First, you will perform a goodness-of-fit test by issuing a series of commands and by executing a Minitab macro. Then you will test whether two categorical variables are independent. In both cases, you use the chi-square distribution.

Objectives

In this tutorial, you learn how to:

* compare an observed distribution of counts to a hypothesized distribution

* construct a Minitab Exec macro

* test whether two categorical variables are independent when the worksheet contains the contingency table counts

* test whether two categorical variables are independent when the worksheet contains the raw data for the two variables

▼ 12.1 Comparing an Observed Distribution of Counts to a Hypothesized Distribution ▲

CASE STUDY: MANAGEMENT — ENTREPRENEURIAL STUDIES (CONTINUED)

Recall that in your sales management class (Tutorial 6), you simulated a week of music sales at a music outlet. The probabilities that you used to generate the sample were the (population) proportion of music sales associated with each of nine music genre. These probabilities, which were found in *The New York Times 1998 Almanac*, are given in the following table.

Genre	Percentage of Sales
1. Rock	.337
2. Country	.152
3. Urban-Contemporary	.125
4. Pop	.096
5. Rap	.092
6. Gospel	.044
7. Classical	.035
8. Jazz	.034
9. Other	.085
	1.000

You decide to anticipate the possibility that your instructor will ask for some kind of verification that the sample came from this population. You decide to do a chi-square *goodness-of-fit* test of the hypotheses:

Null hypothesis, H_0: The sample came from the population specified.

Alternative hypothesis, H_1: The sample came from a population other than the one specified.

To get started:

- Start **Minitab**

- Maximize the **Session window**

- If necessary, enable the **Session command language** and make the output read-only

In Tutorial 6, you saved the worksheet containing your simulated class data as *6Music.mtw*. The file *Music.mtw* contains data from the same procedures you performed in Tutorial 6. In this tutorial, you should work with the data file *Music.mtw*, which is in the Student subdirectory, to ensure that you get the same results as in Tutorial 6.

- Open the worksheet **Music.mtw**

Before analyzing these data, you should save them as a worksheet and this tutorial in a project:

- In the location where you are saving your work, save the worksheet as **12Music**

- Also, save the work you have done thus far in this tutorial in a project named **T12**

The first three columns of the worksheet display the nine numeric and the corresponding nine text values of the music genre (C1 GenreN and C2 Genre, respectively) and the associated probabilities (C3 Prob). C4 Sample and C5 TxSample list the numeric and text genre values from your random sample of 1,000 genre.

Minitab does not have a single command to perform the chi-square goodness-of-fit test, but you can combine a number of commands — each of which you have used before — to perform the test. You decide to use Minitab to perform the chi-square goodness-of-fit calculations using the formula

$$\chi^2 = \sum \frac{(Obs - Exp)^2}{Exp}$$

where Obs and Exp are the observed and expected number of sales for each category (genre), respectively. You then calculate the p-value by comparing the observed chi-square value to a chi-square distribution with $k - 1 = 9 - 1 = 8$ DF (degrees of freedom), where k is the number of categories (genre, in this case).

Use the Tally command to compute the count/frequency of each genre in your sample:

- Choose **Stat > Tables > Tally**

- Select **C4 Sample** as the "Variables"

- Click **OK**

The Session window displays the counts, as shown in Figure 12-1.

FIGURE 12-1

Tally of simulated music sample

```
MTB > Tally 'Sample';
SUBC>   Counts.
```

Summary Statistics for Discrete Variables

Sample	Count
1	338
2	142
3	138
4	96
5	102
6	38
7	41
8	29
9	76
N=	1000

To store these nine sample values and their corresponding counts into the next two columns of your worksheet, C6 and C7:

- Highlight the **nine rows of these data,** and click the **Copy Cells** toolbar button ▣ to copy them onto the Clipboard

- Click the **Current Data window** toolbar button ▣

- Click the **C6 row 1 cell**

- Click the **Paste Cells** toolbar button, and click **OK** to use spaces as delimiters in order to paste the data into the worksheet

- Type **Genre2** and **Observed** as the name row entries for columns C6 and C7

Next, you obtain the expected number of sales (frequencies) under H_0 for each genre by multiplying the genre probabilities (stored in C2 Prob) by the sample size, 1,000:

- Choose **Calc > Calculator**

- Type **Expected** in the "Store result in variable" text box, and press Tab

- Enter, by either clicking or typing, **Prob * 1000** in the "Expression" text box, and press **OK**

The column C8 Expected now lists the expected frequencies for each genre: 337, 152, 125, 96, 92, 44, 35, 34, and 85. The Data window should resemble Figure 12-2.

FIGURE 12-2

The Data window with copy-and-pasted tally results

	C2-T	C3	C4	C5-T	C6	C7	C8	C9
	Genre	Prob	Sample	TxSample	Genre2	Observed	Expected	
1	Rock	0.337	9	Other	1	338	337	
2	Country	0.152	2	Country	2	142	152	
3	Urban-Contemporary	0.125	5	Rap	3	138	125	
4	Pop	0.090	1	Rock	4	98	98	
5	Rap	0.092	4	Pop	5	102	92	
6	Gospel	0.044	3	Urban-Contemporary	6	38	44	
7	Classical	0.035	1	Rock	7	41	35	
8	Jazz	0.034	3	Urban-Contemporary	8	29	34	
9	Other	0.085	8	Jazz	9	76	85	
10			1	Rock				
11			9	Other				
12			9	Other				
13			3	Urban-Contemporary				
14			1	Rock				
15			5	Rap				
16			3	Urban-Contemporary				
17			3	Urban-Contemporary				
18			5	Rap				
19			1	Rock				
20			9	Other				

To compute the chi-square statistic, compute the sum of $(\text{Obs} - \text{Exp})^2/\text{Exp}$ values for each genre:

- Choose **Edit > Edit Last Dialog**

- Type **ChiSq** in the "Store result in variable" text box, and press [Tab]

- Enter, by clicking or typing, **SUM((Observed - Expected)**2 / Expected)** in the "Expression" text box, and press **OK**

The value of the chi-square statistic is 6.63481, as shown in the Data window.

Next, you compute the DF associated with this statistic and store it in a constant:

- Choose **Edit > Edit Last Dialog**

- Type **K1** in the "Store result in variable" text box, and press [Tab]

- Enter, by clicking or typing, **COUNT(Observed) -1** in the "Expression" text box, and press **OK**

- Click the **Session Window** toolbar button 🖳

- Type **name K1 = 'DF'** after the Minitab prompt ("MTB >") to name the DF constant, and press ↵

The expression COUNT(Observed) – 1 will give you one less than the number of categories, which is the number of degrees of freedom for this test of fit. Check in the Info window to confirm that you have created this new constant:

- Choose **Window > Info**

After the listing of the columns, the one constant K1 is listed as having the value 8 and with the name DF.

Next, return to the Session window:

- Choose **Window > Session**

  To compute the p-value associated with the chi-square statistic (6.63481) in C9 ChiSq:

- Choose **Calc > Probability Distributions > Chi-Square**
- Click the **Cumulative Probability** check box, and press Tab
- Select **K1 DF** as the "Degrees of freedom," and press Tab
- Select **C9 ChiSq** as the "Input column," and type **CumProb** in the "Optional storage" text box
- Click **OK**
- Click the **Current Data window** toolbar button ▦

  You observe that the cumulative probability is equal to 0.423503. This is the probability of a value's being less than or equal to the chi-square statistic (6.63481). The p-value is the probability of a value greater than 6.63481, so you must subtract 0.423503 from 1:

- Choose **Calc > Calculator**
- Type **PValue** as the "Store result in variable" and press Tab
- Enter, by either clicking or typing, **1 - CumProb** in the "Expression" text box, and press **OK**

  You note that the p-value is equal to 0.576497 and is stored in C11. You next decide to obtain a summary of your chi-square goodness-of-fit test:

- Choose **Manip > Display Data**
- Select **C7 Observed** through **C11 PValue** and **K1 DF** as the "Columns and constants to display," and press ⏎

  A well-designed display of your test appears in the Session window, as shown in Figure 12-3.

FIGURE 12-3

Chi-square goodness-of-fit output

```
MTB > Print 'Observed'-'PValue' 'DF'.

Data Display

DF    8.00000

Row   Observed   Expected     ChiSq    CumProb     PValue

  1        338        337   6.63481   0.423503   0.576497
  2        142        152
  3        138        125
  4         96         96
  5        102         92
  6         38         44
  7         41         35
  8         29         34
  9         76         85
```

Since the p-value of the chi-square statistic is 0.576497, you should not reject the null hypothesis at any reasonable significance level and should conclude that the results are consistent with the sample being drawn from the population of genre taken from *The New York Times 1998 Almanac*.

Above this output are the Session commands that generated this output, as shown in Figure 12-4.

FIGURE 12-4

Session commands used to generate goodness-of-fit chi-square statistic, DF, and p-value

```
MTB > Name C9 = 'ChiSq'
MTB > Let 'ChiSq' = SUM((Observed - Expected)**2 / Expected)
MTB > Let K1 = COUNT(Observed) - 1
MTB > name K1 = 'DF'
MTB > Name c10 = 'CumProb'
MTB > CDF 'ChiSq' 'CumProb';
SUBC>   ChiSquare 'DF'.
MTB > Name C11 = 'PValue'
MTB > Let 'PValue' = 1 - CumProb
MTB > Print 'Observed'-'PValue' DF'
```

In the next section, you will save and modify this sequence of commands in a special file. This will allow you to perform future chi-square goodness-of-fit tests with a minimal amount of effort. If you do not wish to do this, go to Section 12.3; otherwise, go to the next section. Regardless of your decision, save your work from this section:

- In the location where you are saving your work, save the **12Music.mtw** worksheet

- Click the **Save Project** toolbar button

▼ 12.2   An Exec Macro for Comparing an Observed Distribution to a Hypothesized Distribution ▲

In addition to using Minitab's menu and Session commands, you can also write and store your own sets of commands in files called macros. In this section, you work with *Exec macros*, one of the types of macros available in Minitab (the other type, Global and Local, are more powerful, but available only in the Professional version). You can use Exec macros to perform repetitive analyses and statistical analyses that are not available as commands on Minitab's menus. This macro feature of Minitab essentially gives you the power to "program" in Minitab. (Refer to Help for more information about Exec macros.)

An Exec macro is a series of Minitab commands stored in a file. Exec macro files must be in text (ASCII) format. To use Minitab's Exec macro feature to its fullest, you must know the commands and subcommands by name. To find the Session command equivalent for any menu command, you can consult Help. To find the menu command equivalent for any Session command, you can consult Appendix B, Session Command/Menu Command Equivalents.

▼ **Note** Remember that the Editor > Command Line Editor command provides a quick way to execute commands used earlier in your session or pasted in from another file. Consult Help for further information. ▲

The History window allows you to see the Session command equivalent to every menu command you have issued. To see this:

- Choose **Window > History**

The History window appears. It contains the Session commands shown in Figure 12-4.

In this section, you will use these commands in the History window to create an Exec macro to perform a chi-square goodness-of-fit test for a set of data. You also use the Notepad text editor that comes with Microsoft Windows and was introduced in Tutorial 1. You can find this application in the Accessories folder on the Windows Start menu. To open Notepad:

- Click the Windows 95 **Start** button (this is usually found in the lower left-hand corner of your screen)

- Click **Programs > Accessories > Notepad**

Notepad opens and displays a blank page.

▼ **Note** You can use any word processor to create an Exec macro file and then save it as a text file. Notepad is ideal for this purpose because it always creates text files. ▲

You can type the relevant Session commands into the Notepad. However, an easier approach is to copy and paste them from Minitab's History window:

- Click the **MINITAB Student** button at the bottom of your screen to return to Minitab

- Highlight the **Session commands** shown in Figure 12-4 in the History window, and click the **Copy Cells** toolbar button

- Click the **Untitled - Notepad** button at the bottom of your screen to return to Notepad

- Choose **Edit > Paste** on the Notepad menu bar

A copy of the Minitab Session commands are now in the Notepad. (If your commands don't match those in Figure 12-4, you can edit them in Notepad until they do.)

First, you change the commands so that the ChiSq, CumProb, and PValue variables will be placed in C3, C4, and C5, respectively, by the Exec Macro:

- Highlight the **C9** in the first line, and type **C3**

- Highlight the **C10** in the fifth line, and type **C4**

- Highlight the **C11** in the eighth line, and type **C5**

Next, you want to annotate the Exec macro so that the user knows its restrictions and exactly what the Exec macro expects to find in various columns. To add an annotation to an Exec macro, use the note command. Minitab ignores any information following the word *note*, but prints this information when you run a macro.

- Press Ctrl+Home to place the cursor in the upper-left corner of the Notepad file

- Type **note Chi-Square Goodness-of-Fit Procedure**, and press ↵

- Type **note Procedure assumes observed and expected values are in**, and press ↵

- Type **note Columns 1 and 2 and are named Observed and Expected,** and press ↵

Finally, specify the end of your Exec macro instructions:

- Press Ctrl+End and ↵ to place the cursor at the beginning of the last line of the Notepad file

- Type **end**

The Notepad window should look as shown in Figure 12-5.

FIGURE 12-5

Notepad with chi-square goodness-of-fit Exec macro

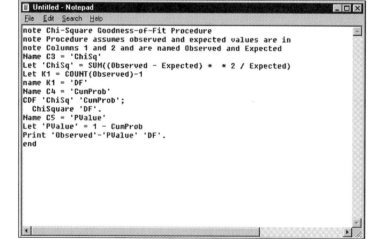

```
note Chi-Square Goodness-of-Fit Procedure
note Procedure assumes observed and expected values are in
note Columns 1 and 2 and are named Observed and Expected
Name C3 = 'ChiSq'
Let 'ChiSq' = SUM((Observed - Expected) * * 2 / Expected)
Let K1 = COUNT(Observed)-1
name K1 = 'DF'
Name C4 = 'CumProb'
CDF 'ChiSq' 'CumProb';
  ChiSquare 'DF'.
Name C5 = 'PValue'
Let 'PValue' = 1 - CumProb
Print 'Observed'-'PValue' 'DF'.
end
```

▼ **Note** You can also add an annotation to an Exec macro by replacing note with #. Information after a # is not printed when you run an Exec macro. This is particularly helpful if you want to remind yourself of the function of commands in the macro, but you don't want these reminders printed when you run the macro. ▲

Next, you verify that each line is correct and then save the Exec macro in a file with the name *Chisqgof.mtb*:

- In the location where you are saving your work, save the Exec macro in a file named **Chisqgof.mtb**

- Choose **File > Exit** from the Notepad menu bar

▼ **Note** When you create an Exec macro with a word processor, you don't need to save it with the *mtb* file extension, but you must save the file in text or ASCII format. ▲

Now return to the Current Data window of Minitab:

- Click the **MINITAB Student** button if you need to return to Minitab

- Click the **Current Data window** toolbar button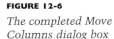

The next step is to erase all but the columns containing the observed and expected values and then move those two sets of values to C1 and C2 in order to make the Data window suitable for the *Chisqgof.mtb* Exec macro:

- Choose **Manip > Erase Variables**

- Select **GenreN, Genre, Prob, Sample, TxSample, Genre2, ChiSq, CumProb, PValue**, and **DF** as the "Columns and constants to erase"

- Click **OK**

- Highlight the two remaining variables, **C7 Observed** and **C8 Expected**

- Choose **Editor > Move Columns**, and click the **Before column C1** option button

The completed Move Columns dialog box should resemble Figure 12-6.

FIGURE 12-6

*The completed Move
Columns dialog box*

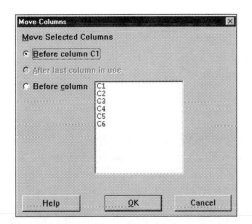

- Click OK

You observe that C1 contains the observed frequencies and C2 the expected frequencies. The Data worksheet is now in the appropriate form for your Exec macro. Next, you save this modified worksheet as *12Music2.mtw* and open *12Music.mtw* so that it is still part of the project:

- Choose **Window > Manage Worksheets**

- Click *12Music.mtw*, click the **Rename** button, and change the worksheet's name to *12Music2.mtw*

- Click the **Open** button, and bring the *12Music.mtw* back into the project

- Click *12Music2.mtw* and then the **Bring to front** button to make that worksheet the active window

- Click **Done**

You are now ready to run the Exec macro (be sure that *12Music2.mtw* is the active worksheet):

- Choose **File > Other Files > Run an Exec**

The first Run an Exec macro dialog box is as shown in Figure 12-7.

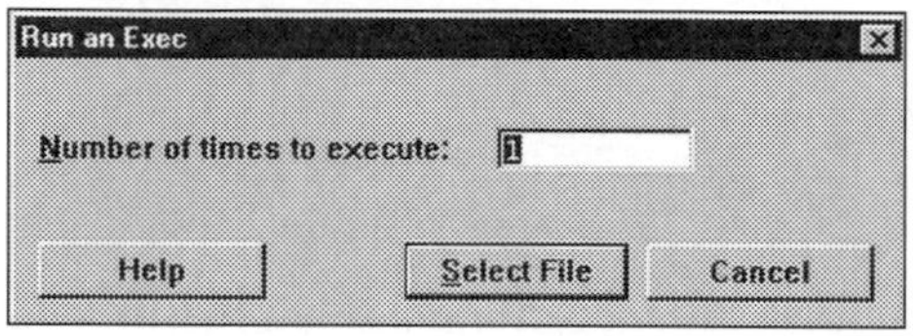

FIGURE 12-7

The first Run an Exec macro dialog box

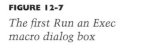

You observe that this first Run an Exec dialog box has a default of 1 time to execute the macro. Since this is the number of times you want to run your Exec macro, you move to the second Run an Exec dialog box:

- Click the **Select File** button

- In the location where you are saving your work, click **Open** to see the file *Chisqgof.mtb* (if it is not in the window already)

Your completed dialog box should look as shown in Figure 12-8.

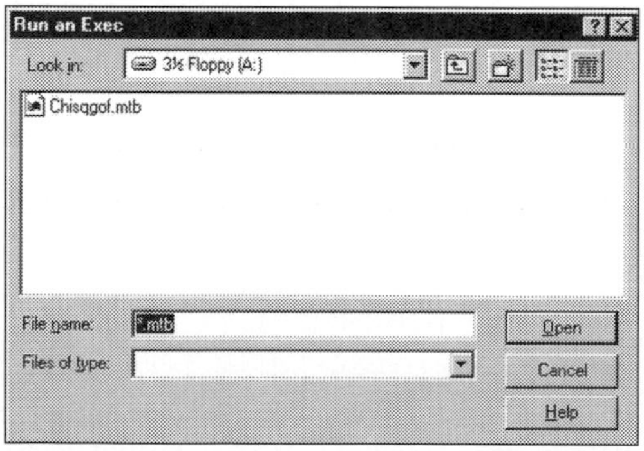

FIGURE 12-8

The second Run an Exec macro dialog box

Finally, open the Exec macro:

- Click on the file **Chisqof.mtb** and click the **Open** button

The Session window appears. Its output is identical to the output produced in Section 12.1, except for two lines explaining that this is a macro and the three lines of notes that were included in the macro. Minitab has executed each command you entered in your Exec macro. For example, it reports the same chi-square statistic and p-value as before.

Your results should be the same. If they aren't, reenter the commands in Notepad, verifying each line as you type it, and then save the file again. When Notepad asks whether you want to replace the existing *Chisqgof.mtb*, click Yes. Notepad erases your previous version and saves the new version using this name. Run the Exec macro and make sure that it works properly before continuing to the next section.

You now have a chi-square goodness-of-fit test Exec macro; it is essentially a new Minitab command. Anytime you need to perform a chi-square goodness-of-fit test, you can use this Exec macro, as long as columns 1 and 2 contain the observed and expected values and are named Observed and Expected.

- In the location where you are saving your work, save the work you have done thus far in this tutorial in the project **T12**

▼ 12.3 Testing the Relationship between Two Categorical Variables in a Contingency Table ▲

CASE STUDY: MARKETING — MARKET RESEARCH

As an intern in a market research firm, you are presented by your supervisor with a 4×5 contingency table based on a well-conducted survey. The table shows the number of individuals who last bought jeans from four major stores, classified according to those individuals' approximate yearly total household income before taxes. Your supervisor asks you to determine if salary level is independent of stores. If the two variables are dependent on each other, differently priced jeans might be heavily marketed at different stores. For example, a store that seems to attract wealthier shoppers might display higher-priced jeans.

You'll be working with the data file *Stores.mtw*, which is in the Student subdirectory:

- Open the worksheet **Stores.mtw**

Before analyzing these data, you should save them as a new worksheet:

- In the location where you are saving your work, save the worksheet as **12Stores**

The Data window displays the contingency table. The first column lists the code number of each store (4, 5, 6, and 10). The next five columns contain the number of individuals who last bought jeans at each store, by income category.

To test for the independence of variables, first formulate the hypotheses:

Null hypothesis, H_0: The variable's income and store are independent.

Alternative hypothesis, H_1: The variable's income and store are dependent.

To run the test:

- Choose **Stat > Tables > Chi-Square Test**

- Select **C2 Under25K** through **C6 75K&Over** as the "Columns containing the table"

The completed Chi-Square Test dialog box should resemble Figure 12-9.

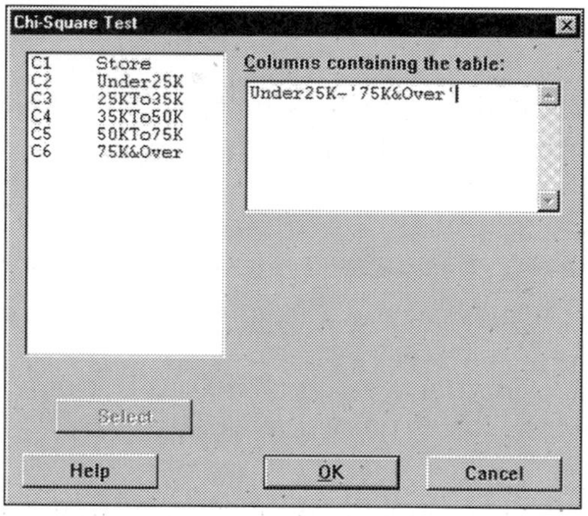

FIGURE 12-9

The completed Chi-Square Test dialog box

- Click **OK**

The Session window displays the results of the chi-square test, as shown in Figure 12-10.

FIGURE 12-10

Chi-square test results

```
MTB > ChiSquare 'Under25K'-'75K&Over'.
```

Chi-Square Test

```
Expected counts are printed below observed counts

      Under25K 25KTo35K 35KTo50K 50KTo75K 75K&Over   Total
  1       14       10       24       12        3        63
        12.77    10.82    19.48    12.77     7.14

  2       21       22       29       15        3        90
        18.25    15.46    27.84    18.25    10.21

  3       11        8       14       17       14        64
        12.98    11.00    19.79    12.98     7.26

  4       13       10       23       15       13        74
        15.00    12.71    22.89    15.00     8.39

Total     59       50       90       59       33       291

Chi-Sq =  0.118 +  0.063 +  1.046 +  0.047 +  2.404 +
          0.415 +  2.763 +  0.049 +  0.578 +  5.088 +
          0.301 +  0.817 +  1.696 +  1.248 +  6.263 +
          0.268 +  0.580 +  0.001 +  0.000 +  2.531 = 26.273
DF = 12, P-Value = 0.010
```

Minitab prints the expected counts below the observed counts for each cell. It then lists the individual chi-square contributions from each cell and sums them to obtain the chi-square statistic, 26.273. From this, you can see which cells contribute the most to the chi-square total.

Note that fewer than expected individuals with incomes of $75,000 and over bought their last pair of jeans at stores 4 and 5 (rows 1 and 2). By contrast, more people than expected in this income bracket made purchases at stores 6 and 10 (rows 3 and 4). The degrees of freedom of the chi-square statistic (DF = 12) and the test's p-value (P-Value = 0.010) appear last. DF is equal to the product of the table's number of rows minus 1, multiplied by the table's number of columns minus 1, in this case, $(4 - 1)*(5 - 1) = 12$. Hence, you reject H_0 at levels greater than this value. You inform your supervisor that store and income are not independent. You also mention that a major contribution of the chi-square statistic comes from individuals whose incomes are $75,000 and over.

- In the location where you are saving your work, save the work you have done thus far in this tutorial in the project **T12**

▼ 12.4 Testing the Relationship between Two Categorical Variables By Using Raw Data ▲

You ask your supervisor if you can examine the actual raw data from which the table was constructed. Using the raw data, you can perform additional analyses, such as calculating contingency table percentages. You can still compute the chi-square statistic from these data.

Your supervisor tells you that the data are stored in the file *Jeans.mtw*, a file that was created by the Professional version of Minitab. She warns you that the file may contain too much data for Minitab to handle.

■ Open the worksheet **Jeans.mtw** from the Student subdirectory

You are immediately informed by the Erase Variables dialog box that the worksheet associated with this file does contain more data, 5,122 elements (cells), than can be processed by *The Student Edition of Minitab for Windows*, which has a limit of 5,000 elements. The dialog box is shown in Figure 12-11.

FIGURE 12-11

The Erase Columns dialog box

Column	Name	Type	Elements
C1	Size	T	394
C2	Age	T	394
C3	Marital	T	394
C4	Earners		394
C5	Employ	T	394
C6	Educ	T	394
C7	Income	T	394
C8	JeanShop		394
C9	PayJean		394
C10	Fashion	T	394
C11	Cost	T	394
C12	Interest	T	394

Total: 5122

Since each variable contains 394 elements, you need to erase at least one variable to bring the number of elements under 5,000. You decide to erase all but the two variables you will use for this tutorial, C7 Income and C8 JeanShop:

■ Highlight **C1 Size** through **C6 Educ**, and click the **Erase** button

■ Highlight **C9 JeanPay** through **C13 Spend**, and click the **Erase** button

■ Click **OK**

Before analyzing these data, you should save them as a worksheet:

■ In the location where you are saving your work, save the worksheet as **12Jeans**

Now there appear to be only two variables in the Data window. You confirm this by examining the Info window and then returning to the Data Window:

- Choose **Window > Info**
- Click the **Current Data window** toolbar button 🖿

▼ **Note** The *Jeans.mtw* data have also been used to create three files: *Jeansa.mtw*, *Jeansb.mtw*, and *Jeansc.mtw*. For this tutorial, you could work with *Jeansb.mtw* because it contains the two variables of interest. ▲

Before performing the chi-square test, you decide to examine the contents of C7 Income and C8 JeanShop by obtaining a Tally of each column:

- Choose **Stat > Tables > Tally**
- Select **C7 Income** and **C8 JeanShop** as the "Variables"
- Click **OK**

The Session window appears with the Tally output, as shown in Figure 12-12.

```
MTB > Tally 'Income' 'JeanShop';
SUBC>   Counts.
```

Summary Statistics for Discrete Variables

Income	Count	JeanShop	Count
100Plus	24	1	6
15to24.9	44	2	17
25to34.9	64	3	13
35to49.9	107	4	66
50to74.9	81	5	95
75to99.9	29	6	69
999	20	7	12
Under15	25	8	5
N=	394	9	11
		10	78
		11	22
		N=	394

The tallies reveal some problems that you will have to deal with before you can replicate the results in the last section. You are told that the 999's in C7 Income represent missing values. Because Minitab uses blanks to indicate a missing value in text data, you need to transform the 999's into blanks. C7 Income also contains seven instead of five income groups. You decide to merge the two highest income groups and then merge the two lowest income groups. This will leave you with the same income groups you worked with earlier.

Finally, you note that the JeanShop column contains codes for 11 stores, not just the stores 4, 5, 6, and 10 in which you are interested. You decide to transform all of the other codes (1, 2, 3, 7, 8, 9, and 11) to missing values so that they will not be used in any analysis. You can use the Manip > Code command to make all of these modifications.

Begin by changing the 999s to blanks (you'll store the transformed data in C14 so that if you ever do want to merge the new variables in this file with other variables in *Jeans.mtw*, you won't have to move columns):

- Choose **Manip > Code > Text to Text**
- Select **C7 Income** as the "Code data from columns," and press [Tab]
- Type **C14** as the "Into columns" variable, and press [Tab]
- Type **999** as the "Original values," press [Tab], and type " " as the "New" value

The completed dialog box resembles Figure 12-13.

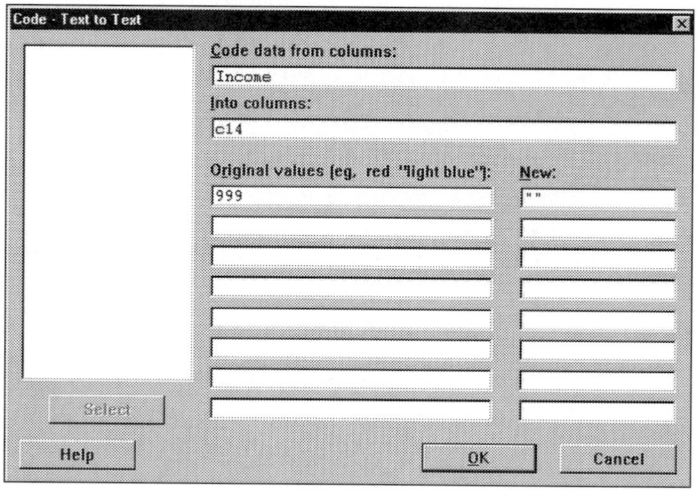

FIGURE 12-13

The completed Code - Text to Text dialog box to create the Income2 variable

- Click **OK**
- Click the **Current data window** toolbar button 🖼
- Type **Income2** in the column header for **C14-T**

Scroll down and notice that the 999's in C7 Income have become blanks in C14 Income2.

Now, collapse the transformed income data into five categories and store the transformed data in a new column, Income3:

- Choose **Manip > Code > Text to Text**
- Select **C14 Income2** as the "Code data from columns" variable, and press [Tab]

- Type **Income3** as the "Into columns" variable, and press Tab

- Type **Under15** and **15to24.9** as the first "Original values," and press Tab (be sure to match the case of the values)

- Type **Under25** as the first "New" value, and press Tab

- Type **75to99.9** and **100Plus** as the second "Original values", and press Tab

- Type **75Plus** as the second "New" value

  Figure 12-14 shows this completed dialog box.

- Click **OK**

  C15 Income3 now contains values that correspond to the five categories present in the contingency table discussed in the previous section.

  Next, code the data in JeanShop so that only the codes for stores 4, 5, 6, and 10 are present; all the other entries will be missing. Recall that for numerical variables, Minitab represents missing values with an asterisk.

- Choose **Manip > Code > Numeric to Numeric**

- Select **C8 JeanShop** as the "Code data from columns" variable, and press Tab

- Type **JeanShp2** as the "Into columns" variable, and press Tab (Minitab will place this variable in C16, the next available column)

- Type **1:3 7:9 11** as the "Original values," press Tab, and type * as the "New" value

  This completed dialog box is shown in Figure 12-15.

FIGURE 12-15

The completed Code - Numeric to Numeric dialog box to create the JeanShp2 variable

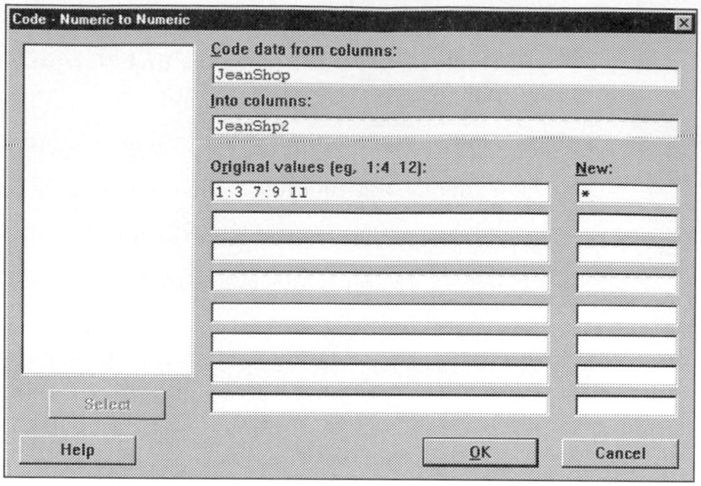

■ Click **OK**

Minitab codes the data for only stores 4, 5, 6, and 10 in C16 JeanShp2; data for the other stores are missing. You may verify this by scrolling down C16 or by using the Tally command.

You are ready to create the contingency table from the data in C15 Income3 and C16 JeanShp2 and to test whether these variables are independent:

■ Choose **Stat > Tables > Cross Tabulation**

■ Select **C15 Income3** and **C16 JeanShp2** as the "Classification variables"

■ Click the **Chi-Square analysis** check box and the **Above and expected value** option button

The completed Cross Tabulation dialog box should look as shown in Figure 12-16.

FIGURE 12-16

The completed Cross Tabulation dialog box for the chi-square test

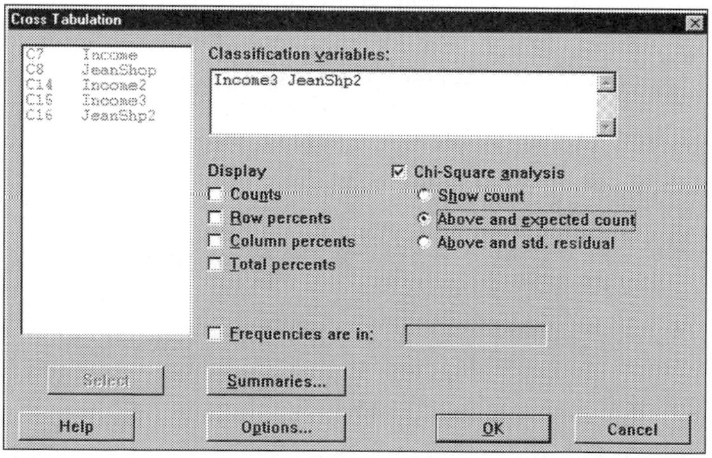

- Click **OK**

Minitab displays the contingency table and chi-square test results in the Session window, as shown in Figure 12-17.

FIGURE 12-17

Initial cross-tabulation contingency table and results of the chi-square test

```
MTB > Table 'Income3' 'JeanShp2';
SUBC>   ChiSquare 2.
```

Tabulated Statistics

Rows: Income3   Columns: JeanShp2

	4	5	6	10	All
25to34.9	10	22	8	10	50
	10.82	15.46	11.00	12.71	50.00
35to49.9	24	29	14	23	90
	19.48	27.84	19.79	22.89	90.00
50to74.9	12	15	17	15	59
	12.77	18.25	12.98	15.00	59.00
75Plus	3	3	14	13	33
	7.14	10.21	7.26	8.39	33.00
Under 25	14	21	11	13	59
	12.77	18.25	12.98	15.00	59.00
All	63	90	64	74	291
	63.00	90.00	64.00	74.00	291.00

Chi-Square = 26.273, DF = 12, P-Value = 0.010

```
    Cell Contents —
              Count
              Exp Freq
```

The rows of the table are the income groups, and the columns are the four stores. This is a 5 x 4 contingency table. For each combination of income group and store, Minitab prints both the number of individuals in that income group who purchased jeans at that store and the expected number, assuming independence. This is indicated by the legend at the foot of the table. You notice, however, that the income groups are not in the order you would like; they are in alphabetical order, the Minitab default. You decide to reorder them:

- Click to **Current Data** window toolbar button

- Click in the **C15 Income3** column header

- Choose **Editor > Set Column > Value Order**

- Click the **User-specified order** option button

- Click in the "Define an order" text box on the right side of the dialog box, and scroll up to reveal the five categories

- Edit the categories so that they are in the order **Under25, 25to34.9, 35to49, 50to74.9**, and **75Plus**

The completed Value Order for C15 (Income 3) dialog box is shown in Figure 12-18.

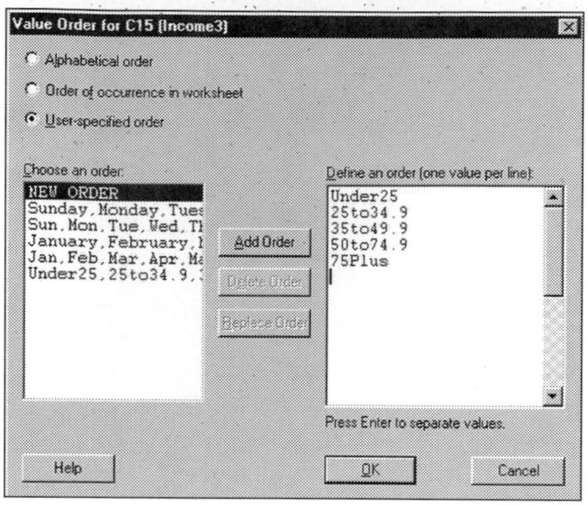

FIGURE 12-18

The completed Value Order for C15 (Income3) dialog box

- Click **OK**

Next, you repeat the chi-square analysis:

- Choose **Stat > Tables > Cross Tabulation**

- Verify that the dialog box has not been changed, and click **OK**

Minitab displays the contingency table and chi-square test results in the Session window, as shown in Figure 12-19.

FIGURE 12-19

Cross-tabulation contingency table and results of the chi-square test, with properly ordered rows

```
MTB > Table 'Income3' 'JeanShp2';
SUBC>    ChiSquare 2.
```

Tabulated Statistics

Rows: Income3   Columns: JeanShp2

	4	5	6	10	All
Under25	14	21	11	13	59
	12.77	18.25	12.98	15.00	59.00
25to34.9	10	22	8	10	50
	10.82	15.46	11.00	12.71	50.00
35to49.9	24	29	14	23	90
	19.48	27.84	19.79	22.89	90.00

FIGURE 12-19 (CONTINUED)

50to74.9	12	15	17	15	59
	12.77	18.25	12.98	15.00	59.00
75Plus	3	3	14	13	33
	7.14	10.21	7.26	8.39	33.00
All	63	90	64	74	291
	63.00	90.00	64.00	74.00	291.00

Chi-Square = 26.273, DF = 12, P-Value = 0.010

Cell Contents —
               Count
               Exp Freq

Minitab now displays the columns in the appropriate order. The chi-square statistic (26.273), the DF for this test (12), and the p-value (0.010) appear after the contingency table. On the basis of the p-value, you reject H_0. Your data indicate that store and income are not independent.

▼ **Note** If you want your contingency table to be formatted like the one in Figure 12-10, with income group as the column variable and store as the row variable, then you need only to switch the order of C15 Income3 and C16 JeanShp2 in the "Classification" variables text box. ▲

You want more detail on the income distribution. In particular, you want to determine the percentage of individuals in each income category:

- Choose **Stat > Tables > Cross Tabulation**
- Click the **Counts, Row percents, Column percents**, and **Total percents** check boxes to select them
- Click the **Chi-Square analysis** check box to deselect it

The completed Cross Tabulation dialog box is as shown in Figure 12-20.

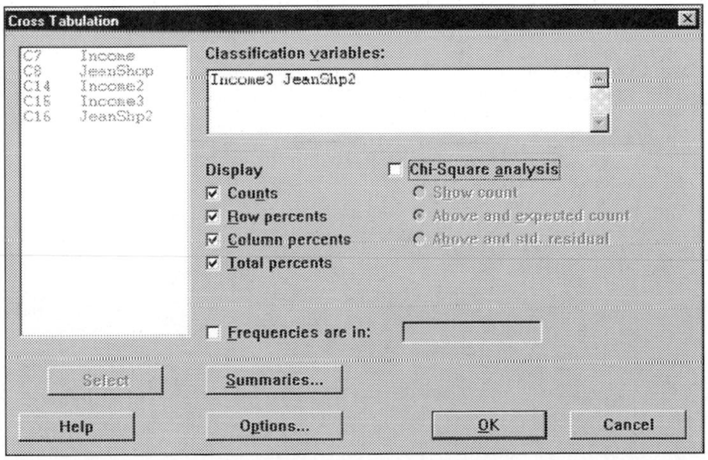

FIGURE 12-20

The completed Cross Tabulation dialog box for percentages

■ Click **OK**

The resulting table is shown in Figure 12-21. Each cell contains the count, the row percent, the column percent, and the total percent, as described by Minitab in its legend at the bottom of the output.

FIGURE 12-21

Percentages of individuals in various categories

```
MTB > Table 'Income3' 'JeanShp2';
SUBC>    Counts;
SUBC>    RowPercents;
SUBC>    ColPercents;
SUBC>    TotPercents.
```

Tabulated Statistics

Rows: Income3   Columns: JeanShp2

	4	5	6	10	All
Under25	14	21	11	13	59
	23.73	35.59	18.64	22.03	100.00
	22.22	23.33	17.19	17.57	20.27
	4.81	7.22	3.78	4.47	20.27
25to34.9	10	22	8	10	50
	20.00	44.00	16.00	20.00	100.00
	15.87	24.44	12.50	13.51	17.18
	3.44	7.56	2.75	3.44	17.18
35to49.9	24	29	14	23	90
	26.67	32.22	15.56	25.56	100.00
	38.10	32.22	21.87	31.08	30.93
	8.25	9.97	4.81	7.90	30.93
50to74.9	12	15	17	15	59
	20.34	25.42	28.81	25.42	100.00
	19.05	16.67	26.56	20.27	20.27
	4.12	5.15	5.84	5.15	20.27
75Plus	3	3	14	13	33
	9.09	9.09	42.42	39.39	100.00
	4.76	3.33	21.87	17.57	11.34
	1.03	1.03	4.81	4.47	11.34
All	63	90	64	74	291
	21.65	30.93	21.99	25.43	100.00
	100.00	100.00	100.00	100.00	100.00
	21.65	30.93	21.99	25.43	100.00

```
Cell Contents —
              Count
              % of Row
              % of Col
              % of Tbl
```

Look at the cell describing individuals who last purchased jeans from store 10 and whose households earn less than $25,000. There are 13 individuals in this group, representing 22.03% of all the individuals with incomes in this category and 17.57% of the store 10 shoppers. The individuals in this cell represent 4.47% of the individuals in the study.

You are particularly interested in how the percentage distribution of income varies between stores and decide to obtain a contingency table with only the column percents.

- Click the **Edit Last Dialog** toolbar button

- Click the **Row percents** and the **Total percents** check boxes to deselect them

- Click **OK**

The contingency table is shown in Figure 12-22.

FIGURE 12-22

Contingency table with column percentages

```
MTB > Table 'Income3' 'JeanShp2';
SUBC>    Counts;
SUBC>    ColPercents.
```

Tabulated Statistics

Rows: Income3   Columns: JeanShp2

	4	5	6	10	All
Under25	14	21	11	13	59
	22.22	23.33	17.19	17.57	20.27
25to34.9	10	22	8	10	50
	15.87	24.44	12.50	13.51	17.18
35to49.9	24	29	14	23	90
	38.10	32.22	21.87	31.08	30.93
50to74.9	12	15	17	15	59
	19.05	16.67	26.56	20.27	20.27
75Plus	3	3	14	13	33
	4.76	3.33	21.87	17.57	11.34
All	63	90	64	74	291
	100.00	100.00	100.00	100.00	100.00

```
Cell Contents —
              Count
              % of Col
```

From this table, you notice that shoppers at stores 6 and 10 tend to be wealthier than those at stores 4 and 5. For example, in store 5 almost 48% (23.33% + 24.44%) of the shoppers are in the lowest two income groups. The corresponding figures for stores 6 and 10 are only 39.69% and 31.08%, respectively. At the other extreme, at store 6, over 48% (26.56% + 21.87%) of the shoppers are in the two highest income groups. The corresponding percentages for stores 4 and 5 are only 23.81% and 20.00%, respectively.

When you rejected the null hypothesis that income group and store were independent, it was precisely because of these differences in the percentage distribution of income by store.

As a result of your analyses, you decide to recommend that management have stores 4 and 5 switch gradually to the cheaper brands of jeans and stores 6 and 10 to the more expensive brands.

▼ **Note** Using the Cross Tabulation command, you can combine a chi-square test of independence with combinations of row, column, and total percentage distributions. However, for clarity and ease of interpretation, it is often better to separate the two analyses, as you did previously. ▲

In this tutorial, you used the chi-square statistic to perform a goodness-of-fit test and tests for variables on categorical data. In addition, you created an Exec macro to perform a statistical analysis that was not available on Minitab's menu.

■ In the location where you are saving your work, save the current project **T12** and then exit **Minitab**

▼ Minitab Command Summary ▲

This section describes the menu and Session commands introduced in, or related to, this tutorial. To find a complete explanation of all commands, use Minitab's Help.

Minitab Menu Commands

Menu	Command	Description
File		
	Other Files	
	Run an Exec	Executes the commands in an Exec file a user-specified number of times.
Edit		
	Command Line Editor	Provides a quick way to execute commands used earlier in your session or pasted in from another file.
Stat		
	Tables	
	Cross Tabulation	Performs a contingency table analysis using raw data consisting of numbers or text from which Minitab computes the contingency table.
	Tally	Calculates a count (or frequency) of each value of a variable.
	Chi-Square Test	Performs contingency table analysis when the worksheet contains the contingency table counts.
Window		
	Manage Worksheets	Performs many operations on Data windows, such as saving, closing, naming, and printing worksheets.

Minitab Session Commands

Command	Description
end	Ends the storage of Minitab commands in an Exec macro.
note	Displays messages to the user on the screen during the execution of an Exec macro.
#	Provides internal documentation to an Exec macro.

Review and Practice

Matching

Match the following terms to their definitions by placing the correct letter next to the term it describes.

_____ DF

_____ Expected frequency

_____ Observed frequency

_____ Chi-square Test

_____ Run an Exec

_____ Total percents

_____ Cross Tabulation

_____ History

_____ Number of categories less 1

_____ (number of rows less 1) * (number of columns less 1)

a. A command on the Tables menu that generates the Chi-Square Test of independence from two categorical variables

b. The number of sample items with a given characteristic

c. A statistic presented by default in the Chi-Square Test output

d. Ratios of observed cell counts to total number of observations in a contingency table multiplied by 100

e. A command on the Tables menu that generates the chi-square test of independence from a table of observed counts

f. Minitab notation for the degrees of freedom of a chi-square statistic

g. Minitab command to invoke a macro

h. Minitab window useful in constructing a macro

i. Degrees of freedom for a chi-square test for independence

j. Degrees of freedom for a chi-square goodness-of-fit test

True/False

Mark the following statements with a *T* or an *F*.

_____ You use the Fit command to perform chi-square goodness-of-fit tests in Minitab.

_____ When computing p-values for the chi-square goodness-of-fit test, you must always store intermediate results as constants.

_____ To combine columns prior to using the Chi-Square Test command, use the Minitab Code command.

_____ Row percents, Column percents, and Total percents are Minitab options available on the Cross Tabulation dialog box that produce percentage summaries.

_____ You can use text data columns with the Cross Tabulation command but not the Tally command.

_____ When you are using the Tally command, you can obtain both the cell's chi-square value and its standardized value by clicking the appropriate options.

_____ Minitab provides the chi-square's p-value when you perform a chi-square test of independence.

_____ When you use Notepad to create files, it saves them in ASCII (text) format.

_____ In addition to the chi-square statistic, Minitab also prints the contribution of each cell when you choose the Chi-Square Test command.

_____ The Cross Tabulation command automatically shows column totals.

Practice Problems

Use Help or Part III, "Exploring Data," of this manual to review the contents of the data sets referred to in the following problems.

1. Open _Lotto.mtw_. Many states have lotto games. In a certain state, you pay $1 and choose six numbers between 1 and 47. If your numbers match those selected, you win. Each Friday, the state publishes a summary of how many times each number has been drawn in all of the drawings. If the drawings are random, then you would expect to see each number the same number of times. _Lotto.mtw_ contains the state lotto information. Rows 1 through 47 contain the frequency with which that number has been drawn over the past three years of a particular state's biweekly lotto drawing. Determine if there is any indication that the drawings are not random.

2. Create an Exec macro that prints out the mean, standard deviation, variance, and mean absolute deviation (MAD) for sample data in C1. Document the macro by using the note Session command and by naming the variable, call it Data, and constants.

3. Open _Prof.mtw_.

   a. Code the instructor's rating variable with these intervals: 1 to 2, 2 to 2.5, 2.5 to 3, 3 up to 3.5, and 3.5 to 4. You might code the ratings in the following order: (3.5:4) code to 5, (3:3.5) code to 4, (2.5:3) code to 3, (2:2.5) code to 2, and (1:2) code to 1. The order is important because Minitab codes sequentially. This ensures that the boundary points are coded to the higher value.

   b. Analyze the data to determine whether the level of the class and the instructor's rating are independent.

4. Open _Carphone.mtw_. Use the _Carphone.mtw_ data to determine whether the presence of a car phone and the occurrence of an accident are independent.

5. Open _Stores.mtw_. To combine categories when using the Cross Tabulation command on the Tables menu, you usually code the variables. To combine categories when using the Chi-Square Test command on the Tables menu, you usually sum variables.

   a. Use the _Stores.mtw_ data to determine whether store and salary are independent when there are three income categories: Under35K, 35KTo50K, and 50K&Over.

   b. Compare your resulting p-value with the one obtained in the tutorial.

6. Open *Note98.mtw*.

   a. Construct a contingency table from the ChipSet and Speed variables. How many 430TX-chip machines have a speed of 233?

   b. Construct a related contingency table with counts, row percents, column percents, and total percents. Explain the meaning of all of the numbers in the cell for 430TX-chip machines with a speed of 233.

   c. Construct another related contingency table that performs a chi-square analysis. What is the value of the test statistic? What is the associated DF?

   d. Explain why it is inappropriate to use the chi-square statistic found in (c).

   e. Verify that the same warning occurs for count data by entering the counts of the contingency table into two columns and using the Chi-Square Test command.

7. Open *Pulsea.mtw*.

   a. Construct a contingency table with Gender as the column variable and Smokes as the row variable. Include column percents. What percent of each gender smokes?

   b. Perform a chi-square test of independence for these two variables. Comment on your answer.

   c. Type the four cell counts into two new columns and use the Stat > Tables > Chi-Square Test command to check if you get the same result as in (b). In what ways does the output in (b) and (c) differ?

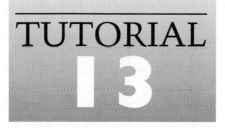

TUTORIAL 13

Analyzing Data with Nonparametric Methods

Until now, the techniques you have used to make inferences about parameters have required random samples and populations that were approximately normally distributed. In this tutorial, you check data for randomness and analyze data from populations that are not assumed to be normally distributed. Techniques that require less stringent assumptions about the nature of the population probability distributions are called *nonparametric statistical methods*.

Objectives

In this tutorial, you will learn how to:

- check a sampling process for randomness
- compare the median of a population to a constant
- compare the medians of two populations
- compare the medians of more than two populations

▼ 13.1 The Runs Test for Randomness ▲

CASE STUDY: METEOROLOGY — SNOWFALL

Since the late 1880s, the U.S. government has collected snowfall measurements. Professor Russell asks your meteorology class to determine whether the yearly amount of snowfall between 1962 and 1997 for a major U.S. city followed a random pattern. The presence of a nonrandom pattern would be of interest to many people, such as municipal authorities who allocate money for snow removal. The data are stored in *Snow.mtw*.

To get started:

- Start **Minitab**

- Maximize the **Session window**

- If necessary, enable the **Session command language** and make the output read-only

You'll be working with the data file *Snow.mtw*, which is in the Student subdirectory:

- Open the worksheet **Snow.mtw**

    C1 Year lists the year for each measurement, and C2 Snowfall shows the amount of snowfall in inches. (C3 Rain is the amount of rainfall in inches corresponding to the actual amount of snowfall.)

    Before analyzing the Snow data, you should save them as a worksheet and this tutorial in a project:

- In the location where you are saving your work, save the worksheet as **13Snow**

- Also, save the work you have done thus far in this tutorial in a project named **T13**

    It is hard to determine by scrolling down to look at the data whether this sequence of 36 snowfall measurements is random. Since the data you are interested in vary over time, you decide to construct a time series plot to get a better picture of how snowfall varies:

- Choose **Graph > Time Series Plot**

- Select **C2 Snowfall** as the first "Y" variable

- Click the **Options** button, and type **1962** in the first "Index" text box

- Press ⏎

    The Time Series Plot dialog box should look as shown in Figure 13-1.

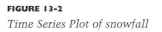

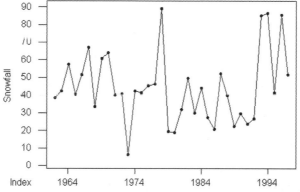

■ Click **OK**

The plot itself is shown in Figure 13-2.

FIGURE 13-2

Time Series Plot of snowfall

By default, each snowfall value is connected to the next one with a straight line. The plot indicates a slight downward trend in the amount of snowfall until 1993 with outlying (i.e., unusual) values in 1973 and 1978. Since 1993, snowfall has increased, although with considerable variability between years. Even with the plot, however, it is difficult to judge whether the pattern of snowfall over the 36 years is a random pattern (a pattern in which what happens in one year does not affect what happens in another year).

To determine whether you have statistical evidence for nonrandomness, you perform a *runs test*. This test is a procedure that helps you determine if the order of the data is random, that is, determined by chance. In some of the tests considered in previous tutorials, you had to assume that the data were randomly ordered. The runs test can be used to verify that assumption.

A *run* is a series of consecutive observations that either fall above a specified constant value or fall on or below the specified constant. The default constant in Minitab is the sample mean. Here, you use Minitab to determine whether the snowfall data have too few or too many runs compared to what you would expect to get if snowfall was "generated" by a truly random process.

First set up the hypotheses:

Null hypothesis, H_0: The values of the sampling process are random.

Alternative hypothesis, H_1: The values of the sampling process are not random.

Now, use Minitab to test the null hypothesis:

- Choose **Stat > Nonparametrics > Runs Test**

- Select **C2 Snowfall** as the "Variables"

The completed Runs Test dialog box looks as shown in Figure 13-3. Minitab gives you the option of specifying some constant other than the mean of the observations as the reference value for determining runs.

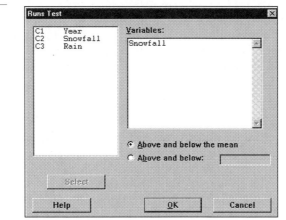

- Click **OK**

The output appears in the Session window, as shown in Figure 13-4.

FIGURE 13-4

The results of the runs test

```
MTB > Runs 'Snowfall'.

Runs Test

    Snowfall

    K =    44.2750


    The observed number of runs =  16
    The expected number of runs = 18.1111
    14 Observations above K   22 below
            The test is significant at  0.4519
            Cannot reject at alpha = 0.05
```

Minitab used the sample mean, $K = 44.2750$, as the constant. In all, there were 16 observed runs. (You can verify this from the raw data.) When there are too many or too few runs, the sample is in nonrandom order.

Minitab calculates that the expected number of runs is 18.1111, assuming a random process, and displays the number of observations above (14) and below (22) the constant. The observed number of runs is close enough to the expected number of runs to produce a p-value for this test of 0.4519, so you cannot reject H_0 at the 0.05 level of significance. You report to your meteorology class that you cannot reject the hypothesis that the pattern of the amount of yearly snowfall is random. Hence, city planners, for example, do not have any evidence on which to base a request for more or less money for snow removal in future years.

▼ **Note** Tutorial 15 discusses additional ways to analyze a time series. ▲

■ In the location where you are saving your work, save the work you have done thus far in this tutorial in the project **T13**

CASE STUDY: HEALTH CARE — CEREAL AND CHOLESTEROL (C0NTINUED)

In Tutorial 8, as a rookie analyst, you analyzed the results of an experiment in which 14 male patients with high levels of cholesterol took part in an experiment to examine whether a diet that included oat bran would reduce cholesterol levels. Each was randomly assigned to a diet that included either corn flakes or oat bran. After two weeks, their low-density lipoprotein (LDL) cholesterol levels were recorded. Each man then repeated this process with the other cereal. You performed a one-tailed, paired t-test on the 14 pairs of LDL results. Since the p-value for this test was 0.003 (less than 0.01), you concluded that the data provided ample evidence that the use of oat bran significantly reduces the mean LDL cholesterol level. The histogram of the 14 differences (shown in Figure 8-11) is skewed slightly to the left, but you knew that the paired t-test is not sensitive to small departures from normality of its differences, so you stuck with your result. However, because you are considering writing up the results of the experiment for publication, you decide to bolster your analysis with both the Sign test and the Wilcoxon test.

In Tutorial 7, you constructed a confidence interval and used a t-test to make inferences about the value of a population mean, under the assumption that the populations were nearly normal. In Tutorial 8, you used a t-test and constructed a confidence interval to make inferences about the value of a population mean of the difference between two dependent populations, again assuming a nearly normal population of differences.

In this tutorial, you will use two of Minitab's nonparametric techniques — the Sign and Wilcoxon tests — to test hypotheses about and find a confidence interval for the median of a population that is not necessarily normal. The Sign test requires only an ordinal measurement scale, while the Wilcoxon test requires at least an interval measurement scale.

You'll be working with the 14 pairs of LDL results that are in the data file *Chol.mtw*, which is in the Student subdirectory:

■ Open the worksheet **Chol.mtw**

In this data set, C1 CornFlke and C2 OatBran contain the LDL level for each of the 14 patients in the study for each cereal, respectively. Before analyzing the Chol data, you should save them as a worksheet:

■ In the location where you are saving your work, save the worksheet as **13Chol**

First, compute the 14 (CornFlke – OatBran) differences:

■ Choose **Calc > Calculator**

- Type **Diff** in the "Store result in variable" text box

- Enter, by clicking or typing, **CornFlke - OatBran** as the "Expression"

- Click **OK**

  Minitab stores the 14 differences in C3 Diff.
  Now, form the hypotheses:

  Null hypothesis, H_0: Population median difference = 0.

  Alternative hypothesis, H_1: Population median difference > 0.

  To perform the Sign test:

- Choose **Stat > Nonparametrics > 1-Sample Sign**

- Select **C3 Diff** as the "Variables"

- Click the **Test median** option button

  Since you are testing a median difference of 0, use the default of 0.0.

- Click the "Alternative" **drop-down list arrow**, and then click **greater than**

  The completed 1-Sample Sign dialog box should look as shown in Figure 13-5.

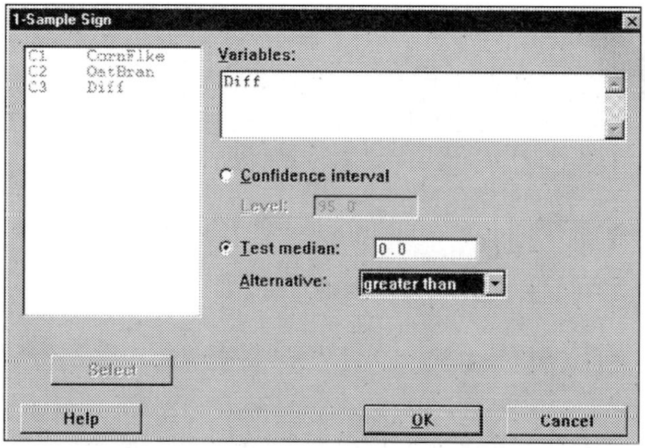

FIGURE 13-5

The completed 1-Sample Sign dialog box

- Click **OK**

  The output in the Session window is shown in Figure 13-6.

FIGURE 13-6

The results of the Sign test

```
MTB > STest 0.0 'Diff';
SUBC>    Alternative 1.
```

Sign Test for Median

```
Sign test of median = 0.00000 versus  >  0.00000

             N  Below  Equal  Above       P    Median
Diff        14      2      0     12  0.0065    0.3600
```

Of the 14 differences, 2 were below 0 and 12 were above. The p-value for this test is 0.0065, so you would reject the null hypothesis at the .05 or .01 level of significance. The sample median of 0.36 suggests that the median LDL cholesterol level is higher with a diet of cornflakes than with a diet of oat bran.

The Sign test uses the binomial distribution with n = 14 (in this case) and p = 0.5 to compute the p-value, 0.0065. (Binomial probabilities were discussed in Tutorial 6.) You can calculate the p-value by computing the probability of two or fewer successes in a binomial experiment, with n = 14 and p = 0.5:

- Choose **Calc > Probability Distributions > Binomial**

- Click the **Cumulative probability** option button, and press ⎚Tab⎚

- Type **14** as the "Number of trials" and **0.5** as the "Probability of success"

- Click the **Input constant** option button, and press ⎚Tab⎚

- Type **2** as the "Input constant," and press ⏎

The output, shown in Figure 13-7, confirms that the probability is indeed 0.0065. If H_0 was true, the probability of getting two or fewer differences less than 0 would be 0.0065. A more likely explanation for this outcome is that H_1 is true and the population median difference is significantly greater than zero.

FIGURE 13-7

Obtaining the p-value as a binomial probability

```
MTB > CDF 2;
SUBC>    Binomial 14 .5.
```

Cumulative Distribution Function

```
Binomial with n = 14 and p = 0.500000

         x      P( X <= x)
      2.00         0.0065
```

▼ 13.3 Estimating the Population Median with the 1-Sample Sign Interval Estimate ▲

You can use Minitab's 1-Sample Sign procedure to find a confidence interval for the unknown population median difference in the LDL cholesterol level. You decide to obtain a 95% confidence interval.

- Choose **Stat > Nonparametrics > 1-Sample Sign**

- Click the **Confidence interval** option button

  Since the default confidence level is 95% you need only:

- Click **OK**

  The resulting confidence interval(s) are shown in Figure 13-8.

FIGURE 13-8

The 1-Sample Sign confidence intervals

```
MTB > SInterval 95.0 'Diff'.
```

Sign Confidence Interval

Sign confidence interval for median

	N	Median	Achieved Confidence	Confidence interval	Position
Diff	14	0.3600	0.9426	(0.1000, 0.7200)	4
			0.9500	(0.0995, 0.7226)	NLI
			0.9871	(0.0900, 0.7700)	3

The output provides three confidence intervals. The top has achieved a confidence level of 0.9426 (below 0.95) and the bottom has achieved a confidence level of 0.9871 (above 0.95). These intervals are based on the 14 differences. For instance, 0.1000 is the fourth smallest difference (in position 4) and 0.7200 is the fourth largest difference — or the eleventh largest (in position 4, counting down). The achieved confidence level for the top interval is $P(4 \leq X \leq 11) = 1 - 2\, P(X \leq 3) = 1 - 2\,(0.0287) = 0.9426$. Here, X is the binomial random variable with n = 14 and p = 0.5. Similarly, 0.0900 and 0.7700 are, respectively, the third smallest and the third largest differences, and the achieved level of confidence for the bottom interval is $P(3 \leq X \leq 12) = 0.9871$. A process called *nonlinear interpolation* (NLI) is used to produce the middle confidence interval (0.0995, 0.7226) with the desired level of confidence.

▼ **Note** You can use the Manip > Sort command to sort the 14 differences. The binomial probability $P(X \leq 3) = 0.0287$ can be obtained by using choosing Calc > Probability Distributions > Binomial and then the Cumulative probability option. ▲

The output suggests that you can be 95% confident that the population median difference in the median LDL cholesterol level for the two cereals lies between 0.0995 and 0.7226.

▼ 13.4 Testing the Population Median with the Wilcoxon Test ▲

Next, you move on to analyze the cholesterol data using the Wilcoxon test and the confidence interval. To perform the Wilcoxon test:

- Choose **Stat > Nonparametrics > 1-Sample Wilcoxon**

- Select **C3 Diff** as the "Variables"

- Click the **Test median** option button

    Since you are testing a median difference of 0, use the default of 0.0.

- Click the "Alternative" **drop-down list arrow**, and click **greater than**

    The completed 1-Sample Wilcoxon dialog box — which looks remarkably similar to the 1-Sample Sign dialog box — should look as shown in Figure 13-9.

FIGURE 13-9

The completed 1-Sample Wilcoxon dialog box

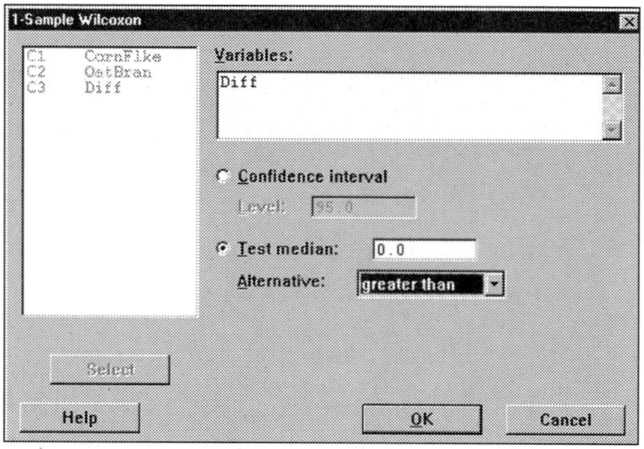

- Click **OK**

    The output should look as shown in Figure 13-10.

FIGURE 13-10

The results of the Wilcoxon test

```
MTB > WTest 0.0 'Diff';
SUBC>    Alternative 1.
```

Wilcoxon Signed Rank Test

Test of median = 0.000000 versus median > 0.000000

	N	N for Test	Wilcoxon Statistic	P	Estimated Median
Diff	14	14	93.0	0.006	0.3900

The p-value for this test is 0.006, so you would again reject the null hypothesis at the .05 or the .01 level of significance. The estimated median of 0.39 suggests that the median LDL cholesterol level is higher with a diet of cornflakes than with a diet of oat bran. Note, however, that the Sign test provided the sample median difference as 0.3600. The value 0.3900 is the median of the pairwise averages. (Pairwise averages — sometimes called Walsh averages — are the averages for each possible pair of values taken from the 14 differences.)

The Wilcoxon test is sometimes called the Wilcoxon Signed Rank test because the test is based on the ranks of the 14 differences rather than the differences themselves.

▼ 13.5   Estimating the Population Median with the Wilcoxon Interval Estimate ▲

The 1-Sample Wilcoxon procedure can be used to obtain a 95% confidence interval for the population median difference.

■ Click the **Edit Last Dialog** toolbar button

■ Click the **Confidence interval** option button, and click **OK**

Minitab displays the 94.8% confidence interval for the median as (0.130, 0.610), as shown in Figure 13-11.

FIGURE 13-11

The 1-Sample Wilcoxon confidence intervals

```
MTB > WInterval 95.0 'Diff'.
```

Wilcoxon Signed Rank Confidence Interval

	N	Estimated Median	Achieved Confidence	Confidence Interval
Diff	14	0.390	94.8	(0.130, 0.610)

For the Wilcoxon procedure, the level of confidence that Minitab generates won't exactly match your request. The interval is based on the distribution of signed ranks that, like the binomial distribution, is discrete. In this case, the closest you can get to 95% is 94.8% confidence. You can be 94.8% confident that the population median difference in the median LDL cholesterol level for the two cereals lies between 0.130 and 0.610.

You feel reassured that all three procedures (the paired t, Sign, and Wilcoxon) support the conclusion that the use of oat bran appears to reduce the LDL cholesterol level.

■ In the location where you are saving your work, save the work you have done thus far in this tutorial in the project *T13*

▼ 13.6 Comparing the Medians of Two Independent Populations ▲

CASE STUDY: SOCIOLOGY — AGE AT DEATH (CONTINUED)

In Tutorial 8, you investigated whether there was a difference in the mean ages at death between "famous" men and "famous" women, as reported in a newspaper. You concluded that there was no significant difference based on the sample. Now you investigate whether there is a difference in the median ages at death between men and women, based on the same data.

In Tutorial 8, you performed t-tests for the equality of two population means, assuming near normality. The Mann-Whitney procedure is the nonparametric counterpart of the independent 2-sample t-test. It uses a 2-sample rank test to compare two population medians. It then computes the corresponding point and confidence interval estimates of the difference between these medians.

You decide to explore this possibility even though the normality assumption appeared reasonable. Some statisticians maintain that if parametric and nonparametric procedures yield the same results, then these results are more credible and the conclusions strengthened.

You'll be working with the data file *Age.mtw*, which is in the Student subdirectory:

■ Open the worksheet **Age.mtw**

C1 DAgeF displays the age at death of 19 females; C2 DAgeM shows the age at death of 18 males.

Before analyzing the Age data, you should save them as a worksheet:

■ In the location where you are saving your work, save the worksheet as **13Age**

You will use the Mann-Whitney nonparametric procedure. First, formulate the hypotheses:

Null hypothesis, H_0: The median ages at death for all famous females and for all famous males are equal.

Alternative hypothesis, H_1: The median ages at death for famous females and for famous males are not equal.

Then use a significance level equal to .05 and perform the test:

■ Choose **Stat > Nonparametrics > Mann-Whitney**

■ Select **C1 DAgeF** as the "First Sample"

■ Select **C2 DAgeM** as the "Second Sample"

The default alternative hypothesis is "not equal" — this is what you want. The completed Mann-Whitney dialog box looks as shown in Figure 13-12.

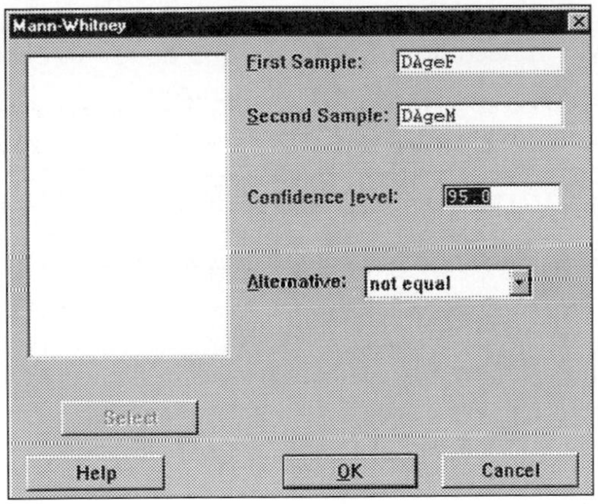

FIGURE 13-12

*The completed Mann-
Whitney dialog box*

- Click **OK**

    The results of the test appear in the Session window and are shown in Figure 13-13.

FIGURE 13-13

*Results of the Mann-
Whitney test*

```
MTB > Mann-Whitney 95.0 'DAgeF' 'DAgeM';
SUBC>    Alternative 0.

Mann-Whitney Confidence Interval and Test

DAgeF     N =  19    Median =      75.00
DAgeM     N =  18    Median =      72.50
Point estimate for ETA1-ETA2 is     2.00
95.3 Percent CI for ETA1-ETA2 is (-8.00,13.00)
W = 375.0
Test of ETA1 = ETA2  vs  ETA1 not = ETA2 is significant at 0.6816
The test is significant at 0.6812 (adjusted for ties)


Cannot reject at alpha = 0.05
```

Minitab first lists medians for each gender and then displays the point estimate (2 years) for the difference (ETA1 – ETA2) in the population medians. Note that this point estimate is not equal to the difference of the two medians. The 95.3% confidence interval for ETA1 – ETA2 ranges from –8.00 to 13.00. Minitab reports a test result of 375.0 and a p-value of 0.6816, so you cannot reject H_0 at the 0.05 level. You have no evidence to reject the equality of the median ages at death for the two genders. Note that this p-value differs from the one produced by the independent 2-sample t-test; this isn't surprising, since the two tests are not equivalent. Although the p-values differ, the conclusions are the same. There doesn't seem to be any significant difference in median ages at death between the two genders. These results are similar to the ones you obtained in Tutorial 8.

The Mann-Whitney test assumes that the two populations have the same shape (which need not be normal). You decide to examine this assumption by constructing a dotplot for each set of ages:

- Choose **Graph > Dotplot**

- Select **C1 DAgeF** and **C2 DAgeM** as the "Variables"

- Click the **Each column constitutes a group** option button

- Click **OK**

The resulting dotplots are shown in Figure 13-14. Both are skewed to the right, with the ages of the males greater than the ages of the females. This graph does not contradict the assumption that the two populations have the same shape.

FIGURE 13-14

Dotplots of the ages at death

Dotplot for DAgeF-DAgeM

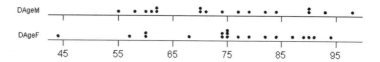

- In the location where you are saving your work, save the work you have done thus far in this tutorial in the project **T13**

▼ 13.7   Comparing the Medians of K Independent Populations By Using the Kruskal-Wallis Test ▲

In Tutorial 9, you used analysis of variance to compare the means of more than two populations. To perform ANOVA, you had to make the parametric assumption of normality of each population. The Kruskal-Wallis H-test is the nonparametric counterpart of one-way ANOVA. It is a generalization of the Mann-Whitney test.

CASE STUDY: CHILD DEVELOPMENT — INFANT ATTENTION SPANS (CONTINUED)

In Tutorial 9, you analyzed the median time that infants spent watching five multicolored designs A, B, C, D, and E. Now you will analyze the same data again. You will run a Kruskal-Wallis test on the data in *Baby.mtw* to test whether there is a difference among the population median attention times for the five designs. You decide to use this test because you have heard that the ANOVA may be more sensitive to departures from normality than the t-test is.

You'll be working with the data file *Baby.mtw*, which is in the Student subdirectory:

- Open the worksheet **Baby.mtw**

The 30 attention times are in C1 Time. The designs are listed in C2 Design.

Before analyzing the Baby data, you should save them as a worksheet:

- In the location where you are saving your work, save the worksheet as **13Baby**

The Kruskal-Wallis procedure requires that the samples be random and independent, with five or more measurements in each (or at least six measurements in one). You must list the data in one column, Response, and the subscripts identifying to which sample an observation belongs in a second column, Factor. For your data, the times in C1 are the response values and the designs in C2 are the factors.

First, formulate the two hypotheses:

Null hypothesis, H_0: The population median attention times for the five designs are equal.

Alternative hypothesis, H_1: The population median attention times for the five designs are not all equal.

To perform the Kruskal-Wallis test:

- Choose **Stat > Nonparametrics > Kruskal-Wallis**

- Select **C1 Time** as the "Response"

- Select **C2 Design** as the "Factor"

The completed Kruskal-Wallis dialog box should look as shown in Figure 13-15.

FIGURE 13-15

The completed Kruskal-Wallis dialog box

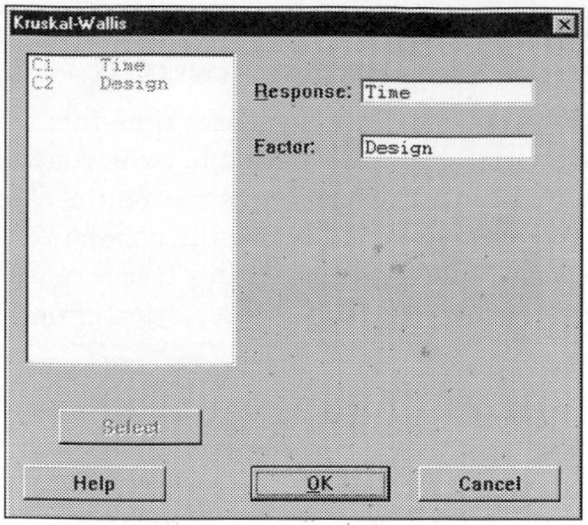

- Click **OK**

  The output in the Session window is shown in Figure 13-16.

FIGURE 13-16

Results of the Kruskal-Wallis test

MTB > Kruskal-Wallis 'Time' 'Design'.

Kruskal-Wallis Test

Kruskal-Wallis Test on Time

Design	N	Median	Ave Rank	Z
A	6	10.400	20.8	1.66
B	6	11.000	24.7	2.88
C	6	9.000	11.0	-1.40
D	6	7.750	7.3	-2.54
E	6	9.350	13.6	-0.60
Overall	30		15.5	

H = 15.84 DF = 4 P = 0.003
H = 15.87 DF = 4 P = 0.003 (adjusted for ties)

Minitab first reports summary statistics for each design. Design B has the largest median time (11.0 seconds); Design D has the smallest (7.75 seconds). The Kruskal-Wallis H-value is 15.84. The p-value corresponding to 15.84 is 0.003. Since there are ties — two or more observations with the same value — Minitab provides another Kruskal-Wallis H-value adjusted for ties, as well as the corresponding p-value. Based on this p-value, you reject the null hypothesis that the population median attention times are the same for the five designs.

The Kruskal-Wallis test, like the Mann-Whitney, assumes that the populations all have the same shape. To check this assumption, you decide to obtain boxplots of the times for the five designs:

- Choose **Graph > Boxplot**

- Select **C1 Time** as the "Y" variable and **C2 Design** as the "X" variable

■ Click **OK**

The graph is shown in Figure 3-17.

FIGURE 13-17

Boxplots of Time by Design

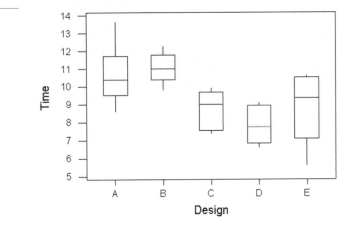

The shapes of the five boxplots are nearly all different, but it is important not to read too much into this. Remember that each boxplot is based on only six values, so the shape can be significantly affected by a single value. You should be concerned, but the evidence against the assumption of equal-shaped populations is not conclusive.

You could use Minitab to perform Mood's Median test, which tests the same hypotheses as the Kruskal-Wallis test. The former is less sensitive than is the Kruskal-Wallis test against outliers, but it is less powerful (less likely to detect important differences) for data from many distributions, including the normal. The Kruskal-Wallis test is more widely used than Mood's Median test.

Minitab can perform nonparametric tests other than those described here. For example, the Friedman test, which is available with the Friedman command, is a nonparametric alternative to the two-way ANOVA with one observation per cell. This test is appropriate in the context of a randomized block experiment. You will find references to this type of experimental design in most introductory texts. Use Help to find out about several nonparametric measures that Minitab will compute — Pairwise Averages, Pairwise Differences, and Pairwise Slopes

In this tutorial, you used the runs test to determine whether a process was random. Then you performed nonparametric procedures that correspond to the parametric procedures introduced in Tutorials 7, 8, and 9. Nonparametric techniques test hypotheses about the median of a single population or compare medians of more than one population; they are useful when the underlying assumption of normality is not justified.

■ In the location where you are saving your work, save the current project **T13** and then exit Minitab

MEDICAL DIAGNOSTICS: Although most of us associate heart failure with older people, it can affect children and infants when the main artery of the heart, the aorta, becomes obstructed and blood cannot flow freely. Doctors treat these blockages by inserting small balloons into the constricted aorta and inflating them to clear the obstruction.

A pediatrician at a midwestern university hospital used the balloon treatment on 30 children, ages 14 days to 13 years, who had obstructed aortas. He monitored their recovery carefully to see what factors would predict whether the operation was a success. One factor the pediatrician used was the measurement of aorta diameter at five points. In a normal aortic valve, the diameters at all five points would be approximately the same and hence the variance in diameter measurements would be close to zero.

The pediatrician used Minitab's Mann-Whitney test to compare diameter variances before and after treatment of two groups of patients: those who eventually required a second balloon treatment and those who did not. The results indicated that the children who would completely recover showed a greater decline in diameter variance from pretreatment levels than those who would require more surgery. This result gave the pediatrician another diagnostic tool to predict whether more treatment would be needed at a later date for a particular patient. Being able to predict patients' future needs enables doctors to better treat them in the present.

This section describes the menu commands introduced in, or related to, this tutorial. To find a complete explanation of all commands, use Minitab's on-line Help.

Minitab Menu Commands

Menu	Command	Description
Stat		
	Nonparametrics	
	1-Sample Sign	Performs a nonparametric 1-sample sign inference (test or confidence level) on a median.
	1-Sample Wilcoxon	Performs a nonparametric Wilcoxon 1-sample inference (test or confidence level) on a median.
	Mann-Whitney	Performs 2-sample nonparametric inference (test and confidence interval) on two medians.
	Kruskal-Wallis	Performs a nonparametric comparison of two or more medians.
	Mood's Median Test	Performs a nonparametric comparison of two or more medians.
	Friedman	Performs a nonparametric analysis of a randomized block experiment.
	Runs Test	Performs a test to evaluate random order of data.
	Pairwise Averages	Computes Walsh averages (the averages of each pair of observations in a column, including the averages of each value with itself).
	Pairwise Differences	Computes the differences between all possible pairs of observations in two columns.
	Pairwise Slopes	Computes the slopes using each pair of data values in two columns.

Review and Practice

Matching

Match the following terms to their definitions by placing the correct letter next to the term it describes.

_____ H

_____ ETA1 – ETA2

_____ Nonparametric

_____ K

_____ Estimated median

_____ Run

_____ Factor

_____ Response

_____ Friedman

_____ Mann-Whitney

a. A series of Minitab statistical techniques that do not assume that the population(s) possess any particular distribution

b. Minitab notation for the difference between two population medians

c. A sequence of observations that share a similar characteristic

d. Minitab notation for the column in which the data are stored for the Kruskal-Wallis command

e. Minitab notation for the test statistic from the Kruskal-Wallis test

f. Minitab notation for the constant used in the runs test to identify a run

g. Minitab name for the statistic equal to the middle value of all pairwise averages of data values

h. Minitab dialog box notation for the subscript column used in the Kruskal-Wallis command

i. Minitab command that performs a nonparametric analysis of a randomized block experiment

j. Minitab command that is the nonparametric counterpart of the 2-sample t-test with independent samples

True/False

Mark the following statements with a *T* or an *F*.

_____ The Runs Test command requires numeric data, since a run is determined by comparing a data value to a number.

_____ You can always use Minitab's nonparametric commands to obtain confidence intervals that correspond to exact levels of confidence.

_____ The Wilcoxon command allows you to perform only two-sided tests.

_____ The Runs Test command allows you to obtain a confidence interval for the population median.

_____ By default, the Wilcoxon command provides confidence intervals as part of the output.

_____ The Kruskal-Wallis command requires the data to be in one column with a subscript identifier in another.

_____ The default null hypothesis value for the median in the Wilcoxon command is zero.

_____ The Runs Test command uses the sample median as the default value to identify runs.

_____ The Mann-Whitney command assumes that the two samples of data are stored in different columns.

_____ The Friedman command performs an analysis that is a nonparametric alternative to the two-way ANOVA with one observation per cell.

Practice Problems

Use Help or Part III, "Exploring Data," of this manual to review the contents of the data sets referred to in the following problems.

1. Open _Snow.mtw._ Recall that the data were presented in chronological order and that there are three outliers. Perform a runs test, which is less sensitive to outliers, on the snowfall data by specifying K equal to the median. Use your results to determine if the snowfall amounts are random.

2. Open _Pay.mtw._ The industry median salary is approximately $29,000.

   a. Use a Wilcoxon test to determine if this company's median salary is comparable to the industry's, with a significance level of .05.

   b. Use a Wilcoxon 95% confidence interval to determine if this company's median salary is comparable to the industry's.

   c. Use a Sign test to determine if this company's median salary is comparable to the industry's, with a significance level of .05.

   d. Use Minitab's ability to compute cumulative binomial probabilities to compute the p-value in (c).

   e. Use a Sign 95% confidence interval to determine if this company's median salary is comparable to the industry's.

   f. Comment on the similarities and differences of the results from the two procedures.

   g. Is it reasonable to assume that these data are from a random sample? How does your answer affect your conclusion?

3. Open _Rivers.mtw._

   a. Determine if the median temperature of the river is different at site 2, which is directly up river from the power plant, than at site 3, which is directly down river from the power plant's discharge from its cooling towers. (You must unstack the Temp column to create new columns that contain site 2 and site 3.

   b. Construct two dotplots to examine whether or not the two populations have the same shape. Do they?

4. Open *Homes.mtw*.

    a. From these data on 150 randomly-selected homes, create a new variable with three categories: homes with 1 bath, homes with 1.5 or 2 baths, and homes with more than 2 baths.

    b. Is the mean acreage the same for these three types of homes?

    c. Is the median acreage the same for these three types of homes?

    d. Should you report the results of (b) or (c)? Briefly explain your answer.

    e. Construct a graph showing a boxplot of acreage for each category. Does the graph suggest that acreage is normally distributed for the three categories?

5. Open *Marks.mtw*.

    a. Use a parametric test to determine if the class performed the same on exams 1 and 2.

    b. Use a non-parametric test to determine if the class performed the same on exams 1 and 2.

    c. Comment on the similarities and differences between the hypotheses and the results of (a) and (b).

    d. Use a parametric test to see if the class performed the same on exams 1, 2, and 3. (*Hint*: You should stack the exam data in one column, store the subscripts in a second column, and create a column that identifies each student.)

    e. Use a non-parametric test to determine if the class performed the same on exams 1, 2, and 3. (*Hint*: Structure your data according to the hint in (d) and use the Friedman test.)

    f. Comment on the similarities and differences between the hypotheses and the results of (d) and (e).

    g. Why were you asked to stack the data in (d)?

    h. Is it reasonable to assume that these data are from a random sample? How does your answer affect your conclusion?

6. Open *Election.mtw*.

    a. Use a runs test to check if the percentage of the vote won by the Democratic Party candidate represents a random process. Use the default constant.

    b. Answer (a) for the Republican Party candidate

    c. Answer (a) for the percentage of the vote won by candidates **other** than those of these two parties.

7. Open *Force.mtw*. Assume that the undergraduate women were randomly selected.

    a. Compute the difference (Force5 – Force45) in C3 and name the difference Diff.

    b. The physical therapist who recorded these data knows that such differences will be considerably greater than zero but wonders if they will exceed 3 pounds. Use the Wilcoxon test to answer this question.

    c. Answer (b) using the 1-Sample Sign test.

8. Open *Age.mtw*. Use the Wilcoxon 1-Sample procedure to test whether the median age at death for all famous women is significantly less than 78.9 years.

9. Minitab does not have a command that computes the Spearman's Rank Correlation Coefficient (rho). This is because the coefficient is fairly straightforward to compute by using existing commands. In fact, Spearman's rho is the correlation between the ranks associated with two variables. Write a short macro that computes and stores the ranks associated with two specified columns of data and then computes the correlation between the two sets of ranks.

TUTORIAL 14

Total Quality Management Tools

Total quality management (TQM) is a philosophy used by many businesses and individuals to improve their processes. The foundation of TQM is making decisions based on accurate and timely data. In this tutorial, you will examine some of Minitab's quality tools that help you detect quality problems and improve your processes. These tools include cause-and-effect diagrams, Pareto charts, and various kinds of control charts. Many of the tools are adaptations of techniques — bar charts and scatter plots, for example — that were examined in earlier tutorials.

Objectives

In this tutorial, you will learn how to:

- create a cause-and-effect diagram

- obtain a Pareto chart

- construct an $\overline{X}$ chart to monitor the mean value of a process

- create a range chart to monitor variability in a process

- produce an individuals chart to monitor individual observations from a process

- construct a moving range chart to monitor variability in a process from individual observations

- create a proportion chart to monitor the proportion from a process

▼ 14.1   Creating a Cause-and-Effect Diagram ▲

CASE STUDY: EDUCATION — FACULTY SURVEY

You did a preliminary analysis of the results of a faculty survey taken by the student government. You have recorded a number of flaws in the survey process and plan an article for the student government newsletter that will summarize your results. You are looking for a structure for organizing the reasons for the flawed process. Minitab offers such a structure, called a *cause-and-effect diagram*, or *fishbone*, that helps you do this.

To get started:

- Start **Minitab**

- Maximize the **Session window**

- If necessary, enable the **Session command language** and make the output read-only

The cause-and-effect diagram lets you graphically represent the factors that influence a problem. The graph is arranged in a structure resembling the skeleton of a fish (hence the alternative name, *fishbone*) and allows for six main factors. By default, these factors are labeled Men, Machines, Materials, Methods, Measures, and the Environment, but some or all can be changed. Experience suggests that these generic labels are suitable for a wide variety of situations. The graph is customized by adding to the diagram specific examples of each factor that may be contributing to the problem. These examples are entered into Minitab from a worksheet.

For the survey process, you decide to use Minitab's default factor labels and to store specific examples (reasons for the flawed survey) of each factor in a file called *Proces.mtw*, which is in the Student subdirectory:

- Open the worksheet *Proces.mtw*

There are six text variables — C1 Men, C2 Machines, C3 Material, C4 Methods, C5 Measurements, and C6 Environment — each listing possible reasons for a flawed survey process.

Before analyzing the Proces data, you should save them as a worksheet and this tutorial in a project:

- In the location where you are saving your work, save the worksheet as *14Proces*

- Also, save the work you have done thus far in this tutorial in a project named *T14*

To construct a cause-and-effect diagram:

- Choose **Stat > Quality Tools > Cause-and-Effect**

- Click in the first "Causes" **text box** and select the variable **C1 Men**

- Repeat this procedure for the next five "Causes" as in Figure 14-1

The labels don't need to be changed because you are using Minitab's defaults. If labels other than these defaults are needed, you can type them after entering the corresponding cause.

- Type **Flawed Process** as the "Effect," and press Tab

- Type **Cause-and-Effect Diagram for Faculty Surveys** in the "Title" text box

The completed dialog box should resemble Figure 14-1.

FIGURE 14-1

The completed Cause-and-Effect Diagram dialog box

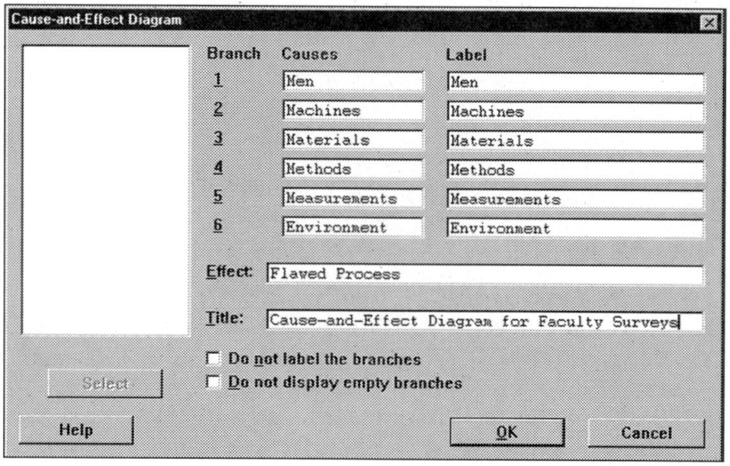

- Press ↵

Minitab produces a cause-and-effect diagram as shown in Figure 14-2.

FIGURE 14-2

Cause-and-effect diagram

Cause-and-Effect Diagram for Faculty Surveys

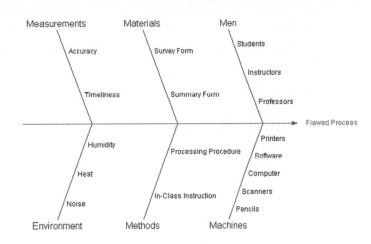

You are pleased with this graphical display. It presents the numerous factors that can affect a flawed survey process. You decide to use this graph as the starting point for a brainstorming session with colleagues to come up with even more areas of concern.

▼ **Note** For convenience, Minitab has two submenus devoted to quality tools, Stat > Quality Tools and Stat > Control Charts. The former includes cause-and-effect diagrams, Pareto charts (which are discussed in the next section), and Run charts, which can be used to detect nonrandom data. The latter produces control charts, which are fundamental quality tools, discussed in Sections 14.3 to 14.8. ▲

▼ 14.2   Using a Pareto Chart ▲

The cause-and-effect diagram in Figure 14-2 certainly presents the possible causes for a flawed survey process in an easy-to-read graphical form. However, the display does not indicate what part of the survey is most flawed. To determine this, you decide to recommend another survey, in which respondents will indicate which factors are negative influences on the survey process. You also decide to recommend that the results of this survey be presented in the form of a Pareto chart. Pareto charts are graphs that combine a bar chart, with the bars ordered from largest to smallest, and an ogive or cumulative polygon. A Pareto chart is often constructed with the bars reflecting the frequency of different defects.

Since you are graduating, you must train a colleague to conduct the survey and prepare the Pareto chart. Your colleague is not well-prepared in statistical methods, so you decide to create a small example to illustrate the use of the Pareto chart. In your example, you assume that 120 students have assessed a proposed questionnaire, responding to the seven areas of concern in the following table. You have also included the counts of the number of students who checked each area of concern.

Area of Concern	Count
1. Too little time for completion	21
2. Ambiguous questions	102
3. Loss of interest because of length	18
4. Little interest in subject	19
5. Inadequate instructions	11
6. Instrument too crowded	25
7. Too many open-ended questions	87

You show your friend how to use Minitab and then how to enter these data and obtain a Pareto chart:

- Choose **File > New**
- Click **OK** for the default Minitab Worksheet
- Enter the following labels into the first seven rows of C1 to represent the seven areas of concern: **Time**, **Ambig**, **Length**, **Subject**, **Instruct**, **Crowded**, and **OpenEnd**
- Enter the corresponding counts into C2: **21, 102, 18, 19, 11, 25, and 87**
- In the header for C1, type **Concerns**
- In the header for C2, type **Counts**

You encourage your colleague to save the data as a worksheet:

- In the location where you are saving your work, save the worksheet as *14Concrn*

To obtain the Pareto chart:

- Choose **Stat > Quality Tools > Pareto Chart**
- Click the **Chart defects table** option button, and press ⎄Tab⎄
- Select **C1 Concerns** as the "Labels in" variable
- Select **C2 Counts** as the "Frequencies in" variable, and press ⎄Tab⎄
- Type **Pareto Chart for Survey Concerns** as the "Title"

At this point, the Pareto Chart dialog box should look as shown in Figure 14-3.

FIGURE 14-3

The completed Pareto Chart dialog box

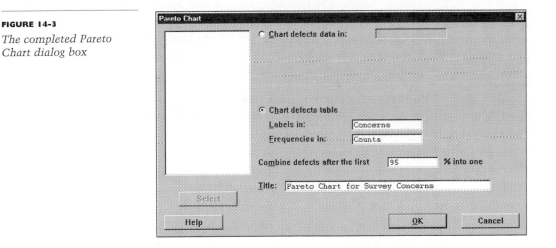

- Click **OK**

The resulting Pareto chart is shown in Figure 14-4.

FIGURE 14-4

Pareto chart for survey concerns

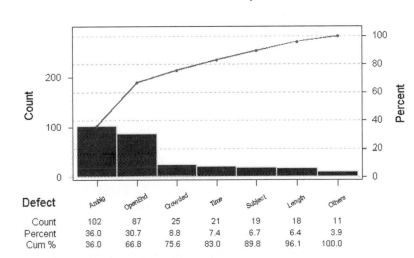

Pareto Chart for Survey Concerns

Defect	Ambig	OpenEnd	Crowded	Time	Subject	Length	Others
Count	102	87	25	21	19	18	11
Percent	36.0	30.7	8.8	7.4	6.7	6.4	3.9
Cum %	36.0	66.8	75.6	83.0	89.8	96.1	100.0

The chart shows the bars for each area of concern arranged from the most frequently occurring to the least frequently occurring. The ogive (cumulative frequency line) shows the progress of the cumulative counts. Beneath the plot are the counts for each area of concern and the corresponding percentages and cumulative percentages.

The chart shows that the two most frequent concerns are ambiguous questions and too many open-ended questions. It shows also that these two occur far more frequently than the others. You can see this by inspecting the bars and by noticing the flattening of the ogive after the second area of concern.

You point out to your colleague that if these data were real, it would make sense to focus improvement efforts on these two concerns. You add that these results are a good illustration of the general use of Pareto charts to distinguish the "vital few" from the "trivial many."

▼ **Note** Minitab allows you to create Pareto charts from raw data as well as from counts. See Help for further information and examples. ▲

- In the location where you are saving your work, save the work you have done thus far in this tutorial in the project *T14*

▼ 14.3 Using Control Charts ▲

CASE STUDY: PRODUCTION — QUALITY CONTROL CHARTS

The instructor of your production course brought three bags of candy to class. Each bag contains 19 "fun packs" of these candies for a total of 57 packs. She identifies each pack and asks the class to imagine that the 57 packs come from a production line and that the class is to evaluate aspects of the production line using various control charts. She informs the class that the weight of each candy should be 2.32 grams, based on product information. She then divides the class into three groups and asks each to measure different characteristics of these candies from all 57 packs.

Group A measures the weight of five candies randomly selected from each pack. It enters these 285 weights into *Candya.mtw*, along with the bag and pack identification numbers.

Group B measures the total weight of each pack. It then measures the weight of the pack paper and computes the weight of the candies in each pack. *Candyb.mtw* contains these three variables along with the bag and pack numbers and the number of candies in each pack.

Group C also records the number of each bag and pack ID, as well as the number of candies in each pack. It also counts the number of red, brown, green, orange, and yellow candies in each pack. It enters its data in *Candyc.mtw*.

The instructor then asks the class to determine whether the production line process is "in control" by constructing control charts relevant to their data sets. A process is *in control* when the mean and variability, or similar characteristics, of the process are stable and any variation in the process is due to random causes.

A *control chart* shows how some aspect of a process varies, usually over time. It normally has statistically determined upper and lower limits. Such charts are among the most widely used of quality tools. Minitab offers 11 control chart types. Quality control technicians use them to monitor processes because they may show when a process is getting out of control. Control charts help manufacturers and members of service industries achieve a high level of quality by meeting certain specifications. In addition, you can use these charts to discover interesting features in a process. In this tutorial, you will construct and interpret five types of Minitab control charts.

▼ 14.4   Constructing an Xbar Chart ▲

Group A sampled five random candies (subgroups of size 5) for 57 packs, weighed each candy, in grams, and placed the results in C3 Weight of *Candya.mtw*, which is located in the Student subdirectory:

- Open the worksheet *Candya.mtw*

    Before analyzing the Candya data, you should save them as a worksheet:

- In the location where you are saving your work, save the worksheet as *14Candya*

    To determine whether the mean of the candy-making process is in control, you decide to produce an X chart to look at the 57 sample means:

- Choose **Stat > Control Charts > Xbar** (the fourth command, not the first)

- Select **C3 Weights** in the "Single column" text box

- Type **5** as the "Subgroup size," and press (Tab)

- Type **2.32** as the "Historical mean"

    The completed Xbar Chart dialog box should resemble that shown in Figure 14-5.

FIGURE 14-5

The completed Xbar Chart dialog box

Xbar Chart

Data are arranged as

○ Single column: `Weights`

Subgroup size: `5`

(use a constant or an ID column)

Historical mean: `2.32` (optional)

Historical sigma: `_____` (optional)

Tests...

Estimate...

S Limits...

Options...

Annotation ▾

Frame ▾

Select

Help

OK

Cancel

■ Click the **Tests** button

Minitab can perform eight different "Tests for Special Causes" on the data. Some are designed to flag an unusual sequence of values. Others flag when a particular number of values fall more than a given number of standard deviations (σs, or sigmas) from the *center line* (in this case, the line corresponding to 2.32 grams). These tests require equal sample sizes within each subgroup. The default is to perform a test that identifies individual points that are more than three sigmas from the center line.

The Tests dialog box is shown in Figure 14-6. Note that there is a brief explanation for each of the eight tests.

FIGURE 14-6

The Tests dialog box

Tests

Tests For Special Causes (default definitions)

○ Perform all eight tests

● Choose specific tests to perform

☑ One point more than 3 sigmas from center line

☐ Nine points in a row on same side of center line

☐ Six points in a row, all increasing or all decreasing

☐ Fourteen points in a row, alternating up and down

☐ Two out of three points more than 2 sigmas from center line (same side)

☐ Four out of five points more than 1 sigma from center line (same side)

☐ Fifteen points in a row within 1 sigma of center line (either side)

☐ Eight points in a row more than 1 sigma from center line (either side)

Help

OK

Cancel

You decide to perform all tests:

■ Click the **Perform all eight tests** option button

■ Click **OK** twice

Minitab computes the 57 sample means (using subgroups of size 5) and plots them on the $\overline{X}$ chart, as shown in Figure 14-7.

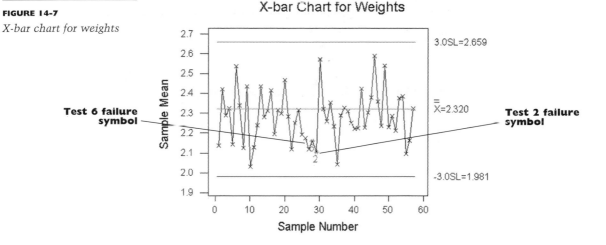

Minitab marks the center line at 2.320. It also places an upper-control-limit line (UCL) at 2.659 and a lower-control-limit line (LCL) at 1.981. Each of these limits is three estimated standard deviations from the center line (3.0SL = 3.0 Sigma Limit). Minitab uses a pooled standard deviation estimate for sigma by default; the pooling is over all subgroups. The $\overline{X}$ chart shows that the process is out of control — nine points have failed Test 2 and four have failed Test 6 — by printing two test failure symbols. To interpret the 6 and 2 test failure symbols, however, you need to look at the Session window and observe the output in Figure 14-8.

- Click the **Session Window** toolbar button ▣

```
MTB > Xbarchart 'Weights' 5;
SUBC>    Mu 2.32;
SUBC>    ScFrame;
SUBC>    ScAnnotation;
SUBC>    Slimits;
SUBC>    Symbol;
SUBC>    Connect;
SUBC>    Test 1 2 3 4 5 6 7 8.
TEST 2. 9 points in a row on same side of center line.
Test Failed at points: 29


TEST 6. 4 out of 5 points more than 1 sigma from center line
        (on one side of CL).
Test Failed at points: 28 29
```

Minitab reports that Test 2 failed at point 29; the nine sample averages before this average were all on one side of the center line. Test 6 failed at points 28 and 29, where Minitab found that four of the five previous sample averages were at least one sigma away from and on the same side of, the center line. Unusual patterns might indicate that the process is drifting away from the target value of 2.32 grams.

You are more than satisfied with this plot. You have learned much about the process from this quality tool.

▼ **Note** You can examine methods for estimating mu and sigma with other than the default values by pressing the Estimate button in the Xbar dialog box. You can examine methods for specifying the control limits by pressing the S Limits button in that dialog box. ▲

▼ 14.5   Constructing a Range Chart ▲

You should investigate the variability of any process because it determines the control limits for the process mean. To ascertain whether the variance of the process is stable and random, you examine the spread in your samples. You can use either the sample range (R) or the sample standard deviation (S) in Minitab to create R and S charts, respectively. For small samples such as this, the R chart is appropriate.

To obtain the R chart for your data:

- Choose **Stat > Control Charts > R**

- Select **C3 Weights** as the "Single column"

- Type **5** as the "Subgroup size"

Notice the direction in parentheses ("Use a constant or an ID column") beneath the "Subgroup size" text box. This is a request that you are either to supply the constant subgroup size, if all subgroup sizes are equal, or specify a column that contains the subgroup sizes, if they are not all equal. The completed R Chart dialog box should resemble that shown in Figure 14-9.

FIGURE 14-9

The completed R Chart dialog box

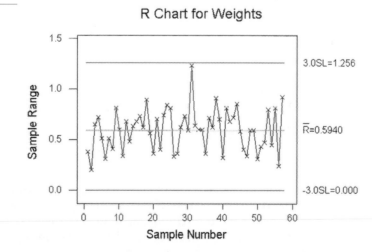

- Click **OK**

Minitab computes the range of each of the 57 groups of five samples and then plots them on the R chart, as shown in Figure 14-10. Minitab draws the center line at 0.5940 (at the average of the sample ranges) and the lower and upper control limits at 0.000 and 1.256, respectively. It draws a lower control limit (LCL) of 0.000, which is often called a *zero-valued control limit* because a LCL of 0 is as low as is possible. The R chart indicates that process variability is not out of control. The observed variation in the range of the candy weights appears to be random.

FIGURE 14-10

R Chart for Weights

You decide to place both the Xbar and the R charts together to better present the data. Use the Xbar-R control chart:

- Choose **Stat > Control Charts > Xbar-R**

- Select **C3 Weights** as the "Variable," type **5** as the "Subgroup size," and press ⌈Tab⌉

- Type **2.32** as the "Historical mean," and press ⟵

  The Xbar-R chart appears as is shown in Figure 14-11.

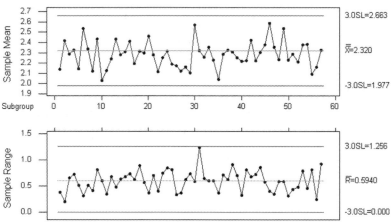

FIGURE 14-11

Xbar-R chart for weights

You are pleased with this chart even though no test results are displayed in the Session window. This is because, by default, the Xbar-R chart command supplies only one test — identifying any mean that is more than three sigmas from the center line — and no mean meets this criteria. Notice that the values for 3.0SL and –3.0SL in the top (Xbar) chart in Figure 14-11 are slightly different from those in Figure 14-7. This is because in the Xbar chart, sigma is estimated by the pooled standard deviation. In the XBar-R chart, sigma is estimated from the subgroup ranges.

You conclude that the candy-making process is prone to some substantial changes in the mean or center, but that it produces consistent weights. You tell your instructor that you would recommend that management meet with the process personnel to determine the sources of the process mean's being out of control. Perhaps together they can identify the causes and avoid the problems in the future.

- In the location where you are saving your work, save the work you have done thus far in this tutorial in the project **T14**

▼ 14.6   Constructing an Individuals Chart ▲

Next, turn your attention to the second group's data. Group B obtained the weights of the 57 fun packs. These values are stored in C6 NetWgt of *Candyb.mtw*, which is located in the Student subdirectory:

- Open the worksheet **Candyb.mtw**

   Before analyzing the Candyb data, you should save them as a worksheet:

- In the location where you are saving your work, save the worksheet as **14Candyb**

   You decide to investigate each pack individually using an *individuals chart*. You specify the historical mean of 20.89 grams for the pack weight to center the chart and the historical sigma of 1.41 grams to determine what fraction of the production process is within the specification limits of 20.89 ± 3 *(1.41) (16.66 and 25.12) grams. Note that for individual values, the control limits are determined by the center line ± 3 σ.

   To obtain the individuals chart:

- Choose **Stat > Control Charts > Individuals**

- Select **C6 NetWgt** as the "Variable"

- Type **20.89** as the "Historical mean," and press Tab

- Type **1.41** as the "Historical sigma"

- Click the **Tests** button

- Click the **Perform all eight tests** option button

- Click **OK**

   The completed Individuals Chart dialog box should resemble that shown in Figure 14-12.

FIGURE 14-12

The completed Individuals Chart dialog box

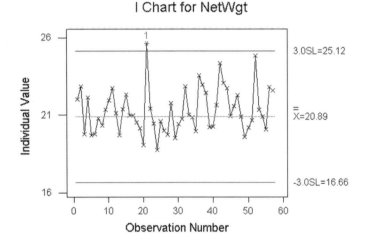

- Click **OK**

  The I (individuals) chart is shown in Figure 14-13.

FIGURE 14-13

I chart for NetWgt

The analysis of the resulting graph is revealing. The Session window shows that point 21 failed Test 1. There appears to be a problem with the twenty-first observation. It has a net weight of 25.62 grams. You contact a member of Group B. She informs you that this pack had a number of crushed candies. You suspect that the damage caused this pack to be outside the specification limits — an interesting discovery found by analyzing the control chart.

▼ 14.7   Constructing a Moving Range Chart ▲

You decide to analyze the variability of the second group's data. In your first investigation, you selected five randomly selected candies. Now you have selected only one pack; you cannot estimate process variability using only one sample. Instead, you use the *moving range* — the range of two or more consecutive observations — to investigate the variability of the process and construct a moving range chart:

- Choose **Stat > Control Charts > Moving Range**

- Select **C6 NetWgt** as the "Variable"

- Type **1.41** as the "Historical sigma"

The completed Moving Range Chart dialog box looks as shown in Figure 14-14.

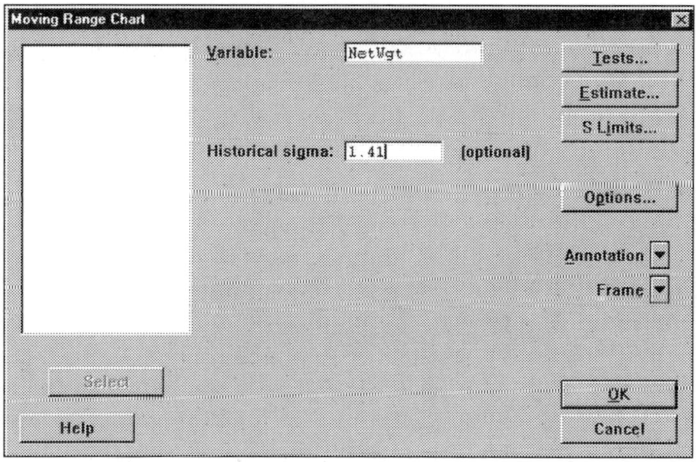

FIGURE 14-14

The completed Moving Range Chart dialog box

- Press ↵

The moving range chart appears in its own window, as shown in Figure 14-15.

FIGURE 14-15

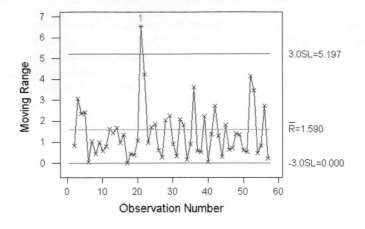

Process variability is not in control, due to the twenty-first pack. Again, your control chart identifies a problem. While this finding agrees with the problem identified by the individuals chart, this type of finding is not always the case. It's a good idea to construct both plots. Minitab lets you do that with a single command, I-MR:

- Choose **Stat > Control Charts > I-MR**

- Select **C6 NetWgt** as the "Variable"

- Type **20.89** as the "Historical mean," and press Tab

- Type **1.41** as the "Historical sigma," and press ←

The I-MR chart appears as shown in Figure 14-16.

FIGURE 14-16

*Initial I-MR chart of
NetWgt*

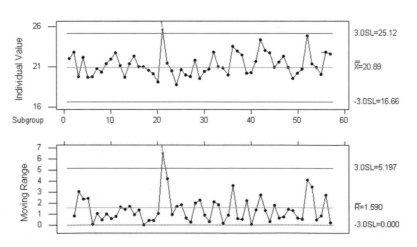

You decide that the test failure symbol may be distracting to the viewer. So you decide to remove all such test failure symbols for the chart:

- Click the **Edit Last Dialog** toolbar ▣
- Click the **Tests** button
- Select the **Choose specific tests to perform** option button, and deselect **One point more than 3 sigmas from center line**
- Click **OK** twice

The resulting chart appears in Figure 14-17.

FIGURE 14-17

Final I-MR chart of NetWgt

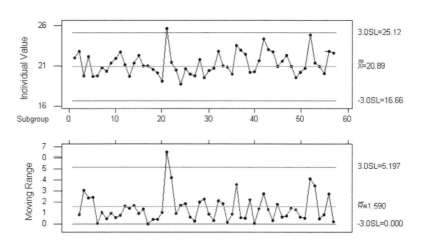

I and MR Chart for NetWgt

You plan to include this combination chart in your final report. It clearly reveals a problem with the twenty-first pack. Since the name of this chart is identical to that of the previous chart, you decide to rename both charts:

- Choose **Window > Manage Graphs**
- Click the first **14Candyb.mtw: I/MR for NetWgt**, click the **Rename** option button, type **Initial** before "I/MR," and click **OK**
- Click the remaining **14Candyb.mtw: I/MR for NetWgt**, click the **Rename** option button, type **Final** before "I/MR," and click **OK**
- Click **Done**
- In the location where you are saving your work, save the work you have done thus far in this tutorial in the project *T14*

▼ 14.8 Constructing a Proportion Chart ▲

Next, you turn to *Candyc.mtw*. You decide to investigate product quality by studying the proportion of defects (such as crushed candies) in each of the 57 packs. This is a common procedure for monitoring the proportion of defective items coming from a production line.

You'll be working with the file *Candyc.mtw*, which is located in the Student subdirectory:

- Open the worksheet **Candyc.mtw**

Before analyzing the Candyc data, you should save them as a worksheet:

- In the location where you are saving your work, save the worksheet as **14Candyc**

Group C entered the number of candies in each pack in C3 Number and the number of defects in each pack in C9 Defects. You can conceptualize this as an *attribute data* problem because each candy is classified as either defective or not. Contrast this type of data to the weight data, which is called *variables data*. To analyze attribute data, you use P (proportion) charts:

- Choose **Stat > Control Charts > P**

- Select **C9 Defects** as the "Variable"

- Click the **Subgroups in** option button, press ⁅Tab⁆, and select **C3 Number** as the "Subgroups in" variable

The completed P Chart dialog box is shown in Figure 14-18.

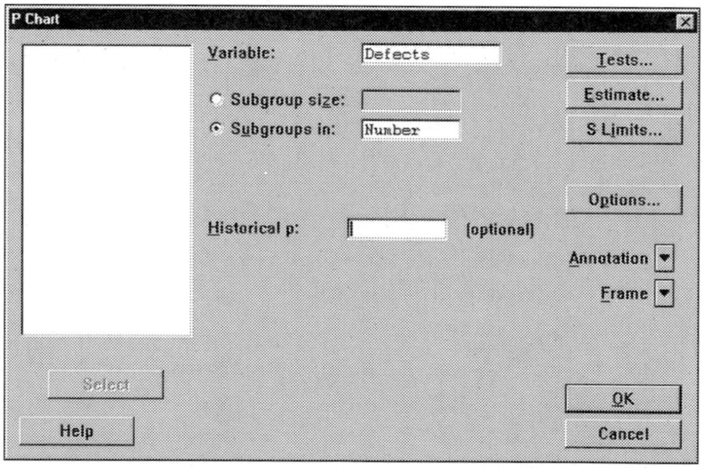

FIGURE 14-18

The completed P Chart dialog box

- Click **OK**

The P chart appears as in Figure 14-19.

FIGURE 14-19

P chart for Defects

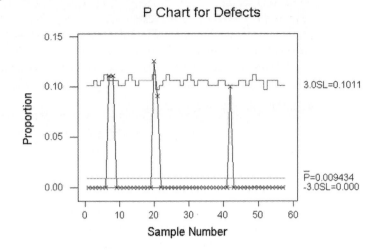

Minitab draws the center line at 0.009434. This is the proportion of defects over all samples combined and is the default value for the center line. It draws a LCL of 0.000, as it did with the R Chart. Minitab displays a *staircased upper control limit* (UCL) at approximately 0.1011, which is a nonconstant control limit that is not a horizontal straight line. The UCL is staircased because there are a different number of candies in each pack. Even though tests cannot be performed, since the UCL is not constant, you identify a problem with three packs (seventh, eighth, and twentieth) based on points that exceed the UCL.

You conclude that this process is not in control. There are too many defective candies among the 57 packs. The charts tell you to recommend that the company determine the cause of the crushed candies immediately so that fewer defects will be produced in the future.

You have seen only a small part of what Minitab can do with its quality tools. Minitab can also chart standard deviations, moving averages, counts (instead of proportions), and counts per unit — all of which are used routinely in the monitoring and analysis of a process.

■ In the location where you are saving your work, save the current project **T14** and exit Minitab

MINITAB AT WORK

QUALITY MANAGEMENT: In the late 1990s, General Electric (GE) chose to use MINITAB statistical software as part of its company-wide "Six Sigma" quality improvement program. GE has set for itself the goal of becoming a Six Sigma quality company — one with virtually defect-free manufacturing, service, and business transaction processes — by the year 2000.

Through its Six Sigma program, which received prominent coverage in *The Wall Street Journal* and *Business Week*, GE aims to improve technological, service, and manufacturing quality across all 12 of its key businesses around the world, namely, aircraft engines, appliances, capital services, electrical distribution and control, information services, lighting, medical systems, motors, NBC, plastics, power Systems, and transportation systems.

A component of GE's quality program is its Supplier Training Program, according to which selected suppliers are provided training in Six Sigma quality improvement methods, including the use of MINITAB as a statistical problem-solving tool. MINITAB training is provided either by GE's internal MINITAB experts or by training specialists from Minitab.

As part of GE's worldwide quality improvement program, MINITAB training has been provided by both GE and Minitab trainers to GE businesses in many countries, including Canada, China, France, Great Britain, Hungary, India, Japan, Malaysia, Mexico, and the United States.

▼
Minitab Command Summary
▲

This section describes the menu commands introduced in, or related to, this tutorial. To find a complete explanation of all commands, use Minitab's on-line Help.

Minitab Menu Commands

Menu	Command	Description
Stat		
	Control Charts	
	Xbar-R	Produces a control chart for subgroup means and a control chart for subgroup ranges.
	Xbar-S	Produces a control chart for subgroup means and a control chart for subgroup standard deviations.
	I-MR	Produces a chart of individual observations and a moving range chart.

Menu	Command	Description
	Control Charts	
	Xbar	Constructs an $\overline{X}$ chart for variables data stored in a column.
	R	Constructs a range chart using the variables data stored in a column.
	S	Constructs a standard deviation chart using the variables data stored in a column.
	Individuals	Constructs an individuals chart using the variables data stored in a column.
	Moving Range	Constructs a moving range chart using the variables data stored in a column.
	EWMA	Constructs an exponentially weighted moving average chart using variables data stored in a column.
	Moving Average	Constructs a moving average chart using variables data stored in a column.
	P	Constructs a proportions defective chart using attribute data stored in a column.
	NP	Constructs a number defective chart using attribute data stored in a column.
	C	Constructs a number of defects per unit chart using attribute data stored in a column for constant sample size.
	U	Constructs a chart of the number of defects per unit sampled using attribute data stored in a column.
	Quality Tools	
	Run Chart	Generates a chart showing individual values and subgroup means or medians and performs tests for nonrandom data.
	Pareto Chart	Generates a Pareto chart — a bar chart with the bars ordered from largest to smallest and combined with an ogive.
	Cause-and-Effect	Generates a cause-and-effect (fishbone) diagram that depicts the potential causes of a problem.

Matching

Match the following terms to their definitions by placing the correct letter next to the term it describes.

_____ Pooled standard deviation sigma

_____ Individuals

_____ Historical sigma

_____ Historical mean

_____ Average range sigma

_____ Tests for Special Causes

_____ Pareto chart

_____ Cause-and-effect diagram

_____ Nonconstant control limit

_____ Zero-valued control limit

a. A dialog box option that fixes the center line at a specified value in a control chart

b. A Minitab dialog box option that fixes the variability value in a control chart at a specified value

c. Minitab's default estimate of variability in the Xbar Chart

d. Minitab's default estimate of variability in the Xbar-R Chart

e. Output showing test results associated with certain control charts

f. Minitab notation that refers to variables data consisting of samples of size 1

g. A staircased limit possible in a P chart

h. A lower control limit that is possible in an MR chart

i. A display that depicts potential causes of a problem

j. A display that includes a bar chart with the bars ordered from largest to smallest

True/False

Mark the following statements with a _T_ or an _F_.

_____ You can directly specify the control limits and center line in all of Minitab's control charts.

_____ A control chart's center line is always the average of its LCL and UCL.

_____ Minitab has an Xbar-MR command.

_____ The Xbar command lets you perform nine special-cause tests.

_____ There are four Tests for Special Causes available with the P chart command.

_____ You can specify multiple columns using the Xbar chart command.

_____ For the P chart, the default center line is the median of the sample proportions.

_____ The Session window displays details of the special-cause tests along with the chart.

_____ All of Minitab's control chart commands require you to specify the subgroup size.

_____ You can request special-cause tests with the Moving Range command.

Practice Problems

Use Help or Part III, "Exploring Data," of this manual to review the contents of the data sets referred to in the following problems.

1. Open *Pubs.mtw*.

   a. Investigate the process mean weight by constructing an [X bar above] control chart. Is the process in control? Briefly explain your answer.

   b. Investigate the variability of the process weight by constructing an R control chart. Is the process in control? Briefly explain your answer.

   c. Construct an Xbar-R control chart for the weights. What are the advantages of using this chart instead of separate control charts? What are the disadvantages?

2. Open *Snow.mtw*. Investigate the yearly snowfall by constructing an I chart and an MR chart. Is the snowfall process in control? Note that there was a major blizzard in 1978, one of the years for which snowfall was measured.

3. In the illustration of P charts in this tutorial, the default option (the proportion of defects over all samples combined) was used to determine the center line and control limits. Redo the analysis by letting Minitab use the specified values of .01 for the "Historical p" and 2 for the "Sigma limit positions" to compute the center line and control limits. Are your results similar? If not, can you explain why?

4. Redo the Xbar control chart in this tutorial but use the Rbar estimate for sigma. Are your results similar? Briefly explain your answer.

5. There are many reasons why you might be late for class.

   a. List reasons why you might be late in six columns in a Minitab worksheet, one column for each of Minitab's Cause-and-Effect default categories (Men, Machines, Materials, Methods, Measures, and Environment).

   b. Construct a cause-and-effect diagram using the six columns you just created.

6. In 1996, the Bureau of Labor Statistics of the U. S. Department of Labor published a report on fatal occupational injuries. Here are the fatality categories and their corresponding numbers in parentheses: assaults and violent acts (1144), contact with objects and equipment (1005), exposure to harmful substance or environments (523), falls (684), fires and explosions(184), transportation incidents (2556), and other (16). Construct a Pareto chart for these fatalities. What do you learn from this chart?

TUTORIAL 15

Time Series Analysis

In Tutorials 10 and 11, you used regression analysis to develop models relating a response variable to one or more predictor variables. When your data consist of observations (responses) recorded over equally spaced intervals of time, regression methods often prove inadequate. With such data, error terms are frequently correlated rather than independent and the data itself is often cyclical in form rather than linear or quadratic. Minitab offers a range of specialized time series tools that help you select an appropriate model and predict or forecast future values for the series.

Objectives

In this tutorial, you will learn how to:

- perform a trend analysis to model and forecast a time series
- perform a classical decomposition to model and forecast a time series
- identify a model using autocorrelation and partial autocorrelation plots
- transform a time series
- use Box-Jenkins autoregressive integrated moving average (ARIMA) techniques to model and forecast a time series
- compare the classical decomposition and ARIMA models
- appreciate that there are other time series modeling and forecasting techniques available in Minitab

▼ 15.1   Performing a Trend Analysis of a Time Series ▲

CASE STUDY: ENVIRONMENT — TEMPERATURE VARIATION

During the summer of 1988, which was one of the hottest on record in the Midwest, a graduate student in environmental science conducted a study for the state Environmental Protection Agency. She studied the impact of an electric generating plant along a river. The Agency was most concerned with the plant's use of river water for cooling. Scientists feared that the plant was raising its temperature and endangering aquatic life in the river. The Agency established a site directly downstream from the cooling discharge outlets of the plant at which they measured the water temperature hourly for 95 consecutive hours.

In this case study, you are an environmental science graduate student working for the Agency on this project. You use time series methods to analyze the problem. You perform the time series analysis in eight phases, given in the following table.

Phase I	Perform a linear trend analysis on the time series.
Phase II	Perform a classical decomposition on the time series using a multiplicative model.
Phase III	Apply the model to forecast future values.
Phase IV	Investigate the autocorrelation and partial autocorrelation structure of the time series to determine an appropriate Box-Jenkins ARIMA model.
Phase V	Transform the data (if necessary) using lags and differences to obtain a stationary time series.
Phase VI	Fit an adequate Box-Jenkins ARIMA model.
Phase VII	Apply the Box-Jenkins ARIMA model to forecast future values.
Phase VIII	Examine the strengths and weaknesses of the multiplicative and Box-Jenkins ARIMA models.

To get started:

- Start **Minitab**

- Maximize the **Session window**

- If necessary, enable the **Session command language** and make the output read-only

You'll be working with the data file *Riverc.mtw*, which is in the Student subdirectory:

- Open the worksheet **Riverc.mtw**

C1 Hour lists the time of day of each measurement, using a 24-hour clock. C2 Temp gives the temperature measurement in °C. The other columns in *Riverc.mtw* contain additional measurements taken at the same time as the temperature. For more information about these other measurements, refer to the description of this file in Help or in Part III, "Exploring Data," of this manual.

Before analyzing these data, you should save them as a worksheet and this tutorial in a project:

- In the location where you are saving your work, save the worksheet as **15Riverc**

- Also, save the work you have done thus far in this tutorial in a project named **T15**

In Tutorials 10 and 11, you used linear regression to model and forecast a response variable based on one or more predictor variables. Plots were used to provide initial insight into the relationship among variables. When the variables form a time series, Minitab provides a number of other techniques especially designed to accomplish the same goals. They appear on the Time Series submenu of the Stat menu.

To obtain an initial picture of any trends in the temperature data over time, you decide to use Minitab's Trend Analysis command. This command is similar to the Fitted Line Plot for simple linear regression because it presents a good combination of graph and numerical information. It allows you to fit one of four models to a time series: a linear model, a quadratic model, an exponential growth model, or an S-curve model. You can store the fitted values and the residuals. In the context of trend analysis, the residuals are called the *detrended* values. An additional option is to generate forecasts of future values of the series. You decide to perform a trend analysis on the temperature, using the Minitab default settings:

- Choose **Stat > Time Series > Trend Analysis**

- Select **C2 Temp** as the "Variable"

The completed Trend Analysis dialog box is as shown in Figure 15-1. Note that the default is a linear model.

FIGURE 15-1

*The completed Trend
Analysis dialog box*

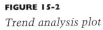

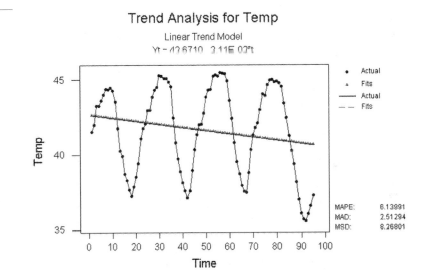

- Click **OK**

  The Trend Analysis plot appears as shown in Figure 15-2.

FIGURE 15-2

Trend analysis plot

Trend Analysis for Temp

Linear Trend Model

Yt = 42.6710 - 2.11E-02*t

Minitab plots the temperature on the vertical axis and the hour on the horizontal axis. All of the time series points are connected with a straight line. The plot indicates a cyclical pattern beginning with temperatures at 2 P.M. around 42 degrees, which rise for the next 8 hours and then fall until they reach a low of about 37 degrees at 7 A.M. (Time equal to 17.) This cycle repeats through the next 24-hour period but with some variation. The peaks and valleys occur roughly 24 hours apart. This suggests that your time series model might include a periodic component. In time series terminology, this is more commonly called a *seasonal component*, even though the cycle might be over hours or over days.

The fitted trend line is also printed. Its equation is below the title, Yt = 42.6710 – 2.11E-02*t. The value 2.11E-02 is scientific notation for 0.0211; it allows the line to be written as 42.6710 – 0.0211*t. The line itself suggests a slight negative trend in the data. In the lower-right corner of the plot are three measures of the adequacy of the fitted model:

1. Mean Absolute Percentage Error (MAPE)

2. Mean Absolute Deviation (MAD) (which you calculated by a series of Minitab commands in Tutorial 2)

3. Mean Squared Deviation (MSD)

The equation and these three measures are also reported in the Session window. (You can get the formulas for these three measures from the glossary in Minitab's Help.)

On the basis of the strong seasonal component and the relatively small value of the slope coefficient (–0.211), you decide to consider another model. Your first choice is a classical decomposition model that will isolate the seasonal, the linear trend, and the error components of the series.

▼ **Note** Instead of the trend analysis that you just performed, you could have used another graph by choosing Stat > Time Series > Time Series Plot or Graph > Time Series Plot, or even Graph > Plot. Because the Trend Analysis provides so much more information than these other graphs, using this command is an example of using the Minitab tool most-suited to your purpose. ▲

■ In the location where you are saving your work, save the work you have done thus far in this tutorial in the project *T15*

▼ 15.2   Performing a Classical Decomposition of a Time Series ▲

The Decomposition command performs a classical decomposition on a time series using either a multiplicative or an additive model. *Classical decomposition* separates the time series into trend, seasonal, and error components by using least-squares analysis, trend analysis, and moving averages. You can also generate forecasts.

From your examination of the time series plot, you decide to use the Decomposition command to obtain the trend, seasonal, and error components of the default multiplicative model. In this model, an observation in the series is represented in the form T*S+E, where T is the trend component, S is the seasonal component, and E is the error component. You decide also to generate forecasts for the next two days (one per hour for 48 hours).

- Choose **Stat > Time Series > Decomposition**

- Select **C2 Temp** as the "Variable"

- Type **24** as the "Seasonal length"

- Click the **Generate forecasts** check box, press Tab, and type **48** as the "Number of forecasts"

- Click the **Storage** button, and click the **Forecasts** check box

- Click the **Help** button in the Decomposition - Storage dialog box to obtain a brief explanation of the quantities that can be stored in this analysis

- Click the **Exit** button to return to the dialog box

- Click **OK**

The completed Decomposition dialog box should resemble that shown in Figure 15-3. The forecasts associated with each observation will be saved.

FIGURE 15-3

The completed Decomposition dialog box

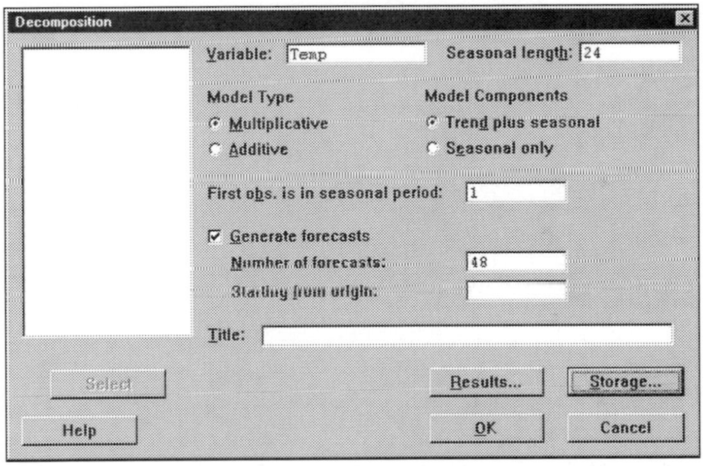

- Click **OK**

Minitab displays the results of the decomposition in the Session window and in three Graph windows. It adds a column, C6 FORE1, that contains the forecasts.

- Click the **Session Window** toolbar button

- Scroll up in the Session window to view the initial results of the decomposition analysis (without the forecasts) that are shown in Figure 15-4

FIGURE 15-4

Decomposition results

```
MTB > Name c6 = 'FORE1'
MTB > %Decomp 'Temp' 24;
SUBC>    Forecasts 48;
SUBC>  Start 1;
SUBC>    Fstore 'FORE1'.
Executing from file: C:\PROGRAM FILES\MTBWINST\MACROS\Decomp.MAC

Macro is running ... please wait
```

Time Series Decomposition

```
Data       Temp
Length     95.0000
NMissing   0


Trend Line Equation
```

$$Yt = 42.6710 - 2.11E-02*t$$

```
Seasonal Indices

Period   Index

    1    1.02167
    2    1.03768
    3    1.04624
    4    1.05749
    5    1.06885
    6    1.07383
    7    1.07158
    8    1.07528
    9    1.07626
   10    1.07279
   11    1.06180
   12    1.02159
   13    0.972796
   14    0.961675
   15    0.932260
   16    0.914849
   17    0.895907
   18    0.887141
   19    0.894304
   20    0.922715
   21    0.954326
   22    0.982207
   23    0.997387
   24    0.999376


Accuracy of Model

MAPE:    2.03659
MAD:     0.83921
MSD:     1.15545
```

Minitab provides the trend line equation $Yt = 42.6710 - 2.11E\text{-}02*t$ and the seasonal indices, which you can combine to obtain predicted and forecasted values. It also indicates the three measures you can use to determine the accuracy of the fitted model: MAPE (2.03659), MAD (0.83921), and MSD (1.15545). Minitab repeats these values in Figure 15-5, which displays a plot of the actual, predicted, and forecasted values along with the trend line.

■ Choose **Window > 15Riverc.mtw: Decomp1**

FIGURE 15-5

Decomposition fit for the Temp graph

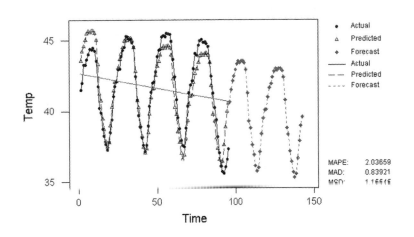

Decomposition Fit for Temp

Notice the legend in the top-right corner. It helps you to distinguish between the actual and predicted values and the forecasts. The graph depicts a slight downward trend, with a 24-hour seasonal component. It also shows the divergence of the predicted values from the actual values at the top of peaks 1, 3, and 4 and at the valley 4 (the last of the 95 observations).

Open the graph that provides a component analysis for Temp (shown in Figure 15-6):

■ Choose **Window > 15Riverc.mtw: Decomp2**

FIGURE 15-6

*Plots showing component
analysis for Temp*

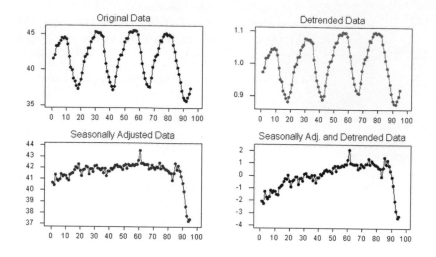

This graph includes plots of the original data, detrended data, seasonally adjusted data, and seasonally adjusted and detrended data. In the plot of the detrended data, the (slight) negative linear trend has been removed. The plot of the seasonally adjusted data shows what the series would look like if there was no seasonal effect. The final graph shows the residuals after the linear trend and the seasonal effects have been removed. The unusual pattern at the end of the last two time series plots dramatizes the fact that the last valley shown in the plot of the original data is deeper than all of the proceeding valleys. The final graph, shown in Figure 15-7, provides a seasonal analysis for Temp.

- Choose **Window > 15Riverc.mtw: Decomp3**

FIGURE 15-7

*Plots showing seasonal
analysis for Temp*

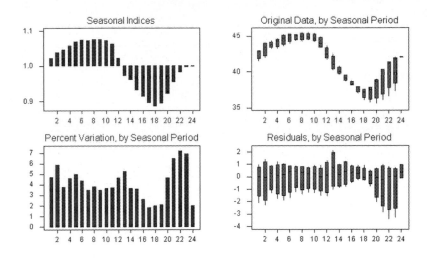

Seasonal Analysis for Temp

The first plot shows the seasonal indices. The next three contain plots of, respectively, the original data, the percent variation, and the residuals. In all four plots, the horizontal axis is the seasonal period. Note the large number of negative residuals present in four of the five last periods in the Residuals plot.

Scroll down in the Session window to view the forecasts resulting from the decomposition analysis, shown in Figure 15-8:

- Click the **Session Window** toolbar button ▦

FIGURE 15-8

Decomposition forecast results

Forecasts

Row	Period	FORE1
1	96	40.6248
2	97	41.5096
3	98	42.1381
4	99	42.4635
5	100	42.8982
6	101	43.3363
7	102	43.5157
8	103	43.4021
9	104	43.5290
10	105	43.5461
11	106	43.3831
12	107	42.9165
13	108	41.2696
14	109	39.2780
15	110	38.8088
16	111	37.6021
17	112	36.8806
18	113	36.0981
19	114	35.7262
20	115	35.9959
21	116	37.1200
22	117	38.3716
23	118	39.4720
24	119	40.0610
25	120	40.1199
26	121	40.9934
27	122	41.6139
28	123	41.9350
29	124	42.3640
30	125	42.7963
31	126	42.9732
32	127	42.8607
33	128	42.9858
34	129	43.0024
35	130	42.8411
36	131	42.3801
37	132	40.7534
38	133	38.7866
39	134	38.3229
40	135	37.1311
41	136	36.4184
42	137	35.6455
43	138	35.2780
44	139	35.5440
45	140	36.6538
46	141	37.8894
47	142	38.9757
48	143	39.5571

These forecasts, which were plotted in Figure 15-5, display the same pattern as your data. They peak between periods 102 and 105. Period 104 corresponds to 9:00 P.M. (the same time you saw a peak in your data).

After this decomposition analysis, you are still concerned about the divergence of the predicted values from the actual values at the top of peaks 1, 3, and 4 and at the bottom of valley 4, all shown in Figure 15-5. You decide to obtain another model and set of forecasts for the same time series. To do so, you plan to examine autocorrelation and partial autocorrelation plots so that you can construct the appropriate ARIMA model. Such models are based to a large extent on the autocorrelational structure present in the data.

- In the location where you are saving your work, save the work you have done thus far in this tutorial in the project *T15*

▼ 15.3 Checking the Autocorrelation and Partial Autocorrelation Plots ▲

For time series data, *autocorrelation* and *partial autocorrelation* measure the degree of relationship between observations k time periods, or *lags*, apart. Plots of these quantities provide valuable information to help you identify an appropriate ARIMA model:

- Choose **Stat > Time Series > Autocorrelation**
- Select **C2 Temp** as the "Series"
- Click the **Number of lags** option button, and press Tab
- Type **24** as the "Number of lags" to tell Minitab to compute and plot 24 autocorrelations

The completed Autocorrelation Function dialog box should look as shown in Figure 15-9.

FIGURE 15-9

The completed Autocorrelation Function dialog box

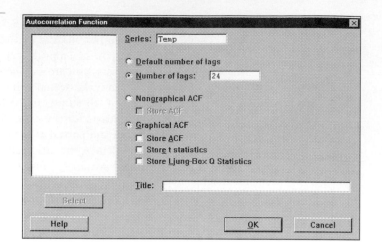

- Click **OK**

  The autocorrelation function plot is shown in Figure 15-10.

FIGURE 15-10

The autocorrelation function plot for Temp

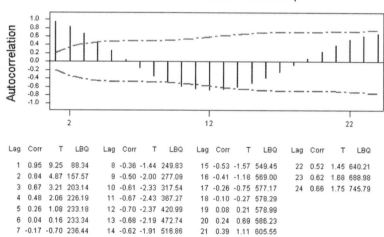

Autocorrelation Function for Temp

Lag	Corr	T	LBQ	Lag	Corr	T	LBQ	Lag	Corr	T	LBQ	Lag	Corr	T	LBQ
1	0.95	9.25	88.34	8	-0.36	-1.44	249.83	15	-0.53	-1.57	549.45	22	0.52	1.45	640.21
2	0.84	4.87	157.57	9	-0.50	-2.00	277.09	16	-0.41	-1.18	569.00	23	0.62	1.68	688.98
3	0.67	3.21	203.14	10	-0.61	-2.33	317.54	17	-0.26	-0.75	577.17	24	0.66	1.75	745.79
4	0.48	2.06	226.19	11	-0.67	-2.43	387.27	18	-0.10	-0.27	578.29				
5	0.26	1.08	233.18	12	-0.70	-2.37	420.99	19	0.08	0.21	578.99				
6	0.04	0.16	233.34	13	-0.68	-2.19	472.74	20	0.24	0.69	586.23				
7	-0.17	-0.70	236.44	14	-0.62	-1.91	516.86	21	0.39	1.11	605.55				

The autocorrelation function plot, indicated by bars at each of the 24 lags, resembles a sine pattern. This suggests that temperatures close in time are strongly and positively correlated, while temperatures about 12 hours apart are highly negatively correlated. (The large positive autocorrelation at lag 24 is indicative of the 24-hour seasonal component.) The pattern in the autocorrelation plot suggests that your ARIMA model may have an *autoregressive (AR)* component. (An AR process of degree k is one in which the current value of the series can be modeled as a linear combination of the k most recent past values for the series.) All of the autocorrelations, except for the first three and several of the negative ones, are within the confidence interval.

Below the graph, a table lists the autocorrelations (Corr), associated t-statistics (T), and associated Ljung-Box Q (LBQ) statistics for each lag. The t-statistics can be used to test the null hypothesis that the autocorrelation at a specific lag equals zero. The LBQ statistics can be used to test the null hypothesis that the autocorrelations for all lags up to a specified value are equal to zero. The three positive, large autocorrelations at lags 1, 2, and 3 suggest an AR component of degree 3 or possibly 2 (that is, the AR component should include 2 or 3 of the most recent past values).

Now construct a plot of the partial autocorrelation function to gather additional information about an appropriate ARIMA model:

- Choose **Stat > Time Series > Partial Autocorrelation**

- Select **C2 Temp** as the "Series"

- Click the **Number of lags** check box, and press Tab

- Type **24** as the "Number of lags" to tell Minitab to compute and plot 24 partial autocorrelations

The completed Partial Autocorrelation Function dialog box should look as shown in Figure 15-11.

FIGURE 15-11

The completed Partial Autocorrelation Function dialog box

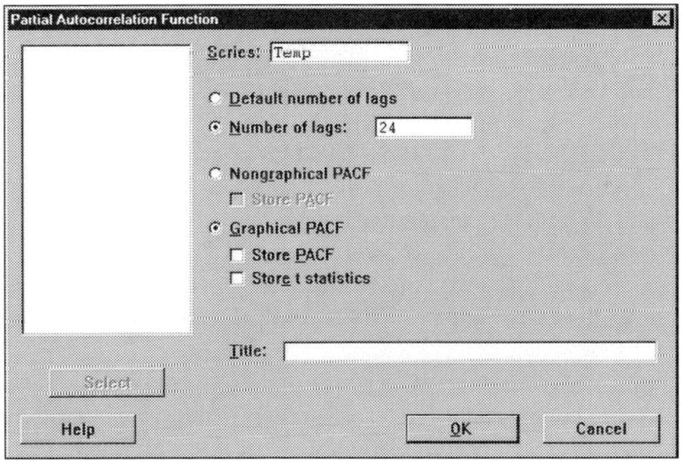

- Click **OK**

The partial autocorrelation function plot is shown in Figure 15-12.

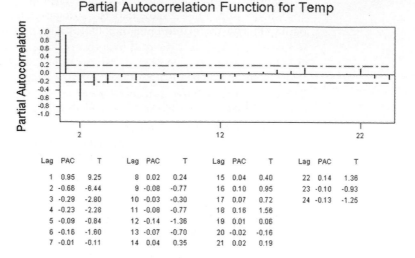

Partial Autocorrelation Function for Temp

Lag	PAC	T	Lag	PAC	T	Lag	PAC	T	Lag	PAC	T
1	0.95	9.25	8	0.02	0.24	15	0.04	0.40	22	0.14	1.36
2	-0.66	-6.44	9	-0.08	-0.77	16	0.10	0.95	23	-0.10	-0.93
3	-0.29	-2.80	10	-0.03	-0.30	17	0.07	0.72	24	-0.13	-1.25
4	-0.23	-2.28	11	-0.08	-0.77	18	0.16	1.56			
5	-0.09	-0.84	12	-0.14	-1.36	19	0.01	0.06			
6	-0.16	-1.60	13	-0.07	-0.70	20	-0.02	-0.16			
7	-0.01	-0.11	14	0.04	0.35	21	0.02	0.19			

The partial autocorrelation plot shows two large partial autocorrelations (spikes) at lags 1 and 2 — this also suggests an AR component of degree 2. Later in this tutorial, you will fit an ARIMA model based on your findings thus far.

■ In the location where you are saving your work, save the work you have done thus far in this tutorial in the project *T15*

▼ 15.4   Transforming a Time Series ▲

The river data are fairly well-behaved, as evidenced by the trend analysis plot in Figure 15-2. If you were to draw a horizontal line at the mean of the series, you would see that the data oscillate with the same cyclical pattern. A time series like this, whose mean and variance do not change with time, is called *stationary*.

Conversely, a series that grows or declines systematically over time is called *nonstationary*. However, by lagging and differencing a nonstationary time series, you can usually make it stationary. To practice using these components, you will obtain the river data's lags and differences, even though they appear almost stationary.

Lagging Data

You can think of *lagging* as *time-shifting*: Each element in a time series plot is shifted to a later point so that it lags behind by the number of time units you specify. When you lag a column in Minitab and store the lagged data, the new column is identical to the former one, except that the entries are shifted down, or lagged, by a specified number of rows. The empty rows at the beginning of the resulting column are filled with *s to indicate missing values. Minitab uses a default lag of 1.

- Choose **Stat > Time Series > Lag**
- Select **C2 Temp** as the "Series"
- Type **Lags** in the "Store lags in" text box

    The completed Lag dialog box should look as shown in Figure 15-13.

FIGURE 15-13

The completed Lag dialog box

Lag	☒

C1	Hour
C2	Temp
C3	PH
C4	Cond
C5	DO
C6	FORE1

Series: Temp

Store lags in: Lags

Lag: 1

Select

Help   OK   Cancel

- Click **OK**
- Click the **Current Data window** toolbar button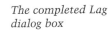

    Compare the temperature data in C2 Temp with the data in column C7 Lags in Figure 15-14. Note that a value in C7 Lags is one row lower than the corresponding value in C2 Temp. The first entry in C7 Lags is missing.

Lagged temperature data

Computing Differences

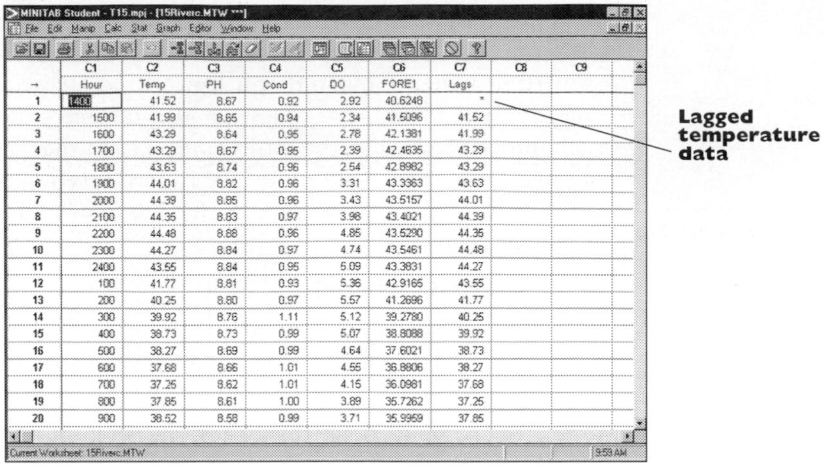

The Differences command computes differences of observations that are a specified lag apart. For example, if you specify a lag of 1, Minitab computes differences between adjacent values in the time series and stores them in a column. To apply the Differences command to the temperature data with differences of lag 1:

- Choose **Stat > Time Series > Differences**

- Select **C2 Temp** as the "Series"

- Type **Diff** as the "Store differences in" variable

    The completed Differences dialog box should look as shown in Figure 15-15.

FIGURE 15-15

The completed Differences dialog box

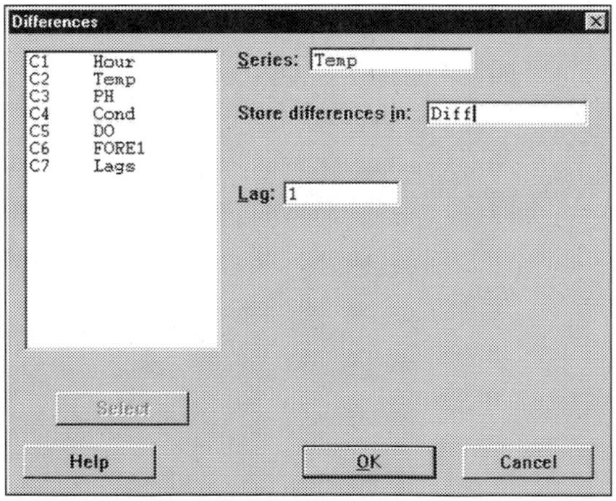

- Click **OK**

C8 Diff contains the differences between adjacent values in the time series for C2 Temp, as shown in Figure 15-16. In other words, C8 Diff is the difference between columns C2 Temp and C7 Lags.

FIGURE 15-16

The Data window with differenced temperature data in C8

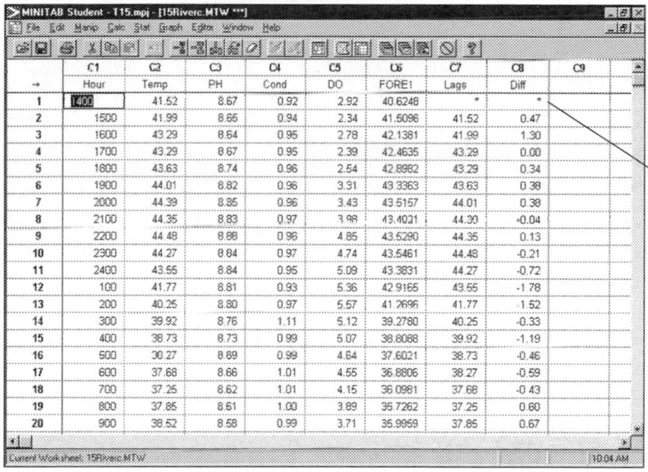

Differenced temperature data

Recall that the shape of your time series plot indicates whether the time series is stationary. Consider taking differences when the time series plot indicates a nonstationary time series. You can then use the resulting differenced data as your time series, plotting the differenced time series to determine if it is stationary.

- In the location where you are saving your work, save the work you have done thus far in this tutorial in the project *T15*

▼ 15.5 Performing a Box-Jenkins ARIMA Analysis of a Time Series ▲

Your investigation of the autocorrelation and partial autocorrelation plots suggested that you should consider an ARIMA model with an AR component of degree 2, called *AR 2*, and a 24-hour seasonal AR component of degree 1, called *SAR 1*. Hoping to keep the model as simple as possible, you first try a model with AR 2 and no seasonality.

Use the ARIMA command to estimate the parameters for this model and investigate its fit:

- Choose **Stat > Time Series > ARIMA**

- Select **C2 Temp** as the "Series," and press Tab

- Type **2** in the "Autoregressive Nonseasonal" text box

The completed ARIMA dialog box should resemble Figure 15-17.

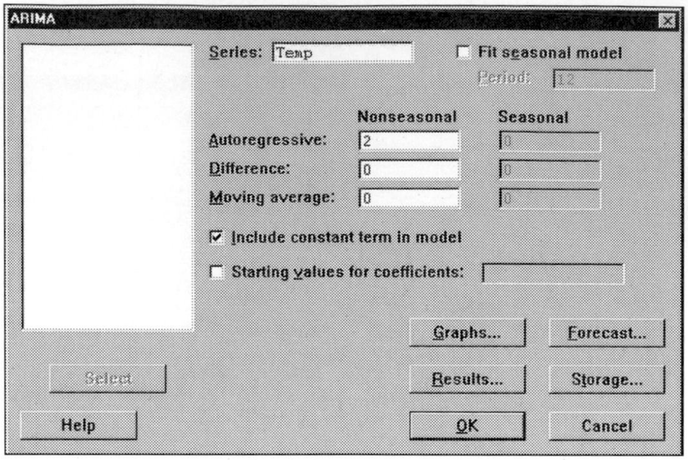

FIGURE 15-17
The completed ARIMA dialog box

▼ **Note** The columns in the dialog box next to Autoregressive, Difference, and Moving average correspond to the nonseasonal and seasonal components of the ARIMA model, respectively. ▲

- Click **OK**
- Scroll up in the Session window to view the results of the ARIMA analysis, which should resemble Figure 15-18

FIGURE 15-18

Iteration estimates from the ARIMA analysis

```
MTB > ARIMA 2 0 0 'Temp';
SUBC>    Constant;
SUBC>    Brief 2.
```

ARIMA Model

ARIMA model for Temp

Estimates at each iteration

Iteration	SSE	Parameters		
0	556.993	0.100	0.100	33.408
1	460.739	0.250	0.020	30.500
2	376.654	0.400	-0.064	27.719
3	301.680	0.550	-0.147	24.946
4	235.673	0.700	-0.231	22.176
5	178.602	0.850	-0.315	19.408
6	130.452	1.000	-0.399	16.643
7	91.073	1.150	-0.482	13.865
8	60.786	1.300	-0.566	11.110
9	39.320	1.450	-0.650	8.351
10	26.746	1.600	-0.734	5.611
11	22.933	1.733	-0.810	3.202
12	22.919	1.742	-0.815	3.069
13	22.919	1.742	-0.816	3.060

Relative change in each estimate less than 0.0010

Minitab fits the model you specify using an iterative process that involves using initial estimates of the parameters to obtain new estimates. The process stops when there are very few change in the values for the estimates from one iteration to the next or when the estimates do not converge after 25 iterations. Minitab provides a history of this iterative process, with the sum of squared errors (SSE) and the parameter estimates for each iteration. In this example, the estimates converge satisfactorily after 13 iterations. In Figure 15-18, the parameter estimates correspond to the two AR 2 components and the constant parameters, respectively.

▼ **Note** Minitab uses the common notation (pdq) × (PDQ) S to specify an ARIMA model. Here (pdq) stands for a nonseasonal model, (PDQ) for a seasonal model, and S for the seasonality. The value p is the order of the autoregressive component, d the number of differences, and q the order of the moving average component of the model. P, D, and Q are similarly defined for the seasonal model. S is the length of a season. You have constructed a (2, 0, 0) (0, 0, 0), 0 ARIMA model. In the absence of a seasonal model, Minitab shortens the model to 2 0 0, which you can see as part of the Session command in Figure 15-18. ▲

Next, Minitab displays the final parameter estimates in detail, as shown in Figure 15-19.

FIGURE 15-19

*Final parameter estimates
from the ARIMA analysis*

```
Final Estimates of Parameters
Type        Coef      StDev        T        P
AR   1    1.7421     0.0629     27.70    0.000
AR   2   -0.8156     0.0639    -12.76    0.000
Constant  3.05969   0.05129     59.66    0.000
Mean      41.6201    0.6977

Number of observations:  95
Residuals:    SS =  22.8842  (backforecasts excluded)
              MS =   0.2487  DF = 92

Modified Box-Pierce (Ljung-Box) Chi-Square statistic
Lag              12       24       36       48
Chi-Square     25.2     48.7     58.4     76.7
DF                9       21       33       45
P-Value       0.003    0.001    0.004    0.002
```

Minitab estimates the first autoregressive coefficient (AR 1) as 1.7421, with a standard deviation of 0.0629 and a t-ratio of 27.70. The second autoregressive coefficient (AR 2) is estimated at –0.8156, with a standard deviation of 0.0639 and a t-ratio of –12.76. The estimated constant term is 3.05969.

You conclude that both the AR 1 and AR 2 parameters are significantly different from zero, since the t-ratios are so large. You could compute the estimated temperature at time T as follows:

$$\text{Temp at time T} = 3.05969 + 1.7421 * \text{Temp (at time T} - 1)$$
$$- 0.8156 * \text{Temp (at time T} - 2)$$

The modified Box-Pierce (Ljung-Box) chi-square statistic, which measures how well the model fits the data, appears last in Figure 15-19. For the following hypotheses, chi-square statistics, and corresponding p-values are computed at lags of 12, 24, 36, and 48:

Null hypothesis H_0: The specified ARIMA model fits the data.

Alternative hypothesis H_1: The specified ARIMA model does not fit the data.

The p-values for these tests are 0.003, 0.001, 0.004, and 0.002, respectively, indicating that each chi-square statistic is significant. You conclude that your specified ARIMA model does not fit the data at most standard levels of significance.

Constructing a Seasonal Model

Based on this lack of fit, you decide to specify a new ARIMA model, (0, 0, 0) (1, 0, 0) (24), that is seasonal:

- Select the **Edit Last Dialog** toolbar button
- Verify that **C2 Temp** is the "Series"

- Click the **Fit seasonal model** check box, and press Tab

- Type **24** as the "Period," and press Tab

- Type **0** in the "Autoregressive: Nonseasonal" text box, and press Tab three times

- Type **1** in the "Autoregressive: Seasonal" text box

The modified ARIMA dialog box should look as shown in Figure 15-20.

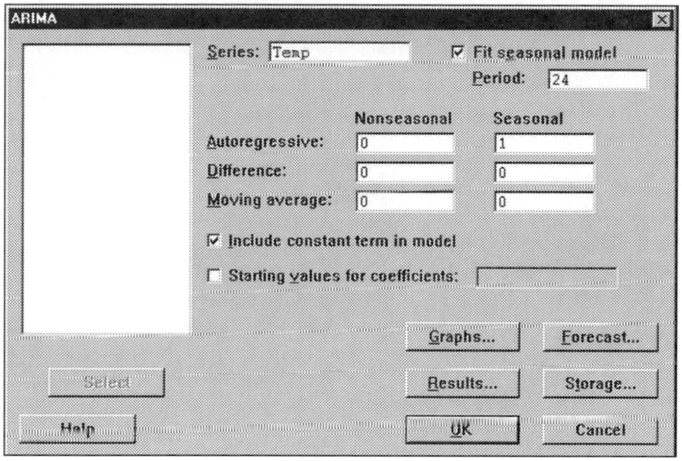

FIGURE 15-20

The completed ARIMA dialog box with the seasonal model

- Click **OK**

Minitab alerts you that it is unable to estimate this model, as shown in Figure 15-21.

FIGURE 15-21

Session window showing seasonal model attempt

```
MTB > ARIMA 0 0 0 1 0 0 24 'Temp';
SUBC>   Constant;
SUBC>   Brief 2.
```

ARIMA Model

ARIMA model for Temp

Estimates at each iteration

Iteration	SSE	Parameters	
0	715.280	0.100	37.584
1	570.425	0.250	31.278
2	443.907	0.400	25.001
3	333.375	0.550	18.729
4	237.159	0.700	12.468
5	154.825	0.850	6.222
6	106.324	1.000	0.000

Unable to reduce sum of squares any further.
* ERROR * Model cannot be estimated with these data.

Now you consult with an Agency statistician. After examining some additional plots, the statistician suggests that you try ARIMA (2, 0, 0) (1, 1, 0) (24):

- Select the **Edit Last Dialog** toolbar button ▣

- Press ⟨Tab⟩ three times, type **2** in the "Autoregressive: Nonseasonal" text box, and then press ⟨Tab⟩ four times

- Type **1** in the "Difference: Seasonal" text box

  The modified ARIMA dialog box should resemble Figure 15-22.

- Click **OK**

  The Session window shows the results of your new model in Figure 15-23.

FIGURE 15-23

*Final parameter estimates
from the ARIMA results
for new model*

```
MTB > ARIMA 2 0 0 1 1 0 24 'Temp';
SUBC>    Constant;
SUBC>    Brief 2.
```

ARIMA Model

```
ARIMA model for Temp

Estimates at each iteration
Iteration      SSE    Parameters
        0   77.8840   0.100    0.100    0.100   -0.002
        1   57.9793   0.250    0.097    0.116   -0.014
        2   42.3752   0.400    0.086    0.126   -0.022
        3   30.5046   0.550    0.070    0.126   -0.027
        4   21.9906   0.700    0.050    0.108   -0.029
        5   16.5296   0.850    0.025    0.059   -0.026
        6   13.8547   1.000   -0.004   -0.058   -0.002
        7   13.7880   1.002   -0.002   -0.107    0.003
        8   13.6610   1.003   -0.002   -0.146   -0.002
        9   13.5726   1.003   -0.000   -0.178   -0.026
       10   13.4953   1.002    0.000   -0.224   -0.021
       11   13.4727   1.001    0.001   -0.255   -0.020
       12   13.4635   1.000    0.002   -0.276   -0.020
       13   13.4592   0.999    0.003   -0.291   -0.020
       14   13.4566   0.998    0.005   -0.300   -0.020
       15   13.4536   0.997    0.006   -0.307   -0.020
       16   13.4484   0.995    0.008   -0.311   -0.020
       17   13.4367   0.994    0.010   -0.314    0.020
       18   13.4064   0.992    0.014   -0.316   -0.018
       19   13.3537   0.991    0.020   -0.317   -0.019
       20   13.3468   0.991    0.024   -0.325   -0.030
       21   13.2687   0.989    0.034   -0.321   -0.028
       22   13.2538   0.991    0.043   -0.327   -0.050
       23   13.1961   0.960    0.096   -0.369   -0.082
       24   13.1644   0.960    0.097   -0.370   -0.082
       25   12.9807   0.967    0.093   -0.369   -0.082
** Convergence criterion not met after 25 iterations.


Final Estimates of Parameters
Type         Coef      StDev        T       P
AR    1     0.9671    0.1245     7.77   0.000
AR    2     0.0927    0.1422     0.65   0.517
SAR  24    -0.3690    0.1526    -2.42   0.018
Constant-0.0820070  -0.0728330   1.13   0.264


Differencing: 0 regular, 1 seasonal of order 24
Number of observations:  Original series 95, after differencing 71
Residuals:    SS = 12.5825  (backforecasts excluded)
              MS =  0.1878  DF = 67


Modified Box-Pierce (Ljung-Box) Chi-Square statistic
Lag              12      24      36      48
Chi-Square     13.9    26.7    39.7    49.4
DF                8      20      32      44
P-Value       0.085   0.144   0.164   0.266
```

The modified Box-Pierce (Ljung-Box) chi-square statistics seem much better for this model. The p-values are now equal to 0.085, 0.144, 0.164, and 0.266. Consequently, you do not reject the hypotheses that this model fits the data.

Note from Figure 15-23 that the iterative process used to obtain parameter estimates was stopped after 25 iterations. To continue the process to possibly obtain more-accurate parameter estimates, you could return to the ARIMA dialog box and enter the final estimates (0.967, 0.093, –0.369, and –0.082) as the starting values for a new round of iterations.

▼ 15.6   Forecasting By Using ARIMA ▲

Once you determine the model, the final step is to forecast future values. Next, you will predict the temperatures for the next 48 hours and then store the forecasts and prediction limits:

- Click the **Edit Last Dialog** toolbar button 🔲
- Verify that the dialog box entries still appear as shown in Figure 15-22
- Click the **Forecast** button

    In the ARIMA - Forecasts dialog box:

- Type **48** as the "Lead" variable, and press ⎡Tab⎤ twice
- Type **AForecst** as the "Forecasts," and press ⎡Tab⎤
- Type **LAForcst** as the "Lower limits," and press ⎡Tab⎤
- Type **UAForcst** as the "Upper limits"

    The completed ARIMA - Forecasts dialog box should resemble Figure 15-24.

FIGURE 15-24

The completed ARIMA - Forecasts dialog box

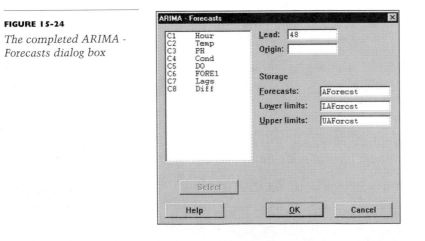

- Click **OK** twice

Minitab displays forecasts with 95% confidence limits in the Session window, as shown in Figure 15-25.

FIGURE 15-25

Forecasts for new model

Forecasts from period 95

Period	Forecast	95 Percent Limits Lower	95 Percent Limits Upper	Actual
96	37.1269	36.2773	37.9764	
97	37.6252	36.4434	38.8071	
98	38.3148	36.8453	39.7843	
99	38.0197	36.2856	39.7538	
100	38.0810	36.0934	40.0686	
101	38.1874	35.9512	40.4236	
102	37.7947	35.3109	40.2784	
103	37.1791	34.4461	39.9122	
104	36.7916	33.8055	39.7777	
105	36.1620	32.9174	39.4066	
106	35.4526	31.9427	38.9626	
107	33.9669	30.1834	37.7504	
108	32.2496	28.1834	36.3159	
109	30.3913	26.0318	34.7508	
110	28.4575	23.7933	33.1217	
111	26.7029	21.7215	31.6843	
112	24.8784	19.5662	30.1906	
113	23.0213	17.3636	28.6790	
114	21.4321	15.4132	27.4510	
115	20.2532	13.8563	26.6502	
116	19.7013	12.9083	26.4943	
117	19.5550	12.3468	26.7631	
118	19.1921	11.5483	26.8359	
119	18.7081	10.6071	26.8092	
120	17.5175	8.7447	26.2903	
121	16.9067	7.4597	26.3537	
122	16.4104	6.2642	26.5566	
123	14.7010	3.9096	25.6525	
124	13.6136	1.9880	25.2391	
125	12.2498	-0.1612	24.6608	
126	10.3824	-2.8480	23.6128	
127	8.2033	-5.8831	22.2897	
128	6.1506	-8.8311	21.1322	
129	3.7823	-12.1366	19.7011	
130	1.2285	-15.6724	18.1294	
131	-2.2698	-20.2005	15.6608	
132	-5.9691	-24.9803	13.0421	
133	-9.9589	-30.1046	10.1868	
134	-14.0681	-35.4056	7.2694	
135	-18.1506	-40.7407	4.4394	
136	-22.5373	-46.4442	1.3697	
137	-27.0944	-52.3864	-1.8024	
138	-31.5523	-58.3015	-4.8030	
139	-35.7192	-64.0021	-7.4364	
140	-39.5750	-69.4722	-9.6777	
141	-43.1511	-74.7481	-11.5540	
142	-47.0313	-80.4185	-13.6441	
143	-51.1369	-86.4097	-15.8642	

Generating a Multiple Time Series Plot

A graph should provide a clearer picture of the same forecasts with 95% confidence intervals. You decide to construct a multiple time series plot:

- Choose **Graph > Time Series Plot**

- Select **C9 AForecst** as the first "Y"

- Select **C10 LAForcst** as the second "Y"

- Select **C11 UAForcst** as the third "Y"

- Scroll up the "Graph variables" text box to verify that the three variables are selected

- Click the "Frame" **drop-down list arrow** and click **Axis**

- Type **ARIMA Forecasts** in the second "Label" text box and click **OK**

- Click the "Frame" **drop-down list arrow** and click **Multiple Graphs**

- Click the **Overlay graphs on the same page** option button

- Click **OK** twice

The graph is shown in Figure 15-26.

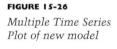
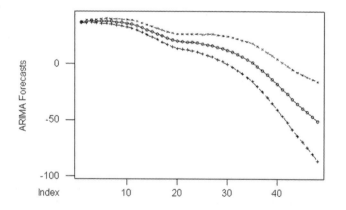

Your forecasts indicate a limited amount of seasonality. Your initial 95% forecast intervals are fairly narrow, with lengths of roughly 2 degrees. Later, the lengths increase to approximately 70 degrees. As you recall from your statistics course, forecast intervals increase in length as you forecast further into the future. You also notice that these forecasts indicate an unreasonable cooling of the river in later periods!

- In the location where you are saving your work, save the work you have done thus far in this tutorial in the project *T15*

▼ 15.7   Comparing the Two Forecasting Models ▲

The forecasts from the classical decomposition and the ARIMA (2, 0, 0) (1, 1, 0) (24) models are different. First, you observe that the initial values of the forecasts for the ARIMA model are much closer to what you would expect based on the last few observations. Second, each set of forecasts produces a distinct pattern, which you can examine by constructing another multiple time series plot with both the FORE1 and AForecst forecast variables:

- Choose **Graph > Time Series Plot**

- Replace the second "Y" text box entry with **C6 FORE1**

- Delete the entry in the third "Y" text box

- Click the "Frame" **drop-down list arrow** and click **Axis**

- Type **Forecasts from Two Models** in the second "Label" text box and click **OK**

- Click **OK** twice

Another graph appears, as shown in Figure 15-27. The ARIMA forecasts are represented by circles and the classical decomposition forecasts by pluses.

Time series plot comparing models

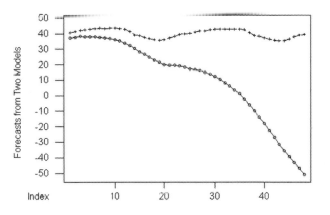

Note that the classical decomposition preserves the seasonality over the 48 forecasts much better than the ARIMA model. It also produces forecast values similar in value and magnitude to the observed data.

You wonder if there might be an even better model for this time series. Your Agency statistician suggests you might try an ARIMA (2, 1, 0) (1, 0, 0) (24) model. Other possibilities might include models using moving averages, single exponential smoothing, double exponential smoothing, or seasonal exponential smoothing. You can implement these procedures by using the Moving Average, Single Exp Smoothing, Double Exp Smoothing, and Winters' Method com-

MINITAB AT WORK

STOCK MARKET: Stock market analysts must be able to model and predict prices accurately to make wise decisions about futures trade contracts. A mathematician in South Carolina used Minitab's ARIMA capability to model the Chicago Board of Trade's wheat contract.

The mathematician assumed that the current wheat contract price is a function of previous price trends; it is this statistical dependence that time series analysts study. He used 1,054 previous wheat contract prices over a period of four years and entered that data into Minitab. Testing several different configurations led him to a successful model that used an autoregressive component of 1, a differencing component of 1, and a moving average of 2.

Once Minitab helps identify a statistically correct model, a stock market or commodities analyst can use Minitab's forecasting capability to predict future wheat contract prices and maybe even make a short-term profit.

mands, respectively, on the Time Series menu. See Minitab's Help for more information about these time series procedures.

In this tutorial, you analyzed a time series with classical decomposition and Box-Jenkins ARIMA techniques. You used a variety of plots, together with lagging and differencing transformations, to help you identify possible models. The interactive nature of Minitab makes it possible to try as many preliminary models as your patience allows before you settle on a final model and begin to make forecasts. The techniques you have seen in this tutorial provide a powerful and flexible forecasting tool that can fit virtually any such model.

- In the location where you are saving your work, save the current project *T15*, and then exit Minitab

Minitab Command Summary

▼
Minitab Command Summary
▲

This section describes the menu commands introduced in, or related to, this tutorial. To find a complete explanation of all menu commands, use Minitab's Help.

Minitab Menu Commands

Menu	Command	Description
Stat		
	Time Series	
	Time Series Plot	Produces a time series plot for one or more columns of data against time.
	Trend Analysis	Uses trend analysis to fit a particular type of trend line to a time series or to detrend a time series.
	Decomposition	Performs classical decomposition on a time series.
	Moving Average	Uses moving averages to smooth out the noise in a time series and forecast future values of the series.
	Single Exp Smoothing	Uses single exponential smoothing to smooth out the noise in a time series.
	Double Exp Smoothing	Performs Holt or Brown double exponential smoothing for a time series.
	Winters' Method	Performs Holt-Winters seasonal exponential smoothing for a time series.
	Differences	Computes the differences between values of a time series that are a specified number of rows apart and stores them in a new column.
	Lag	Shifts the data in a column down a specified number of rows and stores them in a new column.
	Autocorrelation	Computes and produces a graph of the autocorrelations of a time series.
	Partial Autocorrelation	Computes and produces a graph of the partial autocorrelations of a time series.
	Cross Correlation	Computes and produces a graph of the cross correlations between two time series.
	ARIMA	Fits a specified autoregressive integrated moving average model to time series data; also can provide forecasts.

Menu	Command	Description
Graph		
	Time Series Plot	Produces a high-resolution time series plot for one or more columns of data against time on the same axes.

Matching

Match the following terms to their definitions by placing the correct letter next to the term it describes.

_____ Multiplicative

_____ Box-Jenkins

_____ Time Series Plot

_____ Lag

_____ Number of lags

_____ AR 1

_____ Decomposition

_____ Ljung-Box

_____ Stationary

_____ Trend Analysis

a. The option that specifies the number of autocorrelations and partial autocorrelations to compute and display in the autocorrelation and partial autocorrelation plots

b. The default decomposition model

c. The command that shifts a particular column of data down a specified number of rows and saves the results in another column

d. (1, 0, 0) (0, 0, 0) (0)

e. A command found on both the Graph menu and Time Series menu

f. Another name for ARIMA

g. The command that detrends a time series

h. A time series whose mean and variance do not change with time

i. The name of the chi-square statistic you use to test the fit of an ARIMA model

j. The command that allows you to separate the time series into linear trend and seasonal components, as well as error, and provide forecasts.

True/False

Mark the following statements with a *T* or an *F*.

_____ When you use the Differences command, storing the results in a column is optional.

_____ You always produce forecasts of future events when you use the ARIMA command.

_____ A high-resolution time series plot connects sequential points with lines.

_____ Before Minitab can compute differences, you must issue the Lag command.

_____ The ARIMA output contains p-values that determine the significance of the ARIMA model's fit.

_____ An additive model is the default model type with the Decomposition command.

_____ By default the Decomposition command produces nine plots.

_____ Autocorrelation and partial autocorrelation plots always include a test of significance.

_____ MADE, MAP, and MSD are three measures you use to determine the accuracy of the fitted values in classical decomposition.

_____ Use the Trend Analysis command when there is no seasonal component to your series.

Practice Problems

Use Help or Part III, "Exploring Data," of this manual to review the contents of the data sets referred to in the following problems.

1. Open *Sp500.mtw*.

   a. Plot the Close variable.

   b. Perform a trend analysis. Is there a trend component? Is there a seasonal component? Explain your answers.

   c. Perform a classical decomposition. Is there a trend component? Is there a seasonal component? Explain your answers.

2. Open *Riverc.mtw*. Reanalyze the time series in this tutorial using an ARIMA (2, 1, 0) (1, 0, 0) (24) model. How does it compare to the two models considered in the tutorial?

.

3. Open *Riverc.mtw*. In addition to the river's temperature, the state EPA measured three other river characteristics: pH, conductivity, and dissolved oxygen content. The pH (PH) variable indicates the acidity or alkalinity of the water. Perform a time series analysis of pH. Your analysis should follow the approach used in this tutorial. That is, for each characteristic, plot the series and examine the need for a classical decomposition model, fit and forecast a classical decomposition model, obtain the autocorrelation and partial autocorrelation plots, and, finally, fit and forecast an appropriate ARIMA model.

4. Open *Riverb.mtw*. The state EPA monitored several sites in the river study. Site B was directly upriver from the plant's intake pipes. Redo the analysis described in this tutorial using Site B's data, which are stored in *Riverb.mtw*.

5. Open *Riverc2.mtw*, which contains the results of the work you performed in this tutorial. Stack the actual values of the studied time series on top of the fitted values from the classical decomposition and the fitted values from the final ARIMA model. Produce a multiple time series plot of both variables. What does this plot show you?

6. Open *Riverc.mtw*.

   a. Use the Calculator Command to obtain a column identical to C7 Lags in this tutorial.

   b. Use the Calculator Command to obtain a column identical to C8 Diff in this tutorial.

TUTORIAL 16

Data and Information Transfer

Sometimes it is necessary to transfer data to and from Minitab from other applications. Data may have been collected and stored in another package, or you may want to analyze the data with different software. Transferring the data and results also makes it possible to edit them in another application or to combine data and graphs in a professional-looking presentation. In this tutorial, you learn how to export and import data and to transfer data, Session window output, and graphs from Minitab to other popular applications such as Microsoft Excel and Microsoft Word.

Objectives

In this tutorial, you will learn how to:

- export data into text and Excel files

- import data from text and Excel files

- edit Session window text output

- export Session window text output into a Word file

- edit a Minitab high-resolution graph

- export a Minitab high-resolution graph into a Word file

▼ 16.1 Exporting Data ▲

In Tutorial 5, you were asked to write an article about major league baseball ballparks and their effect on the success of the teams that play in them. You gathered some basic data about the capacity of each park, attendance, and team performance in 1997 and when each park was built. A friend has read your article and is interested in whether a park's capacity is explained by the year it was built. You decide to work with him to answer this question. You agree to provide him with the relevant two columns in a file so that he can analyze the data and then to perform a regression analysis yourself and present the results.

To get started:

- Start **Minitab**

- Maximize the **Session window**

- If necessary, enable the **Session command language** and make the output read-only

You'll be working with the Ballpark data in the data file *Ballpark.mtw*, which is located in the Student subdirectory:

- Open the worksheet ***Ballpark.mtw***

- Review the contents of the data set by referring to Help under "data sets"

Before analyzing the Ballpark data, you should save them as a worksheet and this tutorial in a project:

- In the location where you are saving your work, save the worksheet as ***16BP***

- Also, save the work you have done thus far in this tutorial in a project named ***T16***

You decide to erase all but the two variables of interest, ParkBlt and Capacity, and move them to the first two columns:

- Choose **Manip > Erase Variables**

- Select **Team**, **League**, **Attend**, and **Pct** as the "Columns and constants to erase"

- Click **OK**

- Highlight the **C3 ParkBlt** and **C4 Capacity** columns

- Choose **Editor > Move Columns**

- Click the **Before column C1** option button

- Click **OK**

Your worksheet now contains the two variables of interest in C1 and C2, as shown in Figure 16-1.

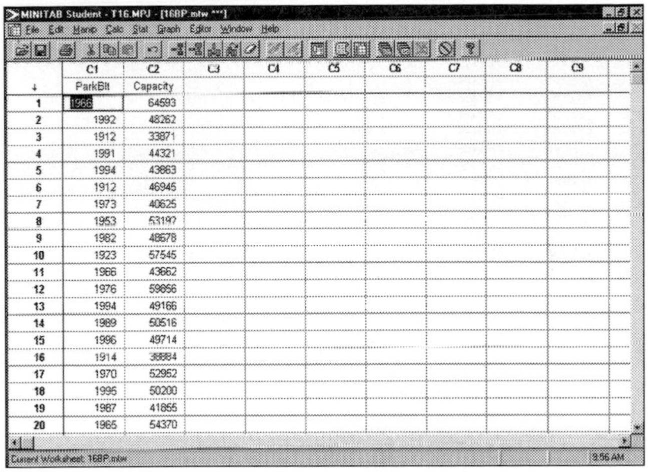

FIGURE 16-1

Data window with two variables of interest

You decide to place these data into a text file. There are several ways to do this. Probably the most practical way for all but extremely large data sets is the *copy-and-paste approach*. You use this technique to copy the data to Notepad:

- Highlight **C1** and **C2**, and click the **Copy Cells** toolbar button ▣

  To open Notepad:

- Choose **Start > Programs > Accessories > Notepad**

- Choose **Edit > Paste** and then **File > Save As**

- In the location where you are saving your work, save the data ***16BP.txt***

You have exported the names and data for the two variables into a text file. Your Notepad file should resemble Figure 16-2.

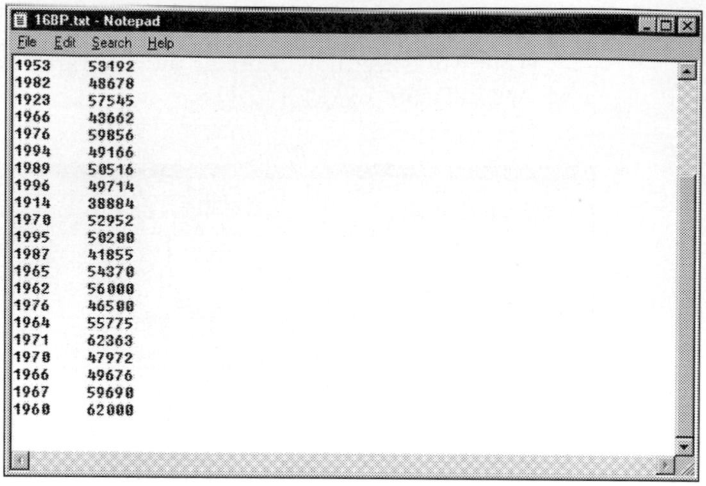

FIGURE 16-2

*Copy-and-paste Notepad
file with two variables of
interest*

- Click **File > Exit**

   The second approach to transferring these variables into a text file is by saving them as a different file type using the File > Save Current Worksheet As command:

- From **Minitab**, choose **File > Save Current Worksheet As**

- Click the "Save as type" **drop-down list arrow**

   Several options are available for saving data. You can save a file in a format compatible with previous versions of Minitab (for example, Minitab 11) or in the Minitab Portable format, a file with the *mtp* extension that can be opened by several different versions of Minitab. In addition, you can save the file in popular spreadsheet and database formats, as you will see later in this tutorial.

   Another option is the text file format, which has the *txt* extension discussed earlier in the manual. The text file format can be read by almost any application, including, in this case, the application your friend wants to use to analyze the data. To save the file in a text format:

- Choose **Text** from the drop-down list

- Click the **Options** button

   The Save Worksheet As - Options dialog box opens, as shown in Figure 16-3.

FIGURE 16-3

*The default Save
Worksheet As - Options
dialog box*

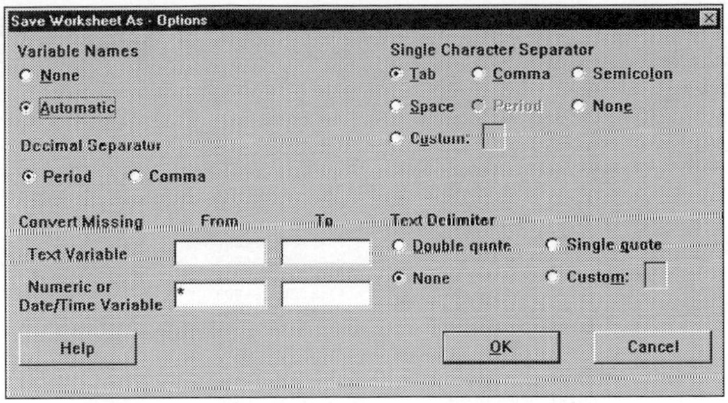

The Save Worksheet As - Options dialog box allows you to control the way Minitab saves the worksheet data in the text file. The Automatic option places the variable names in the first row of the text file, while None omits the column names and just exports the data in the columns. The Single Character Separator options determine the character that will be used to separate columns of data in the text file. A tab is commonly used for this purpose and is Minitab's default setting.

You want to use the default settings, so next you simply return to the Save Current Worksheet As dialog box, designate a name and file type for the file, and save the text file:

- Click **OK**

- In the location where you are saving your work, save the worksheet as *16BP2.txt*

- In response to the warning that "The Worksheet Description cannot be saved for this file type!" click **OK**

Now observe the result of this transfer by opening this text file in Notepad:

- Choose **Start > Programs > Accessories > Notepad**

- From the location where you are saving your work, open the file *16BP2.txt*

The opened file is shown in Figure 16-4. The data in this file have been stored in scientific notation. (For information about this format, consult Minitab's on-line Help.)

```
16bp2.txt - Notepad
File  Edit  Search  Help
ParkBlt Capacity
1.966000000e+003        6.459300000e+004
1.992000000e+003        4.826200000e+004
1.912000000e+003        3.387100000e+004
1.991000000e+003        4.432100000e+004
1.994000000e+003        4.386300000e+004
1.912000000e+003        4.694500000e+004
1.973000000e+003        4.062500000e+004
1.953000000e+003        5.319200000e+004
1.982000000e+003        4.867800000e+004
1.923000000e+003        5.754500000e+004
1.966000000e+003        4.366200000e+004
1.976000000e+003        5.985600000e+004
1.994000000e+003        4.916600000e+004
1.989000000e+003        5.051600000e+004
1.996000000e+003        4.971400000e+004
1.914000000e+003        3.888400000e+004
1.970000000e+003        5.295200000e+004
1.995000000e+003        5.020000000e+004
1.987000000e+003        4.185500000e+004
1.965000000e+003        5.437000000e+004
1.962000000e+003        5.600000000e+004
```

A third approach to export these two variables into a text file is to use the Export Special Text command. This approach allows you to save your data with a user-supplied (FORTRAN-type) format but without the corresponding variable names.

▼ **Note** You can save noncontiguous columns with the Export Special Text command but not with the Save Current Worksheet As command. ▲

You specify an appropriate format by observing that the first variable, ParkBlt, is an integer with a maximum width of 4 digits (designated by I4). The second variable, Capacity, is an integer with a maximum width of 5 digits (I5). The two variables should be separated by one blank space, designated by 1X. Thus you use the following format for this data set: I4, 1X, I5.

- Exit **Notepad**, and return to **Minitab**

- Choose **File > Other Files > Export Special Text**

- Select **ParkBlt** and **Capacity** as the "Columns to export"

- Type **I4, 1X, I5** as the "User-specified format"

The completed Export Special Text dialog box for this command is shown in Figure 16-5.

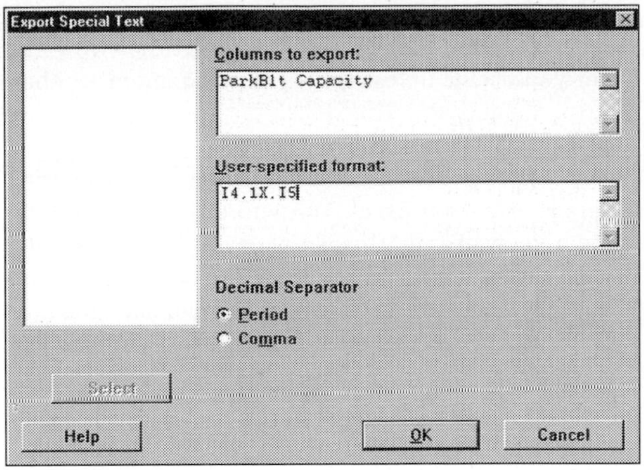

FIGURE 16-5

*The completed Export
Special Text dialog box*

Export Special Text

Columns to export:
ParkBlt Capacity

User-specified format:
I4,1X,I5

Decimal Separator
• Period
○ Comma

Select

Help   OK   Cancel

When you leave this dialog box, you are asked to specify the name, type, and location in which you wish to export these data:

- Click **OK**

- Click the "Save as type" **drop-down list arrow**, and choose **Text Files (*.txt)**

- In the location where you are saving your work, save the file as *16BP3.txt*

- Click **Save**

    Now examine the file's contents using Notepad:

- Choose **Start > Programs > Accessories > Notepad**

- From the location where you are saving your work, open the file *16BP3.txt*
    The opened file is shown in Figure 16-6.

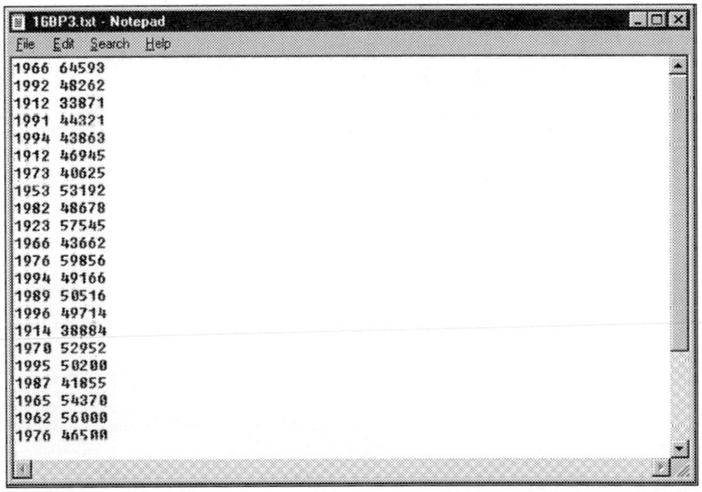

FIGURE 16-6

*Export Special Text
Notepad file with two
variables of interest*

16BP3.txt - Notepad

File Edit Search Help

```
1966 64593
1992 48262
1912 33871
1991 44321
1994 43863
1912 46945
1973 40625
1953 53192
1982 48678
1923 57545
1966 43662
1976 59856
1994 49166
1989 50516
1996 49714
1914 38884
1978 52952
1995 50200
1987 41855
1965 54370
1962 56000
1976 46500
```

Only the data from your worksheet have been transferred into this file.

You could use Notepad to insert the two variable names above the data, but you decide to leave this file and explore another approach to exporting data:

■ Choose **File** > **Exit**

One application that your friend is considering using with the Ballpark data is Microsoft Excel. You will export the 16BP data to an Excel spreadsheet, too. One way to do this is to *copy-and-paste*, similar to what you did previously. For such a small data set, this is again the most practical approach. You highlight the two variables' names and data and copy this information onto the Clipboard. Then you open Excel, paste it into an Excel spreadsheet, and save it as an Excel file.

▼ **Note** One advantage of placing data in an Excel spreadsheet is that you can use its Find and Replace commands to edit the data. Minitab does not have these commands for its Data window (although it does for the Session window). ▲

■ Click the **Current Data window** toolbar button

■ Highlight **C1** and **C2**, and click the **Copy Cells** toolbar button 🔲

■ Choose **Start** > **Programs** > **Microsoft Excel** (your menu selection for Excel may be different; ask your instructor if you need help)

■ Choose **Edit** > **Paste**

■ In the location where you are saving your work, save the file as *16BP.xls*

Your Excel spreadsheet should resemble Figure 16-7. (Your data might still be highlighted.)

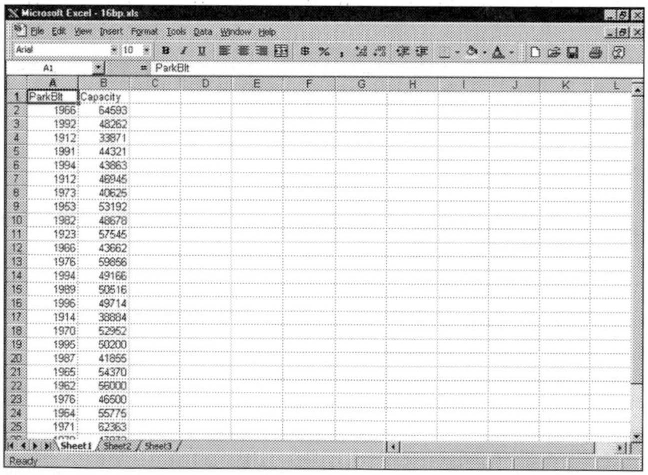

FIGURE 16-7

Copy-and-paste Excel spreadsheet with two variables of interest

■ Choose **File** > **Exit**

You have exported the names and data of the two variables into a Excel file.

Another way to export data to an Excel file is to *use the File > Save Current Worksheet As command*:

- From the Data window, choose **File > Save Current Worksheet As**

- Click the "Save as type" **drop-down list arrow**, and select **Excel**

- In the location where you are saving your work, type *16BP2.xls* as the "File name"

- Click the **Options** button

The Options dialog box, shown in Figure 16-8, is set so that the variable names will be stored in the first row of the Excel spreadsheet (Automatic) and that the standard defaults are employed. You don't need a character separator between the columns for the export because each column of data will become a column in the spreadsheet.

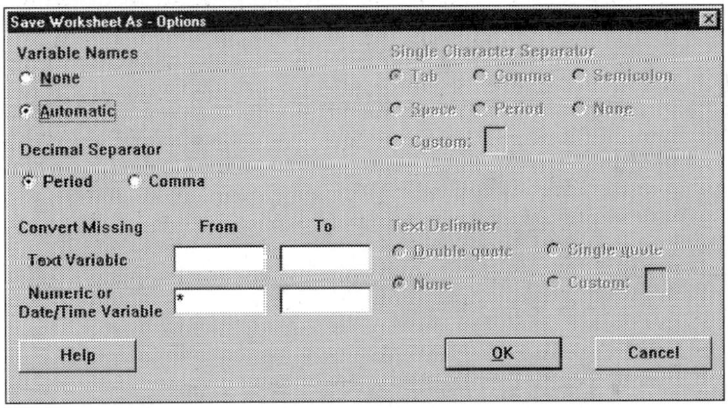

FIGURE 16-8

The default Save Worksheet As - Options dialog box

To create the Excel file:

- Click **OK**, then **Save**, and then **OK**

You have transferred your data from Minitab into both a text file and an Excel file using a variety of approaches. Your friend should now be able to analyze the two columns of data.

▼ 16.2   Importing Data ▲

One outcome of your friend's analysis is likely to be a transformed variable that you will be asked to include in your analysis of the Ballpark data. In anticipation of having to bring this variable back into Minitab, you decide to practice importing data into Minitab from both text and Excel files in a variety of ways.

One approach is to read data from a text file, in this case, the data in *16BP.txt*. These data are shown in Figure 16-2.

However, the easiest way to import such a small data set is to copy-and-paste it:

■ Choose **Start > Programs > Accessories > Notepad**

■ From the location where you are saving your work, open the file *16BP.txt*

■ Highlight the variable names and data

■ Choose **Edit > Copy**

■ Choose **File > Exit** to return to Minitab

■ Choose **File > New**, click on **Minitab Worksheet**, and click **OK** to allow the data to be placed in another worksheet

■ Click the **C1 header cell** and then the **Paste Cells** toolbar button

■ Choose **Window > Manage Worksheets**, click on **Worksheet 2 *****, and click the **Rename** button

■ Type *16BP2.mtw*, click **OK**, and click the **Done** button

Your current Minitab worksheet should resemble Figure 16-9.

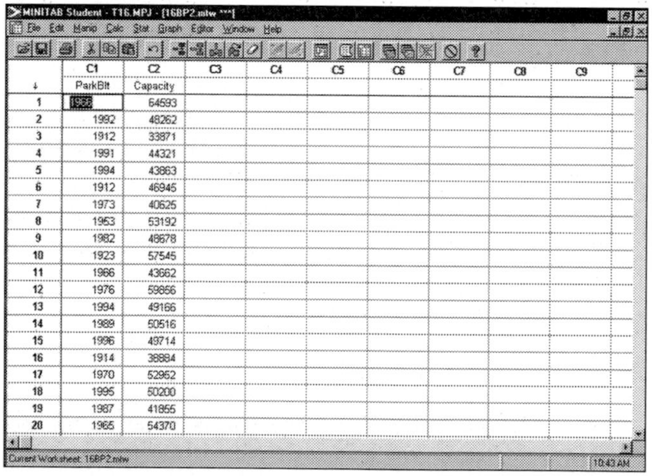

FIGURE 16-9

Copy-and-paste Minitab worksheet with two variables of interest

You have pasted the names and data of the two variables into a Minitab worksheet. Now you decide to import the same data using the Open Worksheet command:

- Choose **File > Open Worksheet**
- From the location where you are saving your work, select **Text(*.txt)** as the "Files of type"
- Select *16BP.txt* from the list of text files that appears but don't open the file yet
- Click the **Options** button

The default Open Worksheet - Options dialog box opens, as shown in Figure 16-10.

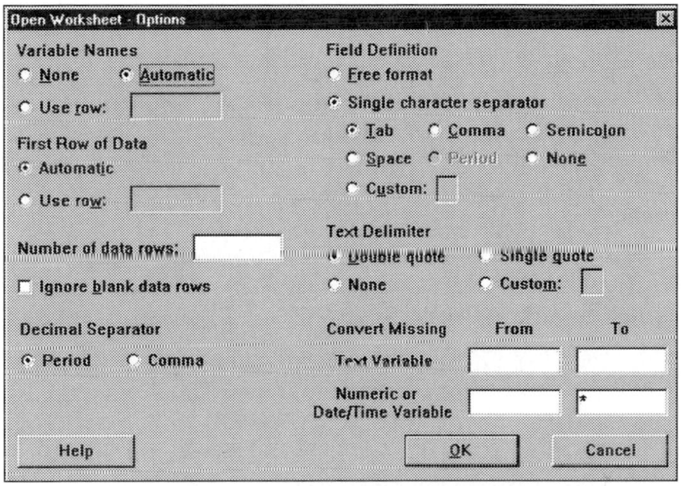

FIGURE 16-10

The default Open Worksheet - Options dialog box

The new Open Worksheet - Options dialog box shown in Figure 16-10 is similar to the Options dialog boxes presented earlier. The defaults match those you used to export your text file earlier. You can change these settings to match the way a text file has been saved so that it will open correctly in Minitab.

Return to the Open Worksheet dialog box, and open the Preview dialog box:

- Click **OK**
- Click the **Preview** button

This Preview dialog box opens, resembling Figure 16-11.

FIGURE 16-11

The Open Worksheet - Preview - 16BP.TXT dialog box

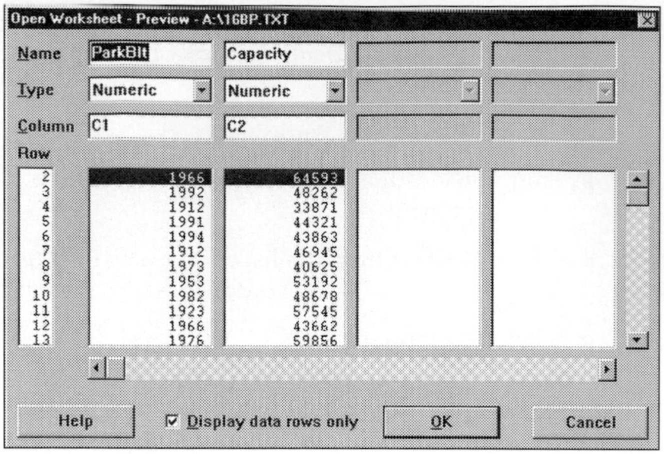

The Preview dialog box allows you to examine your data file before you open it in Minitab. It displays the name, type, and column number for each variable. In addition, you can scroll through the first 100 rows of the data set. If the data are not being read correctly, you can return to the Options dialog box and adjust the settings so that the file is read correctly. This preview can save you a lot of time when you have to import a large data set because it enables you to get it right the first time.

You now are ready to import the data:

■ Click **OK**, and click **Open**

Your data set is placed in a new worksheet *16BP.txt*.

The last approach to import data from a text file is to use the Import Special Text command. This approach is most helpful if you need to solve import problems when the text file is formatted in an unusual way. You know that you can reference Minitab's Help for more details about such formatting, but at this time, you decide to use this approach on the *16BP.txt* file, which has a relatively straightforward format.

First, you need to create a new Minitab worksheet:

■ Choose **File > New**, click on **Minitab Worksheet**, and click **OK** to open a new worksheet

Next, you enter the data needed to import the text:

■ Choose **File > Other Files > Import Special Text**

■ Type **C1** and **C2** as the "Store data in column(s)"

The completed Import Special Text dialog box is shown in Figure 16-12.

FIGURE 16-12

*The completed Import
Special Text dialog box*

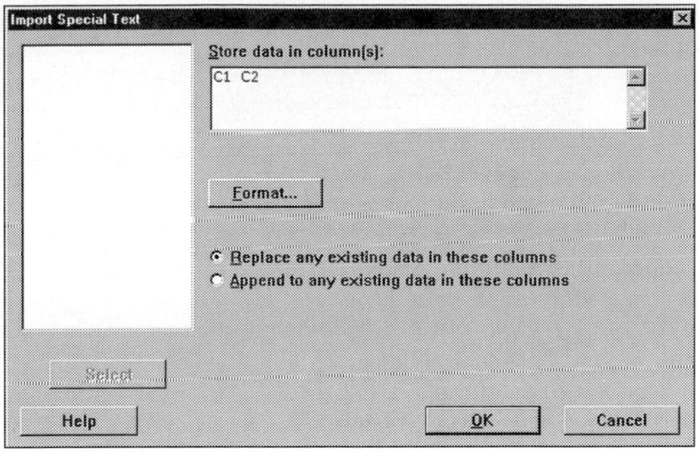

The default is to have the data replace any existing data in these columns. That is why you opened a new Minitab worksheet. There is, however, an option to append the data to any existing data in these columns. Before you import the text, examine the Format dialog box:

■ Click the **Format** button

The Format dialog box opens.

The settings in the Import Special Text - Format dialog box are not correct for the file you are about to import. The data format of the *16BP.txt* file is not blank-delimited; nor is it numeric only. This data set is tab-delimited with the variable names in the first row. So you need to alter Minitab's default:

■ Click the **Tab delimited** option button

The "Column names in first row" check box becomes active.

The completed Import Special Text - Format dialog box resembles Figure 16-13. It also allows you to set how many rows of data you will import, how many initial rows to skip, how the columns are separated, and whether a fixed format was used (as it was when you created the file with Export Special Text).

FIGURE 16-13

*The completed Import
Special Text - Format
dialog box*

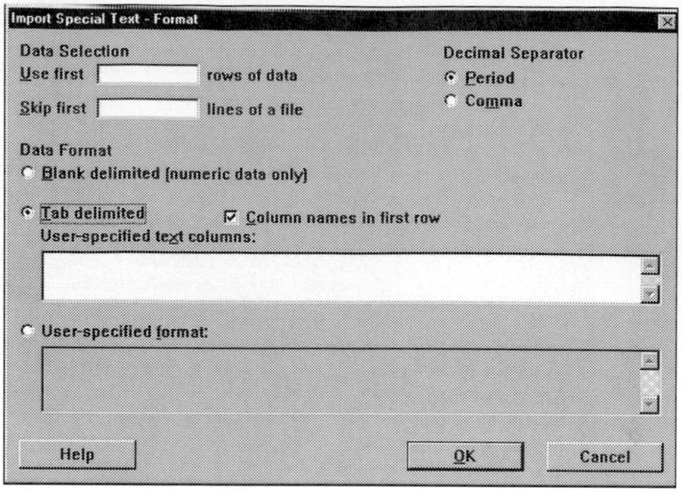

You are now ready to transfer these data into Minitab and name the corresponding worksheet:

■ Click **OK** twice

■ From the location where you are saving your work, select **Text Files (*.txt)** as the "Files of type" and *16BP.txt* as the "File name"

■ Click the **Open** button

■ Choose **Window > Manage Worksheets**, click on **Worksheet 4 ***, and click the **Rename** button

■ Type *16BPIST.mtw* click **OK**, and click the **Done** button

Now suppose that your friend has decided to store the two variables in an Excel spreadsheet such as *16BP.xls*. For such a small data set, the most practical approach is to highlight the two variables' names and data, copy this information to the Clipboard, and paste it into Minitab's data window. Recall that this was also the recommended way to import data from a text file.

An alternative way to bring data from an Excel spreadsheet into Minitab is to use the File > Open Worksheet command:

■ Choose **File > Open Worksheet**

■ Click the "Files of type" **drop-down list arrow**, and select **Excel (*.xls)**

■ From the location where you are saving your work, select *16BP.xls* as the "File name"

Before you open this Excel spreadsheet, you decide to explore the Options and Preview dialog boxes:

■ Click the **Options** button

The Open Worksheet - Options dialog box opens, as shown in Figure 16-14.

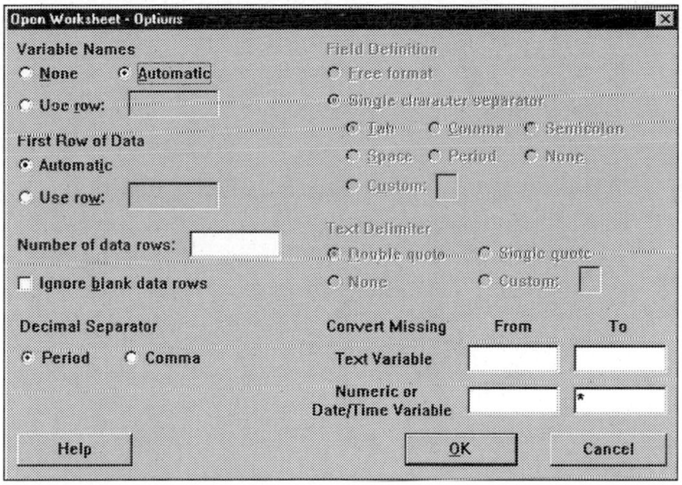

FIGURE 16-14

The default Open Worksheet - Options dialog box

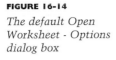

The defaults of Automatic Variable Names and First Row of Data are appropriate because your data have variable names in the first row and the first row of data is in the second row. Note that the upper-right corner is shaded because "File Definition" and "Text Delimiter" are not needed data from an Excel spreadsheet.

- Click **OK** to return to Open Worksheet dialog box

- Click the **Preview** button

Note, as previously, that the Preview dialog box allows you to confirm the name, type, and column of each variable. It also allows you to preview a portion of the data before you enter the data into Minitab.

- Click **OK**

- Click the **Open** button

The results of your efforts are shown in Figure 16-15.

FIGURE 16-15

The Excel Open Worksheet
Minitab worksheet with
two variables of interest

	C1	C2	C3	C4	C5	C6	C7	C8	C9
	ParkBlt	Capacity							
1	1968	64593							
2	1992	48262							
3	1912	33871							
4	1991	44321							
5	1994	43863							
6	1912	46945							
7	1973	40625							
8	1953	53192							
9	1982	48678							
10	1923	57545							
11	1966	43662							
12	1976	59856							
13	1994	49166							
14	1989	50516							
15	1996	49714							
16	1914	38884							
17	1970	52952							
18	1995	50200							
19	1987	41855							
20	1965	54370							

▼ 16.3   Exporting Text ▲

Now that you have learned how to export and import data between Minitab
and two common types of files, you are ready to begin your analysis.

You recognize that determining whether a park's capacity is explained by
the year it was built is a simple linear regression problem. So you want to
obtain the default Minitab regression output:

- Choose **Stat > Regression > Regression**

- Select **Capacity** as the "Response" and **ParkBlt** as the "Predictors"

- Click **OK**

Based on this regression model, you recognize that the year that a park
was built does not affect its capacity. Your decision is based on the low R-
squared value of 1.5%, the relatively high standard error of estimated value of
7634, and the high p-value of 0.531.

You believe, however, that your friend might be confused by the last
block of regression output, the Unusual Observations block. You decide to
remove this information from subsequent regression output even though the
unusual observations can provide valuable information:

- Click the **Edit Last Dialog** toolbar button ⊞

- Click the **Results** button

This dialog box allows you to control the amount of regression output
that is displayed. You change the default so that the unusual observations are
not printed (sequential sums of squares are displayed only for multiple linear
regression):

- Click the **Regression equation, table of coefficients, s, R-squared, and basic analysis of variance** option button

The completed dialog box is shown in Figure 16-16.

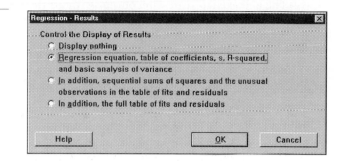

- Click **OK** twice

The abbreviated regression output is shown in Figure 16-17. Note that the Session subcommand Brief 1 indicates that you have requested abbreviated output. Brief 2 is the default, while Brief 0 indicates that you requested no display and Brief 3 indicates that you requested an expanded display.

```
MTB > Regress 'Capacity' 1 'ParkBlt';
SUBC>    Constant;
SUBC>    Brief 1.
```

Regression Analysis

The regression equation is
Capacity = - 23280 + 37.5 ParkBlt

Predictor	Coef	StDev	T	P
Constant	-23280	116220	-0.20	0.843
ParkBlt	37.48	59.07	0.63	0.531

S = 7634   R-Sq = 1.5%   R-Sq(adj) = 0.0%

Analysis of Variance

Source	DF	SS	MS	F	P
Regression	1	23468792	23468792	0.40	0.531
Residual Error	26	1515245198	58278661		
Total	27	1538713990			

You decide to make further modifications in this output so that it is more suitable for presentation to a wider audience. First, you decide to eliminate the Session command language information at the top of the output:

- Choose **Editor > Disable Command Language**
- Click the **Edit Last Dialog** toolbar button 🖼
- Click **OK**

The abbreviated regression output without the Session commands appears as shown in Figure 16-18. (The Minitab "MTB >" prompt also has disappeared from the output.)

FIGURE 16-18

The brief 1 regression output, without the Session commands

Regression Analysis

The regression equation is
Capacity = - 23280 + 37.5 ParkBlt

Predictor	Coef	StDev	T	P
Constant	-23280	116220	-0.20	0.843
ParkBlt	37.48	59.07	0.63	0.531

S = 7634   R-Sq = 1.5%   R-Sq(adj) = 0.0%

Analysis of Variance

ANOVA table

Source	DF	SS	MS	F	P
Regression	1	23468792	23468792	0.40	0.531
Residual Error	26	1515245198	58278661		
Total	27	1538713990			

Then you decide to make the Session window output editable. Recall that you have set the output to be read-only in order to prevent accidental modification of the output. Now you want to reset this option in order to remove the ANOVA table, which doesn't add to the simple linear regression output, and to provide a note about S in its place:

- Choose **Editor > Make Output Editable**
- Highlight the **ANOVA table**, and press ⌨Delete⌨
- Type **Note that S represents the standard error of estimate.**

The resulting output is shown in Figure 16-19.

FIGURE 16-19

The brief 1 regression output, without the Session commands and the ANOVA table but with a note

Regression Analysis

```
The regression equation is
Capacity = - 23280 + 37.5 ParkBlt

Predictor        Coef       StDev          T        P
Constant       -23280      116220      -0.20    0.843
ParkBlt         37.48       59.07       0.63    0.531

S = 7634         R-Sq = 1.5%       R-Sq(adj) = 0.0%

Note that S represents the standard error of estimate.
```

In addition to deleting output and adding comments when the output is editable, you can modify output by cutting, copying, and pasting text and numbers (or searching and replacing for anything in the Session window). You can also specify the font type, style, and size used for output, titles, and comments. The defaults for output are Courier font, Regular style, and 10 size, while the defaults for titles and comments are Arial, Bold, and 12 and Times New Roman, Regular, and 10, respectively.

▼ **Note** For the Minitab output to look right — for example, to ensure that the tables of numbers are properly aligned — you must select a *monospaced* font such as Courier for the code. ▲

You decide to change the title font of this output from Bold to Bold Italic:

- Highlight the title of the abbreviated output, **Regression Analysis**
- Choose **Editor > Select Fonts > Select Title Font**
- Click **Bold Italic** as the "Font style"

The sample output changes. The completed Font dialog box is shown in Figure 16-20.

FIGURE 16-20

The completed Font dialog box

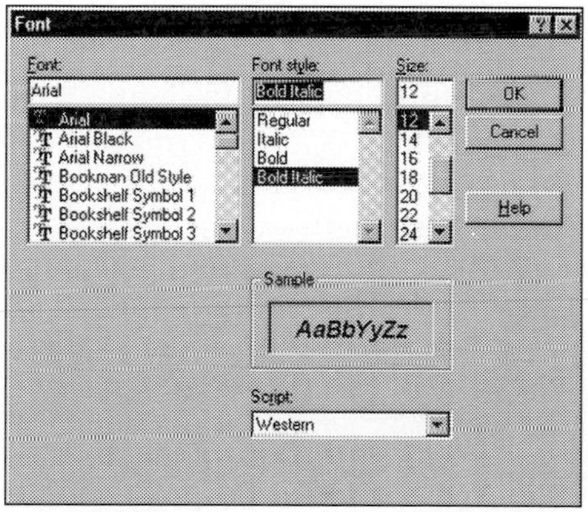

- Click **OK**

With the font change, the modified output is as shown in Figure 16-21.

Regression Analysis

```
The regression equation is
Capacity = - 23280 + 37.5 ParkBlt


Predictor        Coef       StDev          T        P
Constant       -23280      116220      -0.20    0.843
ParkBlt         37.48       59.07       0.63    0.531


S = 7634       R-Sq = 1.5%      R-Sq(adj) = 0.0%


Note that S represents the standard error of estimate.
```

You are now satisfied with your modified regression output. In your opin-ion, it is suitable for a presentation to your friend to a wider audience. It could also be included in a report prepared by a word processor. You decide to place this output into Microsoft Word. Probably the best way to do this is by copying and pasting the output:

- Highlight the **modified output**, and click the **Copy** toolbar button

- Choose **Start > Programs > Microsoft Word** (Your menu selection for Word may be different; ask your instructor if you need help.)

- Choose **Edit > Paste**

The pasted Minitab regression output within Word resembles Figure 16-22.

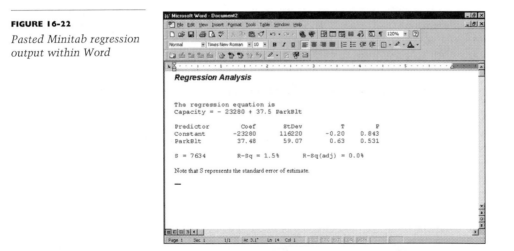

You decide to save this Word file with the name *16BP.doc*:

- Choose **File > Exit**

- Click **Yes** as the response to "Do you want to save changes to Document 1?"

- In the location where you are saving your work, save the file as ***16BP.doc***

Another way to transfer Minitab output into a word processing package such as Word is to place the output into a text file and then open it in Word. You can place the output by copying and pasting the output or by using the File > Save Session Window As command. A disadvantage of this approach is that you lose all font types, styles, and sizes.

You have now prepared your regression output in a format suitable for presentation. In the next section, you will prepare a scatter plot for a similar presentation.

▼ 16.4   Exporting Graphs ▲

In Tutorials 3 and 4, you were introduced to the following three types of Minitab graphs: core, specialty, and character. Most of the subsequent tutorials have involved the use of core and, to a degree, specialty graphs as analysis graphs. You used these high-resolution graphs to assist you in your analyses of a variety of problems. In this section, you will modify an analysis graph that is to be part of a presentation on whether the year a ballpark was built explains its capacity.

Before you produced the regression output in the previous section, you should have plotted the response variable, Capacity, against the predictor, ParkBlt. However, it is never too late to plot data to assist the understanding of an analysis. So you decide to obtain a high-resolution scatter plot of these variables:

- Choose **Graph > Plot**

- Select **Capacity** as the "Y" variable and **ParkBlt** as the "X" variable

- Click **OK**

The resulting scatter plot is shown in Figure 16-23.

FIGURE 16-23

*Default scatter plot of
Capacity against ParkBlt*

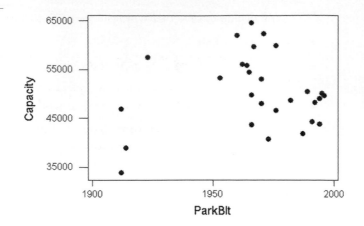

This plot clearly shows why you obtained a poor model in the previous section. There are two clusters of ballparks. The first represents parks built before 1950 and the second, parks built after 1950. In attempting to model both clusters together with a simple linear regression, you do not obtain a good model for either cluster. (Please refer to the Practice Problems for some alternative models for this situation.)

But, while this scatter plot is superb for analysis, it needs to be modified in order to be presented to others. You decide to add a title, a more informative label for the *x*-axis, and a footnote indicating the source of the data. In Minitab, this is best done by using dialog boxes, even though it is possible to edit such a graph.

First, you close the default graph, and then you make the three modifications:

■ Choose **Window > Close All Graphs**, and click **OK**

■ Click the **Edit Last Dialog** toolbar button

■ Click the "Annotation" **drop-down list arrow**, and click **Title**

■ Type **Scatter Plot of Capacity Against ParkBlt** as the "Title," and click **OK**

■ Click the "Frame" **drop-down list arrow**, and click **Axis**

■ Highlight **Auto** in the "Label 1" cell, type **Year Park Built**, and click **OK**

■ Click the "Annotation" **drop-down list arrow**, and click **Footnote**

■ Type **Source: BallPark.mtw** as the "Footnote 1"

■ Click **OK** twice

The modified graph appears as shown in Figure 16-24.

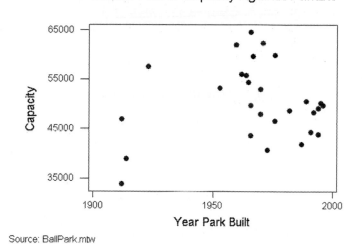

Source: BallPark.mtw

You are more satisfied with this plot but realize it can still be improved. For example, you decide to replace ParkBlt with Year Park Was Built in the Title and to do this by editing the graph.

- Choose **Editor**, and observe that there is a black circle to the left of View

- Choose **Edit** to leave View mode and enter Edit mode

When you are in Graph Edit mode, two palettes appear to the right of the plot. The Tool Palette is in the upper-right corner. It allows you to alter existing portions of the graph, add text to the graph, and draw six geometric entities on the graph. Below it is the Attribute Palette. It allows you to change the attributes of selected objects by clicking on the different tools on the palette. It operates on text, lines and edges, fills, and markers. You will use the first of these two palettes to change the title of your plot, using the Selection Tool button. This allows you to select and resize existing objects and text on a graph.

- Click the **Selection Tool** button (the one that looks like an arrow) on the Tool Palette

- Click the **Title**

A rectangle composed of eight dark squares surrounds the Title, indicating that it is highlighted (click and drag the top bar of each palette to move them if they are covering the graph).

- Double-click the **Title**

A Text dialog box appears.

- Highlight the title, and type **Capacity Against Year Park Built**

  The completed Text dialog box resembles Figure 16-25.

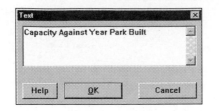

- Click **OK**
- Click anywhere in the graph to remove the eight dark squares

  The edited copy of the graph is as shown in Figure 16-26.

FIGURE 16-26

Edited scatter plot of Capacity against ParkBlt

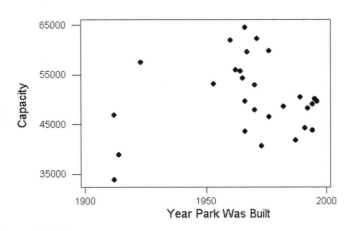

Source: BallPark.mtw

▼ **Note** This is just one of the many editing options available in Minitab. Please refer to Help for more information. ▲

You are pleased with this presentation graph and decide to name it:

- Choose **Window > Manage Graphs**
- Click on **16BP.xls: Plot 'Capacity'*'ParkBlt';**
- Click the **Rename** button

- Type **Plot of Capacity Against ParkBlt**

- Click **OK** and **Done**

Next, you want to transfer this plot into the Word document that contains your edited regression output. This is best done by using the Edit > Copy Graph command. This command copies the graph in the current window to the Clipboard but only after you have returned to View mode. Then you can paste it into Word.

- Choose **Editor > View**

The two palettes disappear.

- Choose **Edit > Copy Graph**

- Choose **Start > Programs > Microsoft Word**

- From the location where you are saving your work, open the file **16BP.doc**

- Press $\boxed{\text{Ctrl}}+\boxed{\text{End}}$ to go to the end of the current Word document

- Choose **Edit > Paste**

The exported graph appears in the Word document, as shown in Figure 16-27.

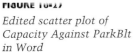

FIGURE 16-27

Edited scatter plot of Capacity Against ParkBlt in Word

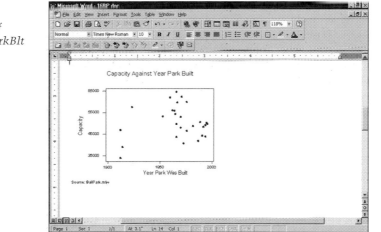

▼ **Note** From Word, you can use OLE editing to modify the Minitab graph by double-clicking on the graph. Minitab's Graph window will open in Edit mode. For information about this editing feature, see Minitab's on-line Help. ▲

To finish this tutorial:

- Save the current document *16BP.doc*, and exit Word

- Save the current project **T16**, and then exit Minitab

You have explored some of Minitab's many capabilities in this and earlier tutorials — but this is only the beginning. As you use Minitab in school or on the job, you will find many new and interesting features that show you just how powerful it is.

▼

**Minitab
Command
Summary**

▲

This section describes the menu commands introduced in, or related to, this tutorial. To find a complete explanation of menu commands, use Minitab's on-line Help.

Minitab Menu Commands

Menu	Command	Description
File		
	Open Worksheet	Copies data from a file, including non-Minitab files, such as text files and Excel spreadsheets and files from earlier releases of Minitab, including versions of Minitab on other platforms, into the current project.
	Save Current Worksheet As	Saves all of the worksheet data in a file, including non-Minitab files, such as text files and Excel spreadsheets, and files for earlier releases of Minitab.
	Other Files	
	Import Special Text	Imports data into specified columns from a text file.
	Export Special Text	Exports data in the specified columns to a text file.
Edit		
	Copy Graph	Copies the graph in the current window to the Clipboard.

Menu	Command	Description
Editor		
	Disable/Enable Command Language	Hides or shows commands in the Session window.
	Make Output Read-Only /Editable	Controls whether the Session window contents can be edited.
	Find	Allows you to locate occurrences of the text you specify. This command is functional only when the Session window is active.
	Replace	Allows you to locate or change a word, phrase, or sequence of characters (regular and special) throughout the entire Session window. This command is functional only when the Session window is active and you have the output in an Editable state.
	Select Fonts Select I/O Font Select Title Font Select Comment Font	Use this dialog box to select how text will be displayed in the Session window. This command is functional only when the Session window is active.
	View	Puts the graph in View mode. This menu item appears only when a Graph window is active.
	Edit	Puts the graph in Edit mode. This menu item appears only when a Graph window is active.
	Move Columns	Moves selected columns. This menu item apears only when a Data window is active.

Matching

Match the following terms to their definitions by placing the correct letter next to the term it describes.

_____ *xls*

_____ Find

_____ *txt*

_____ View

_____ Excel

_____ Courier

_____ Word

_____ Arial

_____ *mtp*

_____ Times New Roman

a. Functional command when the Session window is active

b. Extension associated with a Minitab file that can be opened on all Minitab platforms

c. Functional command when a Graph window is active

d. Popular word processing package

e. Default Minitab output font

f. Popular spreadsheet package

g. Default Minitab Title font

h. Extension associated with text files

i. Default Minitab comment font

j. Extension associated with an Excel spreadsheet

True/False

Mark the following statements with a *T* or an *F*.

_____ You can use the Open Worksheet command to copy data from an Excel spreadsheet.

_____ The default Minitab Title style is Bold.

_____ The Editor > Edit command appears only when a Graph window is active.

_____ You can use a copy-and-paste approach to export data from Minitab to Word.

_____ I represents an integer when you import or export special text.

_____ X represents an exceptional number when you import or export special text.

_____ The File > Save Worksheet command cannot save worksheet data in a file for an earlier release of Minitab.

_____ The View button on the Open Worksheet dialog box allows you to preview a file's contents.

_____ The Adjust button on the Open Worksheet dialog box allows you to change a file's format settings.

_____ You can find and replace data in the Data window.

Practice Problems

Use Help or Part III, "Exploring Data," of this manual to review the contents of the data sets referred to in the following problems.

1. Open *16BP.mtw*. You believe that the introduction of a quadratic term will improve the ballpark model from the case in this tutorial, and you wish to transfer the data related to this term to your friend.

   a. Use Calc > Calculator to create a column equal to the square of the ParkBlt variable. Name it ParkBlt2.

   b. Save the file as *P16BP.mtw*.

   c. Export the ParkBlt, Capacity, and ParkBlt2 variables into a Notepad text file with the same name.

   d. Export the ParkBlt, Capacity, and ParkBlt2 variables into an Excel spread-sheet file with the same name.

2. Open *16BP.txt*.

   a. Your friend believes that the introduction of a variable indicating whether a park was built after 1950 will improve the ballpark model from the case in this tutorial. He wishes to transfer the data related to this variable to you. Enter the indicator variable in *16BP.txt*. (Let 1 represent a park built after 1950.) Name it ParkBltI. Save the file as *P16BPI1.txt*.

   b. Import these data into Minitab using two different approaches. Save the later file as *P16BPI1.mtw*.

   c. Open *16BP.xls* and enter the indicator variable. (Let 1 represent a park built after 1950.) Name it ParkBltI. Save the file as *P16BPI2.xls*.

   d. Import these data into Minitab using two different approaches. Save the later file as *P16BPI2.mtw*.

3. In this problem, you will collect some data and analyze it using three applications.

   a. Collect the following data on you and your siblings, parents, and grandparents: first name, last name, and year of birth.

   b. Place these data into a Notepad file.

   c. Import these data into Minitab using two different approaches.

   d. Create a high-resolution histogram of the year of birth variable. What does this plot tell you?

   e. Edit your histogram so that it is suitable for a presentation.

   f. Obtain a paper copy of your edited histogram.

   g. Export your edited histogram into Word.

4. Open *16BP.mtw*. You believe that the introduction of either a quadratic term or a variable indicating whether a park was built after 1950 will improve the ball-park model from the case in this tutorial.

   a. Use Calc > Calculator to create a column equal to the square of the ParkBlt variable. Name it ParkBlt2. Use Calc > Make Indicator Variables to create an indicator variable. (Let 1 represent a park built after 1950.) Name it ParkBltI. Save the file as *P16BP2I.mtw*.

   b. Perform two multiple regressions on Capacity. The first with ParkBlt and ParkBlt2 as the predictors; the second with ParkBlt and ParkBltI as the predictors. Which of the two regressions do you consider to be the best? Justify your answer.

   c. Edit your Session window output to include your answer to (b).

   d. Export your edited Session window output into Word.

5. Open *MnWage.mtw*.

   a. Plot MinWage against Year. Be sure to use an appropriate stepped connection.

   b. Edit this high-resolution graph so that it is suitable for presentation.

   c. Open a paper copy of your edited plot.

   d. Export your edited plot into Word.

PART III

EXPLORING DATA

This part summarizes all files (data sets and projects) provided in the Student subdirectory of *The Student Edition of Minitab for Windows*. Some of these data sets are not used in the tutorials, so you can explore them to get additional practice.

Each file description includes the following:

- A discussion of the source of the data and its contents

- A listing of each variable's column number and name

- A count of each variable's values and, possibly, its nonmissing values

- A description of each variable

Each project description includes the following:

- A discussion of the project's origin

- An indication of the project's contents

Ads.mtw and Ads2.mtw

This data set contains information about full-page ads in two magazines in 1989, 1991, and 1993. *Ads.mtw* contains only C1–C4, while *Ads2.mtw* adds C5 AdRatio. These files are used in Tutorial 3 (Practice Problems), Tutorial 4 (Practice Problems), Tutorial 5 (Practice Problems), and Tutorial 8 (Practice Problems).

Column	Name	Count	Description
C1	Magazine	24	Magazine
C2	Year	24	Year
C3	Pages	24	Number of pages
C4	FullAds	24	Number of full-page ads
C5	AdRatio	24	Ratio of pages to the number of pages with full-page ads

Age.mtw

To determine the death age reported in a major metropolitan U. S. city, a sociology class randomly selected 37 obituaries from the city's largest newspaper. The sample consists of 18 males and 19 females. This file is used in Tutorial 7, Tutorial 7 (Practice Problems), Tutorial 8, Tutorial 9 (Practice Problems), Tutorial 13, and Tutorial 13 (Practice Problems).

Column	Name	Count	Description
C1	DAgeF	19	Age at death for females
C2	DAgeM	18	Age at death for males

Assess.mtw

Assessors base their home assessments on many different variables. This data set includes a number of those variables, plus the final value of the home and land.

Column	Name	Count	Missing	Description
C1	Land$	81	2	Assessed value of the land
C2	Total$	81	2	Assessed value of the home and the land
C3	Acreage	81	0	Number of acres
C4-T	Height	81	0	Story height (number and type of floors); 1 Story, 1 Stryatk (one story plus attic), 1.5 Story, 2 Stories, 2 Storatk (two stories plus attic), SplitLev (split level), or BiLevel
C5	1stFArea	81	0	Area of first floor, in square feet
C6-T	Exterior	81	0	Exterior condition; Excellnt (excellent), Good, or Average
C7-T	Fuel	81	0	Type of fuel; NatGas (natural gas), Electric, Oil, or Solar
C8	Rooms	81	0	Number of rooms
C9	Bedrooms	81	0	Number of bedrooms
C10	FullBath	81	0	Number of full baths
C11	HalfBath	81	0	Number of half baths
C12	Fireplace	81	0	Number of fireplaces
C13-T	Garage?	81	0	Garage or NoGarag

Baby.mtw

Thirty three month-old infants are randomly divided into five groups of six infants each. The infants in a group are repeatedly shown one of five multicolored designs A, B, C, D, or E. The median time spent watching the design is recorded for each infant. This file is used in Tutorial 9, Tutorial 9 (Practice Problems), and Tutorial 13.

Column	Name	Count	Description
C1	Time	30	Median time spent watching a design
C2-T	Design	30	One of five designs, A, B, C, D, or E

Backpain.mtw

A nurse completing her master's degree thesis collected the following data for a sample of 279 patients who had received treatment for low back pain. This file is used in Tutorial 7, Tutorial 8, and Tutorial 8 (Practice Problems).

Column	Name	Count	Description
C1-T	Gender	279	Patient's gender
C2	Age	279	Patient's age
C3	LostDays	279	Number of workdays lost as a result of low back pain
C4	Cost	279	Cost of treatment for low back pain

Ballpark.mtw

The following data relate to the 28 major league baseball teams that played in the 1997 season. This file is used in Tutorial 5, Tutorial 16, and Tutorial 16 (Practice Problems).

Column	Name	Count	Description
C1-T	Team	28	Name of the team
C2-T	League	28	American or National League
C3	ParkBlt	28	Year that the ballpark was built
C4	Capacity	28	The ballpark's official capacity
C5	Attend	28	Average home attendance for the 1997 season
C6	Pct	28	Winning percentage for the 1997 season

Candya.mtw— Candyc.mtw

Students in a statistics class opened three bags of candy containing individually wrapped snack packs of candies. They determined the average size of each individual candy (*Candya.mtw*), the weight of the packs (*Candyb.mtw*), and the proportion of candies of one color to the others in the pack and the number of defects (*Candyc.mtw*). These files are used in Tutorial 6 (Practice Problems), Tutorial 7 (Practice Problems), Tutorial 1, and Tutorial 14 (Practice Problems).

Candya.mtw

Column	Name	Count	Description
C1	Bag	285	Bag number from which the individually wrapped packs came
C2	Pack	285	Pack identification number
C3	Weights	285	Weight of the individual candies

Candyb.mtw

Column	Name	Count	Description
C1	Bag	57	Bag number from which the individually wrapped packs came
C2	Pack	57	Pack identification number
C3	Number	57	Number of candies in each pack
C4	TotWgt	57	Total weight of the pack
C5	PckWgt	57	Weight of the packaging for each pack
C6	NetWgt	57	Total weight minus the package weight

Candyc.mtw

Column	Name	Count	Description
C1	Bag	57	Bag number from which the individually wrapped packs came
C2	Pack	57	Pack identification number
C3	Number	57	Number of candies in each pack
C4	Red	57	Number of red candies
C5	Brown	57	Number of brown candies
C6	Green	57	Number of green candies
C7	Orange	57	Number of orange candies
C8	Yellow	57	Number of yellow candies
C9	Defects	57	Number of defects

Carphone.mtw

The data in this file are based on a study of the relationship between automobile accidents and the use of cellular phones. This file is used in Tutorial 12 (Practice Problems).

Column	Name	Count	Description
C1-T	Phone?	758	Whether or not the subject owned a cellular phone; Phone or NoPhone
C2-T	Accident	758	Whether or not the subject had an automobile accident during the study period; Accident or NoAccid

Chol.mtw

The values in this data set are the low-density lipoprotein (LDL) cholesterol levels for 14 adult males with high levels of cholesterol. The first value for each person was recorded after two weeks on a diet that included corn flakes and the second, after two weeks on a diet that included oat bran. This file is used in Tutorial 8 and Tutorial 13.

Column	Name	Count	Description
C1	CornFlke	14	LDL level after corn flakes
C2	OatBran	14	LDL level after oat bran

Cpi.mtw

This data set records recent percent changes in the Consumer Price Index (CPI) between 1960 and 1996.

Column	Name	Count	Description
C1	Year	37	Year
C2	CPIChnge	37	Percent change in the Consumer Price Index (CPI)

Crimes.mtw and Crimeu.mtw

This data set contains 1991 violent crime rates for the 50 states and the District of Columbia by U. S. Census division and region. *Crimes.mtw* is stacked. *Crimeu.mtw* contains the same data, unstacked by region (northeast, north central, south, and west). These files are used in Tutorial 5 (Practice Problems), Tutorial 6 (Practice Problems), Tutorial 9 (Practice Problems), and Tutorial 11 (Practice Problems).

Crimes.mtw

Column	Name	Count	Description
C1-T	State	51	State
C2	Division	51	Division (a subdivision of region)
C3	Region	51	Region (the country is divided into four regions)
C4	CrimeRte	51	Violent crime rate per 100,000 people

Crimeu.mtw

Column	Name	Count	Description
C1-T	NEState	9	Northeastern state
C2	NECrime	9	Northeastern crime rate
C3-T	NCState	12	North central state
C4	NCCrime	12	North central crime rate
C5-T	SState	17	Southern state
C6	SCrime	17	Southern crime rate
C7-T	WState	13	Western state
C8	WCrime	13	Western crime rate

Drive.mtw

This data set contains information about a driver education class.

Column	Name	Count	Missing	Description
C1	Max	85	2	Maximum number of students in a class
C2	Init	85	2	Initial number of students who signed up
C3	Dropped	85	2	Number of students who dropped
C4	Replaced	85	2	Number of students who were replaced
C5	Finished	85	2	Number of students who finished the course
C6-T	Type	85	0	Type of class; Auto (automobile) or MCycle (motorcycle)
C7	Order	85	0	Order in which classes were held

Election.mtw

For every presidential election from 1868 to 1996, this data set contains the percentage of the vote won by both the Republican and the Democratic candidates. This file is used in Tutorial 4, Tutorial 4 (Practice Problems), and Tutorial 13 (Practice Problems).

Column	Name	Count	Description
C1	Year	33	Election year
C2	Rep%	33	Percentage of the vote won by the Republican candidate
C3	Dem%	33	Percentage of the vote won by the Democratic candidate

Fball.mtw

The data in *Fball.mtw* come from a newspaper article listing the salaries of all players on a professional football team prior to the start of the 1991 season.

Column	Name	Count	Missing	Description
C1-T	Position	50	0	The position of the player
C2	Expernce	50	0	The years of experience of the player
C3	1990Sal	50	3	The 1990 salary of the player

Column	Name	Count	Missing	Description
C4	1991Sal	50	11	The 1991 salary of the player
C5	1992Sal	50	31	The 1992 salary of the player
C6	Bonus	50	33	The signing bonus the player received

▼

Fja.mtw

▲

A statistician named Frank Anscombe developed these data to illustrate the need for regression diagnostics. When you regress combinations of some of these columns, you get the same regression line. However, if you plot the data, each plot is strikingly different. These results show why you can't depend upon traditional measures for regression. This file is used in Tutorial 11.

Column	Name	Count	Description
C1	X	11	Predictor variable
C2	Y1	11	Response variable
C3	Y2	11	Response variable
C4	Y3	11	Response variable
C5	X4	11	Predictor variable
C6	Y4	11	Response variable

▼

Force.mtw

▲

In an experiment involving 12 undergraduate women, a dynamometer was used to record the strength of the hamstring when the knee is flexed at 5 degrees and then at 45 degrees to the horizontal. The data in C1 and C2 are the force (in pounds) produced in each case. This file is used in Tutorial 13 (Practice Problems).

Column	Name	Count	Description
C1	Force5	12	Force (in pounds) produced by knee flexed at 5 degrees
C2	Force45	12	Force (in pounds) produced by knee flexed at 45 degrees

▼ Gas.mtw ▲

This data set contains a driver's record of gas usage for maintenance records.

Column	Name	Count	Description
C1	GasDay	180	Day on which driver purchased gas (the first is coded as 0)
C2	Mileage	180	Mileage at the time of gas purchase
C3	Gallons	180	Number of gallons purchased
C4	Cost	180	Cost in dollars of gas purchased
C5	MPG	180	Miles per gallon
C6-T	Locale	180	Locale of the gas station; Local or NonLocal

▼ Golf.mtw ▲

A college student, who is also an avid golfer, kept track of his golf scores in the fall of 1991. Based on playing nine holes, he recorded his score, how many greens he hit in regulation, and how many pars or better he made for the nine holes.

Column	Name	Count	Description
C1	Score	22	The score for nine holes of golf
C2	Regltn	22	The number of greens made in the regulation number of strokes
C3	Pars	22	The number of pars or better (birdies, eagles, and so on) made in the nine holes

▼ Height.mtw ▲

A professor in the physiology department of a medical school collected data on the self-reported heights of 60 females in an introductory physiology class. Students were asked to provide their heights (in inches) on the first day of class. This file is used in Tutorial 6.

Column	Name	Count	Description
C1	ID	60	The student's ID number
C2	Heights	60	The self-reported heights, in inches

Homes.mtw

This data set contains real estate data on 150 randomly selected homes. This file is used in Tutorial 4 (Practice Problems), Tutorial 7, Tutorial 8, Tutorial 8 (Practice Problems), Tutorial 10 (Practice Problems), Tutorial 11 (Practice Problems), and Tutorial 13 (Practice Problems).

Column	Name	Count	Description
C1	Price	150	Price
C2	Area	150	Area, in square feet
C3	Acres	150	Acres
C4	Rooms	150	Number of rooms
C5	Baths	150	Number of baths

Jeansa.mtw— Jeansc.mtw and Jeans.mtw

A marketing research firm collected data on individuals who last bought jeans from four major stores. The data are divided into three files. For each file, the value 999 indicates a missing value. *Jeans.mtw* contains all of the data in one file. The number of observations in this file exceeds the maximum number of observations for *The Student Edition of Minitab for Windows*. Thus to analyze the data in this file, you must erase at least one variable immediately after opening this file. These files are used in Tutorial 12.

Jeansa.mtw

Column	Name	Count	Description
C1-T	Size	394	Jean size; Petite, Junior, Misses, or HalfLarg (half sizes or larger sizes)
C2-T	Age	394	Age group; 10to24, 25to34, 35to44, 45to54, 55to64, or 65plus
C3-T	Marital	394	Marital status; Single, DivorSep (divorced or separated), Widowed, Married, or LivAsMar (living as married)
C4	Earners	394	Number of full-time earners

Jeansb.mtw

Column	Name	Count	Description
C5-T	Employ	394	Employment status; FullTime (full-time: 30 or more hours a week), PartTime (part-time: fewer than 30 hours a week), or NotEmpl (not employed)
C6-T	Educ	394	Education completed; GradeSch (grade school or less), SomeHigh (some high school), HighSchl (high school graduate), BusNurTe (business, nursing, or technical school), SomeColl (some college), CollGrad (college graduate), or GradDeg (graduate degree)
C7-T	Income	394	Total yearly pretax income; Under15 (under $15,000), 15to24.9 ($15,000 to $24,999), 25to34.9 ($25,000 to $34,999), 35to49.9 ($35,000 to $49,999), 50to74.9 ($50,000 to $74,999), 75to99.9 ($75,000 to $99,999), or 100plus ($100,000 or more)
C8	JeanShop	394	Identification number of store where last pair of jeans was purchased

Jeansc.mtw

Column	Name	Count	Description
C9	PayJean	394	Price in dollars of last pair of jeans purchased
C10	Fashion	394	*I consider myself to be fashion/style conscious;* DDagree (definitely disagree), Dagree (disagree), SDagree (somewhat disagree), SAgree (somewhat agree), Agree, DAgree (definitely agree)
C11	Cost	394	*I'm very cost conscious when it comes to clothes;* DDagree (definitely disagree), Dagree (disagree), SDagree (somewhat disagree), SAgree (somewhat agree), Agree, DAgree (definitely agree)
C12	Interest	394	*I take more interest in my wardrobe than most women I know;* DDagree (definitely disagree), Dagree (disagree), SDagree (somewhat disagree), SAgree (somewhat agree), Agree, DAgree (definitely agree)

Column	Name	Count	Description
C13	Spend	394	*I spend a lot of money on clothes and (acces sories)*; DDagree (definitcly disagree), Dagree (disagree), SDagree (somewhat disagree), SAgree (somewhat agree), Agree, DAgree (definitely agree)

Lakes.mtw

An extensive study was conducted to determine if the characteristics of lakes in Wisconsin had changed over the last 60 years. Historical data were obtained on 149 lakes between 1925 and 1931. Similar data were obtained on these same lakes between 1979 and 1983.

The collected information included the physical characteristics of the lake, such as maximum depth and surface area, as well as the type of lake. Other variables reported the total area of the lake's watershed and the percentage of the lake that was bog. The data also indicated the amount of development as represented by the number of permanent dwellings within 100 meters of the shore.

In addition, several water quality variables were measured. These included the pH, alkalinity, conductivity, and calcium. Since measurement techniques changed from 1925 to 1979, the data were adjusted to be comparable (the stored data represent the adjusted values).

Column	Name	Count	Missing	Description
C1	LakeID	149	0	An identification number assigned to the lake
C2-T	Type	149	0	The type of lake; seepage, drained, drainage, and spring
C3	Depth	149	0	Maximum lake depth in meters
C4	Area	149	0	Lake surface area in hectares
C5	WSArea	149	0	Watershed area in hectares
C6	%Bog	149	1	Percentage of lake that is bog
C7	DwHist	149	1	Number of lake shore dwellings, circa 1930
C8	DwCurnt	149	0	Number of lake shore dwellings, circa 1980
C9	pHHist	149	0	Historical pH reading
C10	pHCurnt	149	0	Current pH reading
C11	CondHst	149	0	Historical conductivity reading

Column	Name	Count	Missing	Description
C12	CondCur	149	0	Current conductivity reading
C13	AlkHist	149	0	Historical alkalinity reading
C14	AlkCurn	149	0	Current alkalinity reading
C15	CaHist	149	33	Historical calcium reading
C16	CaCurnt	149	0	Current calcium reading

▼ Lang.mtw ▲

One way of measuring people's attitudes toward others is to ask them to evaluate speakers of other languages. However, if the speakers they rate are different, one does not know whether to attribute variability in ratings to the speaker or to the language. To control this factor, Wallace Lambert at McGill University pioneered the *matched guise technique.* Subjects listen to a number of language segments and then rate certain qualities of the speaker, such as friendliness, honesty, and trustworthiness. However, three of the segments they hear are actually the same speaker, using different language "guises." Differences in ratings of that speaker, then, can be attributed to attitudes toward the particular languages and those who speak them.

In the *Lang.mtw* data set, students at an U. S. high school rated five language segments for various qualities on a 1-to-5 bipolar rating scale. (A prior survey asked students which qualities they considered most important for friendship.)

Segment A was the language of a recently arrived immigrant group, Segment C was English, Segment E was French, and Segments B and D were "distracter" languages, which were not included in the data set. Students also filled out questionnaires with their gender, the length of time they lived in the area, and background information about their experiences with other languages.

The immigrant language used was the language of a rather large, recently arrived immigrant population. This study attempted to determine if high school–age students held significantly negative attitudes toward speakers of the immigrants' language. It was predicted that they would have positive attitudes toward English and French.

All questions were answered on a 1-to-5 bipolar rating scale, with 1 the most negative rating (inconsiderate, unfriendly, and so on) and 5 the most positive (considerate, friendly, and so on).

Column	Name	Count	Missing	Description
C1	ImmCons	59	0	Immigrant language: *Is the person considerate?* (1 = inconsiderate, 2 = somewhat inconsiderate, 3 = neutral, 4 = somewhat considerate, 5 = considerate)
C2	ImmFrnd	59	0	Immigrant language: *Is the person friendly?*

Column	Name	Count	Missing	Description
C3	ImmTrst	59	0	Immigrant language: *Is the person trustworthy?*
C4	ImmHon	59	0	Immigrant language: *Is the person honest?*
C5	ImmHlp	59	2	Immigrant language: *Is the person helpful?*
C6	ImmUnd	59	1	Immigrant language: *Is the person understanding?*
C7	ImmResp	59	0	Immigrant language: *Is the person responsible?*
C8-T	Imm?	59	0	*Can you identify this language?* yes or no
C9	EngCons	59	0	English language: *Is the person considerate?*
C10	EngFrnd	59	0	English language: *Is the person friendly?*
C11	EngTrst	59	0	English language: *Is the person trustworthy?*
C12	EngHon	59	0	English language: *Is the person honest?*
C13	EngHlp	59	0	English language: *Is the person helpful?*
C14	EngUnd	59	1	English language: *Is the person understanding?*
C15	EngResp	59	0	English language: *Is the person responsible?*
C16-T	Eng?	59	0	*Can you identify this language?* yes or no
C17	FrnCons	59	1	French language: *Is the person considerate?*
C18	FrnFrnd	59	1	French language: *Is the person friendly?*
C19	FrnTrst	59	1	French language: *Is the person trustworthy?*
C20	FrnHon	59	1	French language: *Is the person honest?*
C21	FrnHlp	59	1	French language: *Is the person helpful?*
C22	FrnUnd	59	2	French language: *Is the person understanding?*
C23	FrnResp	59	1	French language: *Is the person responsible?*
C24-T	Frn?	59	0	*Can you identify this language?* yes or no
C25-T	English?	59	0	*Is English your native language?* yes or no
C26-T	State?	59	0	*Have you lived in this state all of your life?* yes or no
C27-T	LangTime	59	14	*For how many years have you studied a language at school?* 0 ("None"), 0 to 1 years ("0to1yrs"), 1 to 2 years ("1to2yrs"), and 2 or more years ("2+yrs") years
C28-T	2ndLang	59	14	*How, if at all, are you exposed to a language other than English in your home?* NotAtAll (not exposed at all), Speak1 (speak one), Hear1NoU (hear one but do not understand), or Hear1Und (hear one and do understand)

Column	Name	Count	Missing	Description
C29-T	T2ndLang	59	22	*How long have you been exposed to a language other than English in your home?* 0yrs, 1to7yrs, or 8to15yrs
C30-T	Gender	59	17	The student's gender

▼
Lotto.mtw
▲

A state lotto randomly selects six numbers from the numbers 1 through 47. There are two drawings per week. To check whether the drawings are random, a student monitored the game for several years. Based on information provided by the local newspaper, the student determined the number of times each of the numbers 1 through 47 had been drawn over the course of the past three years, for a total of 312 drawings. This file is used in Tutorial 12 (Practice Problems).

Column	Name	Count	Description
C1	Observed	47	The observed number of times each number has been drawn

▼
Marathon.mtw
▲

This data set contains the winning times for the men and for the women running in the Boston Marathon.

Column	Name	Count	Description
C1	YearM	100	Years in which men raced
C2	TimesM	100	The winning times for men
C3	YearW	26	Years in which women raced
C4	TimesW	26	The winning times for women

▼
Marks.mtw
▲

This data set is the grade summary for a social studies class in a secondary school. Three test scores have been recorded for the 24 students in the class. This file is used in Tutorial 2, Tutorial 3 (Practice Problems), and Tutorial 13 (Practice Problems).

Column	Name	Count	Description
C1-T	LastName	24	Student's last name
C2-T	First	24	Student's first name
C3	Test1	24	The score (out of 100) on the first test
C4	Test2	24	The score (out of 100) on the second test
C5	Test3	24	The score (out of 100) on the third test

Masscoll.mtw and Masscol2.mtw

The data in *Masscoll.mtw* are various statistics related to the 56 four-year colleges in Massachusetts for 1995. *Masscol2.mtw* includes all of these variables plus the variables C13 FITS1, C14 RESI1, C15 SRES1, and C16 VSAT**2. These files are used in Tutorial 10 and Tutorial 11 (through *T10.mpj*).

Column	Name	Count	Missing	Description
C1-T	School	56	0	Name of college
C2-T	PubPriv	56	0	Whether the college is public or private
C3	%Top10%	56	7	Percentage of the freshman class that were in the top 10% of their high school graduating class
C4	%Top25%	56	5	Percentage of the freshman class that were in the top 25% of their high school graduating class
C5	%WhoGrad	56	4	Percentage of freshman class that graduate
C6	MSAT	56	3	Median math SAT score for the freshman class
C7	VSAT	56	3	Median verbal SAT score for the freshman class
C8	CSAT	56	3	Median combined math and verbal SAT scores for the freshman class
C9	%Accept	56	0	Percentage of applicants that was accepted by the school

Column	Name	Count	Missing	Description
C10	%Enroll	56	0	Percentage of accepted applicants that enroll
C11	SFRatio	56	0	Student faculty ratio
C12	Tuition	56	0	Out-of-state tuition

▼
Mnwage.mtw
▲

This data set contains information about the minimum wage from 1950 to 1997. This file is used in Tutorial 4 (Practice Problems), Tutorial 5 (Practice Problems), Tutorial 10 (Practice Problems), Tutorial 11 (Practice Problems), and Tutorial 16 (Pratice Problems).

Column	Name	Count	Description
C1	Year	48	Year
C2	MinWage	48	Minimum wage, in dollars

▼
Mort.mtw
▲

This data set contains the mortgage interest rates of six lenders in December 1992 and December 1993.

Column	Name	Count	Description
C1	30Yr1992	6	Interest rate of a 30-year mortgage in 1992
C2	30Yr1993	6	Interest rate of a 30-year mortgage in 1993

▼
Movies.mtw
▲

A student in an economics class collected the following data on 32 movies released in the period 1997–1998.

Column	Name	Count	Description
C1-T	Movie	32	Title of the movie
C2	Opening	32	Gross receipts for the weekend after the movie was released (in millions of dollars)
C3	Budget	32	The total budget for the movie (in millions of dollars)
C4-T	Star?	32	Whether or not the movie has a superstar; Star or NoStar
C5-T	Summer?	32	Whether or not the movie was released in the summer; Summer or NoSummer

Music.mtw

Music.mtw contains a randomly simulated sample of 1,000 music sales in which the genre numbers and names of music (Country, Jazz, and so on) are recorded based on the probabilities of each genre's being selected. This file is used in Getting Started Chapter 3, Tutorial 6 (the data are used, but not the file), and Tutorial 12.

Column	Name	Count	Description
C1	GenreN	9	Numerical designation (1, 2, . . . , 9) of the musical genre
C2-T	Genre	9	Name of the genre
C3	Prob	9	The probability of each genre of music being selected
C4	Sample	1000	The sample of 1,000 genre numbers
C5-T	TxSample	1000	The sample of 1,000 genre names

Niel.mtw

Each year the Nielsen company does an extensive survey of TV-viewing habits of the U. S. population. Many of the surveys are conducted by age and gender because sponsors are interested in how these variables relate to the programs people watch. (For example, see the VPVH data set.)

Column	Name	Count	Missing	Description
C1	Year	25	0	Year
C2	TVStns	25	8	The number of TV stations, both VHF and UHF
C3	NumTVs	25	8	The number of U. S. house holds with TVs, in thousands
C4	Cable	25	11	The number of operating cable stations
C5	Subscbrs	25	9	The number of cable sub scribers, in thousands
C6	Time	25	5	The average number of hours of viewing per TV household per week

Nonprt.mtw and Nonprt2.mtw

This data set contains information about the average number of nonprint displays present on easily seen pages of three different types of newspapers. The easily seen pages are the top half of a full-sized paper's sections and the front and back pages of a tabloid. (The section sizes are all the same.) Nonprt contains just C1 and C2, while Nonprt2 contains an additional column, C3 Maxsize. These files are used in Tutorial 9 (Practice Problems).

Column	Name	Count	Description
C1	AveSize	10	The average size of nonprint displays, in square inches
C2-T	Paper	10	The paper from which the displays come; RegNews (regional newspaper), LocalTab (local tabloid), or NatlNews (national newspaper)
C3	MaxSize	10	Maximum ad size

Note.mtw

This data set contains information about a selection of notebook (portable) computers that were available in 1994.

Column	Name	Count	Missing	Description
C1-T	Chip	24	0	Chip type; DX, SL, or SX
C2	Speed	24	0	Speed, in megahertz
C3	Recharge	24	0	Minutes before battery needs recharging
C4	RAM	24	2	Maximum RAM, in megabytes
C5-T	Monitor	24	0	Monochrome ("Mono") or Color monitor
C6-T	PDevice	24	0	Pointing device; Mouse or Track Ball ("TrkBall")
C7-T	800Num	24	0	Availability of an 800 telephone number; Yes or No
C8	Price	24	0	Price

Note98.mtw

This data set contains information about a selection of notebook (portable) computers available in 1998. This file is used in Tutorial 1 (Practice Problems), Tutorial 2 (Practice Problems), and Tutorial 12 (Practice Problems).

Column	Name	Count	Missing	Description
C1-T	ChipSet	29	0	Chip set
C2	Speed	29	0	Processor speed, in MHz
C3	ChargeOn	29	0	Rated charge time while on, in hours
C4	RAM	29	0	Maximum system RAM, in MB
C5-T	Graphics	29	0	Graphics memory type
C6-T	IPDevice	29	0	Integrated pointing device
C7-T	Support	29	0	Seven day, 24-hour live technical support
C8	Price	29	0	Price

Pay.mtw and Pay2.mtw

This data set contains the salary information of the 11 salaried employees in the sales department of the Temco company. This data set is part of the larger data set *Temco.mtw*, which contains the salary information of all employees in four departments at Temco. *Pay.mtw* contains the first seven variables; *Pay2.mtw* contains these variables (except for C5 Age), plus two more—C8 SalMale (the six male salaries) and C9 SalFem (the five female salaries)—in addition to incorporating the changes made to these data in Tutorial 1. These files are used in Tutorial 1, Tutorial 3, Tutorial 4 (through *T3.mpj*), Tutorial 4 (Practice Problems), Tutorial 7 (Practice Problems), and Tutorial 13 (Practice Problems).

Column	Name	Count	Description
C1	Salary	10	The salary of an employee in the sales department
C2	YrsEm	10	The number of years employed at Temco
C3	PriorYr	10	The number of prior years' experience
C4	Educ	10	Years of education after high school
C5	Age	10	Current age
C6	ID	10	The company identification number for the employee
C7-T	Gender	10	The gender of the employee

Pizza.mtw

This data set contains campus newspaper ratings for 13 pizza shops for two fall semesters. This file is used in Tutorial 1 (the data are used in practice problems, but not the file) and Tutorial 2 (Practice Problems).

Column	Name	Count	Missing	Description
C1-T	Pizzeria	13	0	Pizza shop
C2-T	Type	13	0	Local or Chain
C3	FallRank	13	0	Ranking (first is best)
C4	FallScor	13	0	Score (highest is best)
C5	LSpring	13	3	Scores from previous spring
C6	LFall	13	3	Ranking from previous fall

Proces.mtw

The process of creating, administering, and tallying the student government surveys whose results are in the file *Prof.mtw* involves a number of causes that could contribute to process problems. This file contains six columns corresponding to the six variables used to create a Minitab Cause-and-Effect diagram. This file is used in Tutorial 14.

Column	Name	Count	Description
C1-T	Men	3	Potential process problems caused by people
C2-T	Machines	5	Potential process problems caused by machines
C3-T	Materials	2	Potential process problems caused by materials
C4-T	Methods	2	Potential process problems caused by methods
C5-T	Measurement	2	Potential process problems caused by the measuring process
C6-T	Environment	3	Potential process problems caused by the environment

Prof.mtw

The student government randomly distributed surveys to 15 students in each of 146 sections in a variety of disciplines. The survey asked students to evaluate the course and the instructor. Each participating section received 15 surveys. Some sections returned all 15 surveys, whereas others returned fewer. The results for each section were averaged for use in this worksheet. There are nine columns and 146 rows. Each row presents a summary of the information taken from the 1 to 15 surveys returned by a particular class. This file is used in Getting Started Chapter 4, Tutorial 5 (Practice Problems), Tutorial 7 (Practice Problems), Tutorial 8 (Practice Problems), and Tutorial 12 (Practice Problems).

Column	Name	Count	Missing	Description
C1-T	Dept	146	0	The academic department of the course to which the 15 surveys were distributed
C2	Number	146	0	The course number
C3	Interest	146	0	The section average of the surveyed students' responses to *The course stimulated your interest in this area*; 0 = strongly disagree, 1 = disagree, 2 = neutral, 3 = agree, and 4 = strongly agree
C4	Manner	146	0	The section average of the surveyed students' responses to *The instructor presented course material in an effective manner*; 0 = strongly disagree, 1 = disagree, 2 = neutral, 3 = agree, and 4 = strongly agree
C5	Course	146	0	The section average of the surveyed students' responses to *Overall, I would rate this course as...*; 0 = poor, 1 = below average, 2 = average, 3 = above average, and 4 = excellent
C6	Instrucr	146	0	The section average of the surveyed students' responses to the statement: *Overall, I would rate this instructor as...*; 0 = poor, 1 = below average, 2 = average, 3 = above average, and 4 = excellent
C7	Responds	146	0	The number of completed surveys returned out of the 15 surveys distributed
C8	Size	146	16	The number of students in the section
C9-T	Year	146	0	The level of the course; Freshman, Soph (sophomore), Junior, or Senior

Pubs.mtw

This data set includes information about a series of publications over time. This file is used in Tutorial 14 (Practice Problems).

Column	Name	Count	Description
C1	Volume	84	Volume of publication
C2	Number	84	Number of publication within the volume
C3	Pages	84	Number of pages
C4	Weight	84	Weight, in grams
C5-T	Cover	84	Cover type; PlnBrown (plain brown), GlsyBrwn (glossy brown), PlnGreen (plain green), or GlsyGren (glossy green)
C6-T	Binder	84	Binding status; Binder and NoBinder

Pulsea.mtw

Ninety-two students in a statistics class performed the following experiment. Each student recorded his or her pulse rate and then flipped a coin. If the coin came up heads, the student ran in place for a minute. Otherwise, the student did not. The student then took his or her pulse rate again. The pulse rates and related information about the students are recorded in the following chart. This file is used in Tutorial 1 (Practice Problems), Tutorial 2 (Practice Problems), Tutorial 3 (Practice Problems), Tutorial 4 (Practice Problems), Tutorial 5 (Practice Problems), Tutorial 7 (Practice Problems), Tutorial 8 (Practice Problems), Tutorial 10 (Practice Problems), and Tutorial 12 (Practice Problems).

Column	Name	Count	Missing	Description
C1	Pulse1	92	0	Initial pulse rate
C2	Pulse2	92	0	Second pulse rate
C3-T	Ran	92	0	Whether or not the student ran in place; Ran or Still
C4-T	Smokes	92	0	Smoking status; Smoke or NonSmoke
C5-T	Gender	92	0	Student's gender
C6	Height	92	0	Height in inches
C7	Weight	92	0	Weight in pounds
C8	Activity	92	1	Usual level of activity; Slight, Moderate, or ALot

Radlev.mtw

A television station in southwestern Ohio did a survey to determine the radon levels in homes in its viewing area. Questionnaires and radon detection kits were sent to all viewers who requested them. This file includes the results of only certain questions from the full questionnaire. This file is used in Tutorial 2 (Practice Problems).

Column	Name	Count	Missing	Description
C1	Radon	543	30	Radon measurement, in pico curies
C2	Age	543	60	Age of the house, in years
C3	Days	543	65	Number of days the kit was exposed
C4-T	Insulate	543	9	Amount of insulation in the house; Poor, Average, Excellnt (Excellent), or DontKnow
C5-T	Sump?	543	17	Was the sample taken near a sump pump? yes or no

Ratio.mtw

This data set contains ratios of full-page ads to the number of pages in a magazine (using the data from *Ads.mtw*) from 1989, 1991, and 1993. The first 12 values in C1 AdRatio correspond to a news magazine and the last 12 to a sports magazine. Likewise, the first through fourth values and the thirteenth through sixteenth values correspond to 1989. The other values in C1 AdRatio correspond to the other years. This file is used in Tutorial 9.

Column	Name	Count	Description
C1	AdRatio	24	Ratio of full-page ads to the total number of pages in a magazine

Rivera.mtw— Rivere.mtw, Riverc2, and Rivers.mtw

During the summer of 1988, one of the hottest on record in the midwest, a graduate student in environmental science conducted a study for a state Environmental Protection Agency. She studied the impact of an electric generating plant along a river by observing several water characteristics at five sites along the river. Site 1 was approximately four miles upriver from the electrical plant, about six miles down river from a moderately large midwestern city, and directly down river from a large suburb of this city. Site 2 was directly upriver from the cooling inlets of the plant. Site 3 was directly down river from the cooling discharge outlets of the plant. Site 4 was approximately three-quarters of a mile down river from site 3, and site 5 was approximately six miles down river from site 3.

The Agency was most concerned with the plant's use of river water for cooling. Scientists feared that the plant was raising the temperature of the water and hence endangering the aquatic species that lived in the river.

The student anchored data sounds (battery-operated and self-contained canisters that float in the river) at the five sites and took hourly measurements of the temperature, pH, conductivity, and dissolved oxygen content. She left the devices there for five consecutive days.

These files were used in Tutorial 8 (Practice Problems), Tutorial 13 (Practice Problems), Tutorial 15, and Tutorial 15 (Practice Problems).

Rivera.mtw, Riverb.mtw, Riverc.mtw, Riverd.mtw, and Rivere.mtw

The data sets Rivera through Rivere contain the recordings for each separate site; they therefore do not include the columns C6 Site and C7 Hour1 described below. *Rivers.mtw* contains the recordings from all five sites and includes all of the columns described in the following chart (it also contains the three missing values from Riverb).

Column	Name	Count	Missing	Description
C1	Hour	+	0	The hour of the measurement, using a 24-hour clock
C2	Temp	+	0	The temperature, in °C, of the river at the given hour
C3	pH	+	0	The pH of the river at the given hour
C4	Cond	+	0	The conductivity, in electrical potential, of the river at the given hour
C5	DO	+	0	The dissolved oxygen content of the river at the given hour
C6	Site	478	0	Site
C7	Hour1	478	0	The hour recorded as a number from 1 through 100

+ The counts for the different data sets are Rivera = 95; Riverb = 95; Riverc = 95; Riverd = 96; Rivere = 97; Rivers = 478. Note that Riverb and Rivers have three missing values.

Riverc2.mtw

Riverc2 contains six additional variables.

Column	Name	Count	Missing	Description
C1	Hour	95	0	The hour of the measurement, using a 24-hour clock
C2	Temp	95	0	The temperature, in °C, of the river at the given hour
C3	pH	95	0	The pH of the river at the given hour
C4	Cond	95	0	The conductivity, in electrical potential, of the river at the given hour
C5	DO	95	0	The dissolved oxygen content of the river at the given hour
C6	FORE1	48	0	Forecasts for the next 48 hours
C7	Lags	95	1	Lags
C8	Diff	95	1	Differences
C9	AForecst	48	0	ARIMA forecasts
C10	LAForcst	48	0	Lower limits
C11	UAForcst	48	0	Upper limits

Salary.mtw

A small private college conducts a yearly study of its faculty's salaries. Information on gender, department, years at the school, beginning salary, current salary, and an "experience" variable are recorded. Many other variables are combined to yield an "experience" score. The higher the score, the more experience the person had when he or she first started. The faculty member's current rank is also measured.

Column	Name	Count	Description
C1	ID	171	The college's identification number for the faculty member
C2-T	Gender	171	The gender of the faculty member
C3	StartYr	171	The starting year of the faculty member
C4	DeptCode	171	The department of the faculty member coded as a number

Column	Name	Count	Description
C5	Begin$	171	The starting salary of the faculty member
C6	1991$	171	The current salary (1991) of the faculty member
C7	Expernc	171	The "experience variable" value when the person started at the college
C8-T	RankCode	171	The current rank of the faculty member; Instruct (instructor), AsstProf (assistant professor), AssoProf (associate professor), and Professr (professor)

▼
Salman.mtw
▲

Zoologists housed 14 salamanders in individual cages. During the period of study, they exposed the salamanders to normal conditions and monitored each cage separately. They recorded the activity level in each cage hourly over the course of six days, for a total of 144 hourly assessments. These results were subsequently used to compare other experimental conditions (not included in this data set).

Column	Name	Count	Description
C1	Activity	144	The daily activity level for 14 salamanders

▼
Sbp.mtw
▲

A drug designed to lower systolic blood pressure (SBP) was administered to 12 subjects. The data set contains their SBP before and after the drug was taken.

Column	Name	Count	Description
C1	Before	12	Systolic blood pressure before taking the drug
C2	After	12	Systolic blood pressure after taking the drug

▼
Snow.mtw
▲

This data set contains the total snowfall amounts (in inches) for a large city on the East Coast recorded for the 36 years between 1962 and 1997. This file is used in Tutorial 1 (the data are used in practice problems, but not the file), Tutorial 2 (Practice Problems), Tutorial 3 (Practice Problems), Tutorial 13, Tutorial 13 (Practice Problems), and Tutorial 14 (Practice Problems).

Column	Name	Count	Description
C1	Year	36	Year
C2	Snowfall	36	Snowfall, in inches
C3	Rain	36	The equivalent rainfall, in inches

Sp500.mtw

A professor in a business school at a southern university monitored the stock market over several years. This data set contains 506 consecutive daily high, low, and closing values for the Standard and Poor's 500 Cash (Spot) Index. This file is used in Tutorial 15 (Practice Problems).

Column	Name	Count	Description
C1	High	506	The high value of Standard and Poor's 500 Cash (Spot) Index on a given day
C2	Low	506	The low value of Standard and Poor's 500 Cash (Spot) Index on a given day
C3	Close	506	The closing value of Standard and Poor's 500 Cash (Spot) Index on a given day

Spcar.mtw

This data set consists of fuel economy ratings for 1994 vehicles.

Column	Name	Count	Missing	Description
C1-T	Vehicle	19	0	Manufacturer and model
C2	CT	19	0	Miles per gallon for city driving
C3	HW	19	0	Miles per gallon for highway driving
C4	CM	19	0	Miles per gallon for combination city and highway driving (EPA assumes that 55% of the miles are driven under city conditions)
C5	Cost	19	0	Estimate of the cost of one year's fuel for the vehicle
C6	EngDispl	19	0	Engine displacement in liters
C7	EngCylin	19	0	Number of cylinders

Column	Name	Count	Missing	Description
C8-T	TrnType	19	0	Type of transmission; Automatc (automatic), Manual, or AutoFuel (automatic with fuel-saving device that eliminates slippage)
C9	NumGears	19	0	Number of gears
C10	FuelInfo	19	7	Fuel information; GasGuzTx (gas guzzler tax), PFandGGT (vehicle requires premium fuel and is subject to gas guzzler tax), or PremFuel (vehicle requires premium fuel)

▼
Steals.mtw
▲

Early in the 1991 major league baseball season, Rickey Henderson of the Oakland Athletics baseball team became the stolen base leader, passing Lou Brock. Newspapers reported the number of bases Mr. Henderson stole for each day of the week.

Column	Name	Count	Description
C1-T	Day	7	The day of the week
C2	Bases	7	The total number of bases that Mr. Henderson stole on the given day of the week

▼
Stores.mtw
▲

A marketing research firm collected data on the number of individuals who last bought jeans from four major stores, classified according to their approximate yearly total household income before taxes. This file is used in Tutorial 12 and Tutorial 12 (Practice Problems).

Column	Name	Count	Description
C1	Store	4	Store identification
C2	Under25K	4	The number of individuals earning less than $25,000 who purchased jeans at each store
C3	25KTo35K	4	The number of individuals earning from $25,000 to $35,000 who purchased jeans at each store

Column	Name	Count	Description
C4	35KTo50K	4	The number of individuals earning from $35,000 to $50,000 who purchased jeans at each store
C5	50KTo75K	4	The number of individuals earning from $50,000 to $75,000 who purchased jeans at each store
C6	75K&Over	4	The number of individuals earning more than $75,000 who purchased jeans at each store

T3.mpj

This project is a summary of the work performed in Tutorial 3. It contains numerous graphs that illustrate various aspects of the 3Pay data set. This project file is used in Tutorial 4.

T10.mpj

This project is a summary of the work performed in Tutorial 10. It contains one worksheet, *10Masscol.mtw*, and three graphs: Plot 'Tuition'*'VSAT', Fitted Line Plot without Intervals, and Fitted Line Plot with Intervals. This project file is used in Tutorial 11.

Tbill.mtw

This data set lists the Treasury Bill values for 1991 and 1992.

Column	Name	Count	Description
C1	High	104	High value for a day
C2	Low	104	Low value for a day
C3	Close	104	Closing value

Temco.mtw and Temco2.mtw

This data set contains the salary information for all salaried employees in four departments at the Temco company. *Temco.mtw* contains C1–C8, while *Temco2.mtw* adds four columns that store the fits, the residuals, and the standardized residuals calculated from regressing YrsEm on Salary, and the square of YrsEm. The data set *Pay.mtw* is a subset of this larger data set. These files are used in Tutorial 9 (Practice Problems), Tutorial 10 (Practice Problems), and Tutorial 11 (Practice Problems).

Column	Name	Count	Description
C1	Salary	46	The salary of an employee
C2	Yrs Em	46	The number of years employed at Temco
C3	PriorYr	46	The number of prior years' experience
C4	Educ	46	Years of education after high school
C5	ID	46	The company identification number for the employee
C6	Gender	46	The gender of the employee
C7	Dept	46	The employee's department; Sales, Purchase (purchasing), Advertse (advertising), or Engineer (Engineering)
C8	Super	46	The number of employees supervised by this employee
C9	FITS1	46	Fitted values
C10	RESI1	46	Residuals
C11	SRES1	46	Standardized residuals
C12	Yrs**2	46	Square of YrsEm

▼
Texts.mtw
▲

These data were collected to facilitate analysis of the emphasis on quality control in introductory business and economics statistics texts published between 1989 and 1994.

Column	Name	Count	Missing	Description
C1	Year	52	0	Year of publication
C2	Edition	52	0	Edition
C3	Pages	52	0	Number of pages in text
C4	Chapters	52	0	Number of chapters
C5	QChapter	52	0	Number of quality chapters
C6	QCPages	52	0	Number of pages in quality chapters
C7	QPRatio	52	0	Number of quality pages/ number of pages
C8	QCRatio	52	19	Number of quality chapters/total number of chapters in text

Tvhrs.mtw

This file includes the results of a study of TV-viewing patterns.

Column	Name	Count	Description
C1-T	ID	120	Subject identification number
C2-T	AgeGrp	120	Age group; GradeSch (grade school), CollStu (college student), or 50plus (50 years of age or older)
C3	Age	120	Ages
C4-T	Gender	120	Gender
C5-T	Sesame	120	Whether or not they watched Sesame Street; yes or no
C6	HrsTV	120	Hours spent watching TV in a week
C7	HrsMTV	120	Hours spent watching MTV in a week
C8	HrsNews	120	Hours spent watching news in a week
C9-T	Educ	120	Educational background; SomGrade (some grade school), SomHigh (some high school), HighSchl (high school diploma), SomColl (some college), College (college degree), <=2Grad (two or fewer years of graduate school), >2Grad (more than 2 years of graduate school)

Usdem.mtw

This data set displays U. S. census values, including the estimated population and population density for the decades 1790, 1800, . . . , 1990.

Column	Name	Count	Description
C1	Year	21	Year
C2	Populatn	21	U. S. population, in millions
C3	Density	21	U. S. population density, in people per square mile

Vpvh.mtw

Each year the Nielsen company conducts extensive surveys of TV viewing habits of the U. S. population. Many of the surveys are coded by age and gender groups because sponsors are interested in how these variables affect which programs people watch.

This data set contains the VPVH estimates for several different categories of television programming. The *VPVH estimate* is the estimated number of viewers per 1,000 viewing households tuned to a station or program. This data set includes the 10 VPVH estimates for each of four commonly surveyed gender/age groups (men aged 18 to 34, women aged 18 to 34, men aged 55 +, and women aged 55 +) for the following types of programs: network movies, situation comedies, and sporting events. For the sports program, only data for the two male age groups were given.

This file is used in Tutorial 9 (Practice Problems).

Column	Name	Count	Missing	Description
C1	Movies	40	0	The VPVH data for the top 10 network movies
C2	Comedy	40	0	The VPVH data for the top 10 situation comedies
C3	Sports	40	20	The VPVH data for the top 10 sporting events
C4-T	Group	40	0	The gender/age group; Men18–34, Wom18–34, Men50+, or Wom50+

Wastes.mtw

New and abandoned hazardous waste sites are being discovered across the United States. This data set lists the number of hazardous waste sites found in each region of the country. This file is used in Tutorial 7 (Practice Problems).

Column	Name	Count	Description
C1	NEngland	6	The number of hazardous waste sites in each New England state
C2	MAtlantc	3	The number of hazardous waste sites found in each mid-Atlantic state
C3	ENCentrl	5	The number of hazardous waste sites found in each east-north central state
C4	WNCentrl	7	The number of hazardous waste sites found in each west-north central state
C5	SAtlantc	9	The number of hazardous waste sites found in each southern Atlantic state

Column	Name	Count	Description
C6	ESCentrl	4	The number of hazardous waste sites found in each east-south central state
C7	WSCentrl	4	The number of hazardous waste sites found in each west-south central state
C8	Mountain	8	The number of hazardous waste sites found in each mountain state
C9	Pacific	5	The number of hazardous waste sites found in each Pacific state

Wheat.mtw

A professor in a business school at a southern university studied wheat futures. This data set contains the daily high, low, and closing values for wheat futures for 500 consecutive days, representing approximately 1-1/2 years' worth of data. In addition, the number of wheat future contracts traded on the day is recorded.

Column	Name	Count	Description
C1	High	500	The high value of wheat futures traded on that day
C2	Low	500	The low value of wheat futures traded on that day
C3	Close	500	The closing value of wheat futures traded on that day
C4	Volume	500	The total number of contracts traded on that day

Yogurt.mtw

These data, collected by a research company, show the results of testing 14 brands of plain yogurt. The tests evaluated overall nutritional value, cost per ounce, and the number of calories per serving. This file is used in Tutorial 1 (the data are used, but not the file) and Tutorial 9 (Practice Problems).

Column	Name	Count	Description
C1-T	Rating	14	Nutritional rating; Excellnt (excellent), VeryGood, Good, Fair, or Poor
C2	Cents	14	Cost per ounce, in cents
C3	Cals	14	Calories per 8-oz. serving, in cents

APPENDIX A

Menus and Toolbars

Menus for all Windows

FIGURE A-1

*Manip Menu
(partial view)*

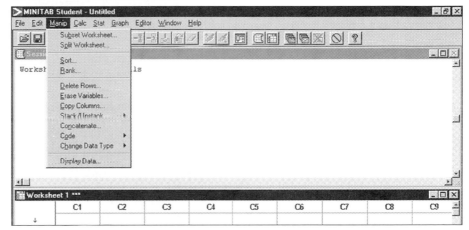

FIGURE A-2

*Calc Menu
(partial view)*

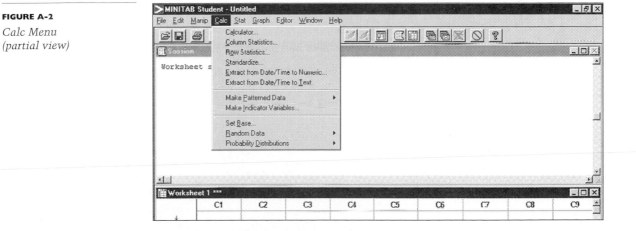

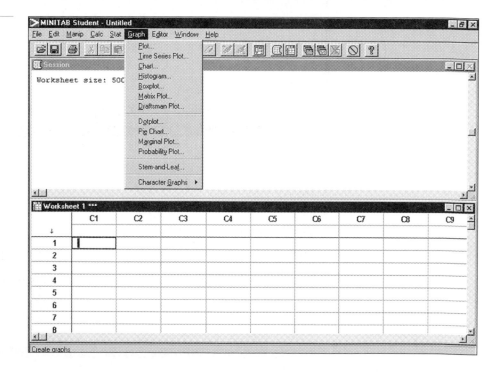

FIGURE A-5
Window Menu (partial view)

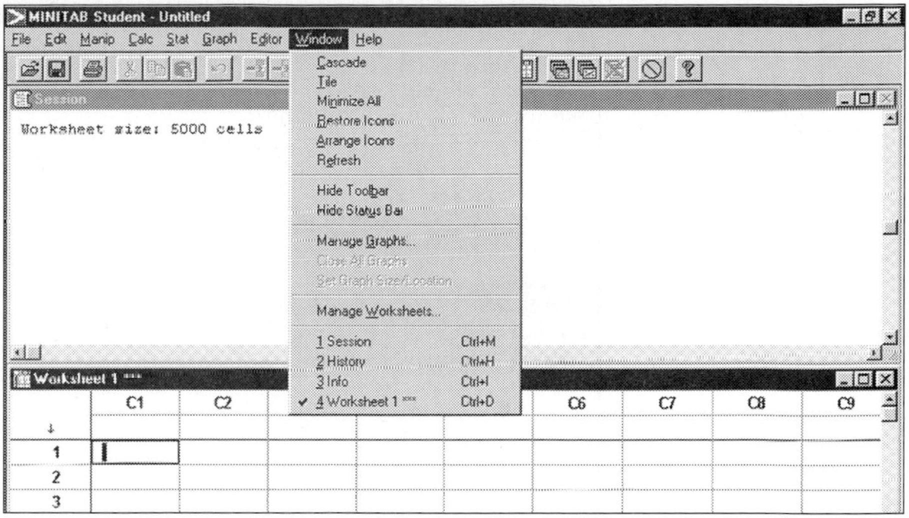

FIGURE A-6
Help Menu (partial view)

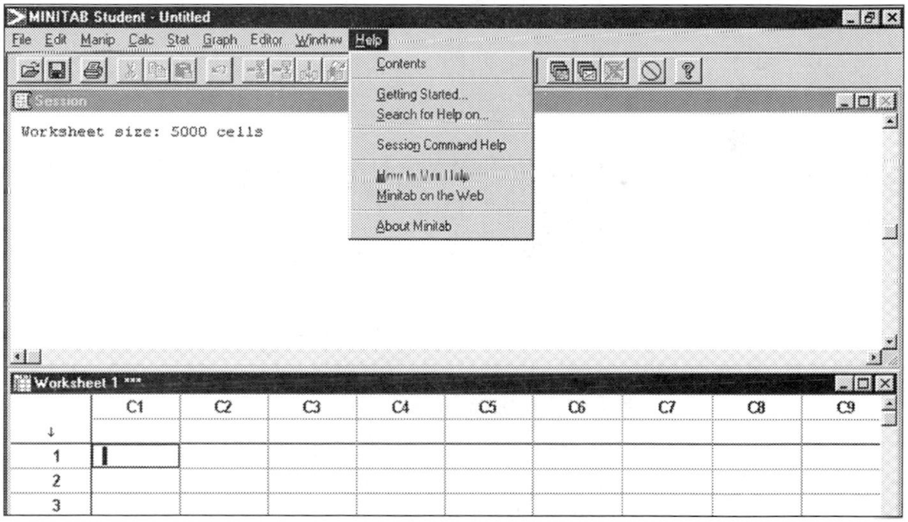

Data Window

FIGURE A-7
Toolbar (partial view)

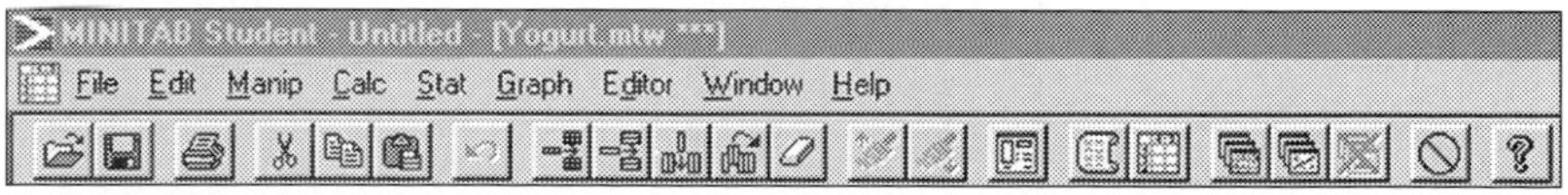

FIGURE A-8
File Menu

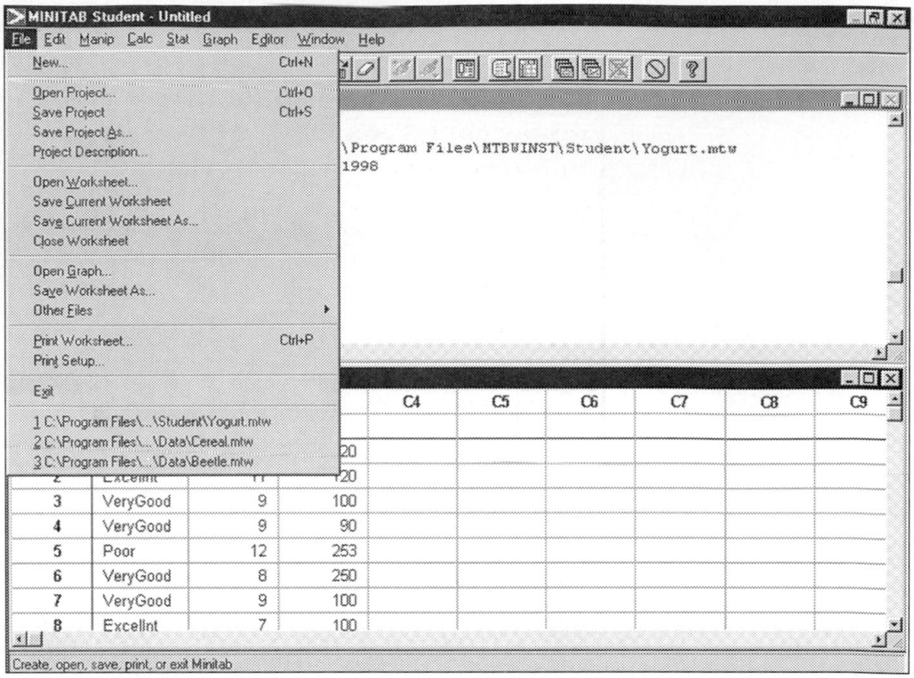

FIGURE A-9
Edit Menu

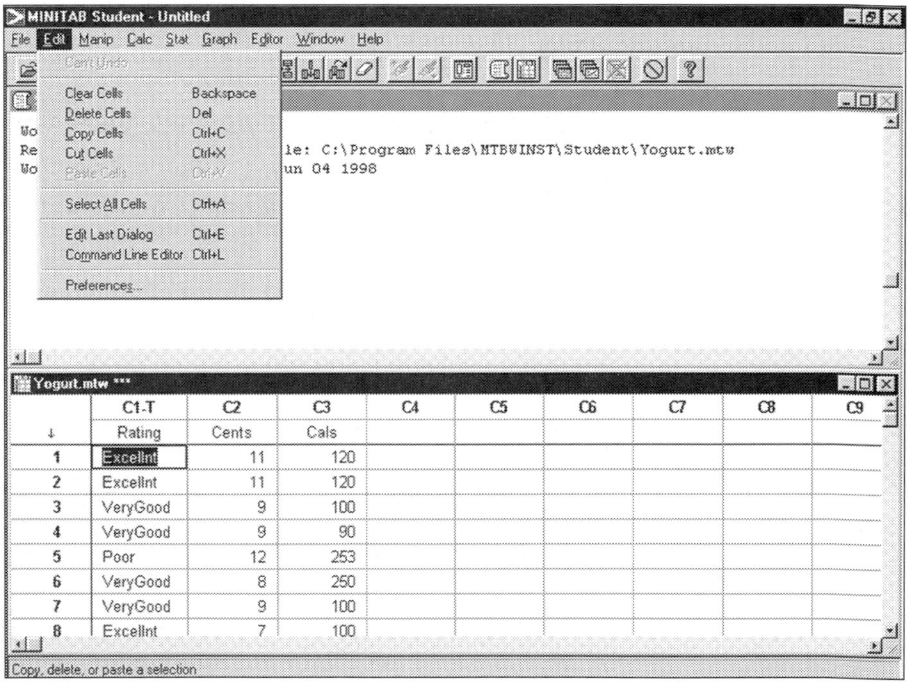

Session Window

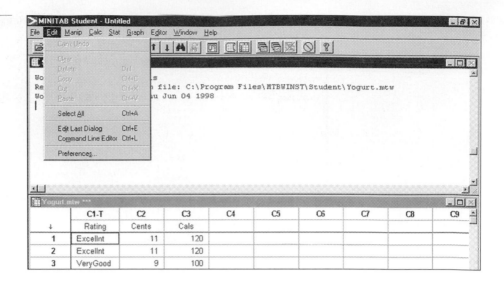

Graph Window

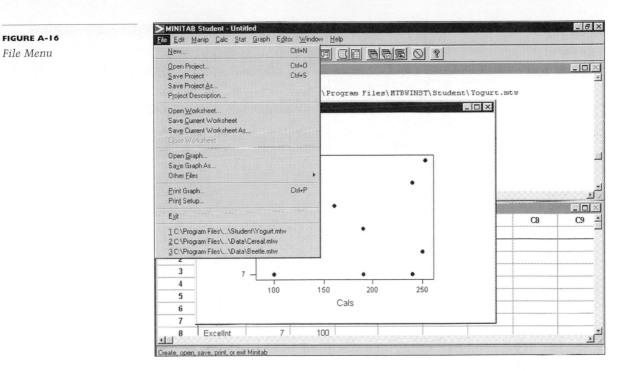

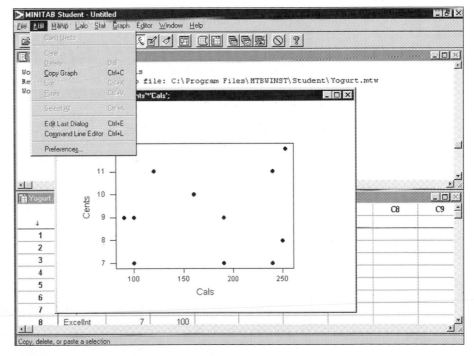

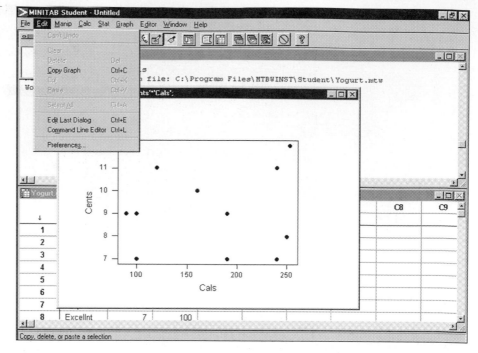

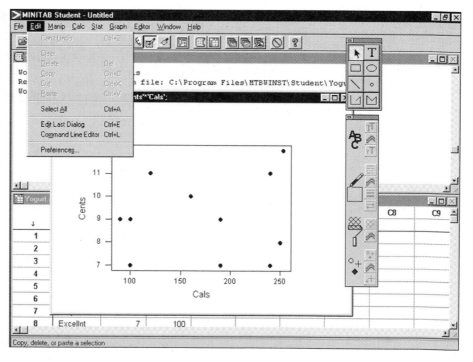

FIGURE A-20

Editor Menu for View mode

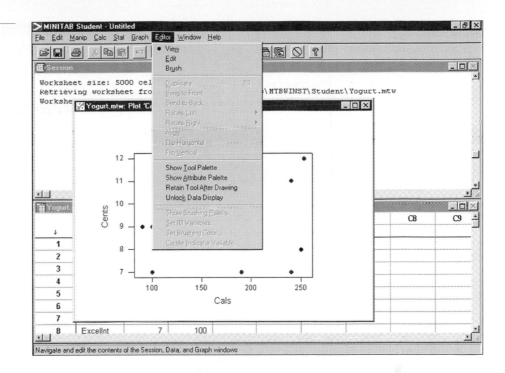

FIGURE A-20

Editor Menu for View mode

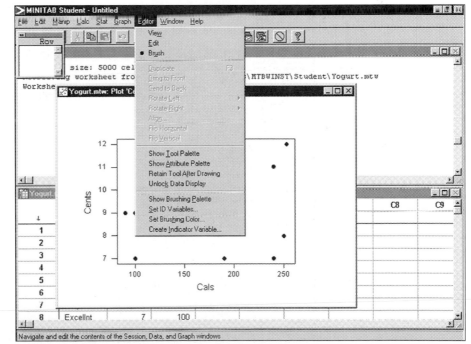

FIGURE A-21

Editor Menu for Brush mode

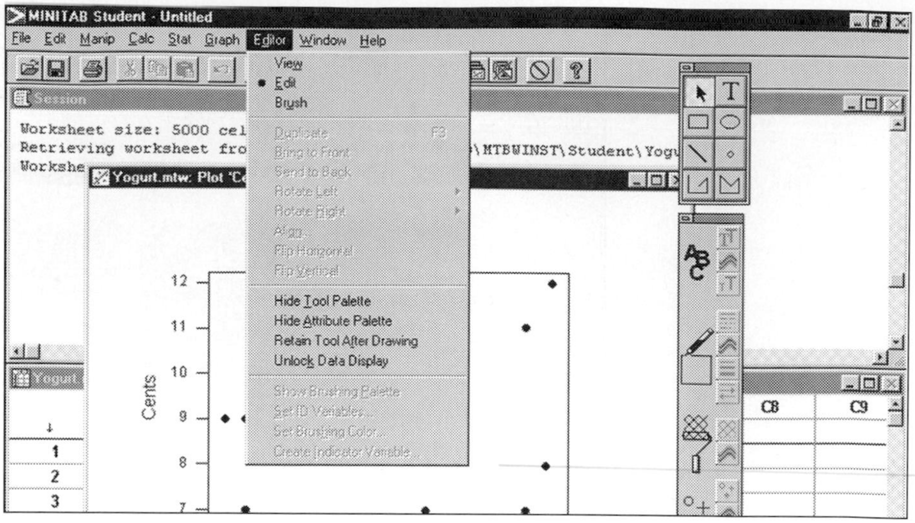

FIGURE A-22
Editor Menu for Edit mode (partial view)

Info Window

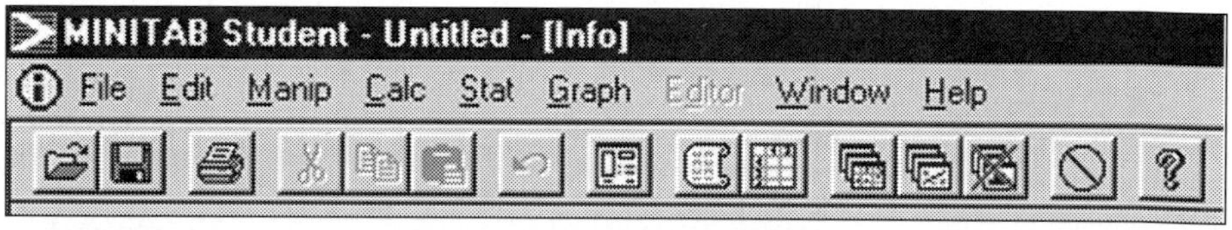

FIGURE A-23
Toolbar (partial view)

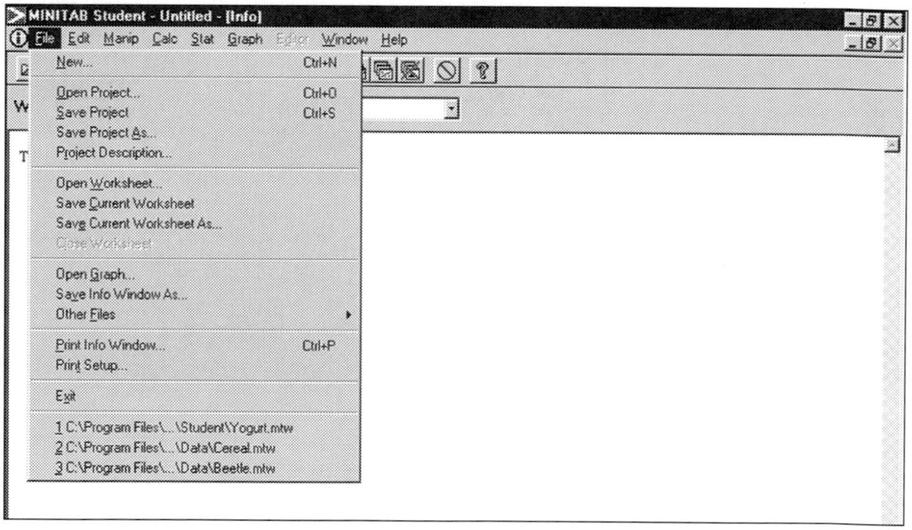

FIGURE A-24
File Menu (partial view)

Info Window

FIGURE A-27

Edit Menu
(partial view)

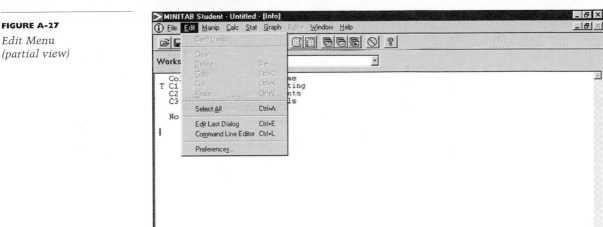

History Window

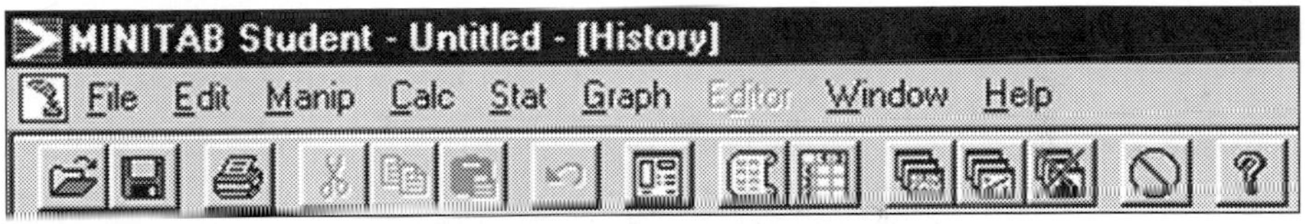

FIGURE A-25

Toolbar
(partial view)

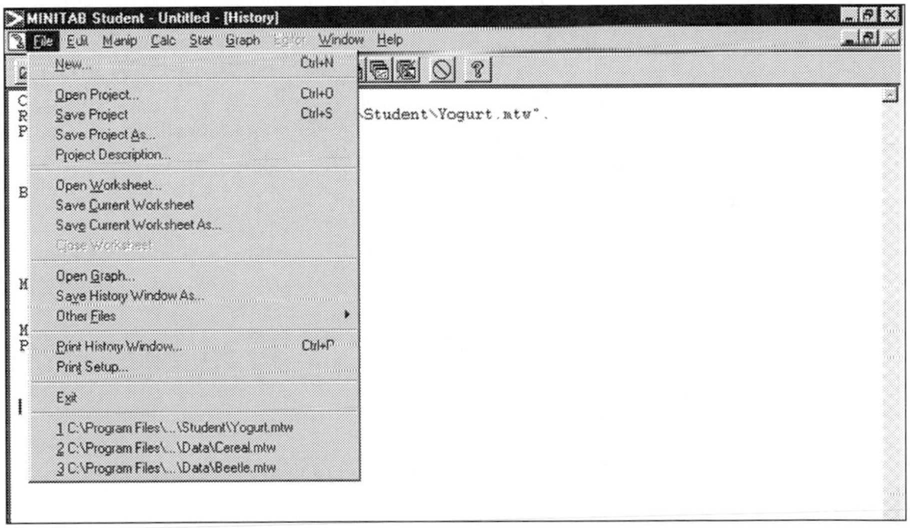

FIGURE A-26

File Menu
(partial view)

History Window

FIGURE A-28

Edit Menu

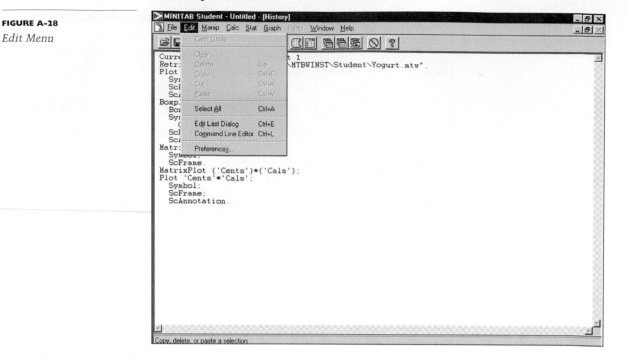

APPENDIX B

Session Command/
Menu Command Equivalents

This appendix is intended for those who are familiar with Minitab and who want to find the menu equivalent for Session commands. The Session commands are listed on the left, and the menu equivalents of those commands are on the right. GPRO in parentheses after a Session command means that the equivalent command produces a high-resolution graph; GSTD in parentheses, a character graph.

The symbol > indicates submenus; for example, Calc > Set Base means "Choose Set Base from the Calc menu." The sequence Stat > Time Series > Autocorrelation means "Choose Time Series and then Autocorrelation from the Stat menu."

Not available in the Student Edition means that that command is available from the menus in the Professional version of Minitab, but is not available (either from the menus or from the Session window) in the Student Edition.

%ACF	Stat > Time Series > Autocorrelation...
%ANOM	*Not available in the Student Edition*
%BANOM	*Not available in the Student Edition*
%BCAPA	*Not available in the Student Edition*
%BOXCOX	*Not available in the Student Edition*
%DECOMP	Stat > Time Series > Decomposition...
%DES	Stat > Time Series > Double Exp Smoothing...
%DESCRIBE	Stat > Basic Statistics > Display Descriptive Statistics...
%DOTPLOT (GPRO)	Graph > Dotplot...
%FFMAIN	*Not available in the Student Edition*
%FISHBONE	Stat > SPC > Cause-and-Effect...
%FITLINE	Stat > Regression > Fitted Line Plot...

%FORM	*Not available in the Student Edition*
%GAGEAOV	*Not available in the Student Edition*
%GAGELIN	*Not available in the Student Edition*
%GAGERUN	*Not available in the Student Edition*
%GAGEXBR	*Not available in the Student Edition*
%GFINT	*Not available in the Student Edition*
%GFMAIN	*Not available in the Student Edition*
%IMRCHART	Stat > Control Charts > I-MR...
%INTERACT	Stat > ANOVA > Interactions Plot...
%INTPLOT	Stat > ANOVA > Interval Plot...
%LDIDENT	*Not available in the Student Edition*
%LDOVIEW	*Not available in the Student Edition*
%MA	Stat > Time Series > Moving Average...
%MAIN	Stat > ANOVA > Main Effects Plot...
%MARGPLOT	Graph > Marginal Plot...
%MESH	*Not available in the Student Edition*
%MULTIVAR	*Not available in the Student Edition*
%NORMPLOT	Stat > Basic Statistics > Normality Test...
%OVERCONT	*Not available in the Student Edition*
%PACF	Stat > Time Series > Partial Autocorrelation...
%PANOM	*Not available in the Student Edition*
%PARETO	Stat > Quality Tools > Pareto Chart...
%PCAPA	*Not available in the Student Edition*
%PIE	Graph > Pie Chart...
%QQPLOT	*Not available in the Student Edition*
%RCAPA	*Not available in the Student Edition*
%RCUSUM	*Not available in the Student Edition*
%RESPLOTS	Stat > Regression > Residual Plots...
%ROBUST	*Not available in the Student Edition*
%ROWTOC	*Not available in the Student Edition*
%RRUN	Stat > Quality Tools > Run Chart..
%RSIXPACK	*Not available in the Student Edition*
%RXBARR	Stat > Control Charts > Xbar-R...
%RXBARS	Stat > Control Charts > Xbar-S...
%RZONE	*Not available in the Student Edition*
%SES	Stat > Time Series > Single Exp Smoothing...
%SYMPLOT	*Not available in the Student Edition*
%TREND	Stat > Time Series > Trend Analysis...
%VARTEST	Stat > ANOVA > Homogeneity of Variance...
%WBCHART	*Not available in the Student Edition*
%WCAPA	*Not available in the Student Edition*
%WINTADD	Stat > Time Series > Winters' Method...
%WINTMULT	Stat > Time Series > Winters' Method...
%XSIXPACK	*Not available in the Student Edition*
%ZMRCHART	*Not available in the Student Edition*
ABORT	Session Command
ABSOLUTE	Calc > Calculator...
ACF	Stat > Time Series > Autocorrelation...
ACOS	Calc > Calculator...
ADD	Calc > Calculator...
ANCOVA	*Not available in the Student Edition*
ANOVA	Stat > ANOVA > Balanced ANOVA...

ANTILOG	Calc > Calculator...
AOVONEWAY	Stat > ANOVA > Oneway (Unstacked)...
ARIMA	Stat > Time Series > ARIMA...
ASIN	Calc > Calculator...
ATAN	Calc > Calculator...
BASE	Calc > Set Base...
BATCH	Session Command
BBDESIGN	*Not available in the Student Edition*
BLOGISTIC	Stat > Regression > Binary Logistic Regression...
BOXPLOT (GPRO)	Graph > Boxplot...
BOXPLOT (GSTD)	Graph > Character Graphs > Boxplot...
BREG	Stat > Regression > Best Subsets...
BRIEF	Session Command
CA	*Not available in the Student Edition*
CCDESIGN	*Not available in the Student Edition*
CCF	Stat > Time Series > Cross Correlation...
CCHART (GPRO)	Stat > Control Charts > C...
CCHART (GSTD)	Session Command
CD	Session Command
CDF	Calc > Probability Distributions > ...
CEILING	Calc > Calculator...
CENTER	Calc > Standardize...
CHART	Graph > Chart...
CHISQUARE	Stat > Tables > Chi-Square Test...
CLUOBS	*Not available in the Student Edition*
CLUVARS	*Not available in the Student Edition*
CODE	Manip > Code...
CONCATENATE	Manip > Concatenate...
CONSTANT	Session Command
CONTOUR (GSTD)	*Not available in the Student Edition*
CONTOURPLOT (GPRO)	*Not available in the Student Edition*
CONVERT	Manip > Code > Use Conversion Table...
COPY	Manip > Copy Columns...
CORRELATION	Stat > Basic Statistics > Correlation...
COS	Calc > Calculator...
COUNT	Calc > Calculator...
	Calc > Column Statistics...
COVARIANCE	Stat > Basic Statistics > Covariance...
CPLOT	*Not available in the Student Edition*
CTABLE	*Not available in the Student Edition*
CTIME	Calc > Calculator...
DATE	Calc > Calculator...
DEFINE	*Not available in the Student Edition*
DEFTEST	*Not available in the Student Edition*
DEGREES	Calc > Calculator...
DELETE	Manip > Delete Rows...
DESCRIBE	Stat > Basic Statistics > Display Descriptive Statistics...
DIAGONAL	*Not available in the Student Edition*
DIFFERENCES	Stat > Time Series > Differences...

DIR	Session Command
DISCRIMINANT	*Not available in the Student Edition*
DIVIDE	Calc > Calculator...
DOTPLOT (GSTD)	Graph > Character Graphs > Dotplot...
DSET	Session Command
DTYPE	*Not available in the Student Edition*
E	Calc > Calculator...
ECHO	Session Command
EIGEN	*Not available in the Student Edition*
END	Session command
ENDLAYOUT	*Not available in the Student Edition*
ERASE	Manip > Erase Variables...
EWMACHART (GPRO)	Stat > Control Charts > EWMA...
EWMACHART (GSTD)	Session Command
EXECUTE	File > Other Files > Run an Exec...
EXPONENTIATE	Calc > Calculator...
FACTOR	*Not available in the Student Edition*
FDESIGN	*Not available in the Student Edition*
FFACTORIAL	*Not available in the Student Edition*
FFDESIGN	*Not available in the Student Edition*
FLOOR	Calc > Calculator...
FRIEDMAN	Stat > Nonparametrics > Friedman...
GAMMA	Calc > Calculator...
GLM	*Not available in the Student Edition*
GPAUSE	Session Command
GPRINT	Session Command
GPRO	Session Command
GSCALE	*Not available in the Student Edition*
GSTD	Session Command
GVIEW	File > Open Graph...
HEIGHT	Graph > Character Graphs > Set Options...
HELP	Help > ...
HISTOGRAM (GPRO)	Graph > Histogram...
HISTOGRAM (GSTD)	Graph > Character Graphs > Histogram...
ICHART (GPRO)	Stat > Control Charts > Individuals...
ICHART (GSTD)	Session Command
IGAMMA	Calc > Calculator...
INDICATOR	Calc > Make Indicator Variables...
INFO	Window > Info
INSERT	Session Command
INVCDF	Calc > Probability Distributions > ...
INVERT	*Not available In the Student Edition*
IW	Session Command
JOURNAL	Window > History
KMEANS	*Not available in the Student Edition*
KRUSKAL-WALLIS	Stat > Nonparametrics > Kruskal-Wallis...
LAG	Calc > Calculator...
	Stat > Time Series > Lag...

LAYOUT	*Not available in the Student Edition*
LET	Calc > Calculator...
LNGAMMA	Calc > Calculator...
LOGE	Calc > Calculator...
LOGTEN	Calc > Calculator...
LPLOT	Graph > Character Graphs > Scatter Plot...
LREGRESSION	*Not available in the Student Edition*
LTABLE	*Not available in the Student Edition*
LTEST	*Not available in the Student Edition*
LVALS	*Not available in the Student Edition*
MACHART (GPRO)	Stat > Control Charts > Moving Average...
MACHART (GSTD)	Session Command
MANN-WHITNEY	Stat > Nonparametrics > Mann-Whitney...
MANOVA	*Not available in the Student Edition*
MATRIXPLOT	Graph > Matrix Plot...
	Graph > Draftsman Plot...
MAXIMUM	Calc > Calculator...
	Calc > Column Statistics...
MCA	*Not available in the Student Edition*
MEAN	Calc > Calculator...
	Calc > Column Statistics...
MEDIAN	Calc > Calculator...
	Calc > Column Statistics...
MINIMUM	Calc > Calculator...
	Calc > Column Statistics...
MISS	Calc > Calculator...
	Calc > Column Statistics...
MIXREG	*Not available in the Student Edition*
MOOD	Stat > Nonparametrics > Mood's Median Test...
MPLOT	Graph > Character Graphs > Multiple Scatter Plot...
MPOLISH	*Not available in the Student Edition*
MRCHART (GPRO)	Stat > Control Charts > Moving Range...
MRCHART (GSTD)	Session Command
MROPT	*Not available in the Student Edition*
MTSPLOT	Graph > Character Graphs > Time Series Plot...
MULTIPLY	Calc > Calculator...
N	Calc > Calculator...
	Calc > Column Statistics...
NAME	Session Command
NEST	*Not available in the Student Edition*
NEW	FIle > New
NEWPAGE	Session Command
NLOGISTIC	*Not available in the Student Edition*
NMISS	Calc > Calculator...
	Calc > Column Statistics...
NOCONSTANT	Session Command
NOECHO	Session Command
NOJOURNAL	Session Command
NOOUTFILE	Session Command
NOTE	Session Command
NOW	Calc > Calculator...
NPCHART (GPRO)	Stat > Control Charts > NP...
NPCHART (GSTD)	Session Command

NSCORES	Calc > Calculator...
NUMERIC	Manip > Change Data Type...
	Calc > Extract from Date/Time to Numeric...
ODBC	*Not available in the Student Edition*
OH	Session Command
OLOGISTIC	*Not available in the Student Edition*
ONEWAY	Stat > ANOVA > Oneway...
OUTFILE	Session Command
OW	Session Command
PACF	Stat > Time Series > Partial Autocorrelation...
PAIR	Stat > Basic Statistics > Paired t...
PARPRODUCTS	Calc > Calculator...
PARSUMS	Calc > Calculator...
PBDESIGN	*Not available in the Student Edition*
PCA	*Not available in the Student Edition*
PCHART (GPRO)	Stat > Control Charts > P...
PCHART (GSTD)	Session Command
PDF	Calc > Probability Distributions > ...
PI	Calc > Calculator...
PLOT (GPRO)	Graph > Plot...
PLOT (GSTD)	Graph > Character Graphs >Scatter Plot...
PLTX	*Not available in the Student Edition*
PONE	Stat > Basic Statistics > 1 Proportion...
POWER	Stat > Power and Sample Size...
PRINT	Manip > Display Data...
PROBIT	*Not available in the Student Edition*
PTWO	Stat > Basic Statistics > 2 Proportions...
RADIANS	Calc > Calculator...
RAISE	Calc > Calculator...
RANDOM	Calc > Random Data > ...
RANGE	Calc > Column Statistics...
RANK	Manip > Rank...
	Calc > Calculator...
RCHART (GPRO)	Stat > Control Charts > R...
RCHART (GSTD)	Session Command
RCOUNT	Calc > Calculator...
	Calc > Row Statistics...
READ	File > Other Files > Import Special Text...
REGRESS	Stat > Regression > Regression...
RESTART	Session Command
RETRIEVE	File > Open Worksheet...
RLINE	*Not available in the Student Edition*
RMAXIMUM	Calc > Calculator...
	Calc > Row Statistics...
RMEAN	Calc > Calculator...
	Calc > Row Statistics...
RMEDIAN	Calc > Calculator...
	Calc > Row Statistics...
RMINIMUM	Calc > Calculator...
	Calc > Row Statistics...
RN	Calc > Calculator...
	Calc > Row Statistics...

RNMISS	Calc > Calculator...
	Calc > Row Statistics...
ROOTOGRAM	*Not available in the Student Edition*
ROUND	Calc > Calculator...
RRANGE	Calc > Calculator...
	Calc > Row Statistics...
RREGRESS	Session Command
RSCONTOUR	*Not available in the Student Edition*
RSMOOTH	*Not available in the Student Edition*
RSREG	*Not available in the Student Edition*
RSSQ	Calc > Calculator...
	Calc > Row Statistics...
RSSURFACE	*Not available in the Student Edition*
RSTDEV	Calc > Calculator...
	Calc > Row Statistics...
RSUM	Calc > Calculator...
	Calc > Row Statistics...
RUNS	Stat > Nonparametrics > Runs Test...
SAMPLE	Calc > Random Data > Sample from Columns...
SAVE	File > Save Worksheet...
	File > Save Worksheet As...
SCDESIGN	*Not available in the Student Edition*
SCHART (GPRO)	Stat > Control Charts > S...
SCHART (GSTD)	Session Command
SET	Calc > Set Patterned Data > Simple Set of Numbers...
SIGNS	Calc > Calculator...
SIN	Calc > Calculator...
SINTERVAL	Stat > Nonparametrics > 1-Sample Sign...
SLDESIGN	*Not available in the Student Edition*
SORT	Manip > Sort...
	Calc > Calculator...
SPLIT	Calc > Split Worksheet...
SQRT	Calc > Calculator...
SSQ	Calc > Calculator...
	Calc > Column Statistics...
STACK	Manip > Stack/Unstack...
STATISTICS	Stat > Descriptive Statistics >
	Store Descriptive Statistics...
STATS	Session Command
STDEV	Calc > Calculator...
	Calc > Column Statistics...
STEM-AND-LEAF	Graph > Character Graphs > Stem-and-Leaf...
STEPWISE	Stat > Regression > Stepwise...
STEST	Stat > Nonparametrics > 1-Sample Sign...
STOP	File > Exit
SUBSET	Calc > Subset Worksheet...
SUBTRACT	Calc > Calculator...
SUM	Calc > Calculator...
	Calc > Column Statistics...
SURFACEPLOT	*Not available in the Student Edition*
TABLE	Stat > Tables > Cross Tabulation...
TALLY	Stat > Tables > Tally...

TAN	Calc > Calculator...
TEXT	Manip > Change Data Type...
	Calc > Extract Day/Time to Text...
	Editor > Set Columns > Width...
TIME	Calc > Calculator...
TINTERVAL	Stat > Basic Statistics > 1-Sample t...
TODAY	Calc > Calculator...
TPLOT	*Not available in the Student Edition*
TRANSPOSE	*Not available in the Student Edition*
TSET	Calc > Make Patterned Data > Text Values...
TSHARE	Session Command
TSPLOT (GPRO)	Stat > Time Series > Time Series Plot...
	Graph > Time Series Plot...
TSPLOT (GSTD)	Graph > Character Graphs > Time Series Plot...
TTEST	Stat > Basic Statistics > 1-Sample t...
TWOSAMPLE	Stat > Basic Statistics > 2-Sample t...
TWOT	Stat > Basic Statistics > 2-Sample t...
TWOWAY	Stat > ANOVA > Twoway...
TYPE	Session Command
UCHART (GPRO)	Stat > Control Charts > U...
UCHART (GSTD)	Session Command
UNSTACK	Manip > Stack/Unstack...
VORDER	Editor > Set Column > Value Order...
WALSH	Stat > Nonparametrics > Pairwise Averages...
WDIFF	Stat > Nonparametrics > Pairwise Differences...
WHEN	Calc > Calculator...
WIDTH	Graph > Character Graphs > Set Options...
WINTERVAL	Stat > Nonparametrics > 1-Sample Wilcoxon...
WOPEN	File > Open Worksheet...
WORKSHEET	File > Open Worksheet...
	File > Close Worksheet
WRITE	File > Other Files > Export Special Text...
WSAVE	File > Save Current Worksheet
	File > Save Current Worksheet As...
WSLOPE	Stat > Nonparametrics > Pairwise Slopes...
WTEST	Stat > Nonparametrics > 1-Sample Wilcoxon...
XBARCHART (GPRO)	Stat > Control Charts > Xbar...
XBARCHART (GSTD)	Session Command
XDACTIVATE	*Not available in the Student Edition*
XDADD	*Not available in the Student Edition*
XDDEACTIVATE	*Not available in the Student Edition*
XDEXEC	*Not available in the Student Edition*
XDGET	*Not available in the Student Edition*
XDREMOVE	*Not available in the Student Edition*
XPWX	*Not available in the Student Edition*
YESNO	Session Command
ZINTERVAL	Stat > Basic Statistics > 1-Sample Z...
ZTEST	Stat > Basic Statistics > 1-Sample Z...

INDEX

Credits

Data Sets:

ADS.MTW and ADS2.MTW; AGE.MTW; ASSESS.MTW; CANDYA.MTWñCANDYC.MTW; DRIVE.MTW; GAS.MTW; NONPRT.MTW and NONPRT2.MTW; PROCES.MTW; PUBS.MTW; RATIO.MTW; TEXTS.MTW; YOGURT.MTW: John D. McKenzie, Jr., Babson College. Reprinted with permission.

CHOL.MTW: Anderson, J.W., Spencer, D.B., Hamilton, C.C., Smith, S.F., Tietyen, J., Bryant, C.A., and Oeltgen, P., "Oat-Bran lowers Serum Total and LDL Cholesterol in Hypercholesterolemic Men," American Journal of Clinical Nutrition, Volume 52, September 1990, 495-499.

CPI.MTW: U.S. Bureau of Labor Statistics, Monthly Labor Review and Handbook of Labor Statistics.

CRIMES.MTW and CRIMESU.MTW: U.S. Federal Bureau of Investigation.

ECLASS.MTW: U.S. Bureau of the Census, Department of Commerce, County Business Patterns.

FBALL.MTW; GOLF.MTW; RIVERA.MTWñRIVERE.MTW and RIVERS.MTW; SALMAN.MTW; STEALS.MTW: Schaefer and Farber, The Student Edition of MINITAB, Release 8. User's Manual © 1992 Addison-Wesley Publishing Co., Reading, MA. Software © 1991 Minitab Inc. Reprinted with permission of Addison-Wesley.

FJA.MTW: Frank Anscombe, Yale University. Reprinted with permission.

HOMES.MTW: Triola and Franklin, Business Statistics, ©†1994 Addison-Wesley Publishing Co., Reading, MA, pp. 772ñ775. Reprinted with permission.

JEANSA.MTW–JEANSC.MTW; STORES.MTW: D. J. Tigert, Babson College. Reprinted with permission.

MNWAGE.MTW: U.S. Department of Labor.

MORT.MTW: Data from Massachusetts Division of Banks.

NIEL.MTW; TVVIEW.MTW; VPVH.MTW: A. C. Nielsen Co. Reprinted with permission.

NOTE.MTW: Data from Byte, March 1994.

PIZZA.MTW: Reprinted with permission from The Rensselaer Polytechnic, student newspaper, Rensselaer Polytechnic Institute.

SNOW.MTW: National Weather Service Office.

SP500.MTW: Used by permission of Standard & Poor's, a division of McGraw-Hill, Inc.

SPCAR.MTW: Environmental Protection Agency.

TBILL.MTW: Data from Dow Jones Tradeline.

TVHRS.MTW: Richard Frost, Babson College. Reprinted with permission.

USDEM.MTW: U.S. Bureau of the Census, Department of Commerce.

WASTES.MTW: Federal Register, October 14, 1992.

Sources

Minitab at Work:

"Forestry" (Tutorial 3): Allegheny National Forest.

"Public Safety" (Tutorial 6): From testimony presented to the Atomic Energy Commission, 1971.

"Retailing" (Tutorial 7): "Survival of Selected Indicator and Pathogenic Bacteria in Refrigerated Pizzas," Journal of Food Protection, Vol. 50, No. 10, October 1987, pp. 859ñ861.

"Scientific Research" (Tutorial 8): Roger Johnson, David Spenny, and Tony Forest, "The Distribution of Supernova Remnants in the Large Magellanic Cloud," Publications of the Astronomical Society of the Pacific, 100:683ñ686, June 1988.

"Human Resources" (Tutorial 10): Robert N. Goldman.

"Education" (Tutorial 12): Allen Shaughnessy and Ronald O. Nickel, "Prescription-Writing Patterns and Errors in a Family Medicine Residency Program," The Journal of Family Practice, Vol. 29, No. 3, 1989, pp. 290ñ295.

"Medical Diagnostics" (Tutorial 13): Patrick Carey and P. Syamasundar Rao, "Remodeling of the Aorta After Successful Balloon Coarctation Angioplasty," Journal of American College of Cardiology, Vol. 14, No. 5, Nov. 1, 1989, pp. 1312–1317.

"Quality Management" (Tutorial 14): Minitab, Inc.

"Stock Market" (Tutorial 15): Albert Parish, "Market Forecasting Models: ARIMA," Technical Analysis of Stocks & Commodities, October 1990, pp.88-96.